THEATRE ROYAL

P.N.

THE HISTORY OF YORK
From Earliest Times to the Year 2000

Edited by

PATRICK NUTTGENS

Patrick Nuttgens

BLACKTHORN PRESS

Blackthorn Press, Blackthorn House
Middleton Rd, Pickering YO18 8AL
United Kingdom

ISBN 0 9535072 8 9

© Patrick Nuttgens et al 2001

ILLUSTRATION CREDITS

The publisher and authors are grateful to the following for help
with providing illustrations:

Borthwick Institute of Historical Research, City of York Art
Gallery, Tate Gallery, Barrie Law, Ronald Willis and Hendon
Publishing Co, City of York Libraries, Andy Liddell, John
Shannon Archive, Fairfax House, York Archaeological Trust,
Trustees of the Chatsworth Settlement, York Civic Trust, The
Dean and Chapter of York, English Heritage National
Monuments Record, Macmillan Publishing, York Evening Press,
C A Lowry, Yorkshire Architectural and Yorkshire
Archaeological Society, Yorkshire Museum

PREFACE

One of the most endearing characteristics of the City of York is that its citizens have rarely, if ever, agreed about its history. In 1661 for example, the Recorder of York, Sir Thomas Widdrington, having collected a lot of historical notes and assembled them under the title of *Analaecta Eboracensia* donated them to the Mayor and Council only to have them brutally rejected. "The shoes of our predecessors are too big for our feet," he was told, and "A good purse is more useful than a long story." The *Analecta* were not published until 1897.

There is no shortage of studies published since that time and the amount of information is almost embarrassing. Among the major studies are the earliest: Drake's *Eboracum* of 1736, Knight's celebrated *History of York* of 1944, the Victoria County History of York of 1961 and the publications of the Royal Commission on Historical Monuments from 1962, of the Yorkshire Philosophical Society from 1825, the York Civic Trust from 1946, the York Archaeological Trust from 1973 and innumerable surveys and reports from York City Council from 1951. It might be argued that further studies are superfluous.

This new book, *The History of York*, is the latest in a series of local histories but it is very distinctive. It brings together in one volume the considered judgements of 10 local scholars, members of the Archaeological Trust, the University of York and local societies. Their chapters from the arrival of the Roman army to the planning controversies of the present day are up to date and authoritative – from the broadest span to the most distinctive detail.

They display the unique characteristics of York both as a city and borough: how layer upon layer of historic development has, as I tried to show in my *York the Continuing City* (1976 onwards), been laid one on top of the other, preserving the old layers below, or sometimes wedged into cracks in the historic infrastructure. In the last century, many more of these layers have been revealed, yielding up their riches of interest and knowledge. There is, therefore, no other city in Britain more capable of illustrating the history of the country, at large, both in terms of its absorbing past or its promise for the future.

Patrick Nuttgens

CONTENTS

Notes on the Authors

Colour Plates

Monochrome Plates

Maps and Illustrations

1. ROMAN YORK
   Patrick Ottaway.
   Introduction 1, The Fortress 4, The Civilian Settlement 14, York in
   the Late Roman Period 30, The End of Roman York 36.

2. ANGLO-SAXON & VIKING-AGE YORK
   Richard Hall
   Introduction 39, Sub-Roman Period 40, Anglian Period 43,
   Anglo-Scandinavian Period 50.

3. EARLY MEDIEVAL YORK.
   Chris Daniell
   Introduction 68, Sources 73, The Nationalities of York 74, The
   Turbulent History of York 78, The Church in York 80, Government
   of the City 88, Living in the City 94, Conclusion 99.

4. LATER MEDIEVAL YORK.
   Barrie Dobson
   The Halcyon Years 100, York and the Crown: Edward I – Richard III
   104, The Urban Economy and the Black Death 114,
   Urban Society: Aliens, Craftsmen and Merchants 120,
   Christianity in the Late Medieval City 130.

5. TUDOR YORK.
   Claire Cross
   Henry VII 141, Church, State and the Pilgrimage of Grace 146,
   Dissolution of the Monasteries 149, Edward VI 156, Mary 159,
   Elizabeth 162, The Revolt of the Earls 165, Catholic Recusancy
   167, Protestantism 170, The Economy 173.

iv

6. SEVENTEENTH CENTURY YORK.
    W. J. Sheils
    Crisis and Conflict 177, Civil Wars and Interregnum 192, A New
    Monarch and a New Role 202.

7. EIGHTEENTH CENTURY YORK.
    Alison Sinclair
    Age of Elegance and Enterprise 212, The Changing Role of the City
    215, Religious Affairs 216, Administrative Role 218, Military Matters
    220, City Government and Politics 223, Contemporary Comment
    224, Nobility and Gentry 226, Merchants, Ministers and Professional
    Men 229, Butchers, Bakers and Comb-Makers 232, Widows,
    Spinsters and Orphans 235, Buildings 237 New Types of
    Building 237, Architectural Style 238, The Suburbs 239,
    Infrastructure Improvements 239, High Roads 240, Navigation
    Improvements 242, Conclusion 243.

8. NINETEENTH CENTURY YORK.
    Edward Royle
    Introduction 244, A Medieval City Transformed 245, Population 248,
    City and Suburbs 249, Economic Development Before the
    Railways 254, The Transport Revolution 256, The Railway Industry
    259, Manufacturing 259, Confectionary and Cocoa 263, Municipal
    Government 264, Politics 270, Religion 271, Education 280,
    Poverty and Health 288, Wealth and Leisure 295.

9. TWENTIETH CENTURY YORK.
    Patrick & Bridget Nuttgens
    Introduction 302, Social Conditions 304, Local Government 310,
    Employment .315, Politics.319, Religion.320, Military and Wartime
    323, The Watershed 326, Communications 327, The Civic Trust and
    Conservation 331, New Uses for Old Buildings 339, Arts and Leisure
    345, Education 347, The University 350, The Millennium .355.

BIBLIOGRAPHY

INDEX

NOTES ON THE AUTHORS

Claire Cross

Like the third Earl of Huntingdon, who was President of the Council in the North in Tudor times, Claire Cross came to York from Leicestershire. She joined the History Department of the new University in 1965 and retired as professor in 2000. She has worked on the late medieval and early modern history of the city and county for many years. She enjoys gardening and travel.

Chris Daniell

Chris Daniell has lived in York over 20 years, originally coming to the University to read History and then staying. He has worked as a historian and archaeologist in York and elsewhere in England. His specialisms include the 12th century and the study of medieval cemeteries. He dislikes gardening and decorating, but enjoys photography and is an active member of St John's Ambulance. He is married to Alison.

Barrie Dobson

Barrie Dobson was Professor of Medieval History at the University of Cambridge from 1988 until his retirement in 1999. He then returned to York where he is now an Honorary Professor of the History Department in the University of York: it was there that he taught for most of his career. As a northerner who has frequently written about church and society in Yorkshire and Durham, he has never lost his enthusiasm for York itself, once capital of the north and now what he calls 'this irresistible battered museum of a city'.

Richard Hall

Richard Hall is an archaeologist who has lived in York since 1974. He has excavated early medieval sites in York and Yorkshire, from the 7th century crypt of Ripon Cathedral to 'The Viking Dig' in Coppergate, York. He is Deputy Director of York Archaeological Trust, Consultant Archaeologist at York Minster, and Honorary Secretary of the Council for British Archaeology. He enjoys reading fiction, particularly the potted autobiographies which introduce authors to their readers.

Patrick & Bridget Nuttgens

Patrick Nuttgens was born in 1930 and educated at the University of Edinburgh. He was one of the first academics to join the new University of York in 1962, and in 1970 became the first Director of Leeds Polytechnic. His books include *York the Continuing City, The Story of Architecture* and *The Art of Learning*. His films include *The Home Front* (BBC series on social housing) and films on Modern Architecture, the Arts and Crafts and Lutyens. His voice on radio will be known to listeners of *A Word in Edgeways* and *Round Britain Quiz*. Patrick lives near York where he writes and paints.

Bridget Nuttgens was born in Kuala Lumpur where her father was in the Malayan Medical Service. She was educated in Scotland, at Edinburgh University, Trinity and All Saints College, Leeds and Leeds Polytechnic. As well as school teaching in both the private and state sector, she has taught adult literacy, English as a second language, and architectural history for Leeds Polytechnic and the WEA. She has worked with her husband on *The Story of Architecture, Understanding Modern Architecture* and *What Should We Teach and How Shoud We Teach It?*

Patrick Ottaway

Patrick has been Senior Field Officer with the York Archaeological Trust for 20 years and in that time has directed a number of excavation and research projects in the city and its region and is especially interested in the Roman period. He is the author of a number of academic and popular books including *Roman York* and teaches for Leeds University. Patrick is a Yorkshireman by birth and proud to live in York with his wife and a faithful whippet named Beauty.

Edward Royle

Ted Royle was born and brought up in Huddersfield but after ten years at the University of Cambridge came back to the north to teach at the University of York where he is now Professor of History. His historical work has been on popular atheism, radical political movements, and religion since the eighteenth century, especially in Yorkshire. He is active in the Historical Association, teaches local history courses at the University, and is a Methodist local preacher.

Bill Sheils

Bill Sheils is Senior Lecturer in History at York University where he has taught for over 20 years. He has written extensively on the reformation in England and has edited a *History of Religion in Britain*, published in 1994. When not teaching and writing, his interests are engaged with sports and his adopted city of York and two of the most memorable occasions he can recall in this respect were the defeats of Arsenal and Manchester United at Bootham Crescent.

Alison Sinclair

Alison Sinclair is an architectural historian who believes that buildings should not be studied in isolation of their historical context. She worked for many years for English Heritage before reaching retirement when she was appointed Honorary Visiting Fellow in the Department of Archaeology at the University of York. She lectures widely on York's buildings and in her spare time enjoys gardening, walking in her local park, music and the theatre.

COLOUR PLATES

Plate 1 Reconstruction view from the south-west of Roman York at about the time of the Emperor Septimius Severus in the years 209-11. The fortress is at the top, and the civilian town is at the bottom; the large public building in the centre is the forum basilica.

Plate 2 Head pot from York, probably intended to represent the Empress Julia Domna (early 3rd century).

Plate 3 Anglian Helmet. Oshere, an otherwise unknown Northumbrian aristocrat, owned this magnificent iron helmet which was made around 750-75. Embellished by brass edging strips and other decorative features, the noseguard has an animal interlace, and a prayer mentioning Oshere is carried on the two brass strips across the crown. Hinged flaps protected the ears, and the neck was surrounded by a curtain of iron mail, its 2000 rings representing a vast expenditure of time and skill. Found at 16-22 Coppergate, it seems to have been deliberately hidden.

Plate 4 Jorvik in 975 – an impressionistic reconstruction of the Anglo-Scandinavian city, looking from the backyards of Coppergate across to the Roman fortress.

Plate 5 York Minster from the West.

Plate 6 *Noah and his Ark.* Panel of the Great East Window (c. 1407), York Minster

Plate 7 The crossing arch of the great church of St Mary's Abbey suppressed in November 1539

Plate 8 'Jacob's Well' in Trinity Lane where Isabel Ward, the last Prioress of Clementhorpe Nunnery is thought to have lived after the Dissolution.

Plate 9 A distant view of the City by Alexander Keirincx, a Dutch artist in the service of Charles I and probably painted during the royal visits of 1639 or 1640, perhaps the earliest view of the city

Plate 10 The main entrance to King's Manor, headquarters of the King's Council in the North until its dissolution in 1641. Note the monogram of James I at the foot of the doorway and the arms of Charles I above, recording royal visits to the city

Plate 11 York Mansion House, the State Room

Plate 12 Richard Boyle, 3rd Earl of Burlington, 1743, by George Knapton

Plate 13 Clifford St, 1905. Clifford Street was built from 1881 when the Water Lanes were demolished and is later Victorian York at its best. The building in the centre is the York Institute of Art, Science and Literature by W.G. Penty (1883-4)

Plate 14 The Yorkshire Museum, built for the Yorkshire Philosophical Society in 1830, architect William Wilkins

Plate 15 Council Housing on Hull Road

Plate 16 York's First New Citizen of the Millennium, Chloe Lucas and her mother Christine.

MONOCHROME PLATES

Plate 1 Peter Addyman (Director of the York Archaeological Trust) inspects the main channel of the Roman sewer which served the legionary fortress baths. (Church Street 1972).

Plate 2 The 'Anglian' Tower, probably 4th century Roman, set into the legionary fortress wall. The Multangular Tower is at the top right. The stone wall on the left belonged to the medieval hospital of St Leonard and the wall on the extreme right is the medieval city wall. The brick building top left is the Public Library.

Plate 3 These two post and wattle buildings, each with a rectangular hearth, were erected on the Coppergate street frontage c.930. They represent the creation of an urban streetscape in *Jorvik*.

Plate 4 A plank-lined cellar, part of a late 10th-century building at Coppergate. The scale by the back door measures 1 metre.

Plate 5 Detail from the archway of St Michael's Church, Spurriergate.

Plate 6 The Great Hall. Merchant Adventurers' Hall.

Plate 7 The Shambles, York's best preserved 'Medieval Street'.

Plate 8 Edmund Grindal, Archbishop of York 1570-76.

Plate 9 Henry Hastings, Third Earl of Huntingdon.

Plate 10 Map of the City of York at the beginning of the 17th century by John Speed showing the large area of gardens and unbuilt space within the city walls at this date, and used as an inset in his *Theatre of the Whole Empire of Great Britain.*

Plate 11A The almshouses in Bootham established by Sir Arthur Ingram in 1630 and largely rebuilt in 1649 following extensive damage during the siege of 1644.

Plate 11B A late 17th century domestic interior for the house of Alderman Thompson, now the front parlour of the Black Swan Inn on Peasholme Green.

Plate 12 John Cossins' Map of York 1748.

Plate 13 Monument to Dr John Dealtry, died 1773, by John Fisher. The inscription was composed by Canon William Mason.

Plate 14 Queen's Staith was still a busy commercial centre in 1900 as these river barges suggest. The new Ouse Bridge of 1820 is in the background.

Plate 15 Map of York in 1901 from Rowntree's *Poverty*.

Plate 16 Prime Minister Tony Blair visits York during the floods of 2000.

MAPS

Roman York and its environs showing the principal areas of settlement, cemeteries (known) and streets (known and conjectured). Drawn by Nick Staley from an original by David Williams with amendments by Glenys Boyles. 7

Roman colonia. 15

Schematic and hypothetical plan of York in c. AD 500. 42

Schematic and hypothetical plan of York in c. AD 850. 49

Schematic and hypothetical plan of York in c. AD 1000. 65

Schematic and hypothetical plan of York in c. AD 1100. 72

Schematic and hypothetical plan of York in c. AD 1300. 102

Schematic and hypothetical plan of York in c. AD 1550. 151

John Speed's 1610 Map of York. See Monochrome Plate 10

John Cossins' Map of York 1748. See Monochrome Plate 12

York 1849. 251

York 1901. See Monochrome Plate 15

York 2000. 357

ILLUSTRATIONS IN THE TEXT

Front End Paper. *York Theatre Royal* by Patrick Nuttgens

1. The Multangular Tower at the south-west corner of the Roman fortress. The small facing stones in the lower half are Roman work while the larger blocks in the upper half are medieval. 4

2. Wellington Row Roman Road. Detail of the cross-section through the 2nd century Roman road make-up, showing large cobbles at the base and layers of fine gravel above (1m / 3' 4" scale). 11

3. 1-9 Micklegate Roman Public Building. Site of the former Queen's Hotel. Monumental stone wall of a public building in the Roman *colonia*. Brick-lined arches, blocked in the 4th century, can be clearly seen. (2m / 6' 6" scale). 17

4.   Mithraic relief (top) was found in Micklegate in 1747 and the dedication tablet from the temple of Serapis was found in Toft Green in 1770. From Wellbeloved's *Eburacum*, 1842. 18

5.   Wellington Row. Roman Stone Building of the late 2nd / early 3rd century. The floor make-up is limestone and mortar, and to the right in the centre is a surviving stone roof support block. Other blocks visible against the walls may have been seats. (2m / 6' 6'" scale). 21

6.   Tanner Row Roman Wooden Building. Late 2nd century Roman timber posts and plank building found at a depth of 14 feet (4.25 m) below ground level. 21

7.   Stone Coffin of Aelia Severa. Once the wife of Caecilius Rufus. She lived 27 years, 9 months and 4 days. The coffin was put in place by Caecilius Musicus, freedman. 26

8. Julia Velva's Tombstone. She died aged 50 years. The stone was set in place by her heir and, presumably husband, Aurelius Mercurialis. 27

9.   Silver penny minted for King Athelstan after he conquered York in 927 – the inscription, in abbreviated Latin reads + EDELSTAN REX TO BRT – Athelstan, king of all Britain. 53

10.   Dedication stone from St Mary Castlegate, York. In mixed Latin and Old English it records that Grim, Aese and another person built the church. The dating formula is broken off, but it may date c. AD 1000. 59

11. Clifford's Tower. 70

12. Norman House Behind Stonegate. 70

13. Reconstruction of the Norman Minster. 81

14. Reconstruction of the Norman Castle. 81

15. Madonna and Child. York Minster. 92

16. York Minster, Manuscript Gospel Book of c. 1000. 92

17. The West Façade of the Merchant Taylors' Hall. c. 1415. 105

18. Walmgate Bar. 105

19. Archbishop Scrope from The Bolton Book of Hours 1420 – 30. 111

20. Lady Row, Goodramgate. 111

21. St William's College of Minstry Chantry Priests. 125

22. The Guildhall of 1447-59 and later Civic Offices. 125

23. York Castle c. 1700 after the destruction of the roof of Clifford's Tower. 140

24. The Thomas Herbert House. 143

25. Holy Trinity, Goodramgate. 143

26. St Andrew's Church, St Andrewgate. 154

27. The Old Ouse Bridge. 154

28 The pulpit and sounding board placed in All Saints, Pavement church in 1634 from which the four civic preachers sustained the puritan temper of the corporation. 184

29. The rebuilt St Mary's Tower on the north-west corner of the old abbey precinct, showing the damage done by the explosion following its mining by the Parliamentary forces in the siege of 1644. 190

30. The simple design of the first purpose built nonconformist chapel in the city contrasts with the ancient parish churches. Situated in St Saviourgate, it was licensed for worship in 1693 by a congregation of Presbyterians and Independents, and remains in use by a Unitarian meeting today. 190

31. An armorial window in the Merchant Taylors' Hall, painted by Henry Gyles c. 1700. 202

32. "A Perspective View of York Castle with part of the Court of Justice and Grand Jury House" c. 1759 by William Lindley. 214

33. "A perspective View of the inside of the Grand Assembly Room in Blake Street", 1759, by William Lindley. The seats were moved in front of the columns in 1751 when it was realised guests could neither see nor be seen, while the seats remained behind the columns, as originally. 214

34. First Water Lane, 1813, by Henry Cave. Henry Cave was drawing master at Mr Lumley's School for Young Ladies at The King's Manor. 222

35. Todd's Book and Print Warehouse, 1797, by Henry Cave. 222

36. Wormalds Cut, created c. 1795 to serve the rear of Walmgate businesses, to the right of the picture. 241

37. Castlegate House, designed by John Carr for Peter Johnson, 1760-62 241

38. Yorkshire Insurance Company fire station 1845. This fire station, designed by G.T. Andrews, was built for the York Fire and Life Insurance Company in St Andrewgate to serve the city of York. 252

39. Duncombe Place was built in 1860 to open up a view of the Minster but, as this photograph of 1910 illustrates, the tower of St Wilfrid's (1864) appears taller. 252

40. The old railway station, designed by G.T. Andrews and opened in 1841. This early-twentieth century view from the city wall is a reminder of the polluted atmosphere of those days. 260

41. The market occupied the new Parliament Street from 1836. This view taken in 1889 from buildings later demolished to make way for Piccadilly, shows the tower of St Wilfrid's church in the background. 260

42. Garden Place was one of the better streets in the Hungate district in about 1904 when these children turned out to have their photograph taken outside the premises of the Hungate Mission (formerly the Wesley Place schoolroom). 262

43. The harmonium is wheeled out from the Skeldergate Wesleyan Mission (opened in 1900) across the road to Beedham's Court, which looks cleaner than when cholera first broke out here in 1832. 273

44. The Primitive Methodist Duke of York Street Mission was opened in 1877. Its annual Harvest Festival brought variety and entertainment to this rather drab district of Layerthorpe. 273

45. Scarcroft School (1896) is the best of six schools designed for the School Board by the York architect, W.H. Brierley. 284

46. The Exhibition Building, architect Edward Taylor (1879) was acquired by the city for its Art Gallery in 1891. 299

47. Stonegate Pedestrian Street. 317

48. New Earswick Folk Hall. 317

49. Lord James of Rusholme. 332

50. Norwich Union Insurance Offices. 332

51. St Sampson's Centre for the Elderly. 341

52. New flats at Bishop's Wharf. 341

53. The Millennium Bridge. 356

Back End Paper. *University of York, Central Hall* by Patrick Nuttgens.

ROMAN YORK

Patrick Ottaway

Introduction

York owes its existence to the Romans. In about the year AD71 Petilius Cerialis, the commander of the Ninth Legion *'Hispana'* chose a site for a fortress on a slightly elevated plateau of land on the north-east bank of the River Ouse. For the next 330 years or so York remained a great military base and it also became the leading civilian town in northern Britain with the rank of provincial capital. The Romans named York *Eboracum* (sometimes rendered *Eburacum*) which may mean 'the place of the yews'. Shortened in most cases to Ebor, the Roman name is still used in many contexts today from the signature of the Archbishop of York, heir to the man named Eborius who was summoned to the Council of Arles by the Emperor Constantine in 314, to the name of the great August race meeting on the Knavesmire in which the feature race is the famous Ebor Handicap.

With their renowned eye for the landscape, the Roman army saw that York enjoyed a number of natural advantages related primarily to communications by both land and water. For a start, York is located on a glacial moraine, a ridge of high ground created by retreating glaciers, which is known to have been used as a routeway running east - west across the low-lying Vale of York for some 2000 years before the Romans arrived. Another land route, now taken by both the A1 and the East Coast Mainline, leads north and encounters no major obstacle able to hold up a campaigning army anywhere in the 45 or so miles (72km) between York and the River Tees. As far as communication by water is concerned, at York the moraine is cut through by the River Ouse, at a point where it may be easily crossed, and, tidal in Roman times, the Ouse provided a navigable route for bringing in supplies and men, via the Humber estuary, from the east coast and North Sea some 40 miles (64km) away. Small boats could also have used the River Foss which approaches York from the north, meeting the Ouse just south of the fortress site. Together the rivers provided a natural defence for the south-east and south-west sides of the fortress which would have been more effective than might appear today because average river level has probably risen by about 10 feet (3m) since Roman times due to the influence of both human settlement and geological factors.

Although York is unusual amongst the principal Roman centres of Britain in not being sited close to an important pre-Roman settlement, this is not to say that the Romans arrived to find a deserted landscape – far from it. In recent years aerial photography and excavation in advance of pipelines, new roads and other developments have revealed numerous pre-Roman Iron Age sites usually characterised by small ditched enclosures and traces of round houses. One example, extensively excavated by the University of Bradford, lay in an area of sandy subsoil at Naburn, 3 miles (5km) south-east of York, but many others have been found on the alluvial clay of the Vale once thought unsuitable for prehistoric agriculture. York itself clearly stood in a managed landscape when the Romans arrived. Research on the well-preserved organic material, including plant remains and snail shells, from recent excavations in the city suggests a mixture of woodland scrub and cleared agricultural land. In short, the Ninth Legion would have encountered a meadowland scene not unlike that to be found on the rural reaches of the Ouse today.

Datable to about the year 100, the earliest written reference to *Eboracum* is as an address on one of the famous wooden writing tablets from Vindolanda, the fort near Hadrian's Wall. This is, however, one of no more than about 30 occurrences of the name in Roman written sources, either documents or inscriptions on stone, and most of these sources tell us little else of historic value. Certain Roman authors describe events which we can assume happened in York, but what is known of the history of Roman York is, none the less, based almost entirely on its physical remains. A few structures, such as the Multangular Tower in Museum Gardens, can still be seen above ground, but for the most part Roman York is buried many feet below the modern city. It survives as demolished buildings interspersed with countless layers, up to 10 feet (3m) thick, of rubble, refuse and other material derived from an enormous range of human activities. Within these layers are vast quantities of pottery, craft debris and objects made from metal, glass, leather and a host of other materials. They also contain biological remains including animal bones, and, where the ground has been waterlogged since Roman times thereby inhibiting the normal decay processes, plants, insects, and even horse manure and the eggs of parasites which live in the human gut!

The discovery of this evidence itself has a long history. Between the early 17th century and the early 20th, structural remains were recorded and artefacts collected by scholars who were strictly speaking antiquarians and connoisseurs rather than archaeologists in the sense that we understand the word today. It was not until the mid 1920s that the first proper archaeological investigations in the city took place when Professor Steuart Miller of Glasgow University set out to determine the history and location of the Roman fortress. In the next 40 years or so excavations in York were for the most part small scale as archaeologists were only able to command limited resources. As far as the Roman period is concerned, work was primarily concerned with the fortress and the cemeteries rather than the civilian settlements which remained largely *terra incognita* until the 1970s.

In 1962 a compendium of all discoveries in Roman York recorded up to that date was published as *Eburacum* by the Royal Commission on Historical Monuments for England in its first volume of the great inventory of the city. This remains the starting point for all academic enquiry into the subject. Subsequently, the Royal Commission was to sponsor one of the most important of all investigations of Roman York, the excavations at York Minster in

3

The Multangular Tower at the west corner of the Roman fortress

1969-72 in advance of the underpinning of the medieval building. Since 1972 Roman York has become part of a programme of research into the history of York in all periods undertaken by the York Archaeological Trust which has been able to put a professional team of archaeologists into the field and conduct some very large-scale and well-resourced excavations, notably in the civilian town south-west of the Ouse. In addition, the Trust has produced a number of important academic and popular publications on the subject, of which a selection are included in the list of further reading suggestions in the bibliography.

The Fortress

The first time a Roman army had set foot in Britain was in the year 55BC when Julius Caesar fought a campaign in the south-east, followed by a second the following year. It was not until AD 43 in the reign of the Emperor Claudius, however, that the Romans set about the permanent conquest of the island. With some 40,000 men at their disposal successive Roman commanders made rapid progress, soon imposing imperial rule on the south-east and south-west of England. Wales took a little longer to subdue and in AD 60-1 the Romans faced a major revolt led by Queen Boudicca. This was only a temporary set-back, however, and in the next ten years Romanised customs and ways of life continued to be adopted by the leaders of the Britons, especially in towns like the provincial capital at London.

An account of the circumstances in which the Ninth Legion advanced north from Lincoln and embarked on the conquest of the native people of the north may be found in the work of the Roman author Cornelius Tacitus. The people who occupied most of the north as far as the Scottish lowlands were known to the Romans as the Brigantes while the Parisi occupied an area roughly the same as the old East Riding of Yorkshire. Tacitus tells us that a conflict between two rival parties in the Brigantian royal house threatened the stability of the Roman province established in the south of Britain in the years since the invasion of AD43. On one side of this conflict was Queen Cartimandua who, for some 20 years, had favoured good relations with the Romans, and on the other was her estranged husband Venutius who led an anti-Roman party. The outbreak of hostilities led to Roman intervention and, as Tacitus put it, 'at the cost of desperate fighting', Cartimandua was rescued from Venutius' forces. There is no independent confirmation of this story and the date of AD69 traditionally given to it is inferred from Tacitus rather than being a verified archaeological date. However, archaeology would seem to confirm that a permanent Roman presence in the north began at about this time. Expansion of the empire in Britain was of a piece with new conquests in Germany and elsewhere undertaken by the recently enthroned emperor, Vespasian, as he sought to consolidate his position.

The Roman legionaries who came to York were heavily armed infantry recruited from the upper echelons of Roman society, the citizens. The opportunity to gain wealth and glory as a legionary was just one of the privileges available to a Roman citizen which were denied to the mass of non-citizens, or *peregrini*, who inhabited the provinces of the empire. They were, however, able to join the Roman army as auxiliary soldiers, in both infantry and cavalry units, and would acquire citizenship when they retired.

Inscriptions tell us the names of two Ninth Legion men stationed in York. That of the standard-bearer Lucius Duccius Rufinus appears on his tombstone now to be seen in the Yorkshire Museum. Below a relief of the man himself dressed in his best parade uniform, we are told that he hailed from *Vienna* (now Vienne) in the Rhone valley. Rufinus was, therefore, typical of the recruits from the Gallic provinces who were entering the army in the late 1st century AD. In other words the Romans who came to York were not necessarily Romans from Rome or even from Italy. The second name we have is that of a clerk, Celerinius Vitalis, which appears on an altar he dedicated to Silvanus, a god of the woods and wild places, very appropriate for a member of an army which probably spent much of its leisure time hunting.

A legion consisted of about 5000 men and was accommodated in a fortress, as opposed to the smaller forts used by the auxiliary units which numbered either 500 or 1000 men. By the late 1st century fortresses had become fairly standardised in form with a playing card-shaped ground plan, usually some 50 acres (20ha) in extent. At York the corners of the fortress are at the four cardinal points (north, south, east and west) and its north-east and north-west sides are still visible in the city's plan as they are followed by the medieval walls. Fortress buildings occupied the spaces between a grid of streets and around the outside ran the defences with a gate at, or near, the centre of each side. At the centre of every Roman fortress stood the headquarters building (*principia*) which had a large central courtyard enclosed by rows of long low buildings on three sides, but on the fourth stood the basilica, a great aisled hall with a row of rooms behind it. These rooms were mostly used as offices, but in the centre was a shrine dedicated to the principal protective deities of the Roman state in which the legionary standards were stored when the soldiers were not out on campaign. At York the basilica is on the north-east side of the courtyard and was *c.*230 feet (70m) long. Part of the

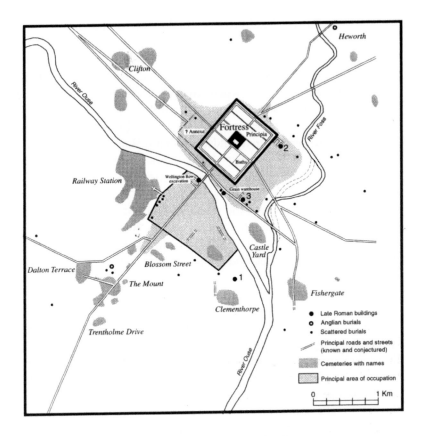

Fig 1. Roman York and its Environs

building was found in excavations at the Minster and one of the 20 columns from the aisle arcades, some 27 feet 6 inches (8.4m) high, found where it fell, in perhaps the 9th century, has been re-erected outside the south door. The lower part of another column can be seen in its original position in the Minster Undercroft. It was in the basilica and adjacent offices that the command and control functions of the legion were exercised and one can imagine the legionary commanders and even Septimius Severus and Constantius I, the two emperors known to have visited York, mounting the raised tribunal to address their troops here.

The fortress headquarters stood on the north-east side of a T-junction between two of the principal streets. Running south-west from this junction, along a line closely followed today by Stonegate, was the *via praetoria* which led to the main gate, or *porta praetoria*, standing where St Helen's Square is now. The second street, the *via principalis*, ran north-west / south-east on a line followed today over much of its length by Petergate. There was a Roman fortress gate under Bootham Bar, one of the city's medieval gates, and another stood at the junction of Petergate and King's Square. A great inscribed stone tablet found nearby, dedicated in AD 107-8 by the Ninth Legion to the Emperor Trajan, may have commemorated the reconstruction of this gate in stone. Another important street, the *via decumana*, led to the main north-east gate of the fortress on a line now followed for part of its length by Chapter House Street, and around the inside of the defences ran the *intervallum* street.

In the years immediately after the legions arrived in York the fortress gates and many other buildings, including the soldiers' barracks, officers' houses, granaries, workshops and the hospital would have been built largely of timber. However, the fortress bath house, known to have occupied a large site in the south quadrant, would for safety and permanence have been built of stone from the start because it used water, perhaps up to 70,000 gallons (317,800 litres) a day, and heat generated in great furnaces fuelled with charcoal. Only a few remains of the bath house have been found, but one of the most spectacular discoveries in Roman York to date has been the main baths sewer which still lies about 15 feet (4.5m) below modern Church Street. *[monochrome plate 1]* The principal channel, fed by a number of side channels, was found over a length of some 150 feet (46m). It is *c.*4'6" (1.40m) high and 2'6" (0.75m) wide, and constructed out of massive blocks of millstone grit and limestone. In places there are round arches which supported walls in the baths above. The sewer's function was to remove water and other waste from the baths and latrines. The water probably came from springs in the region and would have been brought to York in pipes and channels. The Romans used gravity where possible for transporting their water even it meant bringing it from sources at a

8

considerable distance. Proof of this came from examination of the silts in the sewer, which produced the seeds and pollen of plants which prefer limestone subsoil suggesting that some of the springs were at least 12 miles (19km) distant, perhaps in the Malton area, north-east of York.

The usual mode of bathing in Roman style required one to begin by working up a sweat either with exercises or by visiting the *caldarium*, a room heated by hot air which circulated below a floor raised on pillars. Here one oiled one's body and then scraped the sweat, oil and dirt from the skin with a metal tool called a strigil. Part of the York fortress *caldarium* was excavated in 1930 and can still be seen at the aptly named *Roman Bath* public house in St Sampson's Square.

The fortress defences in the late 1st century AD were of the standard Roman type in consisting of a ditch *c.*14'6" (4.4m) wide and 7' (2.10m) deep, and a rampart *c.*10' (3m) high composed of the material dug out of the ditch, and strengthened by timbers and layers of turf. Along the top of the rampart there would have been a timber palisade and, in addition to the four gates, there were watch towers at regular intervals. Although it had defences, it is important to remember that a Roman fortress was not a place which the soldiers expected to defend against an enemy, but one from which they would go out to fight in open country where their superior discipline and weaponry would prove decisive. For this reason roads played a crucial part in the conquest of the north as they enabled the army to travel quickly to places where an enemy might be gathering his forces, and one of the legion's first jobs after arriving in York would have been road construction.

The course of the main Roman roads in the York area is fairly well known. One of them probably followed the route which the Ninth Legion had taken on its original march to York. After crossing the Humber at the northern end of Ermine Street, the army had established a fort on the north bank at Brough on Humber from where York was approached from the south-east via Hayton, near Market Weighton, where an intermediate fort was built. While this may have been the first Roman road to York, the most important, the Roman equivalent of the A1, approached York from the south-west. From Tadcaster, a probable fort site, 9 miles (15km) distant, the road line corresponds closely to the present day A64. As it enters York the road runs a little to the north-west of Tadcaster Road and Blossom Street before entering what was to become the Roman town near Micklegate Bar. From the Bar the road headed north-eastwards in a straight line down to the River Ouse, where there was probably a bridge, before continuing on the same line through the fortress *porta praetoria* and, as the *via praetoria* (described above), terminating at the headquarters building. Excavations at Wellington Row close to the river crossing confirmed that the road had been built in the early years of the Roman presence. It was *c.*33' (10m) wide and constructed with a mounded base of large cobbles with layers of hard-packed gravel above them. A sharp camber allowed rain water to drain off quickly.

Roman roads were used not only for moving troops around the country, but also for transporting supplies, although river transport was usually employed to shift heavy and bulky goods. Along the banks of the Ouse one can imagine rows of warehouses standing next to the wharves where boats brought in the vast quantities of building materials needed for the fortress and, later on, the civilian settlements. Although suitable timber may have been available in woodland quite close to York, building stone had to be sought at least 10 miles (16km) away. To the west magnesian limestone was quarried around Tadcaster, hence its Roman name *Calcaria*, and millstone grit in the Wetherby area or even further afield, while north-east of York, in the Malton area, there were quarries for oolitic limestone.

One reason for the Roman army's choice of York may have been the availability of a good food supply in the native farms on the door step, but additional cereals for bread, the staple of the army diet, as well as other requirements, such as wine and olive oil from the distant Mediterranean would have been brought in by ship. The remains of two successive grain warehouses, both built of timber, were excavated at a site on Coney Street. A remarkable

Wellington Row: Roman Road

discovery in deposits associated with the first structure was a mass of well-preserved grain beetles. It is thought that an uncontrollable infestation had led to the total demolition of the building. In the remains of the second building was a great quantity of charred grain – largely wheat – which is probably testimony to the sort of accidental fire endemic in a settlement of wooden structures.

The legions not only imported supplies to York in these early years, but also made things themselves, including pottery; the poor quality cooking vessels of the native people not being considered suitable. The sophisticated life style of the Roman army meant that it required a wide range of vessels including bowls, storage jars, and flagons. They were made in a distinctive red earthenware, and kilns for pottery, and also for the tiles needed for roofing, are known to have existed to the east of the east corner of the Roman fortress in what is now the Peasholme Green area.

In the years 78 – 84 the Roman fortress at York would have seen a great deal of the Governor of Britain, Gnaeus Agricola, whose career was immortalised in a biography (*The Agricola*) by his son-in-law Tacitus. Agricola completed the conquest of Wales, founding York's sister fortress at Chester, and set about extending the Roman province up to the north of Scotland. He built many forts and roads often, no doubt, using the men of the Ninth Legion as well as the other three legions stationed in Britain at the time. By the early years of the 2nd century, however, with one of the legions withdrawn from Britain, the Romans had pulled the frontier back to a line between the mouth of the River Tyne on the east and the mouth of the Solway on the west. In the early years of the reign of the Emperor Hadrian, who visited Britain in the year 120, and may have passed through York, this line was made into the permanent frontier which now bears his name.

It was at about this time that the garrison in York was changed and the Ninth Legion departed, probably for the fortress at Nijmegen in Holland, to be replaced by the Sixth '*Victrix*'. Initially, it seems that the new legion was heavily involved with construction work on the northern frontier, but by the middle of the 2nd century it was back in York in strength and began a major programme of reconstruction in the fortress. This involved replacing the old timber buildings with stone structures and also the completion, probably in several stages, of a stone wall, with accompanying towers, to strengthen the defences. The fortress wall stood *c.* 16'6" (5m) high and was constructed in front of the original rampart, itself widened and raised in height. Part of the wall can still be seen at the east corner of the fortress along with the base of an earlier corner tower, but much more impressive are the standing remains at the west corner. Here the tower, now known as the Multangular Tower, projects from the line of the wall itself. The projecting part employs a fourteen-sided ground plan from which four sides have been omitted to give access to the second part, rectangular in plan, which lies behind the fortress wall. In all this was a very substantial structure 80 feet (24.3m) long which may originally have stood 35 feet (10.7m) high or even more. An identical tower stood at the south corner of the fortress and between the south and west corners were six interval towers which also projected out from the line of the fortress wall; the form of the south-west gate towers is unknown, but they may have matched the interval towers.

These projecting towers embody new ideas on military fortification as they allowed defenders to fire along the line of the fortress walls at hostile forces attempting to scale or undermine them. Earlier towers stood entirely behind the line of the walls. It is unlikely, however, that the Roman army at York ever expected to be besieged and the south-west defences of the fortress should be seen principally as architecture appropriate to York's pre-eminent status in the north. It was intended to impress local residents and visitors alike with the power of an empire on which the sun would never set.

Impressive though the Multangular Tower and associated stretches of fortress wall still are today, the reconstruction of the south-west defences, and of the north-west defences which was contemporary, is difficult to date accurately. The style of the projecting towers has led some scholars to prefer a late 3rd or even early 4th century date, but a recent review of the evidence from excavations along the line of the defences suggests an early 3rd century date is more likely. It is even possible that construction was set in train during the years 209-11 when the Emperor Septimius Severus used York as his base for pursuing campaigns against the Caledonian tribes in the north of Britain. *[colour plate 1]*

Emperors liked to make their mark on places they had favoured with a visit and Severus had, for a brief period, made York the centre of the whole empire in the sense that much of the apparatus of government accompanied the emperor wherever he went. Not only would Severus have brought a massive retinue of courtiers and officials to York, but we may infer from the contemporary historian Cassius Dio that he also brought his wife, the Empress Julia Domna, and his two sons Geta and Antoninus, the latter usually known as Caracalla on account of the type of cloak he habitually wore.

The Civilian Settlements

Before looking at the history of *Eboracum* after the reign of Severus, we must to go back in time a little and look at the growth of the Roman civilian settlements. The first non-military settlers were probably camp followers, soldiers' families and local people involved in trade with the army. Archaeological investigation suggests that some of them lived on the north-east bank of the Ouse in a zone between the fortress and the rivers while others settled around the main road from the south-west in what is now Dringhouses about 2 miles (3.5km) from the river crossing. Nearer to the crossing point further traces of early buildings have been found including those of a bath house in Fetter Lane and timber structures under the later town baths (see below) in the area of York's first railway station ('The Old Station'). Recovered in this area also were two small bronze plaques, remarkable objects which may have been displayed in a temple or shrine. They bear dedicatory inscriptions, one to the spirits of the governor's residence and the other to Ocean and Tethys, a titan and titaness of Greek legend, made by a man named Demetrius. He is thought to have been the person encountered by the Roman author

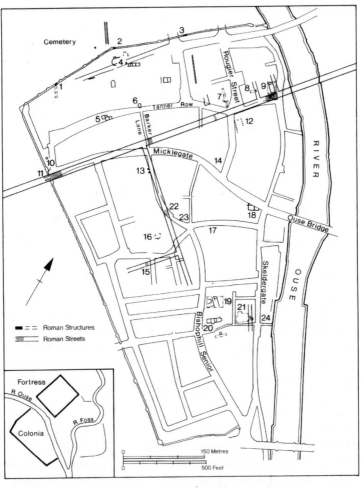

Key to sites:

1-2. Old Station: defences
3. Old Station and Mithraic relief of Arimanius
4. Old Station and Air Raid Control Centre: baths
5. Toft Green: mosaics
6. Temple of Serapis
7. General Accident, Tanner Row: buildings
8. 5 Rougier Street: warehouse and street
9. Wellington Row: main road and buildings
10. Bar Lane: mosaic
11. Micklegate Bar: gate?
12. George Hudson Street: column bases of forum-basilica or temple
13. Trinity Lane: column bases
14. Micklegate/George Hudson Street: Mithraic relief and column bases
15. Bishophill Junior : street and building
16. St Mary Bishophill Junior: house
17. Fetter Lane: baths
18. 1-9 Micklegate: public building
19. 37 Bishophill Senior: houses and terrace
20. St Mary Bishophill Senior: house
21. 58-59 Skeldergate: street and well
22. Trinity Lane: street
23. St Martin's Lane/Trinity Lane: buildings
24. 23-28 Skeldergate: waterfront

Fig 2 York. The Civilian Settlement

15

Plutarch in the years 83-4 when hearing of the man's experiences on a journey to the 'western isles' beyond the ocean.

Although York may already have been put on the map as far as the rest of the Roman world was concerned, excavations have, however, shown that it was not until the mid 2nd century that the Roman civilian settlement south-west of the Ouse began to grow in earnest. In archaeological terms this growth is characterised, firstly, by ditches for drainage and property demarcation, secondly by new streets and, thirdly, by new buildings in both timber and stone. In due course, the settlement would extend over much of the area now enclosed by the medieval city walls which, it appears, probably overlie a circuit of Roman walls.

At the centre of what would have soon appeared as a substantial town by Romano-British standards were the public buildings. The most important of these was the forum. Strictly speaking the word forum means a market place, but it is usually taken to describe a building complex very similar to a military headquarters which had a central courtyard and, on one side, a basilica used for official functions. The location of the York forum is not known for certain, but two rows of column bases observed at the junction of Rougier Street and George Hudson Street in 1898 may have once stood in the basilica. In the basilica itself there would have been a shrine and an altar, found in George Hudson Street, near the column bases, dedicated to the Emperor's *numen*, or sacred essence, and to the *genius*, or spirit, of *Eboracum*, would have been an entirely appropriate part of its appointments.

In addition to the forum, the other essential feature of a Roman town anywhere in the empire was the public bath house. At York there was one in the north-western part of the town which included the largest *caldarium* known in Roman Britain revealed in an excavation immediately before the Second World War. Part of what was probably another bath house, constructed in the early 3rd century, was excavated in 1990 on the site of the former Queen's Hotel on Micklegate. Walls up to 8' (2.5m) thick survived in places to a height of more than 13' (4m) giving a vivid hint of the vanished architectural grandeur of the Roman town.

1-9 Micklegate: Monumental stone wall

A measure of grandeur would also have been apparent in the temples of which there were probably a large number as Roman religion encompassed a great range of ideas and the cult of many different gods and goddesses. They included the long-established members of the classical pantheon such as Jupiter, Juno and Minerva, who had a particular role in the protection of the Roman empire, as well as Mars, Mercury and Venus, all of whom were evidently worshipped in York. The Romans also worshipped their deceased emperors who were thought to be semi-divine beings in life and gods after their death. In important towns the cult was serviced by the *seviri augustales* (literally the 'six men of the emperor') who were usually wealthy freedmen (former slaves). We know of two *seviri* from Roman York. One of them, Marcus Aurelius Lunaris, described himself as a *sevir* of both York and Lincoln on an altar he set up in Bordeaux in the year 237, perhaps in gratitude for a successful trading venture. The other man is Verecundius Diogenes named on a stone coffin, now sadly lost, who was originally from Bourges in Gaul. Remarkably, the coffin

17

of his wife, Julia Fortunata from Sardinia has also been found and can be seen today in the Yorkshire Museum.

Mithras relief and dedication to Serapis

In addition to officially sponsored cults, many others of local or regional deities, such as Arciacus whose name only occurs on an altar from York, were followed by the townsfolk. By the 2nd century, however, there appears to have been growing dissatisfaction with the traditional cults and new religious ideas began to sweep across the empire, principally from the eastern provinces. They were to take root in places like York which had a shifting population of merchants, traders and soldiers. Popular in Britain, because of its appeal to the large military establishment, was the cult of Mithras, a sun god of Persian origin who played a pivotal role in the eternal struggle of good and evil. Every Mithraic temple had a relief showing the god in a characteristic pose slaying the sacred bull from which the blood of life flowed. This can be clearly seen on an example found on Micklegate in the 18th century opposite St Martin cum Gregory church suggesting a Mithraeum stood nearby.

A cult of Egyptian origin is that of Isis and her consort Serapis, and an inscribed tablet found in Toft Green indicates a Serapeum, or temple of Serapis, existed in that area. It was evidently founded by a commander of the Sixth Legion, Claudius Hieronymianus, whose second name suggests he may have been an Egyptian himself. The idea of rebirth after death, which forms a central theme in the cult of Isis, can also be found in that of Cybele, a mother goddess with fertility powers. Her paramour was Atys who is depicted as a shepherd on a tomb monument found on The Mount. In remorse for betraying the goddess with a nymph, Atys castrated himself before dying under a pine tree or, in some versions of the story, being turned into one. Roman sources suggest that the cult involved ceremonies of a dramatic and exuberant nature centring on a spring festival in March. At one point male devotees, probably in a state of drug or drink induced euphoria, emasculated themselves by way of a dedication to the goddess. Whether this took place in York remains unknown!

It is difficult to determine the size of York's population in Roman times, but based on the area known to have been settled, it is likely to have reached about 5000 at its peak (excluding the soldiers). One of the problems of making any sort of estimate is that there is not a great deal known about where the homes of the people of Roman York lay, although it is clear that an important residential area lay in the south-eastern part of the town in what is now Bishophill. In the early 3rd century the steep sloping valley side was terraced in what was clearly a massive undertaking requiring thousands of tons of material and considerable effort to construct. Remains of town houses have been found built on the terrace which would have afforded their residents agreeable river views and boasted such luxuries as under floor heating, private bath houses and rooms decorated with painted wall plaster and marble veneers.

Water for the people of York was usually available at street fountains and evidence for a piped mains supply was found at the Wellington Row site, already referred to in connection with the main road from the south-west. In the mid 2nd century the road was raised in level by 3 feet (c.1m), probably to create a causeway for a bridge or, more likely, for a new bridge over the river. At the same time, lead pipes were laid in a stone-lined trench along one side of the road to carry a mains water supply which must have originated in a distribution centre on high ground to the south-west and probably continued across the bridge to supply the fortress. A pipe recovered in the excavation had an internal diameter of 6" (15cms), the largest known in Roman Britain.

Contemporary with the remodelling of the Roman road at Wellington Row was the construction of a stone building measuring 51 x 34'6" (15.5 x 10.5m) with its longer axis at 90° to the road. The function of this building cannot be identified, but its history is a sort of microcosm of the history of the Roman town as it underwent all sorts of alterations through the late 2nd, 3rd and early 4th centuries after which it was abandoned and partly demolished. In its original form the building possessed a clay oven, probably the source of a fire which seriously damaged the building at the end of the 2nd century. This is evidence once again for one of the principal hazards of Roman town life. What may have been debris from the same fire, or one more or less contemporary with it, was found at a small site nearby (5 Rougier Street) in the form of a thick deposit of burnt grain mixed with charred timber, apparently derived from a warehouse.

In the second half of the 2nd century the main road from the south-west clearly ran through an important commercial zone of Roman York as it approached the River Ouse crossing. On a site on Tanner Row parts of timber buildings were found which had stood immediately to the north-west of a drainage ditch running along the roadside. Roman deposits here were waterlogged; as a result some of the timbers survived revealing numerous details of carpentry techniques including expertly made mortise and tenon joints. In and around the buildings were thick deposits of refuse,

20

Wellington Row: Roman stone building

Tanner Row: Roman timber building

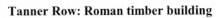

the contents of which have provided some of the best evidence for the crafts practiced in Roman York. Slag from blacksmithing and copper-working occurred in some quantity along with iron tools used in a number of crafts including leatherworking. This was represented by shoe fragments, a complete panel from an army tent and scraps of others. On one of these tent scraps careful cleaning by conservators revealed a graffito scratched into the leather which names the century (an army unit of 80 men) of its commander, the centurion Sollius Julianus. This is probably the same man as Marcus Sollius Julianus who is named on a building stone found on Hadrian's Wall commemorating a stretch of the Wall built by his men. This graffito is therefore a remarkable and intimate testimony to the link between the Sixth Legion on the northern frontier and at its base in York. Other military equipment from the site included a sword, possibly brought to the site for recycling or repair, and fittings from army horse trappings or uniforms.

Good preservation of organic matter meant that the Tanner Row site has produced some of the best evidence for the food supply and diet of the Roman inhabitants of York. Copious animal bones show that the principal source of meat was beef supplemented by a little mutton and pork. Distinctive aspects of the material included the smashed-up limb bones of cattle indicating systematic extraction of marrow used, perhaps, for broth and soup. There were also numerous cattle scapulae (shoulder blades) thought to result from preparing boned-out shoulders of smoked beef, perhaps considered something of a delicacy at the time. The importance of bread and cereal-based foods in Roman diet has already been noted and the charred grain at the Rougier Street site was shown to be 89% spelt wheat and 11% barley which was perhaps used for brewing. A feature of the plant remains from Tanner Row, however, was the diversity of the seeds of field weeds which must have accompanied consignments of cereals and animal feed such as hay. They indicate that York was drawing food from a variety of ecological zones some of which were at least 12½ miles (20km) distant. In addition to locally-produced foodstuffs, others came from further away. They include crabs, perhaps from Bridlington Bay on the east coast, and herring caught in the Humber estuary. From beyond Britain came olives, grapes and figs. Wine from Gaul and olive oil from southern Spain arrived in the great pottery jars known as amphorae. To conclude, the food remains tell us that by the end of the 2nd century the community at York included people with both sophisticated tastes and the wealth to gratify them.

One effect of the increasing demand for food from York, and other towns and forts in the region, was probably the enrichment of some of its landowners, allowing them to espouse a Romanised life style themselves. One manifestation of this was the villa. In a British context a villa may be defined as a Romanised house in a rural setting which usually had a farm attached to it. The main house, at least, would be built largely of stone and enjoy such appointments as heated rooms, baths and mosaic floors. Although the first villas in the south-east of Britain date from the 1st century, the emergence of villas in the north did not get under way until the end of the 2nd century and the buildings remain relatively modest until the 4th. The best-known villa near York is Dalton Parlours near Collingham 11 miles (18 km) to the south-west which has been fully excavated, but others existed at Wilstrop and Kirkby Wharfe, within about 9 miles (14km) west and south-west of York respectively.

Evidence for imports other than food can be inferred from the pottery which is found in vast quantities on excavations, even if the traded goods themselves have not survived. Pride of place amongst wares of continental origin must go to samian, a shiny red tableware imported from various parts of Gaul. Samian was supplemented by so called 'colour-coated' beakers and jars with a shiny purple finish and a low relief decoration which originated in the Rhineland, principally the great Roman city of Cologne. As far as exports from York are concerned, grain and other agricultural products probably made up the bulk of them. In addition, a small contribution was made by objects of jet, a mineral akin to coal which came from the east coast in the Whitby area. Jet can be easily cut and given a high polish; it is also electrostatic which gave it an aura of magic in antiquity. Amongst the commoner items made of jet were beads, bracelets, hair pins and rings, but more elaborate pieces are known including medallion pendants bearing human portraits and gorgon masks which served to repel the evil eye. Although there were other sources of jet in the Roman empire, most of the jet found in the western provinces was probably exported from York.

Amongst the men who were involved in trade at York were Marcus Aurelius Lunaris already named, and Lucius Viducius Placidus from the territory of the Veliocasses, a people who lived around what is now Rouen in northern Gaul. He is referred to as a *negotiator* (merchant) on an inscribed tablet dated to 221. The tablet is witness to a rare British example of building work, in this case of an arch and vaulted passage, which may have formed part of a temple, funded by a wealthy private individual – the sort of thing that is common in other parts of the empire.

Until now we have looked primarily at the civilian town on the south-west bank of the Ouse, but other areas of settlement should not be ignored. Although they have not been extensively explored archaeologically, the most heavily built-up area lay in the zone, already referred to, between the fortress, and the Rivers Foss and Ouse. There is evidence of replanning here in the late 2nd or early 3rd century in that the remains of the Coney Street grain warehouse and other timber structures found on the corner of Coppergate and High Ousegate were overlain by a new street which probably ran along the Ouse bank. A bath house and other buildings have been recorded on the north-east side of this street and inscriptions found on the corner of High Ousegate and Nessgate suggest that there were temples both of the imperial cult and of the god Hercules in that area.

Areas beyond the north-east and north-west defences of the fortress, and east of the River Foss were clearly never densely settled in Roman times, being given over to fields or stock enclosures. South-west of the Ouse, immediately outside the Roman town, it is clear that buildings crowded up to the main road from the south-west for a distance of about 300 yards (273 m). Beyond them lay one of the great cemeteries of Roman York. According to Roman law the dead had to be buried outside areas inhabited by the living. Typically, therefore, cemeteries lined the main roads as they approached settlements. At York large cemeteries were revealed in the 19th century during, for example, suburban development on The Mount and the construction of the railway station in the 1870s. However, although large numbers of jewellery items, pottery vessels and other objects were recovered by local antiquarians, few records were made of the graves themselves and it is difficult to get a detailed picture of the cemeteries' history.

It is clear from research elsewhere in the empire that the cemeteries would have been divided into plots owned by families, occupational groups and other institutions. The rich and powerful usually strove to secure plots in prominent locations close to the roads or on high ground so that their tombstones and mausolea would remind visitors and locals alike of the most important families in the community. Discoveries of tombstones and other funerary monuments suggest that plots close to the main Roman road from the south-west around its highest point, now the junction of the Mount with Albemarle Road and Dalton Terrace, were particularly sought after. However, the cemetery excavated at Trentholme Drive another 330 yards (300m) to the south-west on low-lying ground near what is now the racecourse was probably used by the poorer sections of the community. No tombstones were found here, but there were over 350 graves usually dug just deep enough to inter the body taking little regard to any earlier interments which were casually disturbed and the bones spread about.

Burial practice in Roman York clearly varied a great deal as one would expect in a place which was home to people of diverse geographical origins and whose status in society ranged from the highest ranks of the Roman army and government to the humblest of slaves. For all classes, however, the earliest Roman burials were usually cremations. The body of the deceased was burnt and the remains were then interred in a pottery vessel, or more rarely a glass or lead jar. Cremation fell out of favour during the 2nd century to be replaced by inhumation of the body unburnt. Graves are usually recognisable as bath-shaped pits in which the bodies were often laid to rest in wooden coffins, although only their iron nails survive. In at least some cases the bodies of the dead were buried clothed, although all that usually survives are the jewellery items such as rings and bracelets, and occasionally the iron hobnails of boots and shoes. Votive offerings were sometimes made, for the most part in the form of pottery vessels which probably contained food and drink for the dead on his or her journey to the next world. The skeleton of a female recently found

The Stone Coffin of Aelia Severa

in the Railway Station cemetery was buried with two coins placed over her eyes symbolising the payment to the ferryman who took the dead across the River Styx to the underworld in a version of Roman ideas about death derived from Greek mythology. Scientific examination of the skeleton suggests it was of a woman in her 30s and this is fairly typical of the adult population of Roman Britain, few of whom would have lived beyond their 40s.

A few examples of lead and stone coffins are known from York and sometimes they were clearly placed in mausolea, probably resembling small houses or temples, rather than buried as they bear inscriptions commemorating the names and other details of the deceased which would have been intended for inspection by the living. The remains of a Roman mausoleum, in which there is a skeleton still lying in a stone coffin, can be seen (by arrangement with the property owner) in the cellar of No.104 The Mount. Another mausoleum would have accommodated the family of

Tombstone of Julia Velva

Caecilius Rufus whose wife, Aelia Severa, is named on one of the finest stone coffins from York. In the inscription she is referred to as a member of the *honestiores*, the upper crust of Roman citizens whose menfolk occupied positions of importance in government and administration. We are also told that Aelia Severa's coffin waspaid for by Caecilius Musicus, a slave who had taken on his master's family name on receiving his freedom. One might guess from his second name that he had previously been the household musician.

Grave markers would have been necessary to preserve order in cemeteries, but again only the rich could have stood the expense of a carved tombstone. About 20 have been found in York and they are a fascinating source of evidence for the upper echelons of local society and their customs. As an example we may consider the splendid tombstone of Julia Velva, now to be seen in the Yorkshire Museum. It is made from a block of millstone grit 5'6" (1.6m) high and in the upper half is a scene carved in relief featuring an arched niche intended to portray the apsed (i.e. semi-circular) dining room in a high status house. Within the niche is a group of four figures partaking of a meal. The central figure is presumably Julia Velva who, according to the inscription in the lower half of the tombstone lived to the fairly ripe old age, for Roman times, of 50. Her head and torso alone are visible, but it is clear that she reclines on a couch with a thick mattress and props her head on her left arm. She holds a vessel in her right hand in front of her breast. In front of the couch, viewed from left to right, are, first, a young girl seated on a basket-weave chair clasping a pet bird, next comes a three legged table on which there stand dishes of food, and then a young man, possibly a servant shown small to indicate his inferior status. On the right standing in front of a large table and holding a scroll, is a male figure, presumably the Aurelius Mercurialis named in the inscription as Julia Velva's heir. He is moustached and bearded in the fashion of the early 3rd century and wears a short tunic and mantle. Although at first glance this might seem to an intimate domestic scene, it is actually a powerful statement of family status which shows us what was essentially a public room used by the elite of Roman society to receive guests and clients, and dispense hospitality and patronage.

While funerals were doubtless an everyday occurrence in a town the size of *Eboracum*, one funeral would have captured the attention of the whole Roman empire, that of the Emperor Septimius Severus whose campaign in the north of Britain was brought to an abrupt end by his death in York on February 4th 211. This great event was apparently foretold by a number of omens. Severus is said, for example, to have dreamt that 'he was dragged up into the sky by four eagles'; the eagle, of course, symbolises both Jupiter, the king of heaven, and the empire itself. The demise of an emperor was always regarded as an event of cosmic significance given his place half way between men and gods, and the funeral, attended by the whole imperial family would have been quite splendid. According to Cassius Dio:

'...his body arrayed in military garb was placed upon a pyre, and as a mark of honour the soldiers and his sons ran about it; and as for the soldiers' gifts, those who had things at hand to offer as gifts threw them upon it and his sons applied the fire.'

Severus was presumably cremated somewhere immediately outside York, but was not buried here and we are told that he was taken to Rome in an urn described by Cassius Dio as made of porphyry and in another source as made of gold.

While on the subject of urns, a distinctive artefact of the Severan period in York is the so-called head pot. *[colour plate 2].* It is a vessel made in the shape of a human head, usually female, thought to represent the Empress Julia Domna; a few male heads may represent Caracalla. Head pots were often used for the burial of cremated remains and in view of the semi-divine status of the imperial family what could be better than consigning one's relatives to the hereafter in the care, as it were, of one of its members?

After his funeral Severus's sons Geta and Caracalla immediately returned to Rome to secure their inheritance. In the event rivalry between the brothers soon led to the murder of Geta, and Caracalla reigned supreme until he was himself murdered in 217. Although he has had rather a bad press as an emperor, it was Caracalla that York has to thank for promotion to the rank of a provincial capital when Britain was divided into two provinces. It was probably felt in Rome that undivided Britain with its three legions could pose a threat to the regime if they were commanded by an over-ambitious general. The province of Lower Britain (*Britannia Superior*) had its capital at London and Upper Britain (*Britannia Inferior*) had its capital at York. It is likely that, at the same time, York was given the title of *colonia*, although the only datable reference to York's status in this respect is on the altar, already referred to, dedicated at Bordeaux by Marcus Aurelius Lunaris in the year 237. In origin the title *colonia* referred to a colony of Roman citizens who were expected to promote the interests of the empire, often in newly conquered territory, in return for legal privileges. In Britain there were three *coloniae* established in the 1st century, at Colchester, Gloucester and Lincoln, which were built on the site of legionary fortresses to accommodate retired soldiers. By the early 3rd century when York was designated, *colonia* status was a largely meaningless honour rather like the title 'city' is today.

York was henceforth the seat of the Roman governor of *Britannia Inferior* and the first man known by name to have filled the post was Marcus Antonius Gordianus (Gordian) from Cappadocia (Asia Minor), already fairly elderly in Roman terms at the age of 59 who may well have regarded York as the crowning achievement of his career. Little trace of Gordian's sojourn can be detected in the city's archaeology except for a curious inscribed block, now built into the foundations of the Minster. It appears to refer to a college of *beneficiarii*, soldiers who were entrusted with special missions, which had named themselves after him. One should add that fate was to have another card to play in Gordian's career because in 238, some 20 years after his period in York, when aged 81, he became emperor for a year and even then he died by suicide rather than natural causes!

York in the Late Roman Period

When Marcus Aurelius Lunaris set up his altar of good Yorkshire millstone grit to the presiding goddess of Bordeaux in the year 237, one wonders whether it was with any sense of foreboding that the world he knew was about to be turned upside down. Two years earlier, in 235, the Emperor Severus Alexander, the last of the Severi, died in Mainz to be succeeded by Maximinus the Thracian, a man with no qualification for the job other than the command of a large body of troops. In the next 50 years *Britannia* would be ruled by nearly 40 different emperors, most enjoying only brief reigns, few of whom were capable of organising the defences of an empire under pressure at many different points around its frontiers. In 259 the Gallic provinces, devastated by attacks across the Rhine by hostile armies of a Germanic people known as the Alamanni, broke away under the usurper Postumus who also included Britain and Spain in his domain. In 260 the ruler of the rest of the empire, Valerian, was captured by the Persians in the east dealing what must have been a shattering blow psychologically to the military elite wherever their loyalties lay at the time.

Unlike many of the frontier provinces Britain appears to have avoided the worst of the turmoil afflicting the Roman empire in the mid 3rd century and suffered no major invasions. At the same time, however, the effects of inflation and the disruption of interprovincial trade attendant on political instability led to significant changes in the way the economy operated. This had a particular impact on towns like York which failed to expand any further. Graphic evidence for a changing pattern of its trade can be seen in the pottery and this probably reflects the position with regard to other commodities. Whereas a good range of imported continental wares was available in the 2nd and early 3rd centuries, from the late 3rd century onwards, most pottery was locally produced, the only major source at any distance being the Nene Valley around Peterborough.

Although its economic fortunes may have declined, York did not sink into stagnant obscurity in the late Roman period. It remained a provincial capital and army base throughout the 4th century. In addition, in the year 306, York witnessed an event which heralded one of the most important turning points in the history of the western world: the acclamation as emperor of a young man named Constantine. The background to his rise to power was a revival of the western empire in the late 3rd century due, to a large extent, to a reassertion of imperial authority at the centre which began during the reign of Diocletian (284-305). He appreciated that running the empire was a taxing job for one man at the best of times and so he established a system known as the Tetrarchy, both to lessen the imperial burden and provide for a more ordered succession. There were now to be four emperors, one senior (known as Augustus) and one junior (known as Caesar) for the eastern and western halves of the empire.

Britain's political situation in the late 3rd century had been complicated by the revolt in 285 of Carausius, a Roman naval commander who briefly ruled Britain and part of Gaul. In 293 he was murdered by his finance minister and successor Allectus who in 296 was himself defeated by Constantius I, then the legitimate Caesar in the west. Some ten years later, while campaigning in the north of Britain, Constantius, by now the Augustus in the west, became the second emperor to die in York. On his death the Tetrarchy system demanded that the Caesar in the west, one Flavius Valerius Severus, be promoted Augustus, but, urged on by Crocus, a king of the Alamanni, commanding a force of his Germanic troops with the Roman army in Britain, Constantius's troops voted for his son Constantine. It is not known whether Constantine himself was actually in York when acclaimed as emperor, although one would like to think he was, but he soon left Britain and over the next eighteen years gradually finished off his rivals before emerging in 324 as supreme ruler of the empire.

Constantine I 'the Great' is important in history because he was the first emperor to allow Christians to worship freely, although whether he himself became a Christian is unknown. Indeed, it seems rather unlikely in view of the way that the cult of the emperor as a divine being developed during his reign. We get some flavour of this from the panegyrics which were offered to the emperor on state occasions. One example composed by the poet Eumenius also shows how Britain, as the place where Constantine came to power, was able to bask in some reflected glory. 'Fortunate and happier than all lands because she first saw Constantine Caesar' he wrote, and goes on 'Gracious gods! What means this, that always from some remote end of the world, new deities descend to be universally revered?' Another expression of a 4th century emperor's divine status was the larger than life monumental statue. A limestone head, found in Stonegate in the 19th century, is taken to be from a statue of Constantine which had presumably stood in or near the fortress headquarters.

By the year 391 Christianity in the Roman empire had become so strong that the Emperor Theodosius, a militant Christian, was able to ban the observance of all other cults. It is unclear, however, how many Christians there were in Roman Britain and they may have remained a small minority even in places like York where the population was exposed to new ideas in a way that the rural masses were not. We know, however, that there must have been a Christian community in York since a bishop existed by 314 when Eborius was summoned by Constantine, with three other bishops from Britain, to a Council at Arles to discuss doctrinal matters. Archaeological traces of Christianity are, however, confined to just two artefacts: the first is a tile from the Minster excavations bearing a roughly scratched version of the Christogram, or chi-rho, the first two letters of Christ's name in Greek. The second is a small bone plaque bearing a motto thought to be Christian in sentiment which reads SOROR AVE VIVAS IN DEO (hail sister may you live in God) which was found with a burial in a stone coffin at Sycamore Terrace, off Bootham. There must be some doubt, however, about the significance of these words because, although it is generally thought that Christianity demanded that burials be made without grave furnishing, the Sycamore Terrace burial contained, in addition to the plaque, a glass jug, crystal mirror and jewellery items. An association with Christianity, and the Christian belief in the resurrection on Judgement Day, has also been used to explain the distinctive late Roman practice of embalming the body of the deceased in gypsum (calcium sulphate) before placing it in a lead or stone coffin. There are some 50 gypsum burials known from York, all probably 4th century, but current opinion is that this was simply a fashionable form of interment with no particular religious associations.

York's continuing role as a military base in the 4th century is indicated by a document known as the *Notitia Dignitatum*, a list of official and military dispositions in the Roman empire, probably dating from the early 5th century, but thought to incorporate earlier material. York is named as the base of the Sixth Legion and may also have been the headquarters of an official named in the *Notitia* as the *Dux Britanniarum* (Duke of the Britains) who appears to have commanded all Roman forces in the north. The extent to which York was permanently garrisoned in the 4th century is, however, unclear. The Roman army was no longer organised as it had been when it first arrived in York; legions of infantry were no longer stationed in permanent bases on the frontiers and were no longer assisted by auxiliaries raised in conquered provinces. It was now found more useful to have a mobile field army, largely cavalry, which could be moved to trouble spots as required. Frontiers like Hadrian's Wall were manned by troops known as *limitanei* who formed a militia raised from the local population.

Archaeological evidence for the fortress in the 4th century suggests continued use, but a reduced garrison. Excavations at York Minster revealed some reorganisation of the headquarters basilica in the 4th century, the most striking aspect of which perhaps was the addition of a room at its north-west end which was richly decorated with painted wall plaster (now to be seen in the Minster Undercroft). In addition, there were structural alterations in the barracks north-west of the basilica, but elsewhere there is evidence for the abandonment of some fortress buildings and for the dumping of refuse in and around others. Even the main streets of the 4th century fortress appear to have been poorly maintained. In a series of observations of the *via principalis* in Petergate during sewer repairs in 1998, it was recorded that some 2" (0.05m) of silt had been allowed to accumulate over a gravelled surface of, perhaps, the early 3rd century. However, after about the year 350, the street was reinstated, albeit in a rough and ready fashion, using blocks of stone clearly re-used from demolished buildings in the area. The *intervallum* street was also reinstated at the same time, but a recent observation of the *via decumana* showed that it had probably gone out of use by the beginning of the 4th century and was never resurfaced.

On the fortress defences the ditches appear, in places, to have been redug in the early 4th century, but there is no evidence for any major reconstruction work except for the so-called 'Anglian Tower' *[monochrome plate 2]* located about 200 feet (60m) north-east of the Multangular Tower. It was discovered in 1842 when a tunnel was driven through the city defences by the Recorder of York and it was excavated archaeologically in 1970 when it acquired its name as it was thought, on no very good evidence, to be 7th century. Whilst it may not be Anglian, the structure is clearly a tower and would seem to be an addition to the interval towers on the fortress wall or perhaps a replacement for one a little to the south-west. The tower is striking in being built of roughly coursed and dressed *oolitic* limestone (from the North York Moors) in contrast to the vast majority of fortress buildings which are built of *magnesian* limestone, but it may be argued that if it were post-Roman why is it built of freshly-quarried stone rather than re-used material from what would, by the 7th century, have been redundant fortress structures?

In the civilian settlements the evidence for the 4th century is relatively sparse compared to that for the 2nd and early 3rd centuries. Excavations at Wellington Row showed that the great main road from the south-west was made narrower and the lead water pipes described above were largely ripped out after a series of pits were dug down through the road make-up to reach them. However the water supply appears to have been reinstated, if in a rather less sophisticated form, by means of a remarkable wood-lined trench with vertical sides and a flat base dug along the north-west side of the road. At what date the water finally ceased to flow through the Roman *colonia* is hard to say, but the road itself may have remained in use for some considerable time even after York's imperial status had ended or at least until the bridge collapsed. In the 4th century also it is clear that town houses were newly built while others were enlarged. South-west of the Ouse, in the north-western part of the *colonia*, early 4th century mosaics were revealed at two locations in the 19th century. One of the pavements, found on Toft Green in 1853 has a design theme common on Roman mosaics, that of the spirits of the four seasons who are represented in each corner of the pavement by a female bust accompanied in the case of spring by a swallow, summer by a rake, autumn by a bunch of grapes and winter by a bare bough. In the centre of the mosaic, as a protection against the evil eye, is the gorgon Medusa whose ghastly face turned all who gazed upon it to stone. Another mosaic, this time with a purely geometric pattern, was found in a large reception room with a polygonal apse at one end belonging to a house excavated at Clementhorpe, immediately south-east of the presumed *colonia* defences. On the north-east bank of the Ouse the existence of 4th century houses is implied by mosaics found at St Mary Castlegate and at 21-33 Aldwark.

The identity of the residents of these town houses can never be known and there are no longer even the clues provided by the tombstones of earlier times, but they were probably government officials and retired soldiers. By the 4th century wealthy landowners probably preferred to live on their country estates, rather than in town, and in the York region a number of new villas was established in the early 4th century while others were enlarged and embellished. In the former category may be placed Beadlam, near Helmsley, in the Vale of Pickering where there is the only villa building to be seen today north of the Humber. This is a small house which had heated rooms and a mosaic floor and it stood on the north side of a courtyard surrounded by other buildings. Amongst the villas which were enlarged and embellished are a number in favourable spots on the Wolds such as Langton, near Malton, and Rudston where in the residential block and baths suite were laid mosaics, well known for their representations of Venus and Mercury which bear witness to an abiding interest in classical mythology even in this remote corner of the Roman world.

The End of Roman York

Roman *Britannia* appears to have remained reasonably peaceful and prosperous until the last 20 years or so of the 4th century after which the deterioration in its economic fortunes and security situation was rapid. By the second decade of the 5th century it had ceased to be part of the empire.

A historically recorded event in the later history of Roman Britain occurred in the year 367 when, as we are told by the writer Ammianus Marcellinus, it was the victim of an attack by hostile barbarians, probably from Scotland and Ireland who found the Roman army unequal to repelling them. A senior officer was killed and a general, Fullofaudes, was cut off. In the aftermath the Emperor Valentinian sent a high ranking official, Count

Theodosius, to restore Britain's defences. It is not clear from archaeological evidence what this entailed, although a group of five so-called signal stations on the Yorkshire coast may have been built at this time. They consisted of towers, perhaps about 50–60 feet (15-18m) high, which stood in the centre of a small walled courtyard surrounded by a ditch. The exact function of the signal stations has been much debated, but, in part, they were probably intended to give early warning of sea-borne attackers which could in, due course, be relayed to York.

Dramatic though the attack of 367 sounds, it may have been just one of many and Britain's ability to deal with them was progressively reduced by the removal of Roman forces at the behest of a succession of usurpers seeking to gain the imperial crown. The first of these was Magnus Maximus, a general in Britain who having defeated the Picts, progressed to ruling the western empire from 383 until his murder in 388. One effect of increasing insecurity was to destroy the economic system which had sustained York and towns like it all over Britain. However, a detailed understanding the last years of Roman York is difficult because of the lack of closely datable artefacts in archaeological layers. There are very few coins which can be given a date later than about 402 and, although pottery was probably still made in Roman style in the early 5th century it is difficult to distinguish it from late 4th century material. Having said this, the evidence from the fortress and the civilian settlements does, in general terms, evoke a picture of York in about 400 as a place in which buildings, whether monumental or domestic, were largely deserted, streets were abandoned to encroaching vegetation and rubbish was accumulating around the habitations of the remaining residents.

Although archaeology suggests that Roman York was largely depopulated by the mid 5th century, it can not be assumed it was either entirely deserted or lacking any role in the economy and society of the region. The strategic importance of the river crossing and the value of the fortress and *colonia* defences can not have been lost on any local ruler who inherited the mantle of Roman power in the 5th century. The city was not immediately settled by the Anglian incomers who in the 5th century appear to have been confined to areas east of York. The earliest Anglian activity in York itself takes the form of two late 5th – early 6th century cremation cemeteries. The site at Heworth, which produced over 70 urns, lay adjacent to the Roman road running in an east-north-easterly direction from the fortress *porta decumana*. The other site, from which there are 5-6 urns, lay on The Mount adjacent to the main Roman road to the south-west. The fact that both Anglian cemeteries were sited close to Roman roads and lay within areas of former Roman cemetery may, perhaps, indicate a continuity of sacred associations, although it does not allow one to argue for a continuity of settlement between *Eboracum* and the place which emerges once more into the archaeological and historical record in the early 7th century.

ANGLO-SAXON AND VIKING-AGE YORK

Richard Hall

Introduction

Between the Romans' abandonment of Britain in the early 5th century and the arrival of the Normans in the mid 11th century, York was transformed. By 1066 much of the layout, many of the key functions and several of the major institutions of the medieval and modern town were recognizable. During 650 years York had changed and evolved in response to new political, social, economic and religious requirements. These centuries comprise England's Anglo-Saxon era. However, for convenience in understanding the broad sweep of change, they can be sub-divided into three periods. This "broad-brush" approach of three periods, of approximately equal duration, is helpful because archaeologists who sometimes cannot date their discoveries with precision *are* able to identify types of objects which are typical of one or other of these chronological sub-divisions.

The first is the sub-Roman period of the 5th and 6th centuries, one of the most elusive epochs in York's history. It includes the generations immediately after Rome's withdrawal when local people had to get used to total independence and self-sufficiency. It also embraces the time when pagan Germanic settlers from northern Europe, the Anglo-Saxons, achieved dominance in this region. In recognition of their appearance this period is sometimes also known as the early Anglo-Saxon or pagan Anglo-Saxon period, but because there is *relatively* little evidence for 5th - or 6th - century Anglo-Saxons at York, sub-Roman is the term used here.

The second is what York's archaeologists call the 'Anglian' period. Extending from about 600 to 850, this is the equivalent of what elsewhere in England is called the 'Middle Saxon' period. This was the time when, gradually, the four major Anglo-Saxon kingdoms of Wessex, East Anglia, Mercia and Northumbria were defined, and when Christianity was re-established.

The third period, from about 850 to the Norman conquest, covers the time when Viking armies conquered all of England except Wessex and western Mercia, shared out the land between themselves and settled like minor landed gentry. This extensive Scandinavian influence in England, particularly in Yorkshire, has led to the period being known locally as the 'Anglo-Scandinavian' period; it is also called 'the Viking Age' or the 'late Saxon' period. Alfred, king of Wessex (871-99) and his successors gradually conquered the so-called Danelaw territories, and established a newly united Anglo-Saxon kingdom of England. Under King Aethelred 'the Unready' this kingdom at first withstood renewed Viking attacks in the late 10th century but then succumbed to the Danish king Cnut, whose dynasty ruled in England from 1016 to 1042. English kings were resurrected in the person of Edward the Confessor (1042-66), but his death presented an opportunity for rival foreign contenders to invade England, and resulted ultimately in the Norman conquest.

Sub-Roman Period

The most difficult of these periods for both documentary historians and archaeologists to understand is the first, the sub-Roman period. There are no contemporary written sources which shed light on York between 314 and 627; archaeological evidence, particularly the discovery of coins, clearly shows activity in Roman York continued up to just after 400, but the next three centuries are difficult to identify archaeologically. One explanation for this gap in the archaeological record is that York

40

was deserted soon after 400. Natural catastrophe, in the form of flooding, has sometimes been suggested as a reason, but no trace of any such cataclysmic event has ever been found. The more prosaic explanation for York's decline is that its official links with Rome were severed shortly after 400, when the Roman army left Britain. Without imperial subsidy York's military and administrative functions disappeared, and with them went whatever economic life-line the empire had provided; commercial links with the continent and even regional trade declined as a result. The rich and the important had less reason to be in York; and their absence in turn would have removed the need for others who served and supplied them. Overall a move back into the more dispersed settlement pattern of farms and estates in the countryside took place, where crops for home consumption could be grown. In response to this overall thinning out of the settlement, even the Roman bishop's see might eventually have moved, or simply disappeared.

A variation on this hypothesis suggests that centuries of tradition coupled with York's prestige as a seat of power would have led local leaders to continue to govern the region's population from York, as post-Roman rulers did in sub-Roman towns elsewhere in Britain. It is possible that discoveries made in excavations below and around York Minster in 1967-73 fit this model. There the internal layout and appearance of the great Roman military basilican hall, a structure closely comparable in size to the nave of York Minster, were greatly altered at some time in or after the late 4th century. The activities conducted within this new setting were also radically different from what had gone before, perhaps providing either 'centralized amenities' for townsfolk forced into self sufficiency, or representing the power base of a local sub-Roman authority. Whatever these activities represent, they need not have continued for very long – in instances like this it is often difficult to distinguish between stages in the progression from 'a year or two' to 'a decade or two', 'a generation or two' or even 'a century or two'.

Uncertainty over the dating and duration of this activity at the military heart of Roman York reflects the difficulty

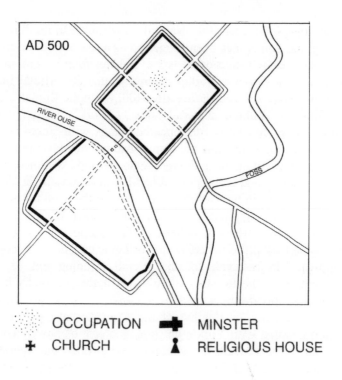

AD 500

RIVER OUSE

FOSS

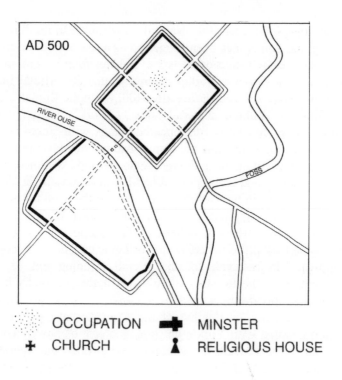 OCCUPATION ✚ MINSTER

✚ CHURCH ⚑ RELIGIOUS HOUSE

archaeologists have in recognizing and dating objects that are characteristic of the 'sub-Roman' 5th and 6th centuries. The Romano-British industries that mass produced pottery, glass, metalwork and other commodities of well known and closely dated types apparently ceased to function as the economic infrastructure which had supported them disappeared after 400. The familiar trappings of everyday life had to change, with locally produced or home-made goods becoming the norm. Perhaps organic materials such as wood and leather, which were readily available and relatively easy to use, became much more common – such materials do not usually survive for long when discarded, and this may help to explain the difficulty in recognising what happened to York's, and the region's, indigenous population in the 5th and 6th centuries.

Anglian Period

In eastern England, the 5th-6th century saw the arrival of immigrants from north-west Europe, the most important of whom were the Anglo-Saxons. Archaeologically their impact is most visible in the adoption of new burial rites, with characteristic pottery urns and fashions in personal jewellery. Cemeteries with these types of object in eastern Yorkshire show that new communities were established there in the mid-late fifth century, and their appearance has also been suggested as a reason for York's desertion at this time, so that it became a ghost-town in a no-go zone separating invading Anglo-Saxons in eastern Yorkshire from defending Britons in kingdoms such as Elmet and Craven to the west.

The idea of a no-go zone seems rather far-fetched, however, and it certainly did not take the Anglo-Saxons very long to penetrate to York. At least two cemeteries with Anglo-Saxon urns have been found outside York, one 550 yards (500 metres) to the south-west at The Mount and one half-a-mile (800 metres) to the north-east at Heworth. They suggest that there were Anglo-Saxon communities living thereabouts by the late 5th century; but they do not prove that York itself was occupied at that time.

The anonymity of York is lifted with events in 627, when Edwin of Deira, Anglo-Saxon king of Northumbria, was baptised in a little wooden church dedicated to St Peter which he had built in York. He was baptised by Bishop Paulinus, one of the band of missionaries originally sent to England from Rome by Pope Gregory in 597. Indeed, it may have been Paulinus's knowledge that York had been the seat of a Roman bishop in the 4th century, rather than any particular vested interest of Edwin's, that determined where in Northumbria the baptism took place, for there is no archaeological evidence that Edwin, or his predecessors, had lived in or used York.

Edwin's church, which *presumably* became Paulinus's cathedral, was dedicated to St Peter and was thus the direct forerunner of York Minster. However, the 1967-73 excavations below the Minster found no traces of Edwin's church, or indeed of any other later pre-Norman church. Gravemarkers dated to the 8th and 9th century were found, however, suggesting that the original cathedral was not far away. It may have stood to the north of York Minster, close to the remains of the medieval Archbishop's palace, in what is now called Dean's Park, or to the south of the Minster, in the vicinity of St Michael-le-Belfrey church, in what had been the courtyard of the Roman *principia*.

After his baptism Edwin began to build a new stone church around the wooden baptistery, but this work was still incomplete when he was killed in battle in 633 and Bishop Paulinus fled to Kent with Edwin's wife and family. Oswald, leader of a rival dynasty from the north Northumbrian kingdom of Bernicia, eventually became king, and the focus of the kingdom shifted northwards, towards the Bernician royal seat at Bamburgh, on the coast of Northumberland. Oswald had spent part of his youth in exile in south-west Scotland; he now invited monks from the Irish/Scottish church founded there by St Columba on the island of Iona to establish a monastic community on the tidal island of Lindisfarne, near Bamburgh, and Lindisfarne also became his bishop's seat. Meanwhile, York may have been virtually deserted once again. Although one of Paulinus's companions, James the Deacon, apparently remained in the vicinity, it was not until Oswald's successor Oswiu decided at the 'synod' of Whitby in 664 to follow Roman rather than Irish/Scottish observances that the bishopric was re-established at York.

By the 660s Edwin's stone church needed restoration, and Bishop Wilfrid leaded the roof, glazed the windows, and suitably renovated it. His successor at York, Bishop Bosa (678/9-706), is credited with founding a religious community. In 735 the bishopric of York was elevated to the status of archbishopric, but the impetus that this event, or a disastrous fire in 741, gave towards further embellishing the church remains unknown. Archbishop Aethelberht (766-779) built a magnificent new church, dedicated to Holy Wisdom, but it is uncertain where it stood. Perhaps it was part of the cathedral complex, but it may have been part of a separate group of churches in the Bishophill area, on the other side of the River Ouse, within the former Roman civilian town. Here, it is suggested, there was a monastic precinct within which were several churches. A decorated stone cross of the 9th century indicates that St Mary Bishophill Junior church had been founded by that time; the nearby St Mary Bishophill Senior (demolished 1963) may have had a similar origin. St Gregory's church in Barker Lane, demolished in the 16th century, had an unusual dedication to Pope Gregory; as the initiator of England's and York's conversion Gregory is most likely to have been venerated through a church dedication in the early centuries after the conversion. Finally, the church of the Holy Trinity, Micklegate, formerly known as Christchurch, may be the successor to Holy Wisdom itself, as those dedications were interchangeable – certainly Christchurch was an enormously important church in the 11th century, when documentary records give us a clear glimpse of its significance.

Either the Minster complex or the Bishophill area was the site of the famous library and school which made York an internationally recognised focus of learning in the later 8th and early 9th centuries. In the church's earliest years James the Deacon is likely to have taught the musical skills for which he was noted, Wilfrid allegedly gave books to St Peter's, and Archbishop Egberht (732-66) taught music, but the library and its use were fostered particularly by the next archbishop, Aethelberht, who collected books and promoted their study. His protégé Alcuin was the York school's most influential pupil, and became master there in 767. He travelled to the continent, and in the 780s left York to join Charlemagne's palace entourage.

The dominance of the church in this discussion of Anglian York accurately reflects the balance of documentary evidence. Eventually, however, the question arises of what, if anything else, was going on in York at this time; and what sort of place was Anglian York. Alcuin's poem 'On the Bishops, Kings and Saints of the Church of York' refers to 'York's high walls and lofty towers', features of its twin defensive shells which it owed to the Romans and which were largely to endure, albeit mostly in renewed form, into the medieval and modern periods.

(Ironically, the so-called 'Anglian Tower', near the west corner 'Multangular' tower of the fortress, is more likely to date to the later Roman era than to the Anglian period). But few other Roman features survived into the modern era, and even parts of the fortress defences themselves have disappeared. Was this the era when they were removed; or did many Roman features survive into Alcuin's lifetime and beyond?

The continuing use of the main gateways through the Roman fortress defences dictated that the approximate lines of the main streets between them should be maintained, in what are today called Stonegate and Petergate, but elsewhere the grid of Roman streets has been swept away. New, post-Roman streets include several that cut at an angle across the Roman alignments, and these could only be established when the originally densely packed Roman buildings had disappeared. This could have happened quite quickly – it is both possible and likely that many of the less substantial Roman buildings in fortress, civilian town and suburbs had become seriously dilapidated or collapsed by 500. More massive, heavily built structures could have lasted longer, but the fallen columns of the Roman fortress basilica illustrate the decay and ruin of what must have been one of Roman York's most imposing buildings. Unfortunately, it is not certain when this took place. Some experts consider that the great basilica, and perhaps other large buildings like it, stood up to and beyond the Viking takeover in 866; others believe it fell in the fifth or sixth century. Its tumble may have been the accidental outcome of neglect and decay leading to structural failure, or may have been deliberately induced by the requirement to obliterate a dangerous ruin. Certainly, at least one other great Roman building seems to have been demolished deliberately. This was a large bath building at 1-9 Micklegate, which seems to have been systematically taken down to only just above ground level; even more surprisingly, the stub walls were apparently used as foundation for a timber structure. Yet again, however, it is not clear when this happened; it may have been in the 4th century, or in the post-Roman period.

Throughout the former Roman city, natural invasion of wind-borne plants and vegetation would have gradually masked any look of dereliction, and what was once townscape may have looked more like an enclosed landscape of houses and fields or allotments by the early 600s. With buildings no longer acting as obstacles to much freer movement within the walls, direct routeways formed diagonally in the fortress between adjacent gates. Goodramgate is part of one such street, running from Kings Square towards a rear gateway, subsequently blocked up and sealed in, behind the Minster; Blake Street is part of another such diagonal between the now invisible south-west gate and the forerunner of Bootham Bar. The Roman bridge across the Ouse, which had run from the foot of Tanner Row to the Guildhall, was another casualty of time – the easiest replacement crossing was at the site of Ouse Bridge, and so the Roman approach from Micklegate Bar had to be roundly deflected on a sweeping curve down Micklegate. None of these developments is at all precisely dated, however. The former Roman *colonia* also seems to have lost a pattern of terracing which had allowed buildings to occupy the quite steep slope up from the river; today this is virtually all masked, and the impression is of a continuous slope.

Within a York cleared of much of the Roman urban infrastructure, as well as in the immediately surrounding former Roman suburbs, not a single 7th-9th century building has been positively identified. In contrast, there is a scatter of 7th-9th century artefacts, which increase in frequency as the centuries pass. Coins are amongst the easiest to identify. Some very rare gold coins were probably struck at a mint in York in the late 7th century. Only a handful are known, and they do not carry the name of a king or a minting place or, indeed, a date; but since three of them were found in York, this seems a likely place of origin for them. When silver replaced gold as the standard for currency, small silver and, later, debased silver coins were produced, known from their Old English names as *sceattas* and *stycas*. Some of them were struck in Northumbria, most probably in York; some bear the names of the kings for whom they were struck, and a smaller number the names of archbishops of York who also had this right. Apart from coins various forms of metal jewellery are probably the most common class of Anglian objects, identifiable and datable both by their form and by their decoration, which often incorporates interlace motifs. Pottery, in contrast, is not the ubiquitous indicator of activity it is in earlier and later periods. Certainly the most splendid object from York's Anglian period is a superb, high quality warrior's helmet of the later 8th century, which provides both an insight into contemporary war gear, and a reminder of the skill of Anglian weapon-smiths. The reasons for it being consigned to earth remain mysterious. *[colour plate 3]*

The quite widespread but not very intensive distribution of Anglian objects of these and other types throughout the Roman walled areas of York could be explained as representing a scatter of residences, occupied by individuals associated with the church, with royalty, or with trade. Such a pattern of occupation is not, by any stretch of the imagination, representative of what we would think of as a town.   It may, however, accurately reflect what could be implied by one of the names given to Anglian York. This is *Eoforwiccaestre*, and it seems obvious that the area within the Roman walls may have been the *caestre*, the defended zone, to which this version of the name referred.   Indeed, it seems probable that the Roman fortress area at least was a royal enclave, its impressive defences giving it a special status and use, appropriate as a royal reserve.

The other name for Anglian York was simply *Eoforwic*; place-name experts believe that this name is the Northumbrian counterpart to a handful of other *-wic* names, including *Lundenwic* ("London-wic"), *Gipeswic* ("Ips-wic") and *Hamwic* ("Southampton-wic"), which seem to have been given to the most important commercial centre in each of the Anglo-Saxon kingdoms. Was this an appropriate name-form for York in the middle-Saxon period of the 7th-mid 9th centuries? Alcuin called York an *emporium*, a seat of commerce by land and sea, and at about the same time a continental writer mentions a colony of Frisians, the international merchant entrepreneurs of their day, based at or near York. The distribution of continental pottery

48

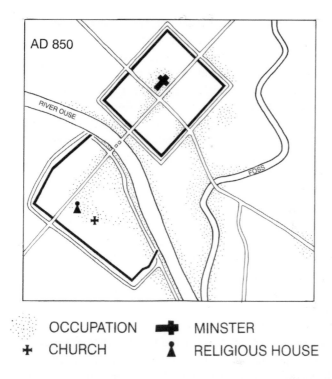

OCCUPATION   ✚ MINSTER
✚ CHURCH   ⌘ RELIGIOUS HOUSE

suggests, not surprisingly, that their activities, or those dealing
with them, were focussed along the River Ouse and, perhaps, the
Foss.

It is at the junction of the two rivers that a settlement
occupied *c*.700-850 has been discovered. Large blocks of land,
one estimated to be 1400 square yards (1200 square metres), were
delineated by ditches or other boundary markers; two or three
long rectangular timber buildings, typically measuring 42-45 feet
(13-14 metres) or more long by 18 feet (5.5 metres) wide, stood
within the plot, aligned on one or other of its main axes. Each of
these buildings, which archaeologists call 'halls', seems to have
had a group of pits dug nearby; these pits were eventually filled
with domestic rubbish, but some may have been originally dug
for other functions, as latrines/cess pits, for storage, or for some
industrial purpose. Certainly, objects were made on the site,

using a wide variety of raw materials, including iron, lead, copper, possibly silver and gold, wool for textile making, bone and antler for combs and other items, wood, leather, furs and animal skins. Domestic chores like grinding grain were carried out but farming or hunting to supplement and vary the diet do not seem to have been concerns of the inhabitants – the animal bone debris is remarkably uniform, and suggests that a regulated supply of meat was made available. However, the Fishergate occupants did benefit from and /or were involved in cross-channel trade with northern France, the Low Countries and the middle Rhineland.

Is this site at Fishergate the *wic* at *Eoforwic*? Well, it may be a part of the *wic*; but it is not particularly like the densely built up areas in *Hamwic*, or so extensive as *Lundenwic*; comparison with Ipswich cannot be made yet. Unique characteristics are not themselves reason to deny the Fishergate site *wic* status; perhaps *Eoforwic* operated differently to its Anglo-Saxon equivalents elsewhere. The Fishergate site could, for example, be interpreted as the York focus to which produce and raw material from one Northumbrian aristocrat's estates were sent to supply the craftsmen, managers and traders who made goods for sale and struck deals for foreign merchandise destined for the aristocratic owner.

Anglo-Scandinavian Period

So far as we know, York/*Eoforwic* was never a target for Viking raiders; yet it was singled out by Viking invaders in 866 as their first target. The 'great heathen army' captured the city on Friday November 1st 866. The choice of All Saints Day, a festival particularly celebrated in York and so a time when the cathedral might have been full of important people, was probably deliberate, with the hope of mopping up as many key figures in one go as possible, and/or of taking ransomable captives. The attack was successful, but the Northumbrian kings Aelle and Osberht were not captured; and when the Viking army returned to York on 21st March 867 after wintering on the Tyne, they had to

Plate 1 The main channel of the Roman fortress baths' sewer

Plate 2 The 'Anglian' Tower

Plate 3 Two post and wattle buildings, Coppergate street frontage c.930

Plate 4 A plank-lined cellar, Coppergate

Plate 5 Detail from the archway of St Michael's Church

Plate 6 The Great Hall. Merchant Adventurers' Hall

Plate 7 The Shambles, York's 'Medieval Street'

Plate 8 Edmund Grindal, Archbishop of York 1570-76

attack and capture York for a second time. On this occasion Aelle and Osberht were killed, although the later (13th-century) story that Aelle was put to death in a snake pit is just that – a story.

After a series of campaigns, largely successful, against the other Anglo-Saxon kingdoms, interspersed with further visits to York in order to keep their new conquest well under control, part of the great Viking army returned to Northumbria in 876. According to a near-contemporary source, the *Anglo-Saxon Chronicle*, their leader Halfdan '*shared out the lands of the Northumbrians and they proceeded to plough and to support themselves*'; according to the '*History of St Cuthbert*', compiled at Durham 1025-50, the Viking army '*rebuilt the city of York, cultivated the land around it, and remained there*'.

Halfdan is not heard of in York again, and indeed the next known king in York was Guthfrith/ Guthred, who ruled from 880/5 until 895, when he was buried at York Minster. The next Viking kings in Northumbria had short reigns, and have no recorded connections with York other than that their coins were apparently minted in the city. Then, from 901/2 until 919 the York mint produced coins which had no king's name; instead they carried the motto 'St Peter's money', sometimes combined with a sword motif and occasionally with a Thor's hammer symbol added as well.

All of this evidence points to several conclusions. The existence of a coin-mint in York, the only one north of the Humber, indicates the city's unique role in the region's economy. The juxtapositioning of Christian Anglo-Saxon and pagan (Scandinavian) references on the coinage suggests a desire by its sponsors to promote an integrated Anglo-Scandinavian identity. The prevalence of Christian messages, particularly focussed on St Peter, patron saint of York Minster, highlights the continuity of the archbishopric of York across this period, and the way in which the church formed links with new Viking leaders. The absence of kings' names may point either to an absence of kings or to the fact that weakness or policy restrained them from claiming the coinage.

At some time between 910 and 919 Ragnall, a Viking from Ireland, captured York, and minted coins which couple his name with that of the city. If his arrival was as late as 919, it was just as York was about to capitulate to the increasingly powerful kings of Wessex, who had already subsumed the west Midlands and had overwhelmed other former Viking kingdoms in East Anglia and the east Midlands. Ragnall managed to maintain the independence of Northumbria and York, affirming the *status quo* at a meeting with King Edward the Elder of Wessex/England at Bakewell (Derbyshire) in 920. On his death in 921 he was succeeded by his relative, Sihtric Caoch ('the Squinty'), who had been king of the Dublin Vikings, and this close link between Dublin and York was to be maintained, intermittently, over the next quarter of a century.

Sihtric briefly used a diplomatic marriage to a daughter of King Edward's in an attempt to stave off even less welcome English advances by Edward's son and heir, King Athelstan, but when Sihtric died in 926/7 Athelstan swept aside the bid for York by Sihtric's relative Guthfrith, King of Dublin, and incorporated York and Northumbria into his own expanding state. He celebrated by issuing coins at York which proclaimed him as 'King of All Britain' and, if William of Malmesbury's 12th-century history is to be believed, it was at York that he welcomed and entertained envoys sent by King Harald 'Fairhair' of Norway, who gave him a fine ship with a gold figurehead, purple sail and gilded shields.

Athelstan, a king both learned and militarily successful, defeated a Scots/Viking coalition which included Olaf, the son of his former rival, Guthfrith, at one of the most famous battles of its era, at *Brunanburh*, in 937. He was the first king of all England to visit York, and maintained his grasp on it continuously until his death in 939. His half brother Edmund then claimed the throne of all England, but Olaf Guthfrithsson seized the chance to install himself as king of Northumbria. He, in 941, was succeeded by his cousin Olaf Sihtricsson. Over the next fifteen years five Scandinavian and two Anglo-Saxon kings ruled Northumbria in a complex patchwork of political and military comings and goings.

Silver Penny minted for King Athelstan

This political turbulence eased as the Viking kings of Dublin were cut down to size by their Irish neighbours, and came to an end in 954 when the exiled Norwegian prince Eric Bloodaxe was expelled for the second and last time by the Northumbrians. King Eadred of Wessex and England regained control, and thenceforth York and Northumbria were always part of a united Anglo-Saxon kingdom.

The three or four generations who spanned the succession of political upheavals from the Vikings' arrival in 866 to the end of Northumbrian independence in 954 also witnessed fundamental changes in the way York looked and functioned. At about the time the Vikings captured York there seems to have been a change in the pattern of where people lived. The Fishergate site, a kilometre downstream of the Roman town at the confluence of the Rivers Ouse and Foss, was abandoned in the mid 9th-century; no coins later than the 860s were found there, but there was no sign of catastrophic destruction. In the Coppergate area, just outside the south-east side of the Roman fortress, there is no clear sign of any occupation between about

AD 400 and the mid 9th century, but sometime in the middle years of the 9th century activity and occupation resumed. By about 900 there are signs that the street line of Coppergate had become fixed. Within a few more decades, by about 930, a regular pattern of plot boundaries had been created, defining property units 18 feet (5·5 metres) wide. Single storey rectangular buildings with walls made of posts and interwoven wattles were erected at the street: the fronts were under the modern pavement, so their full length is unknown but they measured at least 27 feet (8·2 metres) long by 14 feet 6 inches (4.4 metres) wide. They combined living accommodation with workshop space. *[monochrome plate 3]*

The Coppergate site is the only one in York from which such a relatively closely dated sequence of development is known. In contrast to the pre-Viking period, however, there *is* quite a large number of sites at which traces of Anglo-Scandinavian buildings have been recognized. Sometimes the buildings can be confidently attributed to this period because of their relative position in a stratified sequence of occupation that runs from the obviously Roman to the obviously later medieval; sometimes because there is scientifically determined dating evidence; sometimes because there are objects of distinctly and uniquely Anglo-Scandinavian type firmly associated with them; and sometimes because they are of building forms typical of this period. In particular, what archaeologists call 'cellared buildings' or 'semi-basement buildings', constructed from substantial oak planks and beams, appear to have been a favoured type of structure in the later 10th and early 11th century. As well as at the Coppergate excavations they have been seen nearby between Coppergate and High Ousegate, in King's Square and, over the River Ouse, both at the foot of Micklegate and, perhaps, along Skeldergate. *[monochrome plate 4]*

The density of 10th-11th century occupation, revealed most clearly at Coppergate, is also hinted at elsewhere in the city, not just by the frequency of buildings themselves but also by the unusual soil conditions which in several places have preserved their timberwork for over a thousand years. These conditions, which have the appearance of a slightly moist, firm, compacted and aroma-rich peat bog, apparently result from intensive occupation which generates large quantities of organic waste in the form of building debris, household refuse, human cess and animal dung. When discarded in sufficient quantities this heady mixture creates an airtight, oxygen-free deposit in which the usual chemical processes of decay cannot take place. It therefore preserves in virtually perfect condition virtually all the organic materials - the plants, seeds, wood, grain, leather, wool – which were so important to contemporary people. Only horn and linen do not fare well in these anaerobic conditions.

The quantity of Anglo-Scandinavian building remains, and the widespread occurrence of these deeply stratified organic deposits, which could accumulate at the rate of one or two centimetres a year, combine to indicate that Anglo-Scandinavian York was much more like the medieval and modern concept of a town than Anglian York had been. *[colour plate 4]* This difference between pre-Viking and post-Viking York is further emphasized by comparing the variety, quantity and manufacturing techniques of the objects found in and around the Anglo-Scandinavian building, with what is known from the preceding centuries. Anglian objects are relatively few in number and many of them appear either to be home-made or the products of small-scale occasional craftwork, although it has to be admitted that it is impossible to determine accurately the scale of production at the manufacturing site at Fishergate. In contrast, Anglo-Scandinavian objects are often found in very large numbers, and were clearly made in uniform styles which point to professional mass-production by specialist workers.

Nowhere is this seen more clearly than in pottery production, where hand-made Anglian wares were replaced by new forms thrown on a fast wheel and fired in a properly regulated kiln. This technological advance speeded production, gave a more pleasing appearance (soon to be further enhanced when glazed wares were introduced), and opened up the market to standardized cooking pots and other kitchen wares. Again, the makers of wooden cups, who gave Coppergate its name, were 10th-century lathe-turners who produced a uniform series of cups and bowls, the main tablewares of the time. Individuals who had expertise in controlling kilns, ovens and forges for metalworking formed yet another important group of specialists; they established high-temperature industries, and were equally happy to work in lead, copper-alloy, iron, silver or gold, and even to make glass. In all these workshops, and in others such as those of the leatherworkers, antler-workers, barrel-makers and textile workers, the seeds of later medieval craft guilds, with their increasing specializations and demarcations, were sown.

All this production, of course, was a middling process which required both raw materials to fuel it and a market of customers who wanted to acquire these mass-produced items. Both ends of this spectrum must have extended well beyond the boundaries of *Jorvik*, and into an extensive hinterland. York was the only town north of the Humber, and uniquely able to offer this range of both utilitarian and luxury products; its pull, for both suppliers and customers, presumably spread a long way.

Most raw materials needed by York's manufacturers/fabricators were available from the immediately surrounding area, as were the foodstuffs needed to feed a population which, most unusually for the time, was concentrating its productive efforts somewhere other than in farming. Iron ores, lead, wool, flax, wood and timber, antler, animal products of all sorts including meat, milk, hides and bones, grain for bread and brewing, fish and shellfish – all could be brought into York from the estates, land-holdings and farms of the Yorkshire countryside. And back to this countryside might go the products of York's craftsmen, sometimes purchased by the payment of silver, either in coin or by weight.

Not all the goods on sale in Anglo-Scandinavian York were of local origin, however. Foreign contacts which had existed in the pre-Viking period continued, particularly with north-west Europe – wine was still imported from the Rhineland, for example, as was lava for quern stones. Noticeably, however, the geographical range of the import network widened in the late 9th and 10th centuries, reflecting the far-flung overseas contacts to which Scandinavian settlers were accustomed. These contacts brought an enhanced range of exotic goods to York, as well as some surprisingly mundane items. Scandinavia itself contributed walrus ivory from the far north, schist and phyllite sharpening stones from the Eidsborg area in Telemark, central southern Norway, as well as Baltic amber. Soapstone for bowls and ingot moulds originated in the Scandinavian settlement of Shetland, and a handful of other Pictish and Irish objects also reflect Scandinavian trading influence. Silk was brought to York from Byzantium (Istanbul) at the east end of the Mediterranean, to be made up into items such as headscarves; this is proved by the discovery of a group of offcuts and finished pieces at 16-22 Coppergate. A cowrie shell found only in the Red Sea demonstrates contact with the Near East – the shell may have been valued as a lucky charm, but it opens the possibility that other exotic items such as spices, oils or perfumes could have reached *Jorvik* from afar. The furthest travelled item yet found in the Viking-Age city is a coin, an Arab dirham, with an inscription which tells that it was minted in Samarkand in the early 10th century. The fact that it is a contemporary forgery of base metal concealed beneath a silvery looking surface does not mean that it hasn't travelled a long way; further even than the three thousand miles as the crow flies from Samarkand to York, for it surely came to York via Scandinavia, where such (genuine) coins are found in huge numbers. So it doesn't prove a direct link to the modern Uzbekistan, but does indicate the vast geographical extent of Viking Age trade routes.

The departure of Eric Bloodaxe ushered in a period of approximately a quarter of a century when York/Northumbria was relatively peaceful. A year after Eric had disappeared the English king Eadred (946-55) died, but his nephew Eadwig took over the throne of Northumbria, only to be pushed out within two years in favour of his brother Edgar. From 959-75 Edgar ruled all England though a period free from foreign attack that allowed him the nickname of 'the Peaceable'. During this time he promoted religious reforms of monastic communities, which had important repercussions in southern England but little apparent effect in York and Northumbria.

This was, however, a period when an enduring element of York's townscape was established – its multitude of parish churches. Sculptured grave markers dated to the 10th century have been found at several church sites; other churches are mentioned in Domesday Book, or in other late 11th-century documents, and altogether there is convincing evidence that at least some fifteen churches originated before the Norman conquest. There may well have been quite a few more. Only a handful of these have been examined archaeologically; it was excavation, however, which demonstrated that St Helen-on-the-Walls, Aldwark, which was obliterated by demolition in the 1500s, had its origin in a tiny 10th-century single-cell church, and it was excavation which located traces of a timber church built around 1000, St Andrew Fishergate. Most of these new Anglo-Scandinavian churches were built as the private property of their wealthy founders, an expression of status as well as religious belief. The clearest evidence for such private founders is a dedication stone from St Mary Castlegate which names Grim and Aese as two of the proprietors. These rich urban landowners benefited from the tithes paid to their own church, and were therefore likely to be zealous in maintaining the definition of the blocks of land which they owned and from which they could demand these church taxes. Here, then, lies the origin of many of York's parishes; and the distribution of these Anglo-Scandinavian churches also helps us to appreciate the pattern of occupation across the city.

It is striking just how little evidence there is for Anglo-Scandinavian occupation of great swathes of the area of the former Roman fortress, and the parish churches there do not have a demonstrable Anglo-Scandinavian origin. This in particular may reflect the fact that much of the fortress area was in the ownership of the archbishop. Exactly how much, and which bits, are matters for debate, but this ownership may well have effected the types of use made of land here, and influenced where newcomers were able to settle. Apart from grave-markers and other objects from a high-status 10th-11th century cemetery discovered beneath the south transept of the present York

Dedication Stone from St Mary Castlegate

Minster, relatively few Anglo-Scandinavian objects have been found within the fortress over the centuries, either by chance or in controlled excavations. There is some evidence for craft and manufacturing activity in the Minster area, but this is virtually isolated at present, and its setting and circumstance aren't clear. Equally, the discovery that someone in Blake Street, in about 1000, made a trefoil brooch, often considered a classic Scandinavian form, but with a mixture of English and Scandinavian decoration, is exciting but puzzling through being the only evidence for activity there at this time.

Also missing from much of the fortress are anaerobic peaty soils, particularly in its western part. Their absence may reflect this apparent lack of intensive occupation, but it may also relate to a fundamental change in natural topography which today is impossible to detect. From a point within the Roman fortress, in the general vicinity of St Sampson's Square, the natural ground surface sloped away downwards to the east towards the River Foss at an increasing gradient. This encouraged water to seep through the soils in a natural drainage pattern which, in turn, enhanced the preservation conditions hereabouts in a manner impossible for the remainder of the fortress area. Over the centuries, however, starting in the Anglo-Scandinavian era, this slope was levelled up to a much gentler gradient, and it is now barely perceptible in the walk along Parliament Street towards Coppergate. Yet about 16 feet (5 metres) deep below the street is the original base of the Roman fortress wall, 6 feet 9 inches (2.1 metres) of which still stands, cocooned in anaerobic deposits. That gradual accumulation of peaty soils inexorably made the Roman wall appear as less and less of an imposing, insurmountable barrier; it must have eventually become indefensible, and finally it ceased to have any tangible significance. Today its line is recognizable through the pattern of adjacent streets and parish boundaries, but this overall transition from defence to a mere fence may have been a protracted process, and at present its stages are not well understood.

Just how imposing the Roman fortress walls could still be around the year 1000 is well demonstrated at the west corner, where ground level has not changed much since the Roman era. There the Multangular Tower and the adjoining length of wall still stand to a height of about 14 feet 6 inches (4.5 metres), as they must have done in the Anglo-Scandinavian period, although there is evidence from the nearby 'Anglian Tower' site that earth ramparts were thrown up over the walls in the Anglo-Scandinavian period, presumably crowned with a timber palisade. Covered over or not, the south-west wall of the fortress disappears abruptly after a short distance, and a length of medieval wall and rampart runs at a right angle down to the Ouse, leaving the waterfront itself apparently open and undefended. An equivalent re-arrangement of the defences also took place off the opposite corner of the fortress where its north-east wall was at some time extended down to the River Foss to encompass its crossing point at Layerthorpe, just beyond St Cuthbert's church. The Anglo-Scandinavian period seems the most likely time for these crucial alterations to the city's defences.

The short length of new wall near the west corner and this longer extension to the north-east now enclosed large areas of waterfront on both Foss and Ouse, and the Anglo-Scandinavian city developed particularly in the area south-east of the former Roman defences, where two important street systems converged. One main axis continued the line of Micklegate from the north bank of the Ouse, running up Low Ousegate past the church of St Michael's, Spurriergate to the intersection with Coney Street/(Spurriergate)/Newgate (Castlegate). There a series of lanes (now King Street, Cumberland Street and Friargate) gave access to the Ouse at what is now King's Staithe. Staying on the main axis up High Ousegate or Coppergate led on through Pavement with its church of All Saints and, after a zig-zag around St Crux, into Saviourgate and its church of St Saviour, before dropping down past St Cuthbert's to leave the city at Layerthorpe. Once again, it is noticeable how churches were founded at short intervals along this key route during the Anglo-Scandinavian period. The other main axis, having left the fortress at King's Square, where the church of Holy Trinity *may* have already been founded, went via Colliergate or Shambles past the church of St Crux to Fossgate, and thence across Foss Bridge and on into Walmgate.

There are ever-increasing signs that Fossgate and Walmgate, which formed the main route south-east out of *Jorvik*, were built up by the end of the Viking Age. Conceivably development here evolved in two main stages, separated spatially by a feature now recognisable only on maps. This is the curved line, cutting off a loop in the River Foss, which forms the parish boundary of St Denys' church. It is tempting to think that this boundary represents the line of an early defensive embankment; such a fortification would have defended the river crossing at the present Foss Bridge which led to and from the former fortress area. Surviving sculpture suggests that St Denys' church, inside this hypothetical defence, was an Anglo-Scandinavian structure, and excavations just slightly further out down Walmgate have demonstrated that regular plots were in existence by the 11th century, although their origins lay deeper than the base of the investigation. In the 10th century, however, as indeed in the Anglian period, there was occupation well beyond St Denys; excavations at several sites spaced out along the 550 yard (500 metre) long axis up to the 12th-century Walmgate defensive rampart have shown a variety of evidence for Anglo-Scandinavian buildings and industrial or craft activities. It wasn't until the 12th century, however, that Walmgate was enclosed within the medieval defences; before that the street continued south-eastwards, seamlessly merging into what is now the Hull Road and proceeding on towards Stamford Bridge and Beverley.

The Walmgate area was also penetrated by another important route, leading to the city from Fulford, Riccall and Selby. As it approached York this road ran along the northern bank of the Ouse as Fishergate, which then angled northwards along the line of what today is George Street. The churches of All Saints, Fishergate, St Helen Fishergate and St Andrew Fishergate all have Anglo-Scandinavian origins, and emphasize the significance of this part of York. There is also documentary evidence that the archbishop and the king both had interests in the Fishergate/Walmgate area; and the archbishops also had interests immediately across the River Ouse in Clementhorpe. There the church's dedication to St Clement, a saint with sea-faring associations who seems to have been popular with Scandinavians, particularly in 10th-11th century England, suggests that it probably originated in the Anglo-Scandinavian period, if not before.

On this south-western bank of the Ouse, just up-stream from Clementhorpe, it has not yet been possible to gather much evidence for Anglo-Scandinavian occupation within the walled area of the former Roman civilian town. There is, however, sufficient to substantiate the idea that Micklegate, 'the big street', adopted its present sweeping curve either before or during the period. Remains of timber buildings have been found in anaerobic layers near the foot of the street at 1-9 Micklegate, and the churches of Holy Trinity/Christchurch and St Martin, which were either founded or in existence by this time, are on the street line, just as other contemporary churches are elsewhere in the city. If there had indeed been a major monastic focus in the Bishophill area in the pre-Viking period, its assets may have been sub-divided and redistributed to secular owners in the later 9th-10th centuries, and it has been suggested that Bishophill became an important merchants' quarter in *Jorvik,* that St Mary Bishophill Senior was a church where wealthy merchants were buried, and that a grid of streets was deliberately laid out in the Bishophill area, in an act of town planning designed to promote mercantile development, presumably with waterfront facilities for ship-borne trade. All this is possible, but none of it has yet been supported with excavated evidence. There is, however, at least one intriguing place-name to consider. *Divelinestaynes*, the name of a riverside locale off North Street which is first recorded in the 13th century, means 'Dublin stones'; as York's closest political links with Dublin were in the 10th century, it is tempting to see the name as a reflection of Viking-Age trading links; but this cannot be proven, and there is a later, 12th-century reference to ships from Germany and Ireland berthing at York. Nevertheless, a simple 10th-century waterfront construction, consisting of wattlework revetments stabilizing the riverbank or foreshore, has been seen in small-scale excavations there, and is important because it represents our only glimpse of installations that were a key reason for York's importance. It proves, among other things, that the pre-Norman river's edge was 65 feet (20 metres) behind the modern frontage – the Ouse valley was naturally wider, and the river consequently shallower, than it appears today.

Another major reform in the later 10th century was to the system of minting coins; King Edgar introduced a more regularized system of minting in which the names of both the minting place and the moneyer responsible were included on a coin's legend. Henceforth too the design on the coinage was also to be changed at regular intervals of about six years (dropping down to every three years from the 1030s), and when this happened old pennies were withdrawn from currency. The advantage to the royal purse was obvious; the exchange of new coins for old was done at a premium, and in this way the king regularly raised revenue. The advantages for the archaeologist and historian are equally striking. The data-base of moneyer's names, for example, is informative about name-giving habits and, perhaps, the geographical origin of people in the top wealth stratum of society. In York, as many as 75 per cent of the late 10th - and early 11th - century names are of Scandinavian origin; a figure which far outstrips Lincoln, which, although it has the next greatest number, reaches only 50 per cent. Clearly there was a strong Scandinavian influence in *Jorvik*.

Even more significantly, the number of moneyers at work in York exceeded every other of the over seventy minting places in England except London. There could be no more tell-tale statistic of York's economic significance, although there are other pieces of evidence which illuminate these bald figures. It is, admittedly, a 13th-century chronicler, Roger of Wendover, who records that in 974 merchants coming from York landed on Thanet, in Kent, and were robbed; the three hundred year gap and lack of specific corroborative evidence (although the *Anglo-Saxon Chronicle* records that King Edgar ravaged Thanet in 969) makes this entry questionable, though not inherently implausible. There is, however, a contemporary testimony to the commercial importance of *Jorvik*, incorporated in a *Life of St Oswald* written about 1000. It can be translated as follows:

'The city of York is the capital of the whole people of the Northumbrians. Formerly it was nobly built and constructed with strong walls, which have now been left to the ravages of age. The city rejoices, however, in the multitude of its population which, counting men and women but not infants and children, numbers not less than 30,000. The city is crammed beyond expression, and enriched with treasures of merchants, who come from all parts, but above all from the Danish people.'

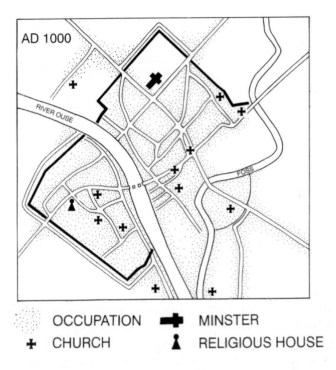

OCCUPATION   ➕ MINSTER

➕ CHURCH   ♟ RELIGIOUS HOUSE

Huge, vibrant and vital though *Jorvik* was, 10th- and 11th-century English kings felt most at home in their southern heartland, and did not often bring their travelling royal court to Northumbria. The independent minded Northumbrians needed supervision, however, and in order to keep a grasp on their northernmost domains the English kings developed a policy of appointing earls of York and Northumbria whom they could entrust with this politically rebellious and factional outpost. Some, like the first earl, Oswulf I, who was appointed after Eric Bloodaxe's departure, were aristocrats from Bernicia who ruled the whole of Northumbria; but the remit of others ran north only to the River Tees. Beyond that, the earls or high reeves of Bamburgh, the traditional Bernician seat of power, sought to maintain their own importance; and they in turn bordered on the Scots, whose eyes were often cast covetously towards

Northumbria. These power blocks had to be dealt with diplomatically, or with military might if necessary. Diplomacy was also required to deal with the archbishops of York, who wielded considerable traditional influence, but not all earls chose that route; Thored, earl in the 970s-980s, is recorded as seizing lands which belonged to the archbishop.

In 980, when Viking raids against England resumed, Edgar's son Aethelred was on the throne. The raids were mainly directed against targets in southern England and the area of the Danelaw was left largely unscathed. King Svein Forkbeard of Denmark took control of these raids in 1003; when Svein died in 1014 and was buried, some say, at York, his son Cnut became the main Viking protagonist, and following the death of both Aethelred and his son Edmund in 1016, Cnut was accepted as King of England. Cnut entrusted one of his Norwegian supporters, Earl Eric of Hlathir, with the earldom of Northumbria and then, after his death, promoted Siward, who held the post for over twenty years. According to the *Anglo-Saxon Chronicle*, after Siward died in York in 1055 his burial was in the church which he had built in *Galmanho* and dedicated to St Olaf. Since Bootham Bar was formerly known as *Galmanlith*, and the Marygate area outside was known as *Earlsburgh*, it seems reasonable to assume that Siward's church is the predecessor of the present St Olave's in Marygate, and that he built it as part of a residential complex, probably fortified, that accounts for the name *Earlsburh*. Siward (and perhaps earls before him) may have been tempted to this location because they could take advantage of a Roman walled enclosure which seems to have formed an annex to the fortress, and which in turn helped to define the walled precinct of the late 11th - century St Mary's Abbey.

On Siward's death Godwin, a powerful southern English earl who was father-in-law to King Edward the Confessor, had his son Tostig emplaced as earl of Northumbria (the names of Tostig and Edward are recorded together on the inscribed sundial at Kirkdale church, North Yorkshire). Tostig was oppressive, and eventually the Northumbrians got him expelled in 1065. He promptly fled and allied himself with the ambitious King Harald

Hardraada of Norway, whose fleet entered the Humber and anchored at Riccall in September 1066. Harald's army advanced towards York, and fought a successful battle against the Northumbrians at Fulford, just south of the city, on 20th September. Harald negotiated a surrender from the men of York, took hostages from the chief citizens (whom Tostig could identify) and then moved off, leaving York intact. On September 25th the army of Tostig's brother Harold, now king of England, swept through York on its way to a surprise attack, hard fought battle and ultimately crushing defeat of the invaders at the Battle of Stamford Bridge. York had weathered the storm; but just two years later it could not withstand the whirlwind of another invader of Viking descent, William the Conqueror.

In 1068 William captured the city and built a castle; after it was recaptured in an English revolt he seized York for a second time, plundering it and desecrating the cathedral. Late in the year, fearing a Danish attack, the Normans set fire to the city. The fire and the extensive destructive earth moving which accompanied the castle building, brought localized change to the city's layout, and further encouraged the new regime to make its mark. This it did, for example, through re-siting and rebuilding the Minster, introducing a new Benedictine monastery of St Mary, and establishing the extensive hospital of St Leonard's. In these matters there is, then, a clear distinction between pre-Norman and Norman York; but the foundations of medieval York were laid in the centuries of Anglo-Saxon and Anglo-Scandinavian rule.

3

EARLY MEDIEVAL YORK

Chris Daniell

Introduction

Before the Battle of Hastings William the Conqueror probably had only the sketchiest - if any - idea of York. He would have known that it had an archbishop and probably that it was a large fortified city in the north of England with Roman origins.

Some sixty years after the Conquest William of Malmesbury gave a short description of York as it was in the eleventh and twelfth centuries with its high walls and churches and especially commented upon the language:

> All the language of the Northumbrians, and especially at York, is so sharp, slitting and frothing and unscape (crude), that we southern men can scarcely understand it.

Even less complimentary was Richard of Devizes's description of York in the late twelfth century: 'York, full of Scotsmen, filthy and treacherous creatures, hardly men' - hardly a flattering advertisement for the greatest city in the north which had an ancient history, thriving mercantile trade and was the seat of the northern archbishop.

At the time of the Conquest, however, such descriptions were in the future. William the Conqueror arrived in York in 1068 at the head of an army of occupation. For over a year there had been a lull in York from the effects of the Battle of Hastings, fought on 14th October 1066, as William consolidated his position in Normandy and the south of England. Upon William's arrival in 1068 the chronicler Orderic Vitalis wrote, 'York was seething with discontent'. For two centuries York had been a Viking city, with Viking roots, culture and the palace of the Viking kings of the region. Visits by the kings of England, based in the south – either peaceful or with military intent – were rare and York was essentially left alone. The arrival of William changed that: he was determined to bring York under his control.

One of William's first actions was to build and garrison a castle in York, followed by a second in 1069. (It is not known which order the castles were built, but the assumption is that the Clifford's Tower castle was the first. York is the only place in the country, with the exception of London, to have two castles built by the Conqueror.) The castles were positioned to control the access into the heart of the city by river, as a chain could be thrown across the river between them. The two castles were of standard Norman design, with a high central mound (a 'motte') on top of which was a keep, and below was a defended area for important buildings and a place of refuge in case of attack (the 'bailey'). The buildings and surrounding defences were all probably made of wood; it was only later in the thirteenth century that a large scale rebuilding of the castles and the city walls in stone took place.

The resentment the people of York felt against this aggressive act was soon made clear. King Swein of Denmark arrived with a large fleet of ships, powerful Anglo-Saxon nobles joined his cause along with the people of York. The castles were attacked and despite a valiant resistance, which included a deliberate setting fire to the city, the castles were burnt to the ground and the garrison massacred. William marched north again in the autumn and devastated the Yorkshire countryside in a military operation now called the Harrying of the North. The scale of the Harrying is now unknown, but it was certainly considered by near contemporaries a devastating campaign even by the standards of the day. The chronicler Orderic Vitalis, citing William the Conqueror's supposed deathbed speech, wrote:

Clifford's Tower

Norman House behind Stonegate

I [William] treated the native inhabitants of the kingdom with unreasonable severity, cruelly oppressed high and low, unjustly disinherited many, and caused the death of thousands by starvation and war, especially in Yorkshire … I descended on the English of the north like a raging lion, and ordered that their homes and crops and furnishings should be burnt at once and their great flocks and herds of cattle and sheep slaughtered everywhere … alas! [I] was the cruel murderer of many thousands, both young and old of this fair people.

There may well be a substantial element of exaggeration in this account as tales got told and embellished. Historians have debated the true scale of the operation and one clue is the large number of villages in Yorkshire described as 'waste' written in the Domesday Book of 1086. Unfortunately there are a large number of reasons why the term 'waste' could be applied to a village, for example it may not have rendered tax. The debate as to ferocity of the Harrying still continues.

Following the Harrying and William's presence in York over Christmas 1069 the rebellion was finally defeated and thereafter the population was quiescent.

The Norman Conquest of York changed the city forever as it started a huge programme of building works within the city. First there were the two castles, the building of which destroyed one of the seven Anglo-Saxon shires in the city. Associated with the larger castle, later called Clifford's Tower, was a dam which blocked the Foss. Where the water flowed out there were several mills, which were later given to the Knights Templar. Behind the dam the build up of water formed the King's Fishpool. The Fishpool, or the Marsh as it was also known, stretched round one side of York forming an impenetrable barrier to invading forces, but also providing a good supply of fish to the city. The low lying areas around the Fishpool were often indicated by the place names, for example there was the church St John's in the Marsh and St Saviour's in St Saviourgate was sometimes called St Saviour's in the Marsh, even though on slightly higher ground.

71

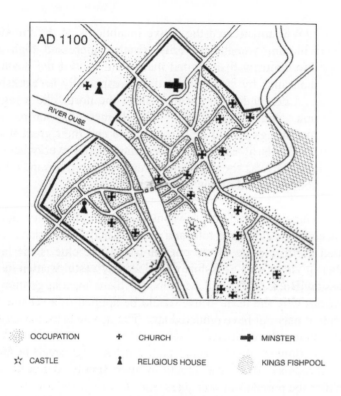

OCCUPATION   +   CHURCH   ⬛ MINSTER

☆ CASTLE   ♟ RELIGIOUS HOUSE   KINGS FISHPOOL

The Fishpool was to have a profound effect upon York's history until the 20th century. Today the only reminder of its existence is in the name Foss Islands Road, indicating the islands which formed within the Fishpool.

The Normans also instigated other massive building campaigns, especially of churches. The Anglo-Scandinavian Minster was dismantled - following the rebel attacks it was in a bad way - and the new Norman Minster was built by Thomas of Bayeux, the new Archbishop of York. Excavations have uncovered the foundations of Thomas's Minster. For many years the plan of Thomas's Minster baffled architectural historians, but recent discoveries in Normandy and at Bayeux have revealed that the plan was probably based upon the church at Bayeux.

The other major building works undertaken before 1100 included St Mary's Abbey and probably the refounded monastery of Holy Trinity on Micklegate in 1089. Initially St Mary's Abbey was founded on a small plot of land just outside the city walls but thereafter it gained in prosperity and size to become the greatest Benedictine abbey of the north.

The building of the castles, the creation of the Fishpool and the building of the churches meant that the character and topography of York dramatically changed. The effects of the Conquest still remain in the present landscape of York.

Sources

During the period from 1066 to 1272 there is a decisive shift in the amount, quality and scale of the available information. In the previous Viking, Anglo-Saxon and Roman centuries archaeology is the key to the history of York, but except in the notable exceptions of the Minster excavations which uncovered the foundations of Thomas's cathedral, it is the written evidence which steadily becomes more plentiful from the Norman Conquest onwards. One of the most remarkable documents ever produced, the Domesday Book of 1086, gives details of who owned what within the city (both on the day of King Edward the Confessor's death and at the date of compilation), the internal organisation (seven shires are mentioned, one of which belonged to the archbishop), and the financial rises and falls of property values. The Domesday Book is a beacon of light illuminating the darkness, but sometimes the information it contains is difficult to interpret. Steadily through the twelfth century the picture of the conditions, people and social networks within the city become clearer as local charters become more plentiful and national records start including significant annual information about York from the mid-twelfth century in the Pipe Rolls. Thereafter in the thirteenth century other national series of records start, such as the Close Rolls, which contain material about York. From the mid-twelfth century architectural remains and art survive in ever greater quantities and are the forerunner of the great explosion of surviving material in the following medieval centuries.

The Nationalities of York

The York that the Normans conquered was made up of many different peoples and races. The root stock, the Celts and Romans, had subsequently been overrun by the Anglo-Saxons, who had subsequently been overrun by the Vikings. Traces of civilisations from the Romans onwards were everywhere to be seen. It is often forgotten that there were large numbers of Roman buildings and structures still standing at the time of the Norman Conquest. The Roman foundations of the city walls behind the Minster were used for the Norman (and later) city walls of York. One Roman building was physically dismantled and used to build the still-standing tower of St Mary's Bishophill Junior church. Following the Romans, the Anglo-Saxons had settled outside the Roman walls, and within had built the first of the many later Cathedral churches. The Vikings lived within the walls and changed the culture and layout of the city for their own purposes, the most obvious impact today is the –gate suffix to many of the street names.

The Normans were the latest group to bring with them their own culture and ideas as an additional overlay to the cultural mix. The Norman population was small in number, but had a profound cultural change for they brought Continental cultural influences with them, including new and dramatic building styles. With the arrival of the Normans the cultural axis shifted from a Viking east-west direction to a Norman north-south axis. Whereas the Vikings culturally looked to their homelands in Scandinavia or for support from the Irish Viking kings, the Normans in York and the north looked to the king in the south for political rule or to the Continental churches and monasteries for their inspiration.

The term Norman is a 'catchall' one, especially in the earliest stages, for a disparate range of people, most of whom were from Normandy, but many of whom were from other areas of France and the low countries. It is noticeable that in the Domesday

Book the term "Frenchman" is invariably used for Normans and other nationalities. The nature and speed of Norman cultural assimilation in York is a difficult to gauge, but one index is that of the use of first names amongst the general population. Although extensive research has not been undertaken on this aspect for York there is initial evidence that Norman first names were given to children in reasonable numbers in the mid-twelfth century. This is highlighted by one of the most powerful twelfth century families in York, that of Lefwin. His father was a shadowy figure called Thorulf and both he and Lefwin had good Viking names. Lefwin's children however, probably born in the middle decades of the twelfth century, had predominantly Norman or Latin names: Hugh, Gerard, Walter and Gilbert. This influence may have come from Lefwin's wife who herself had the Norman name of Juliana le Gras.

To the north lay the Scottish kingdoms, and a grey disputed border area. The English view of the Scots changed through time and whereas it was relatively neutral in the early twelfth century by the end of the century there was strong anti-Scottish feeling in the country, a view perpetrated by Richard of Devizes whose opinion was given at the beginning of the chapter. The indistinctness of the border region led to many disputes and border raids, some more important than others. As the Normans became more settled, their area of power and influence pushed steadily northwards. Initially, York was on the edge of Norman power (shown well by the settlement pattern in Domesday Book - to the north of York the settlements recorded rapidly diminish) with further northern outposts being Richmond and then Durham, with its Norman bishop and abbot.

The founding of monasteries, with their strong continental links, pushed Norman and continental culture and power further and further north. Whitby, Rievaulx, Fountains and Jervaulx form an arc north of York and from them further abbeys and monasteries were founded in the present day Scottish Border region, including Melrose. The border area, and religious life, were still relatively fluid and Aelred, who was brought up at the Scottish court, became abbot of Rievaulx.

The archbishop of York also tried to extend his own authority to cover the north of England and Scotland. Thomas I, in his struggle with Lanfranc during the primacy dispute as to which archbishop took precedence over the over, asserted his claims to the bishoprics of Durham and Worcester, a large part of Lincolnshire, the whole of Scotland, the Hebrides and Orkney. One hundred years later the outcome showed that York only had jurisdiction over the new bishopric based in Carlisle, some rights over the see of Durham and the old territory of Yorkshire and Nottinghamshire. One of the strongest links that York had with the northern regions was with Orkney. There had been bishops of Orkney since the tenth century, but in 1073 the Earl of Orkney, Paul Thorfinsson, sent a cleric called Ralph to be consecrated by Thomas of York, possibly as a challenge to the bishops of Hamburg-Bremen who had traditionally appointed bishops. The link between Orkney and York continued for the first half of the twelfth century with Ralph Novell or Nuell being bishop from 1109 at the earliest to after 1147. However, the people of Orkney objected to having Ralph as bishop and so he was bishop in name only, becoming an assistant to the archbishop of York and the bishop of Durham

As Norman settlement and political domination moved further and further north, York became less and less of a city on the edge of Norman control. The Scottish wars and affairs occasionally were of concern, but were not of lasting importance. In the twelfth century there were two serious Scottish attacks. The first occurred in 1138 when the Scottish army reached within 30 miles of York. Archbishop Thurstan rallied the people of York and nobles from the northern areas and was himself one of the military commanders at the Battle of the Standard (so called because the holy standard of St Cuthbert was carried into battle) where the Scots were comprehensively defeated. The other major campaign in the north occurred in 1173-4 when William, King of Scotland, invaded England and devastated the area down to Alnwick, though there was no direct attack on York itself.

Through the thirteenth century there was little military involvement in Yorkshire and the major rebellion by Simon de

Montfort did not extend into the north. However, York's position as a military base was to change dramatically for Edward I decided to use York as his northern headquarters to attack the Scots.

Even though York was not involved in any direct attack, its strategic and regional importance meant that it had strong defences. As has been mentioned William the Conqueror ordered the first two castles to be built, spanning the river. These castles remained important throughout the twelfth century, but the castle at the junction of the Foss became the more significant of the two. The motte later became known as Clifford's Tower, though the precise reason for its name is unclear, and the castle in general was known as York Castle. The second castle, which is still visible today from Clifford's Tower as a prominent mound across the Ouse, is known as Baile Hill.

As well as the military function the castle was a focus of law and order and was also a base for the sheriff of Yorkshire. The county courts were based within the bailey, with an associated prison. Criminals and traitors were often hanged from the battlements of Clifford's Tower as a visible deterrent.

The walls around the city were patchy. Some walls had survived from the Roman times in various states of disrepair, though the walls behind the Minster, which had been part of the Roman Legionary fortress, were probably in better condition than most. There is little detail about the walls, though there is a reference to the 'walls' or defences being no more than a hedge at the bottom of Walmgate. The gates and bars however were crucial both in terms of defence and trade. It can be argued that the walls of the city were as much about funnelling trade through the bars as about defence, for it was at the bars that tolls were collected for bringing goods into the city. Originally all the bars probably had a barbican on the front, though now only the barbican on Walmgate Bar remains. This feature allowed goods to enter at one end, with a closed gate ahead. The rear gate was then closed and the goods and people were confined until payment was made. The inner door then opened and the people entered the city.

The Turbulent History of York

The history of York is punctuated with outbursts of violence after the Norman Conquest and throughout the twelfth century and thirteenth century. In 1066 there was the Battle of Fulford Gate, which was seen by Chroniclers at the time as severe, though in reality it may have been a bloody skirmish rather than a full-scale battle. The battle was the prelude to the more famous Battle of Stamford Bridge where the Vikings were decisively beaten by King Harold Godwinsson. Fulford Gate may have weakened the Vikings to such an extent that the following battle was lost. Two years later in 1068 there was a major uprising against the Normans by the local population, in the process of which the two castles were burnt down. The chroniclers recorded that the city was also burnt to the ground, although the excavations at Coppergate and elsewhere have found no evidence of widespread burning.

One national rebellion which did affect York was that of the Young King's revolt in 1173-4. The revolt, led by the Henry II's son, the "Young King" Henry, was a national one with the primary theatres of war being the Midlands and the Scottish border where King William of Scotland marched back and forth, attacking the region from Carlisle to Alnwick. York was not directly involved with the fighting but a group of prominent citizens banded together to smuggle arms into the city from Flanders in order to help the supporters of the Young King. The key link between them and the Young King's revolt was probably through the nobleman Roger de Mowbray. Mowbray was fighting for the Scottish king, who had held his son as hostage, and Mowbray also had close personal connections with William de Tickhill, one of the most important people in York. The plot was foiled at the last moment and the citizens involved fined very heavily.

It was during the twelfth century that the most infamous event took place in York's history, the massacre of the Jewish population of the city. The order of events is known in detail. Two eminent Jews, Benedict of York and Josce, attended Richard I's Coronation at Westminster, but were beaten by a mob and thereafter Jews were attacked in cities across England: Norwich; King's Lynn; Stamford; Bury St Edmunds and Lincoln. The antisemitic hysteria was also enflamed in York. Jews were attacked, houses burned and the Jews fled to the safety of the royal castle, only for a siege to be instigated. In dire straits, Rabbi Yomtob of Joigny put forward the suggestion they take their own lives. It was Josce who set the example by cutting the throats of his wife and sons. At daybreak the following morning, the few survivors were tricked out of the castle and massacred by the mob. One of the most shocking aspects of the massacre is that this was not a riot by a crazed mob in the heat of the moment, but was a carefully orchestrated siege which lasted a week. The attackers had enough time to build a siege engine to attack the castle. It is also noticeable that the authorities did very little to control the situation, indeed all law and order seems to have broken down during that week. As well as severe antisemitic feeling there was also a financial dimension, as local nobles were unwilling or unable to repay loans from Jews. The conspirators made their way to the Minster where they seized the Jewish bonds stored at the Minster and burned them in the middle of the church. At the time the surname of one of the local ringleaders, Richard Malbysse, was translated by the Jews as 'evil beast'. The family's name is still known, for Acaster Malbis, one of the villages just outside York, is named after the family.

Once law and order returned the repercussions were quickly felt, with the ring-leaders fleeing the country and those implicated being heavily fined. It is a myth to say that Jews never returned to York for there are many late twelfth and thirteenth century references to them. Many of the richest lived in Coney Street, facing the river near St Martin's Church, and the 'schola' (synagogue) was also located there. Furthermore the Jewish burial ground, just outside the city walls at Jewbury has been carefully excavated. This to date is the only large-scale excavation of a Jewish cemetery in England. The excavations revealed 475 inhumations and it was estimated that the population within Jewish thirteenth century York was approximately 260.

Yet whilst the citizens of York sometimes played a part in

national politics, at other times they were distanced from events elsewhere. During the Anarchy - a period of severe conflict between King Stephen and the Empress Matilda as to who was ruler of England - there were outbreaks of violence in the surrounding districts of York, but the city played little part in the overall events and was outside the main theatre of war. The same was true of the rebellion in the thirteenth century by Simon de Montfort which was based mainly in the Midlands and the South. Armies later came to York during the reign of Edward I when the King, Court and Parliament arrived to orchestrate the Scottish wars.

The Church in York

At no time since the Romans had one race had such a widespread geographical impact in England as the Normans. This is shown by the Domesday Book with its recording of 'Frenchmen' in various towns and villages, and also by the large numbers of clerics who came from, or were trained in, Normandy immediately after the Conquest. One such man was the Norman Thomas of Bayeux who became Archbishop of York after the death of Ealdred, the Anglo-Saxon Archbishop of York. Ealdred was the most important cleric in England immediately after the Conquest, for Stigand, the Archbishop of Canterbury had fled the country and Ealdred had crowned William the Conqueror at Westminster Abbey.

As Archbishop of York Thomas was the single most important person in York after the Conquest. Thomas undertook the rebuilding of the Minster, moving its location from that of the Anglo-Saxon cathedral. The exact location of the Anglo-Saxon cathedral is not known, but its probable location was behind the Norman, and present, Minster. If this assumption is correct then there is the strong image of the Norman cathedral rising in front of the Anglo-Saxon cathedral and dwarfing it in the process. If so, this was a powerful physical representation of the dominance of the Normans, who brought with them new ideas and a forceful image. Only small fragments of Thomas's Cathedral remain, but

Reconstruction of the Norman Minster

Reconstruction of the Norman Castle

one of the most intriguing is a carved capital which is a copy of a capital in Bayeux cathedral. This link strongly suggests that Thomas brought masons from Bayeux, where he had been treasurer, to build the new Minster in York. Sections of Thomas's first Norman Cathedral can still be seen in the undercroft, including a section of wall which still retains its external white rendering, and there is still a small section with the original red lines on to give the impressions of large blocks of stone.

Over the following centuries the Minster was added to and changed. There was a major rebuilding of the choir under the auspices of archbishop Roger of Pont l'Évêque which was probably completed about 1175. The choir has since been extended and rebuilt in the fourteenth century, but there are small remnants built into the fourteenth century walls which show architectural decorative details such as a small piece of chevron ornament and a 'bobbin-like' ornament. Similar styles of decorative ornament have been found at St Mary's Abbey. The south transept was also doubled in size during the last half of the twelfth century and building work continued throughout the thirteenth century, including the north transept, the west aisle and nave and a central tower (which later fell down and was rebuilt). One of the great features of the Minster, the Chapter House, was probably started in the 1260s or 1270s.

The details of the building campaigns can be rather dry, but information about individuals involved are known. Masons' marks - marks on stones presumed to be made by individual masons to show their work - have been found at other ecclesiastical sites and may show how masons moved around the region. One mark in the south transept is also found at Rievaulx Abbey, but seventeen marks are common between York and Byland Abbey, and marks from York also appear at Roche Abbey and Hexham. The masons' names are unknown, though the master carpenter from the thirteenth century campaigns was Gilbert, son of William the Carpenter, who is mentioned as being in the archbishop's service for many years, working both on the Minster and the archbishop's palace at Bishopthorpe. As well as the builders and masons, the stone had to be quarried and transported and in 1233 Robert le Vavasour granted rights in his stone quarry at Tadcaster to the Minster, a valuable right considering the massive building works that were being undertaken throughout the century.

As well as the building of the first Norman Minster, there were two other issues connected with Thomas of Bayeux's time as archbishop: the organisation of the clergy of the Minster and the 'primacy' dispute. Under Thomas of Bayeux the organisation of the Minster clergy was profoundly altered. The church that Thomas was appointed to in 1070 was in an appalling condition. Hugh the Chanter, in his history of the church and archbishops of York, wrote that Thomas 'found everything deserted and waste; of the seven canons (there had been no more), he found three in the burnt city and ruined church.' Thomas rebuilt the church, but he also reorganised the system of living. Hugh wrote:

> 'The canons had long lived in common, but the archbishop, after taking advice, determined to divide some of the lands of St Peter's which were still waste into separate prebends, to leave room for a growing number of canons, each of whom might be eager to build on and cultivate his own share for his own sake. This was done. Then he appointed a dean, treasurer and precentor ...'

The final piece of the jigsaw - the chancellor - was instigated by Archbishop Geoffrey in 1191, to replace the older designation of 'Master of the Schools', though the chancellor's primary role still remained that of supervising the educational and intellectual life of the cathedral.

From living in common, the canons now had their own sources of income, an important part in maintaining the prosperity of the Minster clergy. The system had been set and the number of canons slowly increased and by the early thirteenth century the number was fixed at 36. The wealth of the different prebends varied widely with the treasureship and the prebend of Masham amongst the most lucrative posts in Christendom, renowned even in Rome. Others struggled to make ends meet - St Paul's, on the coast, 'was consumed by the sea'.

The 'primacy' dispute, between the archbishoprics of Canterbury and York as to which was older and had power over the other, had great relevance and intensity to the clergy at the time. Canterbury claimed it was the most important because of its connections with St Augustine who had brought the Christianity of Rome to England. York cited Paulinus as its source of power and authority. The debate was often dramatic, with violent or humorous incidents. The chronicler Roger of Howden recounted how the archbishops of Canterbury and York went to meet a cardinal.

> A dispute arose between the two archbishops … [as to] which of them ought to sit on the right hand of the cardinal; and on the archbishop of York attempting to seat himself there, the servants of the lord archbishop of Canterbury rushed upon him and threw him to the ground, kicked him with their feet and tore his hood.

The cardinal 'took flight' and the meeting never took place. During the twelfth century it was not unusual for much posturing, arguments and occasional violence to break out. Eventually the dispute petered out with the Archbishop of Canterbury having gained the stronger position.

One the determining factors in the debate was the canonisation of Canterbury's martyred archbishop, Thomas Becket. Becket became one of the most influential and revered saints in the Middle Ages and he was a saint with few to rival him in spiritual power. York also had its own saint, the mid-twelfth century archbishop of York, William FitzHerbert. The history of William's canonisation derived from the power politics of his election as archbishop of York. He was the son of Herbert, chamberlain to Henry I and his mother was the half-sister to King Stephen. He also had impeccable York connections: he had been treasurer at the Minster since before 1114 and his family had large estates in Yorkshire. Even though William was successfully elected to the position of archbishop by the canons of the Minster, his election was disputed, mainly by the supporters of the new Cistercian order. The ripples of claim and counter-claim spread to the Papacy in Rome and to St Bernard at Clairvaux. On the one side was royal favour and his uncle, Henry of Blois, Bishop of Winchester, and on the other side the massed ranks of the Cistercians including St Bernard, the pope Eugenius III (a disciple of Bernard) and the Yorkshire Cistercian abbots of Richard of Fountains, William of Rievalux, Ailred, later abbot of Rievalux and Henry Murdac. Eventually the competition proved too strong for William and Henry Murdac replaced William as archbishop. After William had spent several years abroad the situation dramatically reversed in 1153 when Murdac, Bernard and the pope all died. With the major obstacles gone to his election William made a triumphal return into the city. His route took him across Ouse Bridge and the weight of the cheering crowds caused the bridge to collapse. William's presence and the subsequent lack of deaths from drowning were built into one of William's most important miracles. The scene is depicted in the St William Window in York Minster which was made in the early fifteenth century. William's sanctity further increased when he died on the 8 June 1154 after solemn mass. The contemporary rumour quickly grew into fact that he was poisoned. A cult followed and a sumptuous shrine was built. At the Reformation the shrine was destroyed, but parts where discovered in the grounds of the Minster and a reconstruction can be attempted from the remains. Furthermore the shrine itself is depicted in the St William window, along with the Ouse Bridge incident and other of St William's miracles. William was eventually formally canonised in 1227 and his shrine occupied pride of place within the Minster.

Two other archbishops, Walter de Gray (1216-55) and Godfrey de Ludham (1258-65), deserve mention for their tombs were opened revealing some personal items, including a pastoral staff with a head of walrus ivory and a ring in de Gray's tomb, and vestments and chalice in de Ludham's tomb.

Although the archbishop was the most important religious person in the archdiocese, within the city he was but one of a large number of influential clerics. Within the Minster was the Dean, who ran and controlled the chapter, appointments, property and wealth. Relations between the archbishop and chapter were not always easy. Tensions could mount and spill over into the outside world, most notably with the divisions over the election of William FitzHerbert. The Dean and Chapter also had control of the appointments to St Leonard's Hospital.

Between 1066 and 1272 York, like many other towns and cities across England, experienced the growth and influence of the three major religious movements which would continue until the Reformation in the sixteenth century: Benedictine monasticism, the new orders, such as the Cistercians, and then in the thirteenth century the coming of the friars. Each new wave of religious orders were overlays to the existing religious structure of the city.

The two Benedictine monasteries within York were St Mary's Abbey, which was founded just after the Conquest and became the greatest Benedictine monastery in the north of England, and Holy Trinity Micklegate, which was refounded from a house of secular canons (about whom nothing is known) into a house of Benedictine monks. The house was an 'alien' monastery, which meant that it was controlled from outside England, and was one of the family of monasteries dependent upon Marmoutier in France. During the twelfth century other monastic houses were founded in and around York: Clementhorpe nunnery and St Andrew's, Fishergate, a house of Gilbertine monks.

Other monasteries scattered around Yorkshire also had considerable property interests in York, for the city was one of the most important commercial cities in England. The Cistercian abbeys of Rievaulx, Fountains and Bylands all had houses in the city to accommodate visiting clergy and to act as bases for business - especially that of selling wool and skins from their vast flocks of sheep. By the end of the twelfth century the early dynamism of the Cistercian monastic order was diminishing as the monasteries became more settled and had grown.

In the thirteenth century renewed impetus was given to the religious life of the city by a new religious force to arrive in England and York: the friars. They rejected the desire for isolation so favoured by the Cistercians and deliberately based themselves in towns to work amongst the poor and destitute. There were four main orders of friars - the Franciscans (called either Grey Friars - because of their habits - or Friars Minor), the Dominicans (called either Black Friars or Friars Preachers), the Carmelites (White Friars) and the Augustinians (or Austin Friars), all of whom were given land. All four orders rapidly gained acceptance and established a significant presence in York by the middle of the thirteenth century. The locations of their houses were: Franciscans, initial settlement unknown, then settled between Clifford's Tower and the River Ouse; Dominicans, on Toft Green; Carmelites, by the King's Fishpool, and the Augustinians between the River Ouse and the Lendal. The four orders each had their own regions in England, but York was a regional centre for all of them. The Fransciscan region - or custos - based at York included the friaries of Beverley, Scarborough, Lincoln and as far south as Boston in Lincolnshire, though to the north Richmond lay in the custody of Newcastle. Although a great deal is known about the friars in general, little is known about the role of the friars in York until later in the Middle Ages when some indication of their popularity is given by the amount left in wills, a subject which has yet to be fully explored.

The final component to the religious life of the city was the large number of parish churches scattered throughout the city. The early history of these churches is often lost though there are indications (through archaeology and a few inscriptions) that many were built in the eleventh century, especially the smaller ones in less prestigious positions. Archaeological excavations of St Helen on the Walls and All Saints Peasholme Green indicate that the earliest structures were built in the late eleventh century. Few of the founders of churches can be traced, but the church of All Saint's Peasholme Green - built on the margins of York, possibly because there was no other available space - was founded by the ancestors of Ralph Nuvel. It is unfortunate that the ancestors who built the church remain nameless, but Ralph was descended from one of the most prestigious families in York and the church was probably founded around 1100. By the end of the century the city was saturated with about 40 parish churches, along with the monasteries, hospitals and the Minster. Half a century later the four friaries were added to the ecclesiastical equation along with an increasing number of chantry priests based in the churches who were endowed to pray for the souls of the dead.

Government of the City

Virtually nothing is known about the government of the city before the Norman Conquest, though there were probably twelve 'lagaman' or lawmen who ran the city and possibly a sheriff. Both pieces of information come from after the Conquest, but may be extended backwards, though how far back is guesswork. The term sheriff derives from the Anglo-Saxon 'scir gerefa' or 'shire reeve' and it was an institution taken over and adapted by the Normans. It is from the Norman Conquest onwards that the sheriffs are known for Yorkshire, and the sheriffs also controlled the government of York. The first was Gamel, son of Osbern (1066-1068) who may have been the sheriff from Anglo-Saxon times. The sheriff's main roles included the overseeing of justice and collecting the king's revenue (justice was a profitable source of revenue from the fines received), to keep the peace and to organise local defence of the city and region. Until the later twelfth century the information about the sheriffs is fragmentary, but all were powerful people in their own right.

One anomaly in the government of York occurred in Stephen's reign when William Aumale was appointed Earl of York during the Anarchy. This was part of a much bigger strategy by Stephen of appointing earls to cut across the lines of power and influence of the sheriffs. The years 1138-1155 are the only ones in York's history where an Earl of York has had power in the city. (The title of the Duke of York was first used in 1385 when Richard II granted the title to his uncle, Edmund of Langley.)

As well as the sheriff there was an important group of families who had considerable influence within the city. Many of these families stretched back through generations and it has been proposed that the twelve 'lawmen' in the entry written in the Domesday Book of 1086 for York took an active role in leading the affairs of the city. One of the lawmen mentioned in a later document of 1106 was Forne and the family seems to have retained their prominent position within the hierarchy of York for in 1130 Thomas, son of Ulviet son of Forne owed a hunting horse to the king so that he might become an alderman of the York guild. Little is known about this guild except for its existence as early as the reign of Henry I, (and possibly earlier if the Gildgarth mentioned in 1080 was the location of the Gild merchant). If, as is likely, it followed the pattern of other Gild merchant associations in other towns the members paid for economic privileges such as exclusive right to buy or sell in the town - a precursor to the later rights of the Freemen of York.

The city government of York was slowly emerging from the documentary shadows into the limelight. In 1174-5 Thomas of Over Ouse (de Ultra Usam - i.e. from the Micklegate side of the river, and probably the same man as Thomas son of Ulviet) paid a fine of 20 marks (£13 33.) 'for the commune that they wished to make'. No more is known, but the idea of a commune was strong in Flanders and it may have been that overseas trade had encouraged the attempt at a commune in York. How the commune differed from the Gild merchant is unknown.

The most powerful citizens were therefore banding together in order to secure their own self-interests. The sheriff and king demanded taxes off them and similar overseas trading interests brought them together. Slowly the crown began to treat the city as a cohesive unit, giving the merchants privileges and powers. One such family was that of Lefwin and his predecessors and descendants. One descendant, Ralph Nuvel was notable in the history of York for the citizens of York acted in unison to document that Ralph owned the church of All Saints in the Marsh, and with the document they attached a seal - the earliest civic seal of York to survive, and one of the earliest in the country. Other notable families included the Selby family, mayors for many generations, and the Tickhill family. These families can be traced and a detailed picture can be built up of their financial interests and their property holdings. Many of the financial interests of these families were probably mercantile for otherwise their wealth and status are not sufficient from their known property holdings alone to maintain their positions. It is unfortunate that no twelfth century accounts have survived for York traders.

The exact composition of the leaders of the civic government of York is unknown, but one piece of evidence seems so far to have been overlooked. Between 1175 and 1186 William de Stuteville and the Dean and Chapter of the Minster made two agreements, and at the end of both the witnesses included five men termed 'burgesses', presumably of the city of York. The five were Philip son of Baldwin, Thomas son of Richard, Gervase son of Romund, Robert Brun and William son of Sirithe. Work is ongoing to determine their background and influence within the city.

It was from the most powerful group of families that there arose the government of the city. The earliest of York's charters and privileges are now lost, but they can be reconstructed as in 1128 Archbishop Thurstan gave to the burgesses of Beverley the same privileges as the men of York. At some point between 1154-8 Henry II granted York its first royal charter which granted the citizens their liberties and laws, and exemption from the tax called 'lestage' along the coasts. Interestingly the charter states that the rights were the same as granted 'in the time of Henry I', though no charter of Henry I survives. Thereafter the following kings, Richard and John, confirmed these rights, but in 1212 John went a stage further and - for a price - allowed the citizens, rather than the sheriff, to organise and pay the city's annual payment to the Crown, and also allowed the citizens to appoint a mayor. The first known mayor, in 1217, was Hugh Selby. The family thereafter remained one of the most powerful in the city: between 1217 and 1289 Hugh was mayor six times, his son John seven times, and his grandson Nicholas four times. In 1256 the sheriff's powers were further reduced when Henry III granted two more charters to the citizens which dealt with law and justice and effectively deprived the sheriff of all power within the city.

Whilst the mayor and the council controlled areas of the city they did not control all of it as large parts were under other jurisdictions. The castle and its precincts were under the jurisdiction of the sheriff (jurisdiction of Castlegate was disputed). The Dean and Chapter were in control of the Minster's liberty - or the Liberty of St Peter - and also the residences of the canons where ever they lived and the lands held by the Chapter and canons across Yorkshire (153 in all) and further afield. In the second half of the thirteenth century especially, the citizens and churches fought and argued, even to the extent that in 1260 the city was placed under papal interdict because the Mayor had arrested a lady called Annabella and hanged her, even though she was a tenant of the Minster Chapter and the chapter's steward was willing to punish her himself. The citizens also took the law into their own hands by breaking into the house of the Prior of Holy Trinity and carrying off his doors and windows and ill-treating his men.

There was a long running dispute between the citizens of York and St Mary's Abbey. St Mary's had been granted rights in Bootham and Marygate but this sparked off a long running conflict with the civic authorities who regarded the streets, and especially Bootham, as being under their jurisdiction. Looting and bloodshed in 1264 led to St Mary's Abbey building a wall around its precinct for protection, the results of which can still be seen to this day. The dispute was more or less settled in 1354 with Bootham being restored to the city, though disruptions still occasionally occurred.

Little is known in detail of the merchants and their trading activities but it is fair to say that the twelfth and thirteenth centuries laid the foundations for the better documented later Medieval centuries. A few indications of trading activities and trade links are known during the twelfth century and fines for illegal trading activities show that smuggled 'goods' were being brought into the county, and into York, from Flanders. Individual merchants, such as the first mayor, Hugh Selby, exported wool to the Low Countries and imported wine from Anjou. Odd references also reveal Flemings, Bretons, Frenchmen and Italians all trading in York in the thirteenth century.

Madonna and Child. York Minster

York Minster Gospel Book

Trade was helped by the fact that York was an important port in its own right, and in 1203-4 York was ranked seventh in importance amongst ports of the south and east coasts. This was despite the potentially serious difficulties with the tides at York: at certain times of the year if a tide was missed a boat could be stranded for up to two weeks in the city. For this reason through the thirteenth century the growth of Hull meant that traders began to favour Hull as their main port. Even so York remained an important place for ship-building. In 1294-6 York, with 69 ship-wrights, had more than anywhere else in the country. The largest numbers of ship-wrights after York were 50 in London, 38 in both Southampton and Portsmouth, and 35 in Ipswich. These fragmentary indications are all that remain of what must have been a major industry in York.

Internally within the city, guilds and associations began to form. In 1163 the weavers are first recorded as having a trade guild at a price to the King of £10 a year, a sum they dutifully paid until the end of the century. Thereafter their fortunes declined. In 1202 they failed to pay their annual fee, by 1214 they owed £60, by 1219 £80 and by 1279 they owed the enormous sum of £420. Other craft guilds were formed in the late twelfth and thirteenth centuries - by 1180 there were associations of glovers, saddlers and hosiers, and by the end of the thirteenth there were guilds of butchers, drapers and vintners.

A key element to the economic welfare for York in the region and abroad was the annual fair and the weekly markets. The origins of the fairs and markets of York are often lost in antiquity, but during the twelfth century many of them were documented for the first time. The first record of St Peter's or the Lammas Fair held yearly from 3 pm on the 31st July, to 3pm on the 2nd August, is in a grant by Thurstan, Archbishop of York, dated between 1114-1140. The details of the fair are given in Edward I's Quo Warranto Inquisition of 1279

'And when the fair has begun, the bailiffs of the Archbishop will keep the peace in the city and collect tolls and take other profits both on the water and on land just as,

93

at other times, the city bailiffs do. And for the time of the fair he holds infangenth (infangtheif, the ability to catch and sentence criminals, including the ultimate deterrent of death) in his enclosure in York and in his granges in the suburb of that city and a gallows next the suburb, but at other times he does not hold liberty of this kind.'

The fair was one of the great annual occasions of York life and trade, but on a much more regular basis the various weekly markets were held. A 'meat market' is mentioned in the Domesday Book (probably the Shambles) and two markets are known in the twelfth and thirteenth centuries: the market on Pavement or 'Marketshire' and Thursday Market. In the later Middle Ages Thursday Market was principally for the selling of meat.

Living in the City

The government of York was organised by the most rich and powerful of the city and it is they who are best recorded - the mayoral families such as the Selby family and prominent citizens. The bulk of the population go unrecorded or are simply names on witness lists of charters. One of the least represented groups are women. Occasional references are made to them, normally as a 'wife' though sometimes they are persons in their own right, for example Juliana, who was married to Lefwin, left money and four hens to St Mary's Abbey on her death. The role of women generally in York would have been no different to women throughout England - subsumed under their husband's persona in legal and financial matters, unless they were rich or powerful enough to exercise power in their own right. Occasionally widows are known, and some are recorded in financial 'distress' after their husband's death. Servants or the poor are usually ignored, though occasionally a servant might appear in a witness list: Ralph Nuvel's clerk, Thomas, is cited in some of the witness lists.

Religion was an important part of daily life with angels and devils being very real. William of Newbrugh, a twelfth century Chronicler, wrote of several encounters by Ketell, a man gifted with the power to see devils:

> Ketell used to say that some demons were large, robust and crafty, and, when permitted by a superior power extremely hurtful; others were small and contemptible, impotent in strength and dull in understanding

Ketell saw devils all around: a pair were responsible for him falling off his horse; another group planned to attack a village and

> ... he once entered a public house, and saw devils ... in the likeness of apes, sitting on the shoulders of all who were drinking, voiding their spittle into the cups, and deriding the stupidity of these men ... And when prayers were said (as is customary) ... they leaped off affrighted, being unable to endure the virtue of that sacred name.

It is an interesting side-light that prayers were said in the public-house, and at other times if the name of the Saviour was said, the devils backed off.

Fire was also a consideration amongst the crowded wooden houses within York. Most houses did not have an oven but relied for cooking bread either on communal ovens or ovens owned by individuals. Charters and grants also occasionally mention the danger of fire. When Roger the cook and his wife Eva rented a house from Roger de Wynchon, the precentor at the Minster, a clause stated that 'if the buildings are burnt down by fire or are destroyed or deteriorate for any other reason' the house should be rebuilt to the value of 20 marks. However, the most serious fire that was thought to have happened across the city in 1137 when – the argument goes in most histories – York was burnt to the ground by a devastating fire. This has been refuted by Christopher Norton with the intriguing argument that the word 'consecrata' ('consecrated') has been mis-read as 'conflagrata' (conflagration), with the corollary being that there was not a major fire in the city, but there was a major consecration of churches

95

within the city.

Occasional glimpses of life in York can be gathered from charters and the Chronicles. William of Newburgh cites several examples: of boys stoning the hearse of archbishop Gerard because he was accused of witchcraft (is he the only archbishop to have been accused of witchcraft?) and later William cites that young boys were appointed into clerical positions by Archbishop Roger, boys who built

> 'childish houses, to yoke mice in little wagons, to play together indiscriminately'

The image of boys catching mice and harnessing them to small wagons is an amusing one, though the mice probably didn't think so! This reference is the first this author knows to children's games in York. There is only one early reference to plays in York when in the York Minster Statute Book of 1220-5 there is the note:

> 'Item, one will contrive stars with all things pertaining to them except the rushes ...: one on Christmas night for the shepherds and two on Epiphany night if the presentation of the three kings be done'

That the Minster statutes refer to props and that the stars relate to Christmas night and the arrival of the three kings shows the ecclesiastical basis for drama in England, a theme taken up in the later centuries by the glorious cycle of York Mystery Plays.

The routine of life can be broadly mapped out. There were one or two meals per day, with the main meal being eaten early afternoon. Oddly enough, a precise time can be given for 20 March 1140, for on that day there was an eclipse and astronomical calculations showed it occurred at 1.45 pm, when 'almost everywhere it happened that men were sitting down at the dining table'. The year had two patterns to it, the familiar monthly one of January to December, but there was the equally important church year which ran from Advent to Advent, starting on November 30th, with its associated fixed and moveable feast days. The start of the year caused considerable confusion for there were four possible dates, Christmas (probably most common during the late eleventh and early twelfth centuries), the 1st January (the Feast of the Circumcision), the 25th March (the Annunciation or Lady Day) and Easter. The 25th March became more common over the twelfth and thirteenth centuries as the starting point for the year. The days of the week were dedicated to different traditions: fish was eaten on Fridays as meat could not be eaten and, despite church sanction, Sunday was the day for markets. In York the archbishop preached against Sunday trading as late as 1322 when Sunday markets were formally prohibited.

As well as the markets, a large range of wares were sold in the shops around the city. In many areas specialist craftsmen gathered together and their influence can still be seen in the street names of York: Spurriergate, the street of spur makers and Coppergate, the street of the coopers. Trades were also represented by people's surnames: surnames which passed from father to son were rare at the beginning of the twelfth century, and only become common by 1250.

Through archaeological excavations within the city more is known about the living conditions of the period. The environment was one of large amounts of debris and organic material outside and inside houses. Environmental evidence has shown that York during Anglo-Scandinavian and Norman periods had accumulations of filth and rotting matter around the town, whereas in Roman and later-Medieval periods the insects discovered favour cleaner habitats, showing that an effort was made to keep the town clean.

The care of the poor, sick, old and infirm was normally performed within the home, but in certain cases patients could be looked after in St Peter's, renamed after the mid-twelfth century St Leonard's, hospital. Based next to the Minster it was the largest hospital in the north of England. In essence it was a normal house of Augustinian canons, but the care of the sick and elderly transformed it into the largest hospital in the north of England, supposedly with 206 patients, though the numbers probably varied considerably, with the highest number in 1399 of 232 people.

Standards of hygiene were very different to that today with the spread of disease often being associated with sinful actions of the individuals. One particular dread during the twelfth and thirteenth century was the spread of leprosy. One hospital, St Nicholas's Hospital was set up outside Walmgate Bar to house York's lepers outside the city walls.

The range of wealth in the city was vast, with squalor and poverty at one end to the rich and powerful ecclesiastical institutions and lay people at the other. Those with wealth could afford to indulge in the most up-to-date artistic trends of the day. Little now remains in York of these achievements though glimpses can be seen. There are two great collections of material in York. The first is the twelfth and thirteenth century art work in York Minster above ground with the repositioned twelfth century glass high up in the clerestory, and below ground the architecture and sculpture in the undercroft. In the undercroft, which itself has the remains of the magnificent twelfth century pillars with decoration on very similar to the pillars in Durham Cathedral, there are two magnificent pieces of carving, the Doom Stone and the Madonna and Child.

The second great collection is in the Yorkshire Museum where the reconstructed twelfth century sculptures and reconstructed doorway from St Mary's Abbey are displayed. The displays include the remarkable statues of the Apostles and some Old Testament prophets such as Moses, and New Testament figures such as St John.

Elsewhere in the city fragments of architecture can be seen. Four Romanesque church doorways remain: St Margaret's Walmgate; St Denis's church Walmgate; St Nicholas church Laurence St and the door inserted into Ingram's Almhouses in Bootham and said to come form Holy Trinity Micklegate. Unfortunately all have suffered greatly from the ravages of erosion. Generally closed to the public there are the twelfth century columns and vaults of St Leonard's Hospital in the Theatre Royal, but open to everyone is the 'Norman House' behind the frontage of Stonegate. The small section of the masonry built house was discovered in 1939 during the destruction of a later building. Nothing is known of its early history, but in 1376 it belonged to the prebend of Ampleforth and so was probably a prebendal house in the twelfth century as well.

Conclusion

Whilst the living conditions of the poor probably altered very little over the two centuries of this chapter, the status of York had changed dramatically, from that of a conquered and devastated city at the Conquest, to a city which through its merchants and city hierarchy had gained a solid independence from the Crown. When they needed to, the merchants and citizens could act in unison for their own good, and by extension the good of the city, whether by buying chapters or setting up religious or craft guilds. This independence and the power to regulate its own affairs gave the city the springboard needed for the success it gained over the following centuries.

The citizens of the city had also assimilated yet another cultural group to the previous Roman, Anglo-Saxon and Viking groups of the previous centuries. From 1066 they assimilated the Norman culture and they were to assimilate another - the culture of Royalty, Court and Parliament from the south as Edward I marched north to attack Scotland and used York as his base.

LATE MEDIEVAL YORK

Barrie Dobson

'The Halcyon Years: York in the Later Middle Ages, 1272-1485'

'The dial of this city hath a long time gone backwards.' So wrote Sir Thomas Widdrington, Recorder of York and its first real historian, when in 1661 he presented his *Analecta Eboracensia* to the mayor and council. Much to his chagrin, the latter declined this handsome offer on the grounds that they were much more interested in the prospects of a prosperous future than a celebrated past. In their own words, 'Give us leave to tell you that a good purse is more useful to us than a long story'. Over three centuries later it is abundantly clear that the disenchanted York corporation - not for the first or last time - had made a serious error of judgement. For theirs was, as it still is, a city whose future absolutely depends upon its past. Other once famous medieval towns have naturally been confronted with York's post-medieval problem of long periods of waning prestige and declining prosperity; but most of these have long ago either accepted their reduced status with equanimity or have adjusted - like Rome, Venice or London - to new ages in new ways. By contrast, in York the medieval city still tends to rule its modern successor from the grave, through its walls, its street-plan, its Minster and its churches but even more through the emotional attitudes and value-judgements it continues to evoke from its residents and visitors in its latest phase as a beneficiary - and a victim - of a mass tourism which would have astonished all who lived here five and six centuries ago

Accordingly any account of York during the two hundred years between the late thirteenth and late fifteenth centuries should begin by emphasising that it is above all the achievements of those two centuries which not only bring hundreds of thousands of modern tourists to York but are crucial to the economic welfare and indeed survival of those who live in the city. Other contributors to this book might understandably wish to argue that during either the Roman, Anglian, Viking or Norman periods, the fortunes of the city of York were quite as significant for the history of Britain as they were between 1272 and 1485. Nevertheless no one can really deny that it was during those 213 years that the majority of the most powerful and attractive visual memorials York now has to offer its innumerable visitors were initiated, developed or brought to completion.

The achievements of the Plantagenet, Lancastrian and Yorkist city are indeed quite impossible to avoid and ignore half a millennium later. To take only a few examples, these two late medieval centuries were the period when the single most massive architectural enterprise of English Gothic art, the complete rebuilding of York Minster, was brought to a triumphant conclusion; when the city's celebrated walls were brought to their most elaborate state; when the four main bars or gates into those walls were made most lavishly defensible; when the most precious works of secular building in the city, the Halls of the Merchant Taylors and the Merchant Adventurers as well as the civic Common or Guildhall itself, were originally planned and completed; when the city's only major contribution to English literature and drama, the cycle of Corpus Christi mystery plays, was composed and attained its extraordinarily elaborate dramatic form; when the local tradition of glass-painting at York reached its climax of artistic excellence and commercial popularity; and when the city's forty parish churches (no less) were either thoroughly reconstructed, like Holy Trinity, Goodramgate, or All Saints, North Street, or remodelled, refurbished and redecorated

101

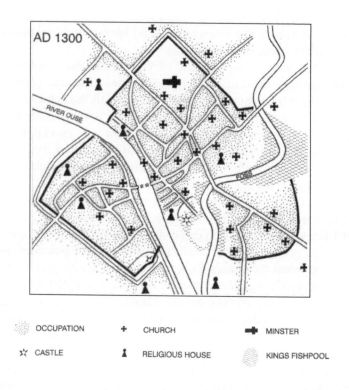

OCCUPATION + CHURCH ✚ MINSTER

☆ CASTLE ⚑ RELIGIOUS HOUSE KINGS FISHPOOL

in conformity with the Decorated and later the Perpendicular architectural fashions of their day. These were the two centuries too (18 May 1396 is the exact date) when the city of York received a charter from King Richard II elevating it to county status in its own right, a privilege previously enjoyed only by London and - very recently - by Bristol. York's acquisition of county status has been interpreted in various ways; but at one level it can certainly be seen as the highest point in the long history of the city's determination to manage its own affairs as autonomously as possible. No man is an island and certainly no town in England, even London, could ever hope to be fully independent from the claims of Crown and national government. However perhaps the major theme underlying the following account of York's development between 1272 and 1485 is that it was during this period, more than ever before or ever afterwards, that the citizens themselves were to a considerable degree in charge of their own destinies and creators of their city's remarkable achievements.

Accordingly, and although the history of York is - like all history - a seamless web, 1272 is in fact an appropriate date with which to begin an exploration of how its citizens came to enjoy those 'halcyon years'. As Chris Daniell has pointed out in the previous chapter, by the beginning of King Edward I's reign in that year, York had long been established as what the twelfth-century chronicler William of Malmesbury styled a 'most populous and metropolitan town' (*urbs amplissima et metropolis*). By present or continental standards, it was admittedly hardly an enormous metropolis, housing fewer inhabitants in fact than modern Selby. In the absence of any reliable statistical evidence before the levying of the three national Poll Taxes a century later (in 1377-81), any attempt to estimate what the total population of the city actually was at the accession of Edward I can only be a more or less speculative guess. However, as thirteenth-century English towns undoubtedly profited from the national demographic expansion of that period, it is not at all implausible that by 1272 York held at least 12,000 inhabitants. It was therefore almost certainly the largest town in the kingdom except for London, already at least five times as large. More certainly still, by the time a new system of national taxation by parliamentary subsidies had been established by the English government a few decades later, the taxable wealth of York (assessed at £1,620 in 1334) was greater than that of any English town except London and Bristol. The seat of one of England's only two archbishoprics since 735 and the commercial emporium of Yorkshire since the Viking period, under Edward I York was to enter - however briefly - a new phase of its history as nothing less than the administrative capital of England.

York and the Crown: Edward I - Richard III

The thirty-five-year long reign of Edward I (1272-1307) has often and rightly been seen as a watershed in the political history of the British Isles. It is undoubtedly a watershed in the history of York. Once most famous as the founder - more accurately the godfather - of parliament, in effect Edward presided over what some recent historians regard as the real genesis of the English state as a sophisticated and well-regulated exploiter of its subjects. In particular, Edward's unprecedented demands for new sources of taxation to finance his never-ending military campaigns against the Welsh, Scots and French created a new type of relationship between the Crown and its boroughs. Needless to say, no English town - not even London, let alone York - was ever powerful enough to defy a king for long. However, by the early fourteenth century there had emerged more explicitly than ever before a sort of unwritten contractual arrangement whereby the mayor and aldermen were increasingly allowed to rule their own city in their own way provided that they preserved a tolerable degree of peace therein and responded adequately to the Crown's demands for assistance in the form of armed men (or ships) and money. At York, as elsewhere in the English counties and major boroughs, it was the insatiable appetites of Edward I and his successors for war taxation which ensured that the citizens would henceforward send two of their number to share the responsibility of conceding that taxation in the newfangled institution of the parliamentary Commons. The result was an ambiguous one. In many ways the governing élite of the city exercised a high degree of self-government; but as a parliamentary as well as 'taxation borough' York was more firmly stitched into the fabric of the English state than ever before.

Edward I's other legacy to the city of York was much less inevitable and more ambiguous still. An intemperate and autocratic ruler, even by the standards of his age, this was a king who had twice tried to coerce the citizens of York itself by using the ultimate sanction of suspending their highly prized

Merchant Taylors' Hall

Walmgate Bar

constitutional liberties. But it was his arbitrary attempts to exploit in his own interests the major dynastic succession crisis north of the Border caused by the fatal accident of Alexander III of Scotland in 1286 which completely transformed not only the previously comparatively tranquil relations between the two kingdoms of England and Scotland but also the strategic importance of York itself. After ten years of intensive diplomatic pressure had failed to bring the Scottish nobility into obedience to his will, in the spring of 1296 Edward I launched the first of his extremely large-scale military expeditions across the Tweed. Edward's attempt to subdue resistance by force, not least by removing the Scottish royal coronation stone at Scone to Westminster Abbey, almost immediately had exactly the opposite effect. By the autumn of the following year, William Wallace had won the battle of Stirling Bridge and inaugurated that struggle for Scottish independence which was only brought to an end when a Scottish king, James VI became James I of England too in 1603. Throughout those three centuries the relationship between the two kingdoms was more often characterised by cold than by hot war; but in either event the city of York found itself taking on a new role as an actual or potential royal base for military operations against the Scots.

At no time in its history was York more heavily involved in the defence of the English realm than during the reigns of Edward I and his son and grandson, Edward II (1307-27) and Edward III (1327-77), all three would-be conquerors of Scotland who were sooner or later forced on to the defensive. Determined to crush the Scottish rebels and aware that he needed a military headquarters as near to the fighting areas as was prudently possible, Edward I actually removed his major governmental offices (the Chancery, Exchequer and central law courts) to York in the summer of 1298. The departments of English central administration were still (just) sufficiently small and rudimentary to be transported more or less en bloc from their usual home at Westminster if not without considerable disturbance to routine. Although the king himself only visited York occasionally during this period, the city was the centre of his war machine and became a rendezvous for the English armies en route to Scotland as well as a major provisioning centre. Meat and grain were stored in the city to supply Edward's armies and the city itself was obliged to make such direct contributions to the English war effort as sending forty crossbowmen to help garrison Stirling castle in 1304. So large were the armies launched against the insubordinate Scots (there were no fewer than 25,000 English foot soldiers at the battle of Falkirk in 1298) that the retailers and especially overseas merchants of York undoubtedly made a handsome profit from their city's position as centre of the nation's affairs.

On the other hand, there is no evidence that Edward I himself ever developed a particular affection for the city. He had expelled the small and by now impoverished Jewish community from York, as from England as a whole, in 1290; and in fact his most enduring contribution to urban development in the north of England was the creation of his new town called Kingston-on-Hull, which eventually, if very gradually, outstripped the commercial enterprise of York's own merchants. In 1305 Edward sent the central departments of government back to Westminster, two years before his death which took place near the Solway Firth at the beginning of yet one last abortive attempt to annihilate Scottish resistance to his will. Where the indomitable Edward I had failed, his feckless son, Edward II, was hardly likely to succeed. Nevertheless it might well be the case that Edward II, however 'chicken-hearted and luckless in war', as a contemporary chronicler called him, knew the city of York more intimately than any English monarch before Richard III. So great was the military threat now posed by the formidable Robert Bruce, king of Scotland from 1306 to 1329, that the new king often visited York during the early years of his reign; and it was through York that he rode to his humiliating defeat at Bannockburn on 24 June 1314. For one of the very few times in English history since the Norman Conquest, an English sovereign had failed in what was universally regarded as his primary duty, the protection of his territory from serious assault and depredation by his subjects' enemies.

Robert Bruce's overwhelming victory at Bannockburn inevitably placed not only the north of England as a whole but York itself at serious risk. Before that battle the inhabitants of the city must have felt sufficiently far from the Tweed to be immune from Scottish invasion. But during the nerve-wracking nine years between 1314 and the conclusion of a thirteen-year truce with Bruce at a great council held at Bishopthorpe in 1323 there was an ever-present possibility that the city might be attacked and even captured by Scottish raiding parties. The worst year was 1319 when the Earl of Moray and James the Black Douglas unexpectedly rode down Swaledale into the Vale of York. A hastily assembled local army marched north from the city, only to be annihilated at Myton-on-Swale three miles east of Boroughbridge. Blinded by the smoke of the straw fires started by the Scots, a motley force of York citizens, priests and even monks was driven helter-skelter backwards into a foaming river. Among the many casualties, alleged to be more than 3,000, was Nicholas Flemyng, the only mayor of York ever killed in action. Three summers later, in 1322, an even greater catastrophe was narrowly avoided. After Edward himself was almost captured in a skirmish between Byland and Rievaulx, another Scottish raiding party actually reached Bootham Bar and terrorised what one or two chroniclers called, rather vaguely, 'the suburbs of the city'. In the event York was not to be subjected to a sustained siege until it was invested by Lord Fairfax and his forces as late as 1644; and it is one of the greater ironies of the city's history that the most famous town walls of medieval England never needed to be put to military use in the middle ages themselves.

Not that late medieval York ever completely lost its role as an ultimate offensive or defensive base against marauding Scots. Not long after the fifteen-year old Edward III succeeded his deposed - and soon assassinated - father in 1327, he too began to pay particular attention to a city in which he must actually have been conceived during the early months of 1312. Much more obviously, Edward realised that York still presented the best possible platform for preparing campaigns against what had now become the traditional foe. By a happy coincidence (a vacancy in the see of Canterbury), the most important royal wedding ever to take place in York - between the young Edward and Queen Philippa of Hainault - was celebrated in the Minster on 24 January 1328. During the next eight years, the central departments of government were once again transferred to York, the Chancery usually to the Minster chapter-house and the Exchequer to the royal castle. Perhaps York was never as close to the centre of national affairs as during these early years of Edward III's reign. The extensive households of the young king and queen occupied large parts of the castle, the Franciscan friary adjacent to the castle and the archbishop's palace at Bishopthorpe. Whether or not, as one chronicler claimed, the almost inconceivable number of no less than 600 royal knights were installed in the precincts of the York Greyfriars in 1327, the presence of so many armed troops in the city certainly led to conflict with York's own citizens and to the shedding of blood in the city's streets. Naturally the unaccustomed presence of large amounts of bullion and plate within the city also led to increased disorder. Bands of robbers clustered around the main roads into and out of the city in the hope of an easy prey; and it has even been suggested that the activities of some of these highwaymen gave birth to the legend of Robin Hood, the most famous outlaw of them all.

But for Edward III, as for his grandfather, the Scots proved easier to defeat than to conquer. During the years between 1335 and 1337, not least because his many expeditions north of the Border were bringing him increasingly diminishing returns, Edward III turned his ambitions to the south and to nothing less than the throne of France. So was inaugurated that Hundred Years' War - as it was much later called - which between 1337 and 1453 was always fought across the Channel and therefore comprised a series of military campaigns where York had naturally much less to offer than previously. Accordingly the royal Exchequer and Court of Common Pleas were sent back from York to Westminster in 1338, from which they returned to the northern city only once more, for a few months in 1392. It was symptomatic of York's changed status in the eyes of the

English monarchy that although no fewer than fifteen parliaments had been summoned to that city between 1298 and 1335, no parliament has ever assembled there since that last date.

Not that York retreated into complete political insignificance after the Hundred Years' War made it absolutely certain - as had always been likely since at least the battle of Hastings - that London rather than York would develop into the political as well as economic capital of the kingdom. However, throughout the tortuous course of the Hundred Years' War it was the common assumption in royal and governmental circles in the Thames valley that as southern England's military resources would henceforward be devoted to expeditions across the English Channel, the inhabitants of the counties north of the Trent should take the responsibility for containing the dangers of aggression from Scotland. In fact the citizens of York rarely played a major part in the protection of the realm themselves. After the 1330s the most effective barrier against Scottish raids into Yorkshire was usually the defence in depth provided by the Northumberland castles of the king, the Percy family and the bishop of Durham. Thus on 13 July 1388 King Richard II sent a letter to John of Gaunt, his uncle and the most powerful of all late medieval magnates, to say that the Scots had invaded England, 'burning and wasting his realm, killing children in their cradles and advancing even as far as the city of York'. But by the time Richard wrote that letter the Scots had already been repelled, nearly 100 miles to the north at the famous battle of Otterburn and by the prompt action not of anyone in York but by the levies raised by Sir Henry ('Hotspur') Percy and the citizens of Newcastle-upon-Tyne.

Although the city of York ceased to be at the geographical centre of national politics after the late 1330s, it was naturally still visited, if at rather erratic intervals, by members of the English royal family. Indeed the visits made there after 1377 by Edward III's grandson and successor, Richard II, were sufficiently frequent and lengthy to give rise to a well-known hypothesis that had he survived the many conflicts with his nobility which eventually led to his deposition in 1399 Richard

110

Archbishop Scrope from the Book of Hours

Lady Row, Goodramgate

would have replaced London by York as England's capital city. On the whole this seems highly unlikely. However, during the last decade of his reign, Richard's quarrelsome relationship with the citizens of London no doubt made him appreciate the hospitality he received at York, where he watched the already famous Corpus Christi mystery plays from a special enclosure near the Minster in 1398. From the mayor and council's point of view, a royal visit to their city offered an ideal opportunity to lobby for privileges and favours from their sovereign. Under the leadership of merchants like the wealthy William Frost, mayor of York no fewer than seven times between 1396 and 1407, the corporation received the most significant of all its many royal charters. In 1393 the city was allowed to elect its own justices of peace and labour; and in 1396 its new status as a county in its own right meant that the sheriff of Yorkshire's jurisdiction over York was henceforward replaced by that of two sheriffs elected by the citizens themselves. As a recent historian has observed, these and other constitutional and judicial changes of the 1390s were as wide-ranging and fundamental for the future of York as the reorganisation of English local authorities in 1974.

Hardly surprisingly, it was exactly in this period, during the last years of Richard II's reign, that the mayor and aldermen began to describe York as 'a city of great reputation, now called the second city of the realm and the Chamber of the King'. Whether either the royal government or the majority of York's inhabitants were much impressed by the short-lived title of 'King's Chamber' is another matter entirely. However closely regulated by the aldermen and their officers, urban society was always prone to outbreaks of sudden disloyalty and violence. In early July 1381, when the news of Wat Tyler's forcible entry into London at the time of the so-called Peasants' Revolt reached York, an armed band led by John Gisburne, an ex-mayor, attacked Bootham Bar in the hope of recapturing political power. Much more startling was the substantial involvement of the inhabitants of York in a large-scale rebellion against the first Lancastrian king, Henry IV, led by Archbishop Richard Scrope during the early summer of 1405. This most politically suicidal act in the entire history of York still seems hard to explain. No doubt a good deal should be made of the citizens' loyalty to their former patron Richard II, deposed nearly six years earlier; and Archbishop Scrope himself was allegedly a very charismatic presence as he walked through the streets of his cathedral city preaching rebellion to an anointed if usurping king. In any case, the archbishop's horrific end, hacked to death at his execution in the fields at Clementhorpe outside the city walls on 8 June 1405 had two important consequences for the city. Although he never received official canonisation by the pope, Scrope proved more effective dead than alive - by creating the most spectacular new devotional cult in the late medieval Minster. Above all, the failure of his revolt and the city' subjection to the royal will - Henry IV eventually pardoned the citizens for a fine of £200 - confirmed that the relationship between citizens and the Crown was too close and too rewarding to be long disrupted, even by that rarest and gravest of acts of disobedience, an armed insurrection.

Throughout the remainder of the fifteenth century the mayor and council of York were accordingly careful never to defy the king of England again. However, after displaying exemplary loyalty to that most successful of English warrior kings, Henry V (who only had time to visit York once, in 1421), the gradual collapse of royal authority during the reign of his son, Henry VI (1422-61) sometimes presented them with extremely difficult problems of choice. All in all, the aldermen of York preferred to negotiate with a powerful and unchallenged sovereign; but during the half-century between 1435 and 1485 they were faced in turn with an incompetent king and then by the dynastic rivalry for the crown now known as the Wars of the Roses. The ferocity of that rivalry must have been brought home to the residents of York with particular force when after the battle of Wakefield on 30 December 1460 Micklegate Bar was adorned with the severed head (decorated with a paper crown) of Richard, duke of York, the father of the two Yorkist kings of England, Edward IV (1461-83) and the notoriously controversial Richard III (1483-5). Since 1471, as the husband of Anne Neville, the heiress of the most formidable of northern magnate families,

113

Richard had usually resided in his Yorkshire power bases at Middleham Castle in Wensleydale and Sheriff Hutton, eight miles north-east of York. Before and after his usurpation of the crown from his nephews in the summer of 1483 he was assiduous in courting the good will of both the city council and the Minster clergy of York. Perhaps the most important reason for such favour was that Richard developed an extraordinarily unusual and ambitious plan to be buried in York rather than at Westminster or Windsor, within an enormous and prestigious chantry chapel - of no less than one hundred chaplains - attached to the Minster. For their part, many if not all of the citizens of York were gratified by the belief that as king of England the most 'special' of all their 'good lords' (their *dominus specialissimus*) might save them from at least some of effects of the long-term economic depression that by the 1480s had the city in its grip. The news that Richard had been 'pitiously slane and murderd, to the grete hevynesse of this Citie' at Bosworth on 22 August 1485 put paid both to that over optimistic hope and to the startling prospect that a city of many medieval monuments might even have come to possess the only royal mausoleum in the north of England.

The Urban Economy and the Black Death

Ironically enough, the greatest beneficiaries of the increasing self-government and administrative complexity of late medieval York are now those of us who wish to recapture the economic realities which lay behind the lives led by our ancestors in that long vanished urban society. For it is only from the reign of Edward I onwards that at last this society gradually begins to be accessible through the records produced within the city itself. Here the critical date is once again 1272, when 'the names of those who have entered the liberty of the city of York' (thirty-six of them in that year) first survive as listed in the city's Freemen's Register. That Register is not only unquestionably the single most invaluable document to be found in the present York City Archives but is also the most impressive and reliable record of its sort to survive from any medieval British town. The great

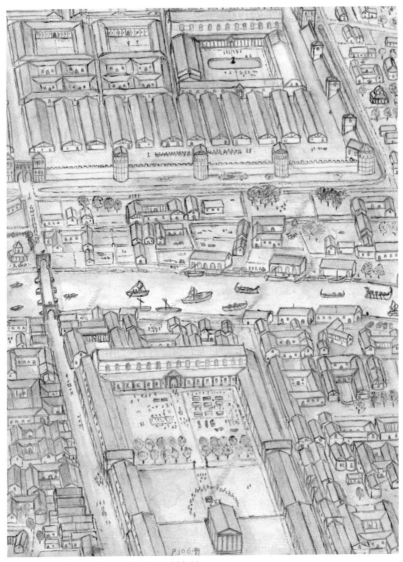

1. Reconstruction of York in the years 209-11.

2. Head pot from York, early third century.

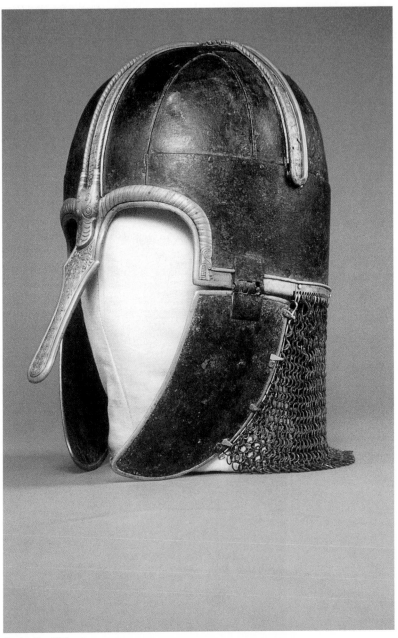

3. Anglian Helmet.

4. Jorvik in 975, from the backyards of Coppergate.

5. York Minster from the West.

6. *Noah and his Ark* Panel of the Great East Window, York Minster.

7. The crossing arch, St Mary's Abbey.

8. 'Jacob's Well' in Trinity Lane.

majority of York's craftsmen earned their livelihood by 'opening windows', that is by selling their own or other manufactured goods from workshops which were also their homes. Because the practice of retail trade in medieval York, as in nearly all medieval towns, was usually restricted to those who had acquired the freedom of the borough, from the 1270s onwards the York Freemen's Register's - which records the names and usually the occupations of the citizens - provides a unique insight into patterns of recruitment and employment within the city walls.

A century later, by the reign of Richard II, the original evidence still accessible in York itself for the life of its inhabitants becomes much greater and more varied still. Although notoriously hazardous to interpret, the last wills and testaments of the more substantial York citizens which begin to survive in the great series of Archbishops' Probate Registers from 1389 onwards (now preserved in the Borthwick Institute of Historical Research) can give an extremely vivid impression of their hopes and fears for this world and the next. By 1400 too the civic administration's own records begin to illuminate the scene even more fully. The first extant civic financial account roll (compiled by the city's three *camerarii* or chamberlains) dates from 1396-97; and by that year the common or town clerk of York was compiling the first of the city's invaluable Memoranda Books. Two generations later, after 1461, there begins to survive an even more remarkable series of volumes, the city of York's own so-called House Books. These record the business conducted at civic council meetings in a wealth of detail unsurpassed - except in London - elsewhere in England at the end of the middle ages.

Although the city of York can therefore boast some of the most valuable urban records left to us from medieval England, only a small proportion of what was once a much larger archive has managed to survive the ravages of time and in particular of the river Ouse, which so often flooded the city council chamber on Old Ouse Bridge. Accordingly much can be known about the careers of the aldermen and overseas merchants of the city but many of the most fundamental features of the economy of the late medieval town remain extremely mysterious, not least the critical issue of the size of the town's population. Like all other British urban corporations, with the solitary exception of Coventry in the early Tudor period, the mayor and aldermen of York never contemplated compiling a census of its inhabitants. Any attempt to trace the demographic history of York in this period is therefore forced to rely, as we have already noticed, on the invaluable but highly controversial returns to the three unpopular national poll taxes levied by the Crown between 1377 and 1381, taxes now most famous because they led directly to the greatest popular revolt in English history, the so-called Peasants' Revolt of 1381. According to the enrolled accounts of these poll taxes still surviving in the Public Record Office, there were exactly 7,248 recorded lay tax-payers within the city in 1377. York was therefore then apparently larger than Bristol, Coventry and Norwich, its three closest rivals among the provincial towns of England, all regional entrepots like itself. But how far do these taxation figures enable us to estimate the total population of men, women and children in the late fourteenth-century city? Although historians are unlikely ever to agree what allowances should be made for the number of children and of beggars in the urban population as well as for widespread tax evasion, it seems not improbable that York held at least 15,000 residents, lay and clerical, when Richard II became king of England. By modern standards, the capital of the medieval north may seem a remarkably small town, not so very much larger than modern Tadcaster or Malton. Perhaps so; but it was to become smaller yet. For a variety of reasons, of which continued outbreaks of bubonic plague (only called the Black Death in the sixteenth century) are the most obvious, the population of York continued to fall or remain highly stagnant for the rest of the middle ages. There may well have been fewer than 10,000 inhabitants of York when this chapter ends, with the death at the battle of Bosworth of Richard III, in 1485.

Two centuries or so earlier, at the time when this account of the late medieval city begins in the 1270s, the population of York city was - as we have already seen - quite possibly twice as large. For in York, as in most of the substantial towns of western Christendom, the sudden onslaught of a new and dreaded *pestilentia*, bubonic plague, was not only the single greatest human calamity in the history of the city but also introduced a period of prolonged demographic attrition. Although late medieval York lacks a detailed contemporary account of the initial catastrophe, it seems clear that the Black Death, most probably imported into England by rats at the port of Weymouth in Dorset during the previous autumn, reached Yorkshire by March 1349. In York itself plague was at its height between late May and late July of that year and proved sufficiently sensitive to the weather to make one chronicler write that it 'followed the course of the sun'. Modern medical opinion does indeed suggest that in this country plague-carrying fleas are always likely to be most actively lethal during the characteristic moist warmth of a typical early summer. No one will ever know for certain how many residents of York died during that horrific year. All in all, it seems more likely than not that the city - like most English towns - suffered a mortality rate of at least 40% in 1349. The register of Archbishop William de la Zouche reveals that almost a half of all the parish priests in and around the city seem to have died between 1349 and 1350. Even more startling is the evidence of the York civic Freemens' Register. During the first half of the fourteenth century an average of some fifty or sixty new citizens were admitted to the franchise every year. In 1350-51 that figure rose to 212, and in 1364-65 to its all-time medieval record figure of 219. There could be no clearer indication that the mayor and aldermen were being forced to admit new citizens in unprecedented numbers in order to fill the gaps left in the ranks of the town's craftsmen by the equally unprecedented mortality of 1349 and the later outbreaks of plague in the 1360s.

Indeed the cruellest paradox in the history of York during its halcyon years was that for two or three generations its prosperity was actually the direct consequence of the most sustained and catastrophic mortality the town has ever known. Death, sudden and painful death, was the spectre which walked the streets of the city, as indeed it walked the streets of all post-

Black Death European cities. From 1349 to the outbreak of a new and formidable viral disease called the 'sweating sickness' in 1485 - and indeed well into the Tudor period too - the residents of York were at continuous risk of early and painful extinction. This was accordingly an age in York's past when the first question a London merchant riding towards Micklegate Bar might ask passers-by was 'wheder ther was any deth within the Citie or not'. It was a period too during which the archbishops, senior Minster clergy and the richer laymen of the town would regularly bolt into the comparative safety of their country retreats 'for the plague that reigneth'. Although only a very small minority of the craftsmen and labourers in York could afford to do likewise, at least one fifteenth-century shoemaker's apprentice received permission 'to depart from his service unto his proper friends until it shall please our Lord Jesu to cease the said plague'.

For at least two centuries after the first outbreak of the bubonic plague in 1349, York can therefore be seen as a medieval and smaller counterpart of a modern Calcutta or Sao Paulo, a Third World city suffering from an appallingly heavy death rate and completely dependent for its survival upon a steady supply of immigrants from the surrounding countryside. For as long as such immigration continued, it could even be argued that the major economic function of late medieval York and England's other major towns was to act as a 'deathtrap' for the English population as a whole. On the other hand, and by an irony which seems to provide the essential clue to the city's achievements in this period, it seems clear that for many years York's deplorable death rate positively promoted the standard of living of the survivors and hence enhanced the prosperity of the town as a whole. One of the most obvious effects of continued epidemics of plague was to remove the least economically productive sections of the city's pre-Black Death population and to increase the *per capita* wealth - and therefore the purchasing power - of those who still remained in a much less crowded town. More significantly still perhaps, as the economic welfare of York - like that of all major urban centres - depended upon supplying its rural hinterland with goods and services which country villages and market towns could not provide for themselves, it naturally profited from the increased demand for such specialised commodities in the north of England as a whole.

Only at that critical point of time when relentlessly continuous mortality in the countryside, probably accompanied by a low birth rate too, began to exhaust the supply of potential rural immigrants from Yorkshire into York did the city's own economy move into a long-term recession. But even in that respect York was more fortunate than the great majority of British towns; for it was only at a comparatively late stage, during the years around 1450, that there are unmistakable signs that its halcyon years were over. At York, as elsewhere, the nature and severity of so-called 'urban decline' in late medieval England presents a series of extremely difficult problems of interpretation. But no reader of the surviving accounts of the proceedings of the city council can doubt that from at least the time of the battle of Towton in 1461, the mayor and aldermen of the city increasingly saw themselves - to use their own words - as 'poor critturs', suffering from the evils of 'decay, poverty, destruction and ruin'. By that decade not only was the rent value of much urban property within the walls in decline but it was also becoming increasingly difficult to find any tenants at all for many tenements and shops. This was the period too when the economic power of the city at last began to be seriously eroded by aggressive competition from the Hanseatic League, from London merchants and from the new woollen textile manufacturing centres at Halifax, Huddersfield and elsewhere in the West Riding. Nor did the mayor and aldermen have much doubt as to the primary reason for their woes. As they complained in an eloquent petition to their new king, Henry VII, on St George's Day 1487, 'ther is not half the nombre of good men within your said Citie as ther hath beene in tymes past'. Ironically enough, that particular lament not only continued to resound in the civic council chamber for centuries to come but also preserved the fabric of medieval York from complete re-development. The city owes its present status as what the present Pope called 'England's most historic city' to exceptional commercial prosperity before the mid-fifteenth century and to prolonged economic stagnation thereafter.

Urban Society: Aliens, Craftsmen and Merchants

Meanwhile, during the century or so between the 1340s and 1440s, economic activity in York may well have been more dynamically self-generated and more nationally significant than it had ever been since the Norman Conquest and was ever to be again. Despite increasing competition from Hull and Newcastle-upon-Tyne, York's single most important function in pre-industrial England was to serve as the north's best service station or hypermarket, the entrepôt through which imported goods were distributed throughout an enormous hinterland. But not only imported goods. For at least three generations after the first attack of the Black Death, York's own manufacturing activity, highly diversified although based more or less exclusively on the small family or household unit, seems to have dominated industrial production in the north. It is therefore all the more fortunate that this is exactly the period when the occupational structure of the city can at last be studied in quite remarkable detail. Whether or not - as seems likely - the years after the Black Death saw a much greater regulation of the labour supply in the city than ever before and the consequent emergence of a ubiquitous system of separate craft guilds, by 1400 the detailed ordinances of those guilds are beginning to survive in great numbers within the folios of the city's Memorandum Books. More revealing still, and more or less unsurpassed in any other English town at this time, is the light which the Freemen's Register, national taxation records and surviving craftsmen's wills throws on how the citizens of York actually earned their living.

Not that we will ever know how all the 15,000 or so inhabitants of York in the later middle ages occupied their time. Many of York's residents will always evade our grasp. Sadly little, for instance, can be known of the numbers and names of the foreigners, then termed aliens, who were hosted or lodged within the city walls. According to the probably not very reliable returns of the national alien subsidy frequently levied upon these non-citizens between 1439 and 1487, the number of resident aliens in York never exceeded 80 (in 1440). By that date the exotic Jewish community in the city, expelled in 1290, was only a memory kept alive by one or two place-names like 'Jewbretgate'. Much the most numerous group of aliens in the fifteenth-century town comprised men and women called 'Deutsch', an infuriatingly vague term which could be applied to German-speaking immigrants from as far north as Alkmaar in Holland and as far south as Vienna in Austria. A handful of alien settlers in York also came from Gascony or northern France (sometimes as prisoners of the Hundred Years' War), others from Ireland and even one or two from Iceland. Thus the entry of Godmondr' Johnson, *'Iselandman'* into the freedom of the city in 1475-6 is an unexpected testimony to the remarkable range of York merchants' overseas enterprise at this period.

Least welcome of all strangers to York were the Scots, so unwelcome indeed that the prospects of a man or woman born north of the Tweed residing in York without royal or civic letters of protection were probably very slim indeed. The fifteenth-century alien subsidy accounts already mentioned reveal a more considerable, if largely 'silent', migration of Scotttish farmers south of the Border than is usually assumed; but true-born Englishmen who were citizens of York were prepared to go to extraordinarily time-consuming and expensive lengths to prove that they were falsely accused of a Scottish ancestry. The most remarkable of all these cases involved no less a figure than the Common Clerk of York, John Harrington, who in 1486 found it necessary to have his English birth certified to the mayor and aldermen by a group of extremely well-connected Yorkshire knights. To an extent still insufficiently appreciated, the cultural as well as economic life of York suffered from the extinction of close personal contacts with Scotland during the late medieval centuries. By contrast the other aliens resident in York, although few in number, often had a considerable impact on the commercial life of the city. Admittedly Henry Wyman, a Hanseatic merchant born in Hamburg, was the last alien mayor of medieval York (for three successive years between 1407 and 1410); and it may well be that York - like England as a whole - became more insular in its attitudes towards the close of the middle ages. However, a detailed inventory of the tools in the workshop of the German John Colan, an alien householder in the city during the 1460s, leaves no doubt that York still offered excellent prospects for immigrant goldsmiths from the Rhineland. Much the most influential of all York's immigrants from mainland Europe was to arrive towards the very end of the middle ages. Fridericus Freez, an immigrant 'docheman' who was admitted to the freedom of York in 1497, established a printing firm there within a generation of Johann Gutenberg's invention of printing by movable type. Who could then have supposed that over forty years later two of Frederick Freez's sons would be burnt together at the stake on the Knavesmire and so provide the city with its first Protestant martyrs to the cause of the English Reformation?

Unlike Frederick Freez and his family, nearly all of York's alien residents will always evade our grasp. But then so too will the very large numbers of English-born non-citizens living in the town, men and women who never had the opportunity to take up the freedom of York and who for that reason were usually styled 'foreigns' by their contemporaries. It is only very occasionally indeed, and usually in the criminal records of the period, that we catch a glimpse of that large pool of under or completely unemployed labour which lay at the bottom of urban society, under-fed, under-nourished and inadequately housed if indeed housed at all. Melancholy and deprived their lot inevitably was. However, as we have seen, it seems likely that there were fewer of them - and that their plight was less completely dismal - after the Black Death than before its first appearance in 1349. By present-day standards substantial householders in late medieval York also employed a remarkably large number of domestic servants, often incomers to the town hired for a year at a time. Household service was naturally also the most common female occupation in the city. Although the women of York were seriously disadvantaged at law and appear in surviving records much less frequently than their fathers and husbands, recent research has done much to suggest that they were the main beneficiaries of the growing shortage of labour in fifteenth-century York. Admittedly, the handful of women who became free of the city were usually either seamstresses or landladies, two honourable but not normally very well rewarded professions. Many more women played an increasingly prominent economic role within the characteristic small-scale family businesses of the period. Not surprisingly indeed, it was as widows that the women of late medieval York were most formidable, and highly desirable prizes too if their first husbands had been prosperous artisans or - above all - merchants of the town.

However, if the female population of late medieval York can only be seen through a glass somewhat darkly, the careers of the adult male freemen of the town are often very well recorded indeed, at least by the standards of the age. At the risk of considerable over-simplification it can be said that the occupations of lay citizens fell into six main categories. The first and largest group, often accounting for almost a quarter of the male taxpayers in the town, were those who worked in one or other branch of the woollen textile industry. The manufacture of woollen cloths and clothing depended upon a host of specialist craftsmen, of whom the most numerous and important were always the weavers and the tailors. There were no fewer than 128 master tailors (not yet styled 'Merchant Taylors') of York when their first recorded ordinances were compiled in 1386-7. Originally a loose-knit fraternity which worshipped at the altar dedicated to St John the Baptist - their patron saint - in the Minster, the York tailors became wealthy and self-confident enough to build their own - still surviving - Guildhall in Aldwark early in the fifteenth century. As, with a few exceptions like Cambridge and St Andrews in Scotland, every medieval British town needed a viable cloth industry to survive at all, the prominence of the textile trades in York is hardly surprising. Much more striking is how completely, at least before the 1460s, York's high quality woollen goods dominated not only

Yorkshire's internal markets but also much of the North Sea and Baltic trade too. It was York-produced cloth exported from Hull which, as will be seen, laid the foundations for the most spectacular mercantile fortunes in the history of the city.

A second group of York citizens, almost 10 per cent of all taxpayers, worked in the leather trades, as skinners, tanners, saddlers or as cordwainers, making shoes. It seems to have been during the century before 1450 that York established its reputation as the main centre for the production of high-quality leather goods in the county. Perhaps the only major drawback was what would now be called an environmental hazard. The process of tanning raw hide into workable leather produced so nauseous a stench that the York tanners were normally required to practise their trade across the river in what is still known as Tanner's Row. Almost as many freemen of the city were involved in the highly varied and indispensable provisioning or victualling trades. As in other late medieval towns, the vociferous shouts of the bakers, butchers and fishmongers dominated the streets and markets of the town; but a city which attracted so many travellers also found employment for unusually large numbers of grocers, spicers, salters and saucemakers as well as the ubiquitous brewers and ale-wives of the city. York was so important a regional centre that it contained exceptionally large numbers of taverners, inn-keepers, hostlers, carters and mariners, the latter unfortunately such transitory visitors to the city that they have left virtually no trace of their crucial role in servicing a city so absolutely dependent upon its transport facilities. As a town which could allegedly (in 1537) provide beds for 1,035 people and stabling for 1,711 horses, the economy of late medieval York was indeed already sensitive to the desirability of a profitable tourist trade.

Yet another prominent group of York citizens, once again about a tenth of the total numbers of freemen, were those who worked in one or other branches of the metal industry. The great majority of these operated at quite an unsophisticated level as girdlers, marshalls, pin-makers, cutlers and - above all - as smiths. However York was unusual among late medieval English towns

St William's College

The Guildhall

in having large numbers of goldsmiths, a lucrative occupation by no means confined to skilled immigrants from the Rhineland. Throughout Yorkshire, and indeed beyond, it was to the metal workers of York that customers would regularly turn for the latest fashions in pewter tableware, for well-made knives and pieces of armour, and for a host of items as small as keys and locks and as large as church bells. The casting of bell metal was in fact the most technologically complex and demanding industrial activity in the medieval city. Successful practitioners of that difficult art might hope to acquire the sort of wealth and prestige which enabled their most celebrated member, Mayor Richard Tunnock, to commission the famous Bellfounder's Window in the north aisle of the Minster nave before his death in 1330. By contrast, few of the many York freemen involved in building work within the city were likely to emerge from the obscurity that went with their generally part-time status. That said, no craftsmen were as crucial to the physical appearance of the town as the triumvirate of stone masons, carpenters and tilers, always - with the plasterers too- the most numerous building workers in the city. More distinctive to York were small groups of more specialised craftsmen, of whom the most celebrated now are the master glaziers who designed the surviving window panels in the Minster and the city's forty parish churches. Of thirty-four medieval glaziers so far identified in York's records, thirty-two seem to have worked exclusively for the institutions of the church. Ironically enough, it was 'John Thornton of Covintry glazier' who in 1405 was awarded the contract to design and complete - within three years - the largest and most ambitious of all York's achievements in stained glass, the Great East Window of the Minster. By contrast, and with a few exceptions like John Chambre 'glasyer' who worked intensively for the Minster with his network of relatives and apprentices before his death in 1437, York's glass painters have left few traces to posterity. But they were numerous and important enough to form one of the fifty or so craft guilds which throughout the fifteenth century 'put on a show' - already a phrase much in use at York - by sponsoring their own pageant at the annual performance of the city's Corpus

Christi play cycle.

The last, and most impressive of those pageants - devoted to the grandest and most sombre of themes, the Day of Judgement itself - was appropriately enough the responsibility of the sixth and much the most dominant of the major occupational groupings in the town, the mercers or overseas merchants of York. Although the medieval usage of the word 'mercer', like the word 'merchant' indeed, can be very ambiguous, there can be no doubt at all that the men who proudly styled themselves *civis et mercator* of the city of York in their wills, legal documents and funeral epitaphs were the real masters of the town. These were men who traded not only in York's own manufactured goods but in all the commodities of internal commerce, especially across the North Sea to the Netherlands and the Baltic. As such, they were the only townsmen of the city, with the exception of the higher Minster clergy and the mendicant friars - who can be said to have had horizons which extended well beyond the city walls. Although only a comparatively small group within the ranks of the city's freemen, certainly less than five per cent of the total, these merchants undoubtedly formed York's dominant political as well as economic élite. Of the eighty-eight different individuals who held the office of mayor between 1399 and 1509, three were drapers, four were grocers and five were dyers - but no less than sixty-eight were merchants or mercers of the city. In law it was the mayor of York who seemed to enjoy near autocratic powers over the citizens; but in practice the mayor usually held his office for one year only (after his election in the Guildhall on 3 February, St Blaise's Day), and was the rotating representative of the close-knit and well-entrenched oligarchy to which he belonged. Not for the first or last time in the history of York this was essentially urban government by a plutocracy.

The overseas merchants of York in its halcyon years were all the more formidable because they wore a double mask. As mayors, aldermen, councillors and the borough's representatives in the parliamentary commons, they controlled the conduct of the city's internal and external affairs: as members of the mercers' fraternity or guild they presided over the city's commercial relations with the outside world. Most of the available evidence, including that of the national customs returns at Hull, indicates that these York overseas merchants were at their most numerous and actively entrepreneurial between the 1370s and the 1440s. Indeed it was their prominence on the York scene which accounted for much of the town's prosperity at this time. Naturally enough, the commercial influence of this merchant élite in the northern capital owed much to new economic developments in late fourteenth-century England as a whole, most obviously the rise of a highly profitable trade in woollen cloth at the expense of the export of raw wool. However, it was the merchants of York rather than of their possible rivals at Boston, Grimsby, Hull, Beverley, Scarborough and even Newcastle-upon-Tyne who proved best able to exploit the commercial opportunities of the reign of Richard II. According to a file of complaints brought by the Hanseatic League against English merchants trading in the Baltic during the 1390s, this was a decade when it seems that there were often twice as many York mercers transacting business in Danzig as there were merchants from either Beverley or Norwich - or even London. It is tempting to suppose that never before nor since has the city played so important a role in English overseas trade. It can be no coincidence that it was during this very period that these York merchants gradually and erratically groped their way towards an appropriate corporate expression of their achievements. In 1430, the fraternity of mercers (already wealthy enough to build its remarkably capacious Hall in Fossgate as early as the late 1350s) received a royal charter incorporating it as a Mercers' Company, receiving its Elizabethan title of 'Company of Merchant Adventurers' only after the years of its most profitable ventures had long since passed.

Ironically enough, it was during the half-century before rather than after Henry VI's charter of 1430 that this galaxy of York mercantile talent seems to have been most active and most conspicuous in the English economy. As recent research has shown, much more can be known about these men as individuals - and as a group - than any other citizens of the town. Even in their case, the heavy mortality of the later middle ages prevented the formation of long-lived merchant dynasties. Theirs was accordingly an oligarchy which could never become too small and exclusive for it was dependent for its survival upon constant replenishment by new recruits from the countryside. Nevertheless this well demarcated urban élite, bound together by ties of kinship and much intermarriage, tended to be dominated by some twenty or thirty especially powerful merchant families. Thus William Graa or Gray, a large-scale wool exporter from Hull in the 1340s and mayor of the city in 1367-8, was the son of John Graa, member of parliament for York at the beginning of the century. William's son, Thomas Graa '*mercator*', became mayor in his turn (in 1375-6 and 1398-9) and fathered a son who was still living in 1429 as Sir John Graa of North Ingleby in Lincolnshire.

Even more spectacular was the wealth of the brothers Robert and Thomas Holme (originally from Holme on the Wolds in the East Riding) who lived on to 1396 and 1406 respectively after holding the mayor's office thirty years earlier. Robert Holme intended to devote the remarkable sum of £400 to the creation of a family chantry in York Minster; but in fact his most enduring monument to posterity has proved to be another chantry chapel, within the church of Holy Trinity, Goodramgate. Now almost totally stripped and denuded, this was the chapel where Robert Holme vainly hoped that his benefaction would maintain twenty-five chaplains for ever - singing masses not only for his own soul and that of his family but also 'that divine worship throughout this city shall be thereby increased'. But for an even more evocative memorial to the mercers who presided over the city's golden age, visitors to York need to make their way to another of its churches, namely All Saints, North Street. There, at the foot of the main east window are the pictures in stained glass of Nicholas Blackburn senior, mayor in 1412-13, and of his son Nicholas Blackburn junior, mayor in 1429-30. Although almost certainly not realistic portraits of the two Blackburns, that particular deficiency would certainly not have perturbed them. For there they are, the wealthiest citizens of their day, immortalized as they would have wished to be immortalized - kneeling in devotion before the figures of York's most popular late medieval saints, the Virgin Mary, St John the Baptist, St Anne and St Christopher. If the Blackburns and their fellow merchants had been told that by the second half of the fifteenth century their city would be - as we have seen - in the throes of economic recession, they would no doubt have been startled. But perhaps not utterly dismayed. As merchants and indeed all the men and women of York contemplated - with an intensity modern society would find impossible to recapture - the terrifying prospects of their lives in the next world, it was the perceived truth of the Christian religion which obsessed them most of all.

Christianity in the Late Medieval City

By 1272 all the major institutions of the Christian church in the city of York, unrivalled in England except at London and Canterbury, were already well established and much visited. Most obviously of all, not only had there been a cathedral there since 625 but the later medieval archbishops and cathedral canons were wealthy enough to have already embarked upon the first of a series of ambitious building campaigns which ended with the complete replacement of an immense Romanesque cathedral by an even larger Gothic successor. When, on 9 January 1284 Edward I, his wife Queen Eleanor, ten bishops and numerous magnates attended the translation of the bones of St William of York from the nave to their new resting place behind the High Altar, the two sumptuously decorated cathedral transepts had already been in place for thirty years and a magnificent new chapter house was about to follow. Seven years later, on 6 April 1291, Archbishop John le Romeyn laid the foundation stone of the massive Gothic nave, so large a project that its wooden roof was only completed seventy years later, shortly after the first outbreak of the Black Death. Thereafter, by a long and often interrupted process, the Minster's master masons designed and built a luxuriously decorated Lady Chapel and Choir, completed in time for the cathedral's crowning glory, the Great East

Window, to be inserted between 1405 and 1408. Yet another sixty years elapsed before the Minster's three great towers were all thoroughly reconstructed; and only after the cathedral's reconsecration in 1472 was it finally more or less free of scaffolding at the conclusion of the most sustained architectural enterprise ever conducted in northern England. As a permanent memorial to the changing architectural fashions in England between the early thirteenth and late fifteenth century, York Minster - in John Ruskin's phrase - is still 'the Acropolis of English Gothic'. *[colour plate 5]*

Like all medieval cathedrals, York Minster had many functions to fulfil, not all of them easy to reconcile with one another. As the *matrix ecclesia* or mother church of England's largest diocese it was the scene of the most elaborate acts of communal and choral worship in Yorkshire as well as presenting to the believer a symbol of the heavenly mansion awaiting him or her in the next world. More specifically still, since 735 the Minster had been the seat, the *cathedra* of one of England's only two archbishoprics. However the primates of the ecclesiastical province of York were so powerful and so wealthy that their importance as pastors of their dioceses and as experienced administrators (usually canon lawyers) in the service of the Crown quite transcended their role in the city itself. In fact the late medieval archbishops of York were nearly always to be found at Westminster or in their manor houses at Bishopthorpe, Cawood and Scrooby in Nottinghamshire rather than in their York palace, of which only fragmentary remains together with its chapel - now the Minster Library - still survive north of the Minster. To all intents and purposes it was therefore the dean and chapter and not the archbishop who directed the affairs, including the building works, of the cathedral. Between 1294 and the Reformation the Minster chapter comprised thirty-six canons, nearly all of whom enjoyed extremely valuable revenues from the landed estates and tithes which comprised their individual prebends. Thus the 'golden prebend' of Masham was worth £120 a year when held by the future Archbishop George Neville in the mid-fifteenth century; and the dean of York - with an annual income of more than £300 - held the richest non-episcopal benefice in England. As these canonries and prebends carried no responsibility for the cure of souls, they could be held by absentee clergy. The inevitable result was that the great majority of York Minster canons were royal or episcopal officials in the south of England who rarely visited York at all. It is easy to forget that not the least important function of a medieval cathedral was to act as an agency for the transfer of wealth from the profits of agriculture in the parishes to sustain the expenses of the kingdom's bureaucracy, of university colleges in Oxford and Cambridge and of the cathedral's own absentee canons too.

Only a small handful of York's thirty-six canons therefore committed themselves to life-long service in the Minster by taking up residence there. Those who did so, only seven or eight in the 1370s and as few as two or three a century later, were all the more influential figures in the city as well as the diocese of York because there were so few of them. Most spectacular of all was the wealth of those residentiary canons who also held office as the dean, the treasurer or the archdeacon of Richmond. Thus among the many exceptionally opulent legacies in his will of May 1414, Master John Newton, treasurer of the Minster from 1393 to 1414, bequeathed to the abbot of St Mary's, York, not only his ship or barge but a large lead-smelting furnace at Poppleton. John Newton, his colleagues and his successors are more or less completely forgotten today. However, of all the residents of late medieval York, there can be little doubt that these were the men who maintained the biggest households, possessed the largest private libraries and had the greatest access to liquid capital and to political influence. Thus in the 1480s when Richard III usurped the throne, he was at pains to court the good will of Dean Robert Booth and Canons William Poteman and Thomas Portyngton: it was this powerful triumvirate which not only directed the cumbersome machinery of the diocese but supervised the lesser Minster clergy in York itself. Of the latter, the thirty-six vicars choral deputised for the absentee canons by taking on the responsibility for communal worship in the cathedral choir: since the 1250s they had lived in chambers within the so-called

Bedern south-east of the cathedral precinct and became a powerful and at times unruly corporation in their own right. Between the 1370s and 1470s another group of clerks, the chaplains who sang masses at private chantries within the Minster, increased from twelve to almost twenty. In 1461 they too were incorporated as a college ('of Persons having Chantries in the metropolitical church of York'), now known as St William's College, immediately east of the cathedral. Until the Reformation the presence of these and other cathedral clergy within the walls of York naturally did much to enhance the prestige of the city - and to protect it from the worst effects of economic adversity. When the anniversary of the death of Archbishop Henry Bowet was celebrated in the Minster in 1424, at least eighty-two members of the cathedral clergy were present. Only seven were canons, but there were thirty-six vicars choral, sixteen chantry chaplains, six deacons, five thurifers (incense-burners), two sacrists, three vestry clerks as well as seven boy choristers.

York's other great ecclesiastical corporation, the community of Benedictine monks at St Mary's Abbey in Bootham, was almost as large as the Minster. It is unfortunately infinitely less well recorded. Because almost all of its internal records were destroyed after its surrender to Henry VIII in November 1539 virtually nothing can be known about the realities of monastic life within the St Mary's Abbey cloister. What is certain is that throughout the later middle ages its annual net income of at least £2,000 made it one of the ten richest monasteries in the country, with a wealth unrivalled by any ecclesiastical corporation in the north, even by Durham cathedral priory or Fountains Abbey. Like the Minster, this too was a religious community sufficiently well-endowed to take the exceptional step of rebuilding its entire church - from 1270 onwards - in exceptionally graceful Gothic Decorated style. The abbots of St Mary's, living in their increasingly spacious and sumptuous apartments, now incorporated within the King's Manor, were among the most powerful monastic prelates in the realm. Their extremely conspicuous wealth made them ideally well qualified to play both an important diplomatic role as English envoys to the church councils of Christendom and also a now more famous legendary role still, as the avaricious and 'ryche abbot here besyde Of Seynt Mari Abbey' outwitted by the greenwood outlaw in the *Lytell Geste of Robyn Hode*. The presence of such a formidable abbot and community of Black Monks just outside Bootham Bar posed a serious threat to the trading and marketing monopolies of the mayor and citizens of York; but after a long series of bitter conflicts on this issue, in 1354 the authority of the abbot over the economic life of the city was largely confined to the abbey precincts and the street of Marygate in Bootham. By the fifteenth century, St Mary's Abbey, with its sixty or more monks, its 200 or so servants as well as its boarding school for perhaps as many as fifty young scholars, was a positive asset to the city's welfare.

None of the other religious houses whose precincts honeycombed the city in the later middle ages were of anything like as much economic or religious significance as St Mary's Abbey. However, both the Benedictine priory of Holy Trinity in Micklegate and the Gilbertine priory of St Andrew survived the economic disaster of the Black Death: the former usually housed some ten or a dozen monks during the fifteenth century while recent archaeological investigation has shown that St Andrew's priory was rebuilt on a much more modest scale as its complement of Gilbertine canons contracted to three or four. The city of York's only nunnery, located immediately south of the city walls and dedicated to St Clement, also survived, if it hardly flourished, with a community of about ten nuns, often recruited from younger daughters of gentry families in the vicinity of the town. Much more significant for the social as well as religious life of late medieval York was the colossal Hospital of St Leonard, whose extensive if fragmentary remains can still be traced between the present Theatre Royal and the Multangular Tower. St Leonard's was one of the largest and richest hospitals in the country, capable of housing two hundred sick persons of both sexes as well as a large clerical staff even after its fortunes declined from the time of the Black Death. It is an even more intriguing tribute to the city's position as regional ecclesiastical centre that by the fifteenth century it also possessed well over twenty smaller hospitals, the great majority being almshouses or *maisons dieu*, whose inmates were committed to praying for the souls of their founders, usually canons and merchants of York.

More influential still, although no longer visible and very poorly documented too, were the friaries of the city. York was one of the thirteen towns in England where all four of the major mendicant orders established convents, the Franciscans or Grey Friars near the royal castle, the Dominicans or Black Friars on the site of the city's first railway station near Toft Green, the Carmelites or White Friars in Hungate with a quay on the river Foss, and the Augustinian or Austin Friars by the river between Guildhall and Lendal Tower. During the decades immediately after the foundation of the Austin convent by Lord Scrope of Upsall in 1272, each of these friaries seems to have housed as many as forty to fifty inmates. Although these figures tended to fall to less than twenty friars in each convent by the later fifteenth century, the mendicant population of the city continued to have a much greater impact on the spiritual life of the townsmen and their families than is usually acknowledged. All in all, and despite many opinions to the contrary, they probably retained their reputation as the most literate, best-educated and most accessible members of the religious orders until the very end. At York the friars were in great demand within the town not only as the most celebrated preachers in an age when sermons were the most frequent agencies of mass communication but also as intermediaries in purgatory for the dying and dead. Few residents of the city - if they could afford it - were unaware of the desirability of making bequests (like that of Dame Joan Chamberleyn in January 1502) of '6s. 8d. to every howse of Frears within the citie of York, goynge with ther crossis in procession from the howse of my inhabitacion'.

Much more significant for the practice of religion by the residents of York were the forty or so parish churches of the city, of which slightly fewer than half still survive and many of those only in a very truncated form. With a larger collection of parish churches than any other medieval English towns except London, Winchester and Norwich, it could well be argued that after the Black Death introduced drastic population decline York had become seriously 'over churched'. It is certainly true that of the thirty-nine churches recorded in a civic jury's report of May 1428, only St Olave's, St Michael-le-Belfrey and St Crux, Fossgate enjoyed fully adequate revenues in their own right. Not that the comparative poverty of the income enjoyed by the city's rectors and vicars did much to inhibit the extensive reconstruction and rebuilding of their churches. However neglected and even vandalised in subsequent centuries, the present physical appearance of all nineteen of the city's surviving pre-Reformation churches would still be immediately familiar to our later medieval predecessors. Despite the lack of any medieval church wardens' accounts, it seems absolutely clear that York is no exception to the general rule that it was in the fifteenth century that Englishmen and women gave most generously to the fabric of their parish churches. It was to those churches much more often than to the Minster or the many monasteries, hospitals and friaries of the city, that the laity of York offered their most impressive witness to their faith; and it was in those parish churches too that they wished not only to be buried but also to be remembered before God and man, certainly for as long as they could provide the necessary funds - and if possible for ever.

How could it be otherwise? To an extent now almost impossible to imagine, the religious life of the men and women of late medieval York was dominated by a belief in the terrors of hell and the possibility of redemption through purgatory. An intensely personal desire for salvation underlay most private acts of devotion in the town, not least the new emphasis on the spiritual credit to be earned by the acts of corporal mercy so graphically portrayed in the celebrated stained glass window of about 1420 which Nicholas Blackburn senior gave to his parish church of All Saints, North Street. Above all, the conviction that vicarious intercession for the souls of the dead would speed their passage towards paradise gradually created an immense and elaborate network of so-called chantry foundations, within which one or occasionally more priest chaplains would be employed to sing (*cantare*) masses for the deceased and his family according to the terms of his chantry foundation or last will and testament. The great majority of York men and women could only afford a temporary chantry, of which the most common type was an obit whereby the deceased was remembered at a mass celebrated for a specified number of years on the anniversary of his death. York citizens with greater means would often fund a chantry chaplain for a number of years. Thus in 1497 the York mayor Robert Johnson bequeathed £35 so that 'an honest prest shall synge at the alter of our said Lady daily, by the space of 7 yeres…and then caste holy water upon my grave'.

Much more expensive still, and much better documented too, were the perpetual chantries of the city, perpetual because their founders had bequeathed a sufficiently large endowment to support - or so they vainly hoped - one or more priests until the Day of Judgement. Record has been discovered of at least 140 different perpetual chantries in late medieval York, of which nearly sixty were located in the Minster and approximately eighty in the parish churches. Needless to say, a parishioner had to possess very substantial wealth indeed to endow such foundations; and the chantries of the city were accordingly a memorial to the most prominent citizens, and especially the merchants and the mayors, of the town. The last six laymen ever to found a perpetual chantry in York (John Carr; Sir John and William Gilliot; Thomas Nelson; Sir Richard York; and Sir Richard Wartre) were all overseas merchants who held office as mayor between 1448 and 1490. So thoroughly were all the York - and English - chantries destroyed by the Protestant reformers of the 1540s that little visible evidence still survives to remind us that they once existed. Nor is this particularly surprising. The great majority of the chantries in York's parish churches were not housed in separate chapels but were dispersed at various altars, before which masses and prayers were offered daily for the souls of the deceased by chaplains who often only received a stipend of as little as £5 per annum. Not that such apparently *ad hoc* arrangements prevented chantries from being fundamental to the religious routines in the city. For an archbishop of York chantries must have seemed the least significant of all the ecclesiastical institutions under his authority; but for many laymen in the city they were the most important means whereby they could express their own family devotion and display their ability to influence church affairs themselves. As founders, descendants and patrons of their family chantries, merchants like the Graas, Holmes and Blackburns had a vested interest in their prosperity, both material and spiritual. So too did the city council itself. In 1388 Mayor William Selby declared publicly that the prayers of the city's 300 or more parish priests and chantry chaplains 'are to be especially devoted to the citizens of the city, their patrons and their masters'. An audacious claim perhaps; but in practice many residents of York had already begun to believe that the welfare of their parish church could no longer be left exclusively to churchmen. Long before the Reformation the laity of the city were inextricably involved in influencing, directing and indeed criticising the prevailing conduct of the Christian life.

But it is easy to forget that the religious and other attractions of the city were in some ways even more important - as they still are - to its visitors than to its parishioners. Throughout the later middle ages, as today, the single most important reason for visiting York at all was to admire and marvel at its Minster, the largest Gothic cathedral in England. Pilgrims and tourists rarely leave much trace of their expeditions in historical records; and of the innumerable visitors to York Minster between the late thirteenth and late fifteenth centuries, very few indeed convey a vivid impression of what they found. One of those who did so was - somewhat unexpectedly - a woman - 'John of Brunham's daughter of King's Lynn', better known as Margery Kempe, that restless and religiously tormented burgess's daughter whose dictated autobiographical reminiscences were rediscovered as recently as 1934. It was after her first pilgrimage to St William's shrine at the Minster, 'on a Friday on Midsummer Eve (in 1413) in right hot weather as this creature was coming from York-ward carrying a bottle with beer in her hand and her husband a cake in his bosom' that the husband in question finally complied with

Margery's request that he should 'never meddle with her again'. But it was of a subsequent visit to the Minster perhaps seven or eight years later that Margery tells us most. After disturbing the routines of a crowded cathedral with her 'great weeping, boisterous sobbing and loud crying', she was interviewed by the archbishop of York, Henry Bowet, at his palace of Cawood eight miles down the river Ouse. Far from obeying the archbishop's order 'that thou wilt neither teach nor challenge the people in my diocese', Margery reminded him that 'God Almighty forbiddeth not, sir, that we shall speak of Him.'

The 'Book of Margery Kempe', probably written in the late 1430s, is hardly likely to be typical of the female spirituality of late medieval England. Nevertheless perhaps the most profound development in the religious history of York during this period is indeed that an increasing number of women as well as men did begin to speak - and think - of God and the salvation offered by Jesus Christ more intensely than the inhabitants of the city had ever done before. Like Queen Elizabeth I, historians should be wary of believing that they can ever penetrate the mysteries of the human soul. However, enough evidence survives at York and other English towns to suggest that a fundamental change in human sensibility probably did occur between the 1270s and the 1480s. Only then did Christianity become a deeply felt religion of the people at large, only then does one encounter what a French historian has called 'the personalization of the divine fact'. Such an 'interiorization' (to use another clumsy expression) of the religious experience did not inevitably result in revolutionary ideology or outright heresy. Admittedly Margery Kempe's hysterical scenes in York Minster led to the accusation that she was herself a Lollard; but in fact, and as far as we can tell, the city and diocese of York were remarkably free from the fiercely evangelical heretical movement founded by John Wycliffe and propagated by his Lollard disciples both before and after his own death at Lutterworth on the last day of December 1384. Although this greatest of all English heresiarchs was a Yorkshire clerk from the hamlet of Wycliffe on the southern bank of the river Tees who received holy orders in

York Castle

the Dominican friary church at York in 1350-1, his doctrinal and other heresies seem to have had much less impact in Yorkshire than in southern England and the Midlands. That said, and by a paradox which seems central to our understanding of late medieval religion in York as elsewhere in the country, the pastoral and evangelical efforts of many of its archbishops and clergy seem to have been only too successful in making their parishioners increasingly conscious of the gap between spiritual ideal and current ecclesiastical practice. Can one best explain the apparently otherwise inexplicable by suggesting that the success of the Protestant Reformation in York was itself an indirect tribute to the depth of Christian feeling already present in the late medieval city?   But for the answer to that fundamental and difficult question we need to consider the turbulent religious development of the city after the battle of Bosworth and under the Tudor monarchs. A new chapter in the history of York is about to begin.

5

YORK UNDER THE TUDORS: DEFIANCE AND SUBMISSION

Claire Cross

Henry VII

On 23 August 1485, the day after the Battle of Bosworth, at the instigation of the Mayor, Nicholas Lancaster and other long time adherents of Richard III, the city council recorded in its minute book how the king, 'late mercifully reigning upon us, ... through great treason of the Duke of Norfolk and many other that turned against him with many other lords and nobles of these north parts, was piteously slain and murdered, to the great heaviness of this city.'

For many years before he had usurped the throne, indeed ever since 1471 when on his acquisition of the Neville inheritance he had set up his household at Middleham and Sheriff Hutton castles, the governors and a significant section of the populace of York had pinned their hopes upon Richard Duke of Gloucester. The overthrow of a monarch with close ties to the region by a Tudor king with no links at all to the north of England augured badly for the city, and time and again the corporation was called upon to prove its loyalty to the new regime. Yet in the long term the equivocal nature of the city's allegiance worked in its favour, since the national government in its efforts to assert its authority over the region found it imperative to create a permanent outpost at York. This enabled the city, almost despite itself, to preserve and in certain respects strengthen its status as the capital of the north of England, a position it succeeded in maintaining until 1642.

Towards the end of the fifteenth century York desperately needed a royal benefactor and the largesse such a patron could bestow. A city, which in the fourteenth century had been a thriving manufacturing town as well as a centre of commerce and trade, was now a mere shadow of its past greatness. That golden age would never return, though it took the corporation decades if not centuries to accept the unpalatable reality and resign itself to the fact that the city's future lay in the service industries and not in cloth production, responsible for much of its wealth in the high middle ages.

On the accession of Henry VII York could not hide the all too visible signs of its decay. The townspeople were rattling like peas in a pod in a city now far too large for their needs; even at lowered rents landlords were failing to attract tenants and there were derelict houses in nearly every street. The city's population had peaked in 1400 at about 15,000, making it the largest city in England outside London. Over the ensuing century and a half it had almost halved to around 8,000, which placed York well behind Norwich, Bristol, Exeter, Salisbury and perhaps Newcastle.

A fall in population does not invariably signify decline. Most major towns experienced serious problems in the late middle ages, but the depression in York seems to have been worse than elsewhere in the north of England because of the almost total loss of the cloth industry. From the fourteenth century weavers had been moving out of a highly regulated city to unincorporated townships in the West Riding like Halifax, Wakefield and Leeds, where they could live at less expense and work unhindered by restrictive practices. Economically weak, vulnerable politically, York in 1485 was in an extremely precarious situation.

Having backed the losing side in the Wars of the Roses the corporation realised that it had no choice but to make peace with Henry Tudor and before the end of August 1485 started seeking the new king's favour. Its determination to preserve its independence, nevertheless, remained strong, and when Henry VII and his chief agent in the north, the Earl of Northumberland, began

The Thomas Herbert House, Pavement

Holy Trinity, Goodramgate

143

nominating candidates to fill the vacant offices of Recorder and Town Clerk, previously held by supporters of Richard III, the council insisted upon appointing its own candidates. When, therefore, less than a year after his accession, the news broke of the king's intention to visit York, the corporation felt under considerable pressure to establish the city's good faith.

The city sheriffs and two aldermen with sixty horses met Henry VII in 1486 at Tadcaster bridge, the boundary of the Ainsty, to conduct him to the city. At Bilborough Cross the Mayor and the rest of the aldermen in scarlet gowns, the town clerk and common council in violet, the chamberlains in mulberry and many inhabitants on horseback in red waited upon the king and brought him to Dringhouses to be greeted by yet more citizens. Closer to the city at St James's chapel on the Mount local children had their chance to acclaim Henry before the start of pageants specially devised for the occasion. The first spectacle staged at Micklegate Bar depicted a red and white rose to symbolise the union of the hitherto opposing houses of York and Lancaster, after which Ebrauke, the mythical founder of York, submitted to the king his 'city, key and crown to rule and redress'.

Processing down Micklegate Henry encountered at Ousebridge the six royal predecessors who bore his name followed by Solomon, who exhorted him to govern his 'realm righteously by politic providence'. At yet another scene outside the Guildhall in Coney Street David yielded the king the sword of victory. The celebrations culminated in Stonegate where none other than the Virgin Mary promised Henry 'to sue to my son to send you his grace'.

Despite this brave attempt to assert the legitimacy of the Tudor line, the very next year Lambert Simnel led a revolt challenging Henry's right to the throne. Having quelled the pretender's forces without too much difficulty, on 30 July 1487 the king accompanied by a thousand noblemen in military array entered York to be welcomed for a second time by the Mayor and corporation at Micklegate Bar 'giving due lovings unto Almighty God for the great fortune, noble triumph and victory which it hath pleased his Godhead to grant unto your highness, subduing your rebels and enemies at this time...' The sudden nature of this visit prevented the corporation from commissioning new pageants as they had done in the previous year; instead at the king's suggestion, they staged a performance of the traditional Corpus Christi plays which Henry watched from Thomas Scott's house in Coney Street. Then, after the trial and execution of several rebels, in acknowledgement of the city's loyalty in the recent crisis the king knighted the Mayor, William Todde, and another senior alderman.

While Henry may have gained the allegiance of the city council the townspeople periodically continued to defy the government. In 1489 many of York's inhabitants sided with North Riding agitators, who had murdered the fourth Earl of Northumberland near Thirsk as he was trying to impose royal taxation, and then compelled the corporation to give them military assistance, an action for which the city had subsequently to seek the king's pardon. During an almost ten year altercation between the citizens and the vicars choral of the Minster over pasturing beasts on meadows adjoining the city Henry threatened to take York's government into his own hands if the Mayor could not keep the peace. He intervened yet again in 1504 when the commons rioted against the corporation over another perceived infringement of their rights.

Throughout the first two decades of the sixteenth century the corporation continued to have difficulty in maintaining order. For the crown the solution lay in strengthening the civic oligarchy and curtailing the powers of the commons. A contested mayoral election in 1517 presented Henry VIII with the opportunity to revoke the city's latest charter and to issue a replacement which curtailed the powers of the common council responsible for nominating the Mayor. This virtual exclusion of the commons from all aspects of local elections made the corporation far less susceptible to popular pressure for centuries to come.

York's fortunes in the sixteenth century reached their nadir in the reigns of Henry VII and Henry VIII. During the 1530s the council could not balance its budget, for several years in succession returning an annual deficit until it completely overhauled its accounting system. Even the central government acknowledged the city's plight and regularly reduced its taxation assessments and other financial commitments fixed at the height of its medieval prosperity. The almost total loss of the textile industry had made York increasingly dependent upon its role as a supplier of labour and goods to local institutions of which the church was far and away the most important. Any weakening of the church automatically affected the local economy, and the crown's attack upon ecclesiastical revenues in the 1530s posed a new threat to an already beleaguered city.

Church, State and the Pilgrimage of Grace

As the seat of the archbishop of both the diocese and the northern province, York had for centuries greatly benefited from the physical presence of the church in its midst. The Minster with its residentiary canons and vicars choral and vast array of chantry priests stood at the apex of the pyramid. Then came the local religious houses, St Mary's Abbey, Holy Trinity Priory, St Leonard's Hospital, St Andrew's Priory, Clementhorpe Nunnery and the four convents of friars. A further thirty monasteries from throughout the whole of the north of England had found it advantageous to acquire a base within the walls. The city in addition still possessed no fewer than forty parish churches each with its complement of two or three priests. These all required a constant supply of labour and food from local sources quite apart from more occasional ecclesiastical necessities such as vestments, ornaments and plate, while to meet the demand for liturgical books a printing press had been set up in York at the turn of the century.

At first Henry VIII's ecclesiastical revolution seems to have had little direct effect upon the city. As instructed by Thomas Cromwell, in 1534 and 1535 Archbishop Lee preached against papal supremacy in the Minster before the assembled clerical and civic dignitaries, and in obedience to the parliamentary statute the clergy duly recognised Henry's sovereignty over the church. The climate of opinion, however, changed when an impoverished king began casting envious eyes on the wealth of the church. In 1535 the monasteries alone were receiving from their lands almost double the average annual income of the crown, and to engage in an active foreign policy Henry desperately required alternative sources of revenue.

Royal officials charged with surveying the national assets of the church reached York in January 1536, and within months of the production of their report Parliament passed an Act to dissolve religious houses worth less than £200 a year and vest all their lands in the crown. Several York institutions fell into this category, and in the summer of 1536 both Clementhorpe Nunnery just outside the walls and Holy Trinity Priory in Micklegate were suppressed.

A riot broke out in York in late August during a performance of the play of St Thomas, followed the next month by a serious quarrel with possible religious implications in the Merchant Adventurers' hall, and the city appears to have already been in a volatile state before the insurrection, popularly known as the Pilgrimage of Grace, began at Beverley in early October 1536. Incited by monks recently expelled from some Lincolnshire houses and other clerics fearful that they might soon share the same fate, the townspeople of Beverley had needed little encouragement to rebel against their hated overlord, the archbishop of York. Having forced the Yorkshire lawyer, Robert Aske, to become their captain, the insurgents quickly spread the revolt to much of the East Riding. Driven from the beginning by two not always compatible aims, to protect the rights of the church and to prevent the imposition of new taxation, they then marched upon York in the hope of wringing concessions from the government.

On 9 October Lord Darcy commanded the Mayor, William Harrington, in the king's name to take up arms against the rebels, but his order came too late; the York commons rose on 11 October, and the archbishop immediately fled to Pontefract castle. Bereft of outside aid, the Mayor capitulated and on the afternoon of 16 October Robert Aske at the head of some four or five thousand horsemen passed through the city to the Minster where the Treasurer, Lancelot Collins, and the rest of the cathedral clergy ceremonially conducted him to the high altar. After Evensong had ended, Aske posted on the cathedral doors an order restoring monks and nuns to the houses from which they had been recently expelled. During the three days he spent in the city, he lodged with his commanders at the house of Sir George Lawson who until that date had enjoyed a double career as an important government servant and a leading alderman. In addition to Lancelot Collins, the prior of the nearby Augustinian friars, John Aske, and John Pickering, the prior of the York Dominicans, both publicly backed his crusade.

Just after Aske had left York, on 20 October a younger brother of the Earl of Northumberland, Sir Thomas Percy, and a band of some ten thousand men with the reluctant abbot of St Mary's at their head rode 'gorgeously' 'through the king's highness's city of York in complete harness with feathers trimmed', the commons displaying 'such affection towards him as they showed towards none other.' Percy together with Sir Nicholas Fairfax, Sir Oswald Wolsthrope and George Lumley also briefly made Lawson's house their headquarters before moving south to join Aske.

In December the city sent a delegation to the conference at Pontefract between the Pilgrims and the king's representative, the Duke of Norfolk, which on the proclamation of a royal pardon brought the first part of the rebellion to an end. Although York avoided any involvement in the risings which broke out afresh early in the new year, news of an impending royal visit caused much alarm in the city, and in February 1537 the corporation anxiously sought the advice of the Duke of Norfolk and the archbishop on the best means of regaining their monarch's favour. To intimidate his subjects yet further Henry decided later in the year to return Robert Aske, after his trial and sentence in London, to die in York 'where he was in his greatest and most frantic glory'. Witnessed by large crowds, his execution took place at Clifford's Tower on 12 July 1537.

In the event Henry postponed his northern progress for four years, giving the corporation time to confer with the city of Lincoln, similarly implicated in the rebellion, on the best way to assuage his wrath. The encounter with the king finally occurred on 15 September 1541 when the Mayor, aldermen, and councillors with a multitude of the most discreet commoners and representatives of the Ainsty, clad this time not in scarlet but in a fine 'sad tawney', assembled at Fulford Cross to meet Henry, his new bride, Katherine Howard, and the rest of the royal party. With the entire York contingent humbly kneeling on their knees, the Recorder in a long oration acknowledged their 'most odious offence of traitorous rebellion'. Affirming their repentance 'from the bottoms of our stomachs', he went on to pledge their goods and bodies in the king's service 'to the utter effusion of our hearts' blood'. Henry then graciously accepted their gift of £140 in gold, and declared his willingness for a reconciliation.

The Pilgrimage of Grace brought home to the king the urgent necessity for much stricter control over the north. His father had tended to govern the region through the Council in the North, which could trace its origins back to the administrative chamber set up by the Duke of Gloucester in 1471 to manage his newly acquired Yorkshire and Cumberland estates. In the seemingly less troubled atmosphere of the first part of his reign Henry VIII had allowed the council to fall into disuse, but now, having experienced at first hand the threat posed by the north to the very existence of the Tudor state, he resolved to revive the institution. After reorganising the council and granting it a permanent staff, the crown in 1538 appointed as its president the Yorkshire born Robert Holgate, at the time the nonresident bishop of Llandaff. Under Holgate's direction it embarked upon the daunting task of enforcing government policy throughout the whole of the north of England.

Dissolution of the Monasteries

The king's determination to persist with the dissolution of the monasteries in the wake of the defeat of the Pilgrimage of Grace made the subjugation of the north all the more pressing. In the summer of 1537 Henry authorised the confiscation of the lands and sites of certain northern religious houses such as Jervaulx, Sawley and Bridlington, whose abbots and priors had been convicted of treason for their dealings with the rebels after the

December pardon. Then a little over a year later his ministers turned their attention to York, and under the guise of 'voluntary' surrenders induced all the city's surviving religious houses to submit to the crown. The small Gilbertine Priory of St Andrew in Fishergate was the first to capitulate in November 1538, followed in December by the second and final dissolution of the considerably larger Benedictine Priory of Holy Trinity, Micklegate. The suppression of the very much poorer four York friaries, the Dominicans on Toft Green, the Franciscans by the Castle, the Augustinians near the Guildhall and the Carmelites north of Fossgate, also all took place before Christmas. Then after a year's respite in late November and early December 1539 the axe finally descended upon the city's two richest foundations, St Mary's Abbey and St Leonard's Hospital.

Quite apart from the very many servants employed by these houses, the dissolution resulted in the expropriation of approaching one hundred and fifty York monks, canons, nuns and friars. With a community of fifty monks, St Mary's Abbey alone contributed a third of this total, Holy Trinity Priory adding a further nine monks, St Andrew's Priory four canons, St Leonard's Hospital eight brothers and four sisters, Clementhorpe Priory eight nuns and the Dominican, Franciscan, Carmelite and Augustinian convents around sixty friars between them. On the assumption that those wishing to persevere in the religious life could transfer to another house, apart from the respective heads of the two institutions, the state in 1536 made no financial provision at all for the Holy Trinity monks or the Clementhorpe nuns. The friars, except for the warden of the Franciscans, similarly went empty away. By virtue of the fact that they had vacated their monasteries after 1536, the rest of the York monks and canons fared better, obtaining pensions proportionate to the annual income of their houses. This meant that the abbot of St Mary's secured an annuity of 400 marks, the prior of St Andrew's £10 a year and the already very wealthy master of St Leonard's a dwelling house within the former hospital, Beningborough Grange worth in excess of £26 annually and £100 in goods and cash. Their communities did less well, the monks of St Mary's receiving pensions of

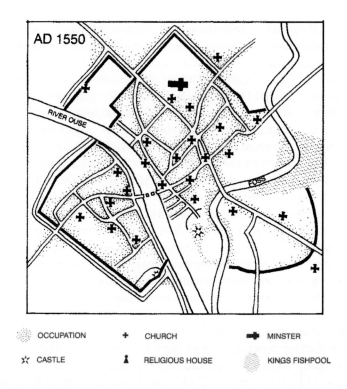

AD 1550

RIVER OUSE

FOSS

OCCUPATION   ✚ CHURCH   ⬛➤ MINSTER

☆ CASTLE   ⚑ RELIGIOUS HOUSE   KINGS FISHPOOL

between £5 and £10 a head according to seniority, the canons of St Andrew's annuities of £4, the brothers of St Leonard's annual stipends ranging from £5 to approaching £7 and the sisters a little over £4 a piece.

While eviction from their communities cannot have been other than traumatic for those who had believed they had entered them for life, from a purely economic standpoint few if any of the former York monks faced destitution, particularly since they could now take livings in the secular church. The richest foundations in the city furthermore had the resources to look after their own. Guy Kelsaye from St Mary's gained the presentation to the Abbey's living of Wilby in Norfolk which he resigned in 1553 in favour of another former member of the house, while a third St Mary's monk, Thomas Marse, acquired the Abbey's rectory of Hargham in the same county.

Especially important for their influence upon the subsequent religious history of York were those former monks and friars who settled in the city itself. The Holy Trinity monk, William Gryme, became rector of the parish of Holy Trinity in Micklegate; Richard Barwicke and Thomas Baynes, both monks of St Mary's, obtained the livings of St Saviour and St Mary, Castlegate respectively. Two brothers of St Leonard's in succession occupied the rectory of St Denys in Walmgate, previously owned by the hospital, while the York Gilbertine, John Hodgeson, procured the living of St Mary, Bishophill Junior. Though only one former York friar, George Bellerby, the last vicar of the very poor parish of St Wilfrid, achieved the security of a parochial benefice at least a dozen others earned a precarious livelihood in the city as chantry or stipendiary priests. Out of sympathy with new theological ideas, nearly all these former monks, canons and friars remained in the city for the rest of their lives, a bar to any fundamental religious change.

Quite apart from its impact upon the individuals most nearly concerned, the dissolution of the monasteries crucially affected many other aspects of the city's existence. The cessation of the daily round of monastic worship and the dispersal of their communities left some of York's most magnificent ecclesiastical monuments without any function or purpose, and the abbey church of St Mary's, which rivalled the Minster in size and grandeur, the infirmary chapel of St Leonard's hospital, the smaller priory churches of St Andrew's and Clementhorpe and the four great friary churches all became redundant. The nave of Holy Trinity Priory church alone survived and this only because local parishioners had established rights to worship there before the Reformation. Their roofs stripped of lead the other churches soon fell into ruin, valued chiefly as quarries for constructing or repairing buildings elsewhere in the city. *[colour plate 7]*

This seeming lack of concern for the destruction of a major part of York's ecclesiastical heritage can perhaps be traced back to the fact that the city's inhabitants had always looked first to their parish churches. Judging from the bequests they made when they died, hardly any citizens had formed close associations with local monasteries, though their attitude towards the friaries had been very different, with few wealthy testators failing to commission the four mendicant orders to accompany their bodies to the grave and celebrate masses for the health of their souls. They had now to cope without these clerical funeral directors for the future.

The monasteries had also occasionally provided opportunities for local boys to rise in the world. It would never again be possible for a Micklegate boy to join his neighbourhood monastery as had been the case of the last prior of Holy Trinity, Robert Speght. After the dissolution clerics could attain high promotion in the church only after a long period of study at one of the two universities. As part of its charitable functions St Mary's Abbey had kept a boarding house for fifty poor scholars attending the Minster school, and St Leonard's hospital had maintained another grammar school: the city lost both institutions in 1540. In the later middle ages York had possessed important libraries; these now also fell under suspicion as a source of support for claims of papal supremacy. On his visit to York in 1534 the antiquary John Leland found the Minster had already disposed of most of its books. The surrender of St Mary's Abbey resulted in the dispersal of its library, while that of the Austin friars, known to have contained over 600 volumes in the late fourteenth century, also disappeared in the same decade. It is just possible that the last warden of the Franciscans, Dr William Vavasour, salvaged from his friary the eight score printed books and unspecified number of manuscripts he mentioned in his will.

While relatively few York inhabitants can have taken advantage at first hand of the educational opportunities offered by their religious houses, and even fewer have aspired to place a child in a local religious community, all must have been conscious of the economic and social benefits the city derived from these institutions. The monasteries in particular had employed large numbers of servants from York and its hinterland: some may have gone on to serve the new owners, but others may well have lost their livelihood. While St Mary's Abbey distributed far less charitable relief than might have been anticipated from such a wealthy foundation, and the poor derived relatively little from the

St Andrew's Church, St Andrewgate

The Old Ouse Bridge

much less well endowed Holy Trinity, St Andrew's and Clementhorpe priories, St Leonard's Hospital fell into a totally different category. Even though the expansion of the intercessory side of the institution in the later middle ages at the expense of its nursing functions had caused a marked decline in the numbers receiving care, the corporation's failure to save the hospital left an unfilled vacuum in civic provision for the sick and the aged for centuries to come.

In addition to their precincts, which in the case of St Mary's Abbey, St Leonard's Hospital and Holy Trinity Priory occupied large tracts of the city, the local monasteries owned many urban messuages and tenements. Consequently at the dissolution an unprecedented number of buildings came on to the property market within a very short space of time. The crown retained St Mary's Abbey until the early nineteenth century, but very soon alienated most of the other monastic sites. In the 1540s Sir Leonard Beckwith, a Yorkshire gentleman and government servant, leased and later bought Holy Trinity Priory, his relative, Ralph Beckwith, acquired the Carmelite friary, and Alderman Richard Goldthorpe gained possession of both Clementhorpe Nunnery and St Andrew's Priory. Within two decades of the dissolution another royal official and city councillor, Sir George Lawson, succeeded in converting his lease of the Augustinian Friary into a sale, while the Franciscan Friary went first to the Harper family, and then after a generation to Alderman Robert Brooke. Early in Elizabeth's reign Laurence Green of York obtained the Dominican Friary, and, after a series of lessees, St Leonard's Hospital some years later passed into the hands of the Savile family.

In 1545 the London financier, Sir Richard Gresham, paid the crown a little over £1,200 for about a quarter of York's housing stock previously in monastic ownership, and over the next two decades began selling these tenements to local men, instructing his executors to liquidate the remainder after his death. It took the best part of a generation to redistribute the property, now broken up into very small lots, but even by the death of Henry VIII there seemed little prospect of the church ever recovering its former possessions.

Only one man tried to make some reparation for all this destruction, dispersal of property and loss of charitable institutions. With so many avenues closed by the ideological conflicts of the times education remained a neutral area, attractive to both Catholics and Protestants, and in 1546 Archbishop Holgate founded three grammar schools, one at his birthplace of Hemsworth in the West Riding, one at Old Malton and one in York. Modelling his curriculum on the one given by Colet to St Paul's school in London, Holgate required his headmaster to be skilled 'in the Hebrew, Greek and Latin tongues' and expected him to conduct his pupils to the Minster on Sundays where, with the offices still being sung in Latin, they were 'devoutly to say their matins together and seven psalms or to be reading of Scriptures... and to be other ways well occupied during the time of service in the said church.'

Edward VI

The accession of Edward VI in 1547 set the seal upon the religious revolution. A convinced Protestant unlike his father, the young prince soon began making his designs clear. In his last years Henry VIII had authorised a survey of collegiate churches and the much smaller chantry foundations within parish churches offering intercessory masses in perpetuity for their founders' souls, but had died before the Act of Parliament intended to suppress these institutions could take effect. The first parliament of the new reign now passed a second Act, this time containing an explicit denial of the doctrine of purgatory, to authorise the confiscation of chantries by the crown.

It may well be that of all the Reformation legislation this Act affected the generality of the laity more than any other. Just before the outbreak of the Pilgrimage of Grace Archbishop Lee had assured Henry VIII's advisors that northerners had accepted the king's supremacy over the church and the abolition of papal authority but warned that they clung tenaciously to the medieval doctrine of purgatory. Though supporters of the royal supremacy, Lee and his suffragan bishop, Robert Pursglove, had themselves

156

remained conservative in theology. They had discouraged the preaching of innovatory Protestant beliefs within the diocese, and the very few York people holding unorthodox views at this period seem almost all to have been foreigners. As a matter of course in the 1530s and 1540s York testators were still investing in masses to be said for their souls after their deaths by a whole army of chantry priests, recently augmented by dispossessed monks and friars. The 1548 Act in consequence descended upon a city ill prepared for radical change.

Although the corporation had procured an Act of Parliament in 1536 to dissolve certain municipal chantries on the grounds that their income was no longer sufficient to support a priest, this in no sense demonstrated any local disenchantment with the institution. When they reached York in 1548 the Edwardian commissioners found that there were around a hundred chantries still functioning in the city, almost equally divided between the Minster and the parish churches. The Minster now lost St Sepulchre's College, built on to the north wall of the nave to accommodate twelve prebendaries and their deputies intended exclusively to pray for the dead. The other casualty was St William's College, established much more recently by the dean and chapter to regulate the chantry priests attached to the many different altars in the Minster. At the same time the crown seized the endowments of chantries in all the parish churches. In 1549 some of the inhabitants of Seamer and Wintringham in the East Riding tried forcibly to resist the expropriation of their chantries but, perhaps mindful of their recent royal visitation, the people of York kept their feelings to themselves.

The corporation, meanwhile, claiming that the city had neither the population nor the wealth to maintain forty churches, had obtained a private Act of Parliament in 1547 to reduce the number of parishes within the walls to a still generous twenty-five. The complicated process of amalgamating parishes continued all through the reign and beyond, adding yet further to the disruption created by the dissolution of the chantries.

Some chantry priests, like Peter Glenton, the former Augustinian friar, with a chantry in the Minster and another in St

Helen's, Stonegate, the former Dominican, Thomas Richardson, who served a chantry in the now redundant church of St Peter the Little, and the former Franciscan, Ralph Clayton, a chantry priest in St Mary, Castlegate, found themselves dispossessed for the second time. Thomas Grayson, very probably the son of William Grayson, wiredrawer of York, originally a canon of Newburgh Priory until its surrender in 1539, now lost the chantry he had subsequently acquired in the Minster. Despite his local connections he then had no choice but to serve as a curate for a decade in St Lawrence's parish before securing the benefice of St Martin, Coney Street at the beginning of Elizabeth's reign.

All the city parishes seem to have complied with national legislation without any open challenge, taking down their altars and substituting communion tables, removing and destroying statues, replacing wall paintings of saints with sentences from the scriptures. On the appointment of Robert Holgate, already President of the Council in the North, as Archbishop of York in 1544 basic tenets of Protestant theology began to be systematically expounded in the Minster for the first time. In his injunctions of 1552 Holgate enjoined regular attendance at the divinity lecture upon the junior cathedral clergy, who in addition had to learn every week a chapter of St Paul's epistles in Erasmus's new Latin translation, beginning with the epistle to the Romans. He also decreed that singing in the choir should be plain and distinct, banned organ playing during service time and ordered biblical texts to be inscribed above the high altar. Even more importantly for the future he required the dean and chapter to provide the Minster Library not only with recent editions of the collected works of the ancient doctors of the church but also with new Protestant biblical commentaries by continental theologians such as Musculus, Brenz, Bullinger and Calvin.

These archiepiscopal injunctions failed to impress the Duke of Northumberland who required an even more explicit demonstration of Holgate's adherence to the principles of the Edwardian Reformation. The 1549 Act of Parliament had removed the obligation of compulsory celibacy from the English clergy, and, it seems chiefly to prove his Protestant credentials, in January

1550 the archbishop, at the age of sixty-eight, in a public ceremony married a local gentlewoman, Barbara Wentworth. Intended to scotch rumours that he entertained papist sympathies, to the undisguised glee of some of his conservative clergy this action landed Holgate in an embarrassing legal quandary. Within months of the wedding an impoverished Yorkshire gentleman, Anthony Norman, began a suit against the archbishop in the Privy Council for the restitution of his conjugal rights. Barbara Wentworth had indeed married Norman when both parties were children, but his appeal misfired on the production of evidence that she had resolutely refused to give her consent after coming of age, and Holgate retained his wife till the end of the reign. Some of the Minster prebendaries and vicars choral also married at this time, but very significantly virtually none of the city clergy availed themselves of this new dispensation. It may very well be that outside the environs of the Minster Protestant teachings had made little headway in most of the city parishes before the death of Edward VI.

Mary

On the Duke of Northumberland's failure to divert the succession in favour of the Protestant Lady Jane Grey, in late July 1553 York corporation promptly recognised Mary Tudor, welcoming the accession of 'so noble, godly and most rightful a queen'. Robert Parkyn, a conservative priest of Adwick le Street near Doncaster, recorded how, even before the first Parliament of the reign had assembled in Westminster, in the north of England priests had once more spontaneously begun celebrating the mass. The government authorities moved swiftly against Holgate, dispatching him to the Tower in October 1553 and then the ensuing March depriving him from his see for infringing his vow of celibacy. By this date a broken man, he renounced his marriage, asserting that his fellow bishops in the Edwardian period had been 'much further gone amiss in religion than he was and with obstinacy'. Having returned to the old faith and offered the crown a thousand pounds in restitution for his past crimes, he regained his liberty in January 1555 and lived out his final days as a Catholic priest in the house in St Sepulchre's parish in London which had come into his possession as the last master of the Gilbertines.

In York itself some evangelicals in the Minster, the sole bastion of Protestantism in the city, proved much more constant in their opinions, and for the first time in the sixteenth century the chapter was riven on ideological lines. Seven prebendaries, William Clayborough, Thomas Cottesford, Robert Watson, Henry Williams, Miles Wilson, Thomas Wilson and William Perepointe, and three vicars choral, Robert Cragges, Walter Lancaster and Peter Walker, all forfeited their offices for having married in the Edwardian period. Cottesford preferred exile rather than compromising his beliefs; having regained his canonry in 1560, Thomas Wilson went on to pursue an active career in the Elizabethan Protestant church.

The rest of the chapter cooperated with their new, albeit absentee archbishop, Nicolas Heath, in the restoration of Catholic services and ceremonial, somewhat belatedly in 1557 allocating funds for repainting the high altar and setting up statues of the Virgin and St John on the rood. Some leading citizens also felt moved to participate in this refurbishment of the Minster; in return for prayers for his soul Alderman George Gale in 1556 left a frontal cloth embroidered with a gold representation of the resurrection, while the following year one of the city's most substantial beneficiaries from the purchase of former monastic property, Sir Leonard Beckwith, presented a green and red sarcenet processional canopy for the blessed sacrament.

In obedience to the decrees recently promulgated at the Synod of Westminster, and perhaps also to counter the influence of Archbishop Holgate's school, in 1557 the dean and chapter founded, or refounded a grammar school for fifty boys in the former hospital in the Horsefair. Conscious of the importance of education in the doctrinal battles of the age, they intended its pupils should play their part in putting 'to flight the rapacious wolves, that is devilish men, ill-understanding the Catholic faith, from the sheepfolds of the sheep entrusted to them'.

Outside the Close in the city itself the veneer of Protestantism seems to have rapidly disappeared. Of the many civic clergy unconnected with the Minster only one is known to have married. As early as November 1553 the corporation ordered an altar to be set up in St Thomas's Hospital, and the following February reintroduced into the cycle of the Mystery Plays the pageants portraying the death, assumption and coronation of the Virgin. Very few heresy trials occurred in York, apart from that of a York gentleman, Christopher Kelke, charged with Lollardy in November 1555, and not a single Protestant martyr was burnt in the city. Both during Wyatt's revolt in 1554 and again in 1557 on the seizure of Scarborough Castle by the rebels, the city never wavered in its loyalty to Mary, and the imperial ambassador even informed Charles V that the queen contemplated moving to York to live among Catholic people. In this much more sympathetic climate the corporation tried to obtain the restoration of St Leonard's Hospital. Unable to afford so costly a concession, the crown instead sanctioned several reductions in the city's tax assessments.

The Catholic renewal came to an abrupt halt in the autumn of 1558 when Cardinal Pole, perhaps the queen herself and certainly many of her churchmen and senior officials fell victim to the sweating sickness. The mortality crises of the years 1557-9, the worst of the century for York as for the nation as a whole, overshadowed the final years of the reign. Throughout the first half of the sixteenth century the city had suffered from recurrent epidemics of the bubonic plague, with particularly severe episodes between 1549 and 1552, but the sweating sickness, probably a particularly virulent form of influenza, struck a population with no inbuilt immunity. While the plague disproportionately affected the lower orders who had no choice but to live in cramped and insanitary sectors of the city, this 'new ague' infected rich and poor alike, causing the deaths of at least a dozen councillors as well as a number of clergy. More York citizens made their wills in 1558 than in any other year in the sixteenth century, and the contemporary statesman, Sir Thomas Smith, may not have greatly exaggerated matters when he claimed that between 1557 and 1559 'the third part of the men of England were consumed'.

Elizabeth

York, nevertheless, overcame this devastation more quickly than might have been expected. Slowly and at first imperceptibly the city's economic position began to recover after Elizabeth's peaceful succession to the throne on 17 November 1558. This improvement, however, came at a price, as decade after decade the central government tightened its grip upon the corporation. Although it had recognised the new monarch without prevarication, the ensuing change in religion gave the state cause yet again to doubt the city's allegiance, and the unwillingness of some of the leading Minster clergy to accept the religious settlement, passed by Parliament in the first year of the new reign, increased this distrust yet further.

In 1559 Archbishop Nicholas Heath together with all the rest of the English bishops continued to uphold the Pope's headship over the church, and in so doing set the dean and chapter an example they had not received in the earlier crises in the Tudor church. When royal commissioners dispatched to enforce the Act of Supremacy reached the diocese in the summer of 1559 the suffragan Bishop of Nottingham and prebendary of Wistow, Robert Pursglove, refused to recognise the queen as the supreme governor of the English church and retired, 'stiff in papistry', to Ugthorpe in the North Riding. The Chancellor, Geoffrey Downes, who with Pursglove had taken a prominent part in the Marian restoration of Catholicism, took a similar stand. They were joined by the Succentor, Roger Marshall, and the Archdeacon of York, George Palmes, a member of the Naburn gentry family which remained part of the local Catholic community till late in the eighteenth century. This purge of about half the chapter deprived the Minster of most of its chief officers.

By reorganising and strengthening the Council in the North and creating a new ecclesiastical court concerned primarily with the enforcement of religious conformity the central government took two important steps in the first years of the reign to combat the influence of these alienated intellectuals and to prevent future unrest. While the Council in the North had been located in the King's Manor since 1540, in its early days it had routinely held its judicial sessions at Newcastle, Durham and Hull in addition to York. The crown's decision, therefore, to sanction its permanent establishment in York in 1561 had important implications for the city. The council implemented central government policies from York, and it was to its court in York that suitors came to seek justice in criminal and civil cases from all over the region. To cope with the rapidly increasing bureaucracy from this time onwards successive presidents began enlarging the former abbot's house of St Mary's Abbey to create at the King's Manor chambers adorned with renaissance decoration fit for a royal governor. The High Commission Court for the northern province, the outward manifestation of the royal supremacy in the region, which included the President of the Council of the North as well as the Archbishop among its members, also began operating in York in 1561 and was very soon similarly summoning complainants and defendants to the city for the whole area from the Humber to the Scottish Border. The two institutions between them guaranteed York's position as the administrative and judicial capital of the north until 1642.

At first in the 1560s the pace of change seemed slow, particularly for the reformers who aspired to erect a Protestant commonwealth in the city. Her first candidate having died before he could take up his post, the queen failed to appoint a new archbishop of York to replace Heath until the beginning of 1561. When he belatedly took possession of his see Thomas Young found he had to work with ecclesiastical administrators apathetic at best to the new religious settlement. Nicholas Wotton, simultaneously Dean of Canterbury and Dean of York, did not reside within the northern province and it seems to have been left to the new chancellor, Richard Barnes, to revive Protestant preaching in the Minster. It was not until the appointment of Matthew Hutton on Wotton's death in 1567 that the chapter acquired an active and resident Protestant Dean. Within a year

Hutton was making his presence felt within the city, prohibiting the corporation from performing the Creed Play in which he had discovered much which disagreed 'with the sincerity of the gospel'. Both the Chancellor and the Dean had wives, an outward and very visible sign of their commitment to Protestantism, and Mrs Barnes and Mrs Hutton with their families came to live in the Close. Like the queen herself, some York conservatives did not take kindly to the new ways, and in 1570 no less a man than Alderman Allen had to answer to the Archbishop for disparaging a sermon he had heard in the Minster in defence of clerical marriage.

Unlike the prebendaries the city clergy almost to a man complied with the religious settlement of 1559 and took the oath acknowledging the queen's authority over the English church. Although the city parishes obediently once more removed altars, took down images and whitewashed the interior of their churches the adherence of many citizens to Protestantism still seems to have been little more than skin deep. In 1562 some gentlemen dining with Alderman William Coupland wagered that the crucifix with Mary and John would be set up in all churches again within the year, and in 1564 Archbishop Young estimated that only two of the city's thirteen aldermen favoured the new religion. In 1567 the ecclesiastical lawyer and alderman, Thomas Standeven, declared himself a 'member of Christ's Catholic church' and asked for the prayers of the Virgin Mary and the saints in his will. In addition to distributing a penny dole to sixteen hundred paupers, at his death in 1568 Alderman William Coupland arranged a near approximation to a traditional Catholic funeral in St Sampson's church with five great wax candles burning about his hearse and thirteen poor men in black gowns with torches accompanying his body to the grave. Isabel Ward, the last prioress of Clementhorpe, who had settled in the city after the dissolution, reputedly in 'Jacob's Well' in Trinity Lane, also made no attempt to disguise her beliefs at her death in the summer of 1569. Having besought 'the blessed Virgin Mary and all the holy company of heaven to pray for me', put aside £5 for Catholic ceremonies at her funeral, and given money and plate to her Ellerker cousins and household possessions to her servant, she bestowed the proceeds from the sale of the remainder of her goods to the poor. *[colour plate 8]*

The Revolt of the Earls

These indications of religious conservatism may well have led the Earls of Northumberland, Cumberland and Westmorland to expect much of this only 'halfly reformed' city in the autumn of 1569. As with the Pilgrimage of Grace the causes of the Revolt of the Earls were as much political and economic as religious. The prestige of the old noble families of Percy, Clifford and Neville had suffered through their failure to obtain the high government office to which they felt themselves entitled, while the flight of Mary Queen of Scots into England in the spring of 1568 and her subsequent detention in Bolton Castle in Wensleydale had added a new dimension to an already politically charged situation. The exposure the following year of the secret plan for a marriage between the Scottish queen and Thomas Howard, Duke of Norfolk, the most senior member of the ancient nobility of England, precipitated the revolt. Elizabeth, seeing the plot as a bid to determine the succession to the English throne, possibly even as an attempted deposition, summoned Northumberland, Cumberland and Westmorland to Westminster. The Earls in reply raised their tenants on their hereditary lands and began marching south, and having occupied Durham in November, threw out the Protestant prebendaries and reintroduced the mass. Outside the four most northerly counties of Cumberland, Westmorland, Northumberland and Durham the rebels gained nothing like the same amount of popular support as the Pilgrims had done a generation earlier. Once they reached Ripon, their troops began melting away in the face of much superior government forces and the Earls had no choice but to retreat back to their heartlands before escaping to the continent.

For a brief moment the rebellion seemed to offer the possibility of replacing a Protestant with a Catholic queen, and as soon as news of the revolt reached Rome the Pope early in 1570 issued a bull excommunicating Elizabeth, stripping her of her 'pretended title' and releasing her subjects from their allegiance. While it appeared too late to affect the outcome of the rising, it gave the government grounds for regarding English Catholics as potential if not actual traitors to the English state.

The corporation, having learnt its lesson in 1537, in 1569 took resolute action against the Rebellion of the Earls. The revolt, nevertheless, by compelling the central government once again to reassert its authority in the region marked a watershed in the history of York and indeed of the whole of the north of England. First the opportune death of Archbishop Young allowed the crown in April 1570 to appoint Edmund Grindal as his successor. An energetic, evangelical Protestant who equated loyalty to the state with commitment to Protestantism, Grindal from the start went out of his way to attract preaching ministers to the province. Probably in response to interventions from cathedral dignitaries, in 1570 the corporation for the first time ordered householders to send two members of their families to attend sermons in the Minster on Sundays and holidays. Stiffened by Grindal, the High Commission court at this stage took a much stronger line against conservatives who had previously conformed but were now refusing even to attend their parish church. When in 1572, to the consternation of his more Protestant fellow aldermen, the Mayor, William Allen, had the temerity to sponsor a performance of the Corpus Christi cycle, the High Commission intervened to ban both the traditional Christmas interludes and any further presentations of the Mystery Plays. Sensing the time to be ripe to force the townspeople to engage with the ideology of the Elizabethan age, the Minster clergy refused any longer to tolerate these reminders of York's Catholic past. In the person of the new President of the Council in the North they soon perceived that they had gained a highly influential ally for the cause.

Having recalled Thomas Radcliffe, Earl of Sussex, for his failure to avert the Rebellion of the Earls, in the autumn of 1572 Elizabeth named her very Protestant cousin, Henry Hastings, third Earl of Huntingdon as his replacement as President of the Council in the North. *[monochrome plate 9]* Under the guidance of the privy council, and in close collaboration with a series of Calvinist archbishops, Huntingdon administered the north for more than two decades, fully integrating it at last into the Tudor state. At all times under the eye of the Lord President, York experienced this supervision at close quarters, and finally came to understand that civic prosperity could be attained only through total obedience to the central government.

Catholic Recusancy

From the beginning Huntingdon considered it his duty to secure the city's loyalty to the crown, seeing Catholic dissidents as the chief threat to this allegiance. In 1559, however grudgingly, the priests in the city parishes had accepted the Elizabethan church settlement and carried almost all the members of their congregations with them. The Act of Uniformity passed together with the Act of Supremacy in the first Parliament of the reign had imposed the obligation of church attendance on Sundays and holy days upon the entire nation and all the evidence suggests that until the Rebellion of the Earls virtually all York's inhabitants complied with the law. Thirty-two defaulters appeared in court after an archiepiscopal visitation of the city in 1568, but they all seem subsequently to have been present at services in their parish church. Apart from the Minster prebendaries, who had left York after their deprivation in 1559, a principled stand against participating in what they considered heretical worship seems to have been limited to the households of two medical doctors, Thomas Vavasour and Roger Lee.

Early in the next decade, however, the teachings of the Catholic Counter-Reformation reached the city. Early in the reign some university scholars, who had gone into exile to avoid conforming to the new Protestant regime, set up an English college at Douai in the Low Countries where, at first almost exclusively by their published writings, and later by training a new generation of English Catholic priests, they strove to win the nation back to the old religion. From Douai the English Catholic laity received clear and unambiguous instruction that they should under no circumstances endanger their eternal salvation by associating in any way whatever with the heretical state church.

Henry Cumberford, the Marian precentor of Lichfield

Cathedral, jailed in York for recusancy for some six or seven years from 1570, together with the Cambridge educated Master of Archbishop Holgate's school, John Fletcher, were among the first to propagate Counter Reformation beliefs in the city, and in some wards they fell on very fertile ground. As early as 1573 Thomas Oldcorne, a tiler from St Sampson's parish, confessed that he had not come to church for the previous year and a half nor received holy communion because he believed 'that the religion now established is not according to God's Word nor is not Catholic, and that he is persuaded that after the consecration the body of Christ is really present in the sacrament'. In 1574 the first contingent of young English priests from seminaries at Douai and Rome returned to their native land to minister to these groups of hard line Catholics.

Even at its strongest in the last quarter of the sixteenth century the York Catholic community may never have been very large, numbering no more than a hundred believers at most, but its importance bore little relation to its size. For at least a generation recusancy permeated all levels of urban society from the aldermanic elite to the very poor and gained the sympathy of many reluctant conformists. The existence of such a body in York at the very time when the nation was drifting into a war with Catholic Spain and when English Protestants automatically regarded the seminary priests as agents of the papacy and traitors to the English state could not but be of the greatest concern to the Archbishop and the Lord President.

At first the High Commission concentrated primarily upon the city council, in 1577 severely reprimanding several civic leaders including the Mayor, John Dineley, for their leniency towards Catholic recusancy. Worse followed in 1579 when Robert Cripling came to serve his turn as mayor. Like Dineley married to a Catholic wife, Cripling, who in the past had not disguised his dislike of Protestant preachers, now refused to take any punitive action against Catholics. In retaliation the Council in the North took the unprecedented step of imprisoning a Lord Mayor during his term of office. Even this exercise of naked power failed to excise all traces of conservatism in high places. In the manner of his Catholic predecessors the aged Alderman John Bean in 1579, having implored the Holy Trinity to pardon his sins, on the day of his burial in his parish church of St Martin's, Micklegate, arranged for the huge sum of £100 to be spent on mourning gowns, poor relief and poor maidens' marriages. Dineley, Cripling and Bean, however, represented a passing generation. Although they kept their ties with Catholic family members, no councillors after 1580 openly expressed support for the old religion and from this date onwards the corporation cooperated fully with the policies of the queen's representatives in church and state.

This placed the corporation at odds with some of the governed, since until the end of the reign Catholicism remained a cause for which some citizens below the level of the aldermen and councillors were still prepared to suffer and even die. The majority of York Catholics did not have the means to pay the fines of one shilling a week for absence from church imposed by the 1559 Act of Uniformity, let alone the prohibitive sum of £20 a month set down in the new Act of 1581. Consequently most had to accept the alternative which the Acts provided, lengthy periods of imprisonment in often filthy and unhealthy gaols. Between 1580 and 1594 the High Commission sent thirty recusant wives or widows to York Castle or other prisons where over a third died from disease. Recusant women were always in the majority, but some York men such as Ambrose Cooke and William Tessimond, saddlers, the apothecary John Wright, the miller George Pole, and the locksmith William Bowman among others also paid dearly for their allegiance to the Catholic cause.

In an age which found it impossible to distinguish between religion and politics the Act of 1581 made celebrating mass a capital offence while that of 1585 expelled all Jesuits and seminary priests from the kingdom upon pain of death. From 1582 until the end of 1595 thirty priests were tried and executed in the north, the majority at the Tyburn on the Knavesmire. The 1581 Act also prescribed the death penalty for lay people convicted of sheltering priests, though in practice judges hardly ever enforced this sanction. Because of the uniqueness of the event, therefore, and also because its victim was a woman, the martyrdom of Margaret

Clitherow evoked universal repulsion.

Born into a conservative background, Margaret Middleton had observed the state religion both as a girl in St Martin's parish in Coney Street and for a time after her marriage to John Clitherow, a prosperous butcher in the Shambles. Then, after witnessing the death of the Earl of Northumberland, she seems in the early 1570s to have been converted to Catholicism by Dr Vavasour's wife. Imprisoned numerous times for failing to attend her parish church of Holy Trinity, King's Court, she made use of her new found leisure to learn to read and to say her service in Latin. When at liberty she loved nothing more than to make a pilgrimage to the Tyburn where the seminary priests had died. When she appeared before the civil authorities yet again in 1585 for avoiding Protestant worship she would almost certainly have been sentenced to another period in prison, had she not for a reason which has never been fully explained refused to allow her case to proceed to a trial. At this stage she may not have understood that being pressed to death, rather than execution at the stake, was the automatic penalty at the common law for such an offence. The Assize Judges, the Mayor and councillors, and certain Protestant ministers stressed the barbarity of the sentence to try to get her to make a token gesture of conformity, but all in vain. Arrayed as a bride awaiting her bridegroom, she died in the York Tollbooth on 25 March 1586.

Protestantism

While Catholic apologists understandably looked with hatred upon the perpetrators of the northern persecution, Protestants regarded the queen's representatives in a very different light. To them men like Huntingdon, Grindal, *[monochrome plate 8]* Sandys and Hutton came to liberate the region, and to transform its capital into a city upon the hill. From the outset the geography of York militated against their grand design. Despite the amalgamations earlier in the century the city still retained a disproportionate number of tiny parishes, its situation all the more anomalous when compared with other northern towns: Newcastle possessed four parishes, Hull two and Leeds only one. The very low income of the individual churches, most of which had been valued at less than £10 in 1535, offered little inducement for graduates to settle in the city when for the first time a university education was coming to be seen as a necessity for a Protestant minister. For the greater part of Elizabeth's reign most if not all of the city clergy had neither the qualifications nor it seems the inclination to supply a regular round of Protestant preaching to which the people of Hull had been exposed since 1560 when councillors had attracted Melchior Smith to the town.

Single handedly the Lord President took it upon himself to remedy the situation, in 1579 urging upon the corporation the advantages of establishing a civic preacher. The Mayor, Robert Cripling, expressed no enthusiasm for the scheme, pointing out that York with its archbishop and cathedral chapter differed greatly from Newcastle and Hull: members of the corporation would go to the Minster to hear sermons, but they did not see the necessity for raising funds to maintain a preacher. Ignoring such arguments, Huntingdon persisted in his plans, and later in the year induced the corporation to approve the proposal in principle, and by the following year the city had collected sufficient contributions to pay a civic preacher the substantial salary of £30 a year. The first lecturer proved a disappointment, leaving York soon after his arrival, but his successor, Richard Harwood, preaching in season and out of season during a ministry of over thirty years, more than fulfilled his patron's expectations.

As a new generation of councillors came to the fore the corporation itself increasingly took the initiative in matters of religious reform. Six months before the Rising of the Earls, Alderman Robert Pacocke, whom Archbishop Young in 1564 had considered 'no favourer' of religion, acknowledged that salvation came through the death of Christ alone, and that 'all the works that ever I have done or could do' were 'of themselves of none effect or worthy to attain any favour at God's hands'. In 1578 the corporation resolved to destroy medieval representations of the mass in the windows of St Thomas's hospital outside Micklegate bar, and in the ensuing twenty years introduced measures to

171

promote sabbath observance, prohibit drinking in service time and the opening of shops on Sundays.

The presence of a little band of Frenchmen in the city helped promote this emergent Puritanism. Three or four Huguenots had settled in York by the latter part of the century, and at least one, Ferdinando Phawghney, married an English wife. Phawghney's Calvinist convictions appealed to several of the city's governing elite, Alderman Laurence Robinson choosing the Frenchman to be the godfather of one of his sons. At his death in 1589 Robinson expressed his hope of salvation by the merits of Christ's death and his assurance of being 'a member of his most beautiful, comfortable and glorious church'. As well as giving continental biblical commentaries to two York ministers, Phawghney himself, when he died in 1595, bestowed £6 over three years 'for the maintenance of the preaching of God's word at my parish of All Hallows'. Two years later Alderman Robert Askwith followed his lead with the request 'that a godly sermon shall be made at my burial by Mr Harwood or some other well learned man'. Alderman Robert Brooke, the founder of a highly influential family in the city during the seventeenth century, in his will of 1598 summed up the thinking of this new breed of York civic leaders, proclaiming, 'my only trust is to be saved by the death and passion of my redeemer Jesu Christ, who shed his most precious blood for my sins and the sins of the whole world of so many as trust to be saved by his most cruel death and bloodshedding, for it was for our sakes to appease the wrath of God the father that he had against mankind for the disobedience of our forefather Adam...'

Slowly and almost imperceptibly the theology of the Minster dignitaries and the civic lecturer began to have an effect not only upon the city elite but also upon some much humbler citizens. The Elizabethan incumbent of St John's, Ousebridge very unusually recorded the religious inclinations of some of his more noteworthy parishioners. The very aged Margaret Metcalfe, widow of Anthony Metcalfe of Wensley, at her death in October 1579 'wholly and fully reposed her whole confidence and trust in the death and passion of Jesus Christ' and 'was heartily sorry that she was so superstitiously and popishly bent in times past'. Two decades later the vicar particularly commended the octogenarian Andrew Watson for his knowledge of religion and frequent attendance at his parish church and Edward Wilcock, a former servant of the lawyer, John Moore, for his 'godly, faithful and ... Christian end.'

The war with Spain, which lasted for much of the latter part of the century, may well have played its part in these more positive attitudes towards the national church, for in common with much of the rest of the country a sense of patriotism seems to have gripped the population of late Tudor York. No fewer than 1,300 inhabitants voluntarily signed the Bond of Association in 1584 to defend the queen's life against the machinations of her enemies. In August 1586 the citizens celebrated Elizabeth's escape from assassination with a sermon and general communion in at the Minster, followed by street parties and bonfires late into the night 'with great rejoicing and singing of psalms, and ringing of bells'. More and more in the common mind allegiance to the crown was coming to be identified with adherence to Protestantism.

Certainly for the third Earl of Huntingdon devotion to Protestantism and loyalty to the queen were two sides of a single coin. As he lay dying at the King's Manor in December 1595 he held up his hands and prayed 'God bless Queen Elizabeth, God save Queen Elizabeth'. In the obituary he wrote for his brother, Sir Francis Hastings gave pride of place to his love for the gospel, recalling how 'he never set a straying foot in any place where he did not labour at the least to settle the preaching of the word to the people'. To Huntingdon, perhaps more than to any other man, the city owed its integration into the Protestant culture of the nation.

The Economy

Although politics and religion had dominated its policies during Huntingdon's twenty-three years as Lord President, the Council in the North had also done its best to promote the city's economy. As the reign of Elizabeth was drawing to its close York had become a very different city materially from what it had been at the accession of Henry VII. The century's long depression had lifted at last. During the forty years the Council in the North had been permanently established at the King's Manor the city had benefited greatly from the suitors and visitors it attracted to York. These in their turn had generated welcome custom for local bakers, butchers, brewers, tailors, drapers, shoemakers, glovers and many others, creating so great a demand for accommodation that sixty-four inns had been established in the city by 1596. The luxury trades had also expanded and York goldsmiths, silversmiths, pewterers and stationers now found a ready market for their products.

The end of the mid Tudor inflation and the return of a sound national currency had materially contributed to this recovery. The corporation had cleared its debts by the beginning of Elizabeth's reign and stayed solvent for the rest of the century. Within a year of the destruction of the medieval bridge over the river Ouse by flooding in the winter of 1565 it raised sufficient funds to build a fine, single-span replacement. Very gradually it also showed signs of returning confidence in other areas, selling urban tenements to invest in much more lucrative manorial rights in villages outside the city.

York merchants were among the first to experience this new prosperity. Even though the corporation had failed to stem the migration of weavers to West Riding townships, they still continued to buy and sell Yorkshire cloth, and profited even more from the trade in lead from the Richmondshire and Craven fields. They dealt on a wide scale in foodstuffs for which York remained the largest centre for the whole of the Yorkshire region, and in addition regularly imported luxury goods from London and overseas to meet the needs of the northern nobility and gentry.

Long distance trade had also revived and the city had strengthened its position as a distribution centre for much of the north and the northern midlands with good communications with London by road as well as by sea. York furthermore still possessed the capacity to dominate its main outport, the Privy Council in the 1580s estimating the city's overseas trade at three times that of Hull. The merchants guild, renamed the Merchant

Adventurers Company in the royal charter of 1581, now concentrated upon importing iron, pitch, hemp and flax from northern Germany and the Baltic. Commerce at home and abroad had resulted in a considerable accumulation of capital in the city to make money lending a major source of income in late Elizabethan York.

The century as a whole saw little alteration in the ways in which the freemen earned their living, with merchants still controlling the city at the end of the period as they had at the beginning. In this respect York differed from more industrialised inland cities like Norwich or Worcester where large numbers of inhabitants were engaged in the textile trades. York tailors, drapers, boot and shoe makers and glovers continued to meet local demand, but failed to go on to develop specialist markets as their counterparts in Coventry and Northampton were doing. Food production figured largely in the city with bakers and butchers in positions of influence, although York butchers never gained the predominance they achieved in the same period in Leicester. While they received few large scale commissions, the building trades at least retained their former importance. Only in the service industries had major new business begun to emerge with innholding, a relatively insignificant craft in 1500, becoming one of the major occupations in the city by 1600.

The improving economic climate of the second half of the sixteenth century affected York's previously stagnant population. Despite constant migration into the city, outbreaks of plague and the sweating sickness had prevented any significant population growth in the first half of the sixteenth century, but the number of inhabitants within the walls began to increase from around Elizabeth's accession, in most years the majority of surviving parish registers showing a small excess of births over deaths. In marked contrast to the earlier period there were no major epidemics in York for some forty years after 1560 so allowing this growth to continue unchecked. The rise in population, however, to approach perhaps 12,000 in 1600 can only have been attained by massive immigration. Once more as in the high middle ages prospects of employment were drawing streams of migrants into the city.

This movement of population had presented the corporation with massive problems. Well before the 1572 Act of Parliament the city had taken a census of its poor, and gone on to control begging licences and to relieve the impotent and aged by weekly poor assessments. In the next decade it had set up a workhouse, where the unemployed participated in a series of loss making schemes of spinning and weaving, in addition to a house of correction for those whose would not work. These measures failed, however, to check the number of poor people flocking to the city and by the end of the century the corporation was driven to dispatching immigrant paupers back to their last place of residence. As in the middle ages extremes of wealth and poverty existed side by side and the poor greatly outnumbered the rich; but few would have denied the fact that the city was a far more dynamic and optimistic place in which to live at the end of Elizabeth's reign than it had been for more than a century.

Compelled by a succession of Tudor monarchs over the course of a hundred years to accept the direct supervision of a royal governor in place of earlier sporadic intervention from Westminster the city fathers, if not all the inhabitants of York, had eventually learnt not to kick against the pricks. The Council in the North, which had battled long and hard with the forces of local conservatism, triumphed in the end as the city finally realised that civic advancement could come only through cooperation with the policies of the central government. In 1485 the corporation had reacted with grief and apprehension to the fall of the Yorkist dynasty; on the death of Elizabeth Tudor in March 1603 it set immediate plans in motion to greet the Stuart line.

6

YORK IN THE SEVENTEENTH CENTURY

W J Sheils

Crisis and Conflict

The death of Elizabeth I and the accession of James VI of Scotland placed York in a potentially advantageous position. Although they remained separate kingdoms, the union of the Crowns of England and Scotland produced a new political environment and York, as the principal city in the north of England, occupied a central position in the territories governed by the new king. York was one of the first major cities to welcome James when he stopped off on his way south, and the royal monogram can still be seen carved at the foot of the doorway in King's Manor, seat of royal government in the north, where the new king stayed and was entertained. *[colour plate 10]* There was some speculation afoot that the city might become the new capital, but this owed more to regional fancy than to any serious view of government, and James, and his Scottish followers, were soon enticed by the wealth and opportunities which they found on their arrival in London. The brief moment of euphoria and excitement passed, to be followed by a dark chapter in the city's history with the arrival of plague in the early summer of 1604.

As early as July 1603 the corporation had restricted trade with known affected areas, to which they later added the important port of Hull, much used by York merchants, when that city was discovered to have the infection. Watches were placed on the walls and the bars were locked at night in an attempt to place a *cordon sanitaire* around the city, and a number of traders, including one William Morton, were prosecuted for transporting their goods over the city walls under cover of darkness during the late summer and autumn. The winter months brought some lifting of restrictions, and trade with London was restored provided wares were not bought from houses known to be infected, but the threat returned with the spring. In March the watch was renewed, vagrants were prevented from entering within the walls and the poor were prohibited from begging. By May, however, plague had entered the city, and on 1 June the mayor sent a letter to the city's MPs in London listing 17 households known to be infected. The council set up plague lodges outside the city walls for those infected, and also set about the killing of cats and dogs, who were thought to carry the infection on their coats. Despite these precautions the plague proved impossible to control and the council tried to prevent fellow councillors from fleeing the city, an order which proved ineffectual, with the result that between 16 July and 21 September the council failed to meet. The impact was severe; an estimate of 1639 indicates that 3512 people, over a third of the population, died in the summer and autumn of 1604, and the psychological impact of this can be gauged from the entry in the parish register of St Olave's church just outside the walls in which it was recorded that between August and December 'people dyed so fast that they could not be well nombred'. An epidemic of these proportions meant that no sector of the community was immune from its impact; the plague started on the west bank of the river but soon spread through all parishes in the city, wealthy as well as poor, with only Michael le Belfrey, which included the Minster Yard, escaping the worst of the ravages. The human impact can be seen in the entries from the parish of Holy Trinity Goodramgate, where fifty-one burials were recorded in the month of September, destroying whole households such as the Braithwaites; Margaret was buried on 4 September to be followed by James on 11, Anne on 17 and Edward on 22, with his daughters Mary and Sybil being

Plate 9 Henry Hastings, Third Earl of Huntingdon

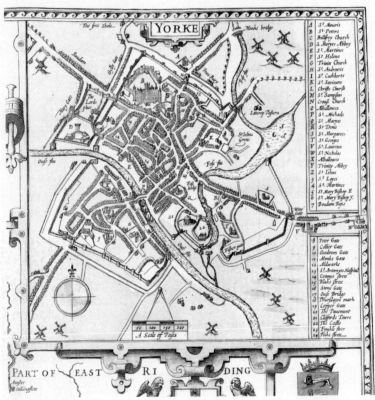

Plate 10 John Speed's map of York

Plate 11A The almshouses in Bootham

Plate 11B The house of Alderman Thompson

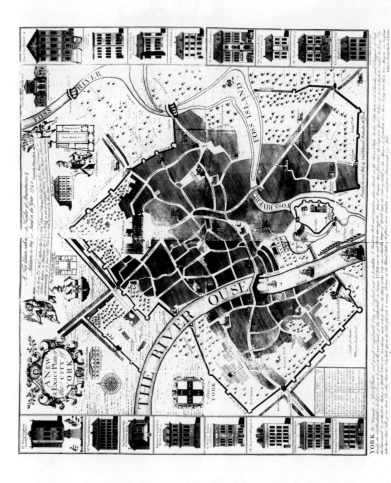

Plate 12 John Cossins' Map of York 1748

Plate 13 Monument to Dr John Dealtry

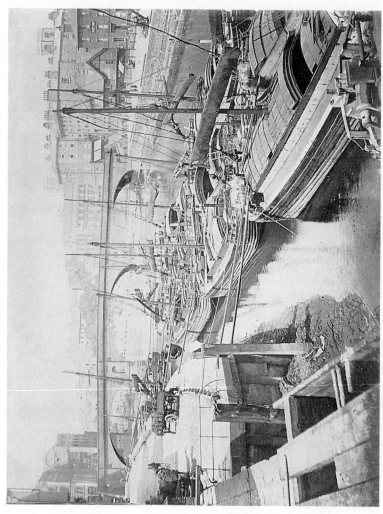

Plate 14 Queen's Staith in 1900

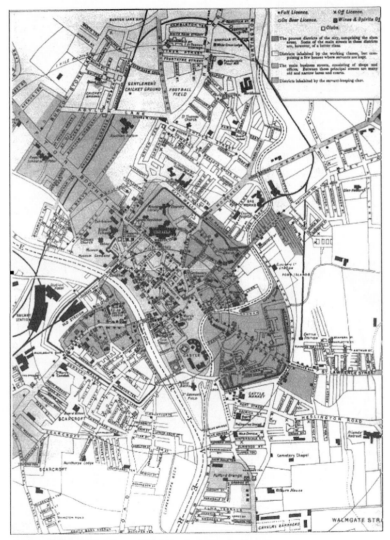

Plate 15 Map of York in 1901 from Rowntree's *Poverty*

Plate 16 Prime Minister Tony Blair visits York during the floods of 2000

buried on 1 October. Nor were the Braithwaites alone, almost half the deaths came from households recording three or more burials. At the height of the epidemic the city demonstrated signs of social stress when the residents of Marygate, a 'sore infected' street, objected to their richer neighbours within the walls denying them access to food and attempted to break out of the cordon put around them. They were only dispersed when a gun was fired and one of their number injured. Whether similar disturbances took place elsewhere cannot be certain. Our only evidence for this incident comes from a subsequent deposition by the injured party who later sought poor relief from the authorities. The winter of 1604-5 brought some relief, and mortality returned to normal levels in the early months of 1605, with the last recorded plague burial being noted at All Saints Pavement on 30 April.

Fortunately, York was not to see an epidemic of these proportions again, though the threat of plague was present in 1610, 1624-6 and 1637, and plague itself broke out in 1631 but was successfully contained within the parish of St Lawrence, on the east side of the city beyond the walls. On this occasion preventive measures were more effective and the direct involvement of Thomas Wentworth, as President of the King's Council in the North, enforced their implementation, with the inhabitants of Walmgate 'shutt up in their own severall houses and their back door lock upp or nayled upp and their fore doors also lock upp on the day'. Although the plague seemed to have been controlled by November 1631 restrictions on movement within the city continued until March 1632, and only a handful of plague deaths were recorded in these months.

These examples were typical of the experience of most larger towns in the period, and show the uncertain conditions under which most people lived their lives. Even in normal times infant and child mortality were high, with an average of four out of ten children dying before they reached the age of ten years in even prosperous parishes like St Michael le Belfrey and St Martin Coney Street throughout the century. Human misery was never far from the surface of the Early Stuart town but, even following the calamity of 1604-5, what is remarkable is the speed with which it

179

was able to recover. What had been disaster for some proved an opportunity for others: those who left the city soon returned, migrants flocked to York to take the place of those who had died, and the shortage of skills and the availability of housing enabled the young to set up home and start new families. Baptisms were higher in the decade following the plague than in the years before, and admissions to the freedom of the city almost doubled in 1605, thus replacing the traders and craftsmen lost. Housing was soon re-occupied, with the same number of houses contributing to the parish rates for 1605 in Holy Trinity, Goodramgate as had done in the previous years. Though it is hard for us to imagine today, by 1610 it was as if the plague of 1604 had never happened; life had returned to normal, outwardly at least.

The new arrivals to the city came from a variety of places; as was usual the unskilled and the labourers were mostly drawn from the surrounding countryside, but the evidence of apprenticeships to the Merchant Taylors' guild shows that many skilled workers came from further afield, and in particular reminds us of the enduring trading links which York had with the Dales through the wool trade carried down the river systems and shipped abroad through the city. Many of the new apprentices, such as Francis Atkinson from Melmerby, indentured to William Maison on 24 November 1606, and George Chaytor from Wensley, came from parishes in Wensleydale and parts of Cumbria which in the later Middle Ages had been great grazing lands owned by the monasteries. York continued to be a magnet for the young and aspiring throughout the region, it was a place of opportunity and the regional capital at the hub of a distribution network which covered most of the north of England. In addition to this market function the city was a centre of ecclesiastical and civil administration and, as such, the provider of professional services to an extensive hinterland. The walls may well have formed a physical and jurisdictional barrier between town and country, but in economic and social terms the relationship between York and its rural hinterland remained one of mutual dependence.

The importance of York's market function is best illustrated by the admissions to freedom granted by the city, for the freemen were the citizenry on whose efforts the prosperity of the whole community depended. During the first half of the century admissions were dominated by four craft groups who comprised almost three quarters of the freemen; they belonged to the distributive trades, those employed in food and drink, and the clothing and leather crafts, while much of the remaining 25% was taken up with textile workers, metalworkers and those employed in the building and joinery crafts. Tailors and merchants consistently appeared at the head of the craft lists, followed by cordwainers and a variety of butchers, bakers and innkeepers. The pattern remained broadly the same during the second half of the century, though the royal charter granted to the Merchant Taylors in 1662 distorted the figures somewhat, when the labourers emerged as a significant element in the economy, being the largest group of freemen admitted in the last quarter of the century. In all, the economic prosperity of the city depended to a large degree on its distributive trades and cloth, although no longer manufactured in the city, remained essential to its prosperity, the cloth merchants being among the richest sectors of society. Although York's role in overseas trade declined in these years the merchant community was sufficiently secure in its position to rebuild part of the Merchant Adventurers Hall, incorporating an imposing entrance with their coat of arms which can still be seen in Fossgate. The trade they engaged in was mostly with the Low Countries and the Baltic, the latter through the Eastland Company, and in 1640 the seven leading merchants, all of them alderman, were substantial traders each dealing in goods worth over £4000 a year. Next in importance after the merchants were the food and drink trades, no doubt catering for the clientele who came to the markets and fairs and also to the increasing numbers who came to the city to sue in the courts or to seek the advice of the lawyers who served the church and civil courts. Between them these courts heard over 2000 cases a year as well as conducting the everyday business of proving wills and registering contracts and, in that way, brought a good deal of business into the city. After 1660 the reduction in status of the church courts and the abolition of the Council in the North reduced the importance of York as a legal and administrative centre, and it is no surprise to see that this was accompanied by a decline in the numbers of freemen innholders. These innholders were of course the elite of the craft and for the ordinary residents of the city it would be the numerous alehouses and brewing establishments, often run as a form of by-employment by the wives or other family members of freemen following other crafts, which were the most common resorts for refreshment. We know that at the beginning of the period three-quarters of the brewers and tapsters recorded combined that activity with another source of income. The decline of the food and drink trades after 1660 was compensated for by the increasing diversity of occupation available by the end of the century, reflected not only in the emergence of the labourers as a large group of freemen but also by the appearance of providers of luxury goods and services for the gentry and commercially prosperous classes throughout the north: bookbinders, clockmakers, goldsmiths, painter/stainers, and musicians could all be numbered in double figures by the 1690s. Their presence, and that of George Clay, an instrument maker admitted in 1679, and John Hale, a tobacco cutter admitted two years later, indicates the beginnings of a new phase in the history of the city which will form the subject of the next chapter. During the 17th century, however, York's market economy remained its chief source of economic well being and, for the most part, its freemen prospered, but the absence of any substantial manufacturing activity meant that the city itself did not grow significantly in population in these years. The 12,400 people recorded in 1700 represented a modest increase on the figure of about 10,000, which is the best approximation we have for 1600, suggesting a relatively stable community. As we shall see, that stability was also reflected in its political institutions, but the impression gained from general trends and from the superficial surface impressions recorded by many visitors to the city in these years conceal an eventful history.

The political institutions of York did not change greatly in this period, although issues like the Civil Wars and the accession of the catholic King James II is 1685, affected the day to day conditions of politics massively. As is to be expected, politics followed economics and the leaders of York's government reflected the importance of the trading community in the city. Merchants filled the office of mayor, the chief magistrate of the city, on sixty occasions during the century and, of the 29 alderman elected between 1603 and 1644, 18 were merchants. The importance of the cloth trade was further reflected in the eleven drapers who occupied the mayoral chair before 1700, and these figures demonstrate the narrow base from which the city recruited its governors. Merchants also dominated the sheriff's office, comprising almost half of those elected, but here there is evidence of a wider distribution, for the remaining sheriffs came from 27 different occupational groups, including butchers, cordwainers and masons. City government was in the hands of relatively few families, and although there were divisions on matters of principle, they comprised a close-knit oligarchy often related by blood or marriage, as were the Breareys and the Harrisons. Although successive generations followed each other in office, it was rare for this to go on for more that three, for among the fruits of civic office were access to county society or the purchase of landed estates. Edward Thompson owned land at Sheriff Hutton and later generations settled at Escrick Park, though the family continued to play an active part in civic affairs well into the 18th century. The Robinsons, an aldermanic family early in the century, achieved the highest office in the county when Sir William, by then living at Newby Park, was High Sheriff of Yorkshire in 1639, whilst his son became MP for York in 1660, and a nephew lord mayor in 1700. The Thompsons and the Robinsons were two of the more spectacular cases of civic elites entering county, and even national, politics, but others well known in the city, the Geldarts, Dickinsons, and Herberts provide further proof of the close link between town and country in this period. Nor were those links always in one direction, for county families also looked to the city; Sir William Ingram's son married the daughter of a mayor, Thomas Marshall, and another mayor, William Allanson married into the Tancred family of Wensleydale. Those links were to become more important to the city as the century progressed, but before considering the later period we should turn to events in the first four decades of the century.

Although a York citizen played a key role at the heart of national politics in 1605, when the gunpowder plotter Guy Fawkes, son of a York lawyer and former pupil of St Peter's School, was

arrested in the cellars of the Houses of Parliament on 5 November, national events did not impinge directly on civic politics to any significant degree before 1640. That is not to say, however, that the city was not the location of some of the most fundamental divisions in English society at that time. One of the chief characteristics of York's history in these years is the emergence of a committed puritan or godly leadership in the city; it was encouraged by successive archbishops in Matthew Hutton (archbishop 1595-1606) and Tobie Matthew (archbishop 1606-1628), sustained by active preaching from puritan clergy like Edmund Bunney, whose memorial is still to be seen on the south wall of the Minster choir, and intensified by the survival of Catholicism among the population and the activities of missionary priests among them. In

All Saints Church Pavement

the years up to 1628 this godly preaching was encouraged by the Minster authorities also, and the corporation built on late 16th century initiatives in financing a preaching ministry. In 1607 the city preacher, Richard Harwood, was authorised to preach wherever he could find the largest congregation and was encouraged to follow his Sunday sermon with the puritan practice of an exercise, or further exposition of the text with other clergy

184

present, in the afternoons. By 1624, when Henry Ayscough was appointed, the preacher was providing a Sunday sermon at All Saints, Pavement, and preaching a monthly afternoon sermon in the parish church of the current lord mayor, and by 1628 these afternoon sermons had become weekly, with an assistant preacher appointed to help out. In additions to these the corporation were generous in paying for occasional sermons by preachers of whom they approved, but 1628 was to prove to be the high point of this activity. In that year archbishop Matthew died, to be succeeded by a succession of primates of a very different stamp. This was compounded in the following year when relations broke down between Parliament and Charles I, and the king decided to rule without Parliament, instigating eleven years of personal rule marked by conflict over the royal prerogative and Parliamentary privilege, especially in the raising of taxes such as Ship Money. These national tensions were mirrored in the local context by a series of conflicts between corporation and dean and chapter over matters of precedence and jurisdiction.

Archbishops Harsnett and Neile were Arminians in churchmanship, and placed order and the sacraments above preaching as the hallmarks of a true church. Their policies represented a challenge to the religious practice which had become established in the city over the previous generation, and several of the York parochial clergy found themselves in trouble with the ecclesiastical courts during the 1630s. The corporation, in order better to secure the funding of their preachers, set out to purchase the patronage of two parishes, All Saints Pavement and St Saviour, and they were successful in 1632, appointing the preacher and his assistant to the livings. At the archbishop's visitation the following year, however, both men were reported for failing to say the set prayers authorised in the Book of Common Prayer, and they were joined in this offence by the clergy of eight other city parishes. Clearly, battle lines were drawn up between the church authorities and a significant sector of the city clergy, who could rely on the support of the corporation for their preaching. The case of John Birchill, rector of St Martin cum Gregory in Micklegate is probably the best way of illustrating these conflicts. Birchill succeeded two earlier puritan ministers in the parish, where the congregation clearly shared their ministers' views, for the churchwardens were presented to the court for concealing Birchill's nonconformity and several parishioners, including three alderman, were charged with irreverence in the church, which was ordered to be rearranged, or 'beautified', to comply with the standards of Arminian churchmanship. Birchill himself was charged with a range of offences, including departing from the Book of Common Prayer, refusing to baptise with the sign of the cross, giving communion to individuals who were not members of his parish and thereby drawing them away from their rightful pastor, and holding conventicles, or unauthorised prayer and preaching meetings, in the city and elsewhere. It is clear that Birchill's following went beyond the boundaries of his own parish, including even the families of Minster dignitaries, and, as such, threatened the established religious institutions. The case against Birchill dragged on through the courts for six years, disturbing his congregation, which included a number of families from the governing classes of the city, including the Hoyles, Breareys and Tophams, and was very disruptive to civic peace.

Other parishes were also affected by religious disputes and several householders in four of them refused to pay their rates for the 'beautifying' of the churches demanded by archbishop Neile, in one case the churchwarden of St Cuthbert's being beaten up by an angry parishioner when he asked for his contribution. The preaching activity of the puritans was supported by legislation from the council, including the suspension of traditional civic feasts in 1621, and strict orders for the observance of the sabbath, despite the reissue of the Book of Sports, which licensed Sunday games, in 1633. It was in that year also that the city had another royal visit when Charles I came to King's Manor on his way to his coronation as King of Scotland in Edinburgh. Charles, of course, was a supporter of the Arminian bishops, and when in York ordered the removal of some unsightly pews from the Minster and the demolition of some houses built up against its walls. Charles also assisted the cathedral authorities in their policies by granting them £1000 to set up an organ, to gild and colour the altar screen, and to provide new plate and altar cloths. In this context, therefore, the religious disputes discussed above, apparently trivial to modern minds, had direct political repercussions, and were repeated up and down the country where godly corporations saw their traditional rights threatened by what they considered an aggressive religious minority whose views were, in the minds of the puritans, tainted by popery. In a city like York, where there was a residual and active Roman Catholic community of about sixty people, and in an area where the Catholic sympathies of several gentry families were well known, this fear was particularly potent.

In the city itself these disputes were aggravated by rows over jurisdiction between the corporation and the Minster, which still claimed extensive privileges over sizeable areas of York, Minster Yard, Bedern and Davy Hall, whilst the Dean and Chapter was also a major city landlord. The city had been granted a new charter on 19 July 1632 which extended its authority over some outlying villages formerly belonged to the jurisdiction of the dean and chapter who, not unnaturally, challenged the new charter. The dispute eventually reared its head in public over seating in the Minster when Archdeacon Whickham placed a stall in the cathedral choir higher than that of the lord mayor. The indignation of the corporation was unbounded and they decided to boycott the Minster entirely until the archdeacon, on the orders of central government in London, apologised. Seating of course was only the occasion and not the cause of such disputes, for the corporation saw the privileges of the dean and chapter as a serious threat to its ability to regulate the economic and civil life of the city: tradesmen could set up in business within the chapter liberties without securing the freedom of the city, and criminals and petty offenders against regulations could escape the magistrates by residing in those same liberties. What lay at the heart of these arguments therefore were legitimate concerns over authority, and disagreement over the way in which society should be ordered. To the godly a strict and scripturally based discipline was the true blueprint for society, and among the surviving signs of their concerns we still have the fine pulpit placed in All Saints, Pavement by the corporation in 1634, with its inscriptions from the

Epistle to Timothy, 'PREACH THE WORD BE INSTANT IN SEASON AND OUT OF SEASON' and from Proverbs, 'WHERE THERE IS NO VISION THE PEOPLE PERISH'. Also at All Saints an annual sermon continues to be preached which was established by Mistress Moseley in 1634, whilst scholars can still use the fine collection of over 3,000 the books belonging to archbishop Matthew which was bequeathed by his widow in 1629 to provide a library for the Minster.

The events so far described chiefly concern the upper sectors of York society, but concern for the poor was another hallmark of the puritan conscience, whether motivated by the demands of Christian charity or the imperatives of social control. The Poor Law of 1601 had placed the responsibility for relief of the poor on the parishes nationally. In York the parish officers were supervised by the corporation who organised an annual survey or 'view' of the poor in each ward of the city. Some of these records survive and we know that in 1632/3 there were 294 paupers in receipt of relief, as well as a further 181 children, probably orphans following the 1631 plague. Of these paupers the greater part was found in Walmgate Ward, a pattern repeated in 1637/8 when the figure for Walmgate was three times higher than that for the more prosperous Bootham Ward. The city clearly had its wealthier and its poorer areas but, unlike modern cities, rich and poor were found in all parishes and streets so that social segregation was not an option and all could come face to face with the consequences of destitution, among their neighbours if not their family. Like other towns of the period York made some attempts to relieve poverty by providing work for the poor, by spinning and weaving in St George's house in 1620, or by providing materials for outwork in 1627 from storehouses in the obsolete medieval buildings of St Anthony's Hall and St Thomas's Hospital, and these initiatives were increased, under direction from the Privy Council in London, during the 1630s. Poor relief dealt with paupers, but large sections of the population hovered on the edge of or close to pauperism and an accident or the death of a parent could easily plunge a whole household into destitution. For these cases private charity supplemented statutory obligations and parishes received endowments from their wealthier citizens for bread doles, for apprenticing poor children, for helping craftsmen to set up in business and to assist poor widows. Most of these were modest sums of money, like the rent charge for the poor of St John's Ousebridge derived from bequests by James Wright in 1635 and Samuel Brearey in 1644, but there were some examples of substantial gifts, like that of £100 for the poor of St Crux by William Weddall in 1618. The most substantial form of charitable bequest, however, was the establishment of an almshouse, and the seventeenth century was a notable period for such initiatives, three being set up in York before 1640. Two were set up by members of the city elites, Thomas Watters Hospital, comprising seven cottages under one roof in 1609, was probably located in the old haberdashers' guild hall which was repaired and made habitable in 1627, and Thomas Agar's Hospital in Monkgate, founded for six poor widows in 1631. The third almshouse was established by Sir Arthur Ingram in Bootham, and reminds us that it was not just the civic elite who were moved to act in this way. The building, which still stands in Bootham, was erected between 1630 and 1632 and was designed to house ten poor widows, who were to receive £5 a year each and a new gown every three years, and a small chapel was provided with an 'honest and able man' to read prayers there. Following damage during the siege of 1644 it was rebuilt in 1649. The right of nomination of places in the almshouse remained with Sir Arthur's friends and relatives and the responsibility for maintaining the building and paying the widows' dues devolved to his son, a fact which was to cause problems later in the century when the Ingrams no longer played an active role in the city. *[monochrome plate 11A]*

Sir Arthur was Secretary to the Council in the North from 1613 and a key figure in royal administration in the region. In addition to his almshouses he was responsible for the greatest building works undertaken in the city in the early part of the century. The son of a Yorkshire merchant who had prospered in London, Ingram made a fortune in the customs service and became one of the richest men in the kingdom, acquiring over 40 manors in Yorkshire, including those of Sheriff Hutton and Temple Newsam,

St Mary's Tower

Nonconformist Chapel, St Saviourgate

where he also undertook major building projects. The Council in the North met in King's Manor, premises which underwent extensive improvements in these years undertaken by two Lord Presidents: Edmund, Lord Sheffield claimed that he had spent over £3,000 on the building when he gave up the presidency in 1625, and his contributions include the fine doorway bearing the arms of Charles I which marks the present entrance, and another which bears his coat of arms; Thomas Wentworth, the arrogant and ill-fated earl of Strafford, was Lord President from 1628 and built a new wing on the south-west side of the courtyard, with a chapel and a gallery, as well as the long gallery which joins the south and north wings and forms the end of the first courtyard today. The Council acted as a court of law and its presence provided work for about thirty lawyers and officials as well as another hundred or so clerks, servants, cooks and grooms, so that servicing the needs of its members played a significant part in the local economy. As the Council's secretary Ingram had offices in Petergate opposite the west front of the Minster, but immediately took on the remainder of a long lease on the former prebendal house of South Cave, in Precentor's Lane opposite his offices. He and his brother were appointed wardens of the archbishop's palace and prison in 1616, and in 1618 he was granted a lease of the palace site in Minster Yard, 'it being utterly ruinous, waste and decayed'. He took further leases of lands in what is now the Dean's Park, and thus acquired a site on which to build an impressive residence and gardens, incorporating a small courtyard, rooms as large as the main rooms in the King's Manor, and extensive grounds furnished with a bowling green, tennis court, and statuary which attracted comment from visitors to the city like John Aston who in 1639 described the figures as 'images of lyons, beares, apes and the like, both beasts and birds which, from the topp of the steeple please the eye, but otherwise are showes onely to delight children'. Aston's dismissive tone is echoed by Ingram's modern biographer, who described the building as a 'typical house of the parvenu, with no expense spared'. Ingram's house stood alongside another former prebendal residence, the Treasurer's House, newly built in the early years of the century by Sir George Young, son of a former

191

archbishop, and together these buildings made Minster Yard an imposing testimonial to new wealth and modern architecture.

Parvenu or not Ingram made his mark not only on York's townscape, but also on its social scene. The house offered hospitality to the Mayor and aldermen in 1636, and the King dined there in April 1639, and again during the autumn of 1640 when Ingram's steward recorded 'great meals and all lords this week' and a bill for the week of £77 5s. 3d (£77. 26p). It was probably during this visit that the king had a view of York painted by Alexander Keirincx in which the towers and spires of the city churches can be picked out behind the stretch of wall on the western edge of town. *[colour plate 9]* During these visits the city was briefly host to the armies set to fight the Scots, and felt threatened by their continued presence outside the walls on Clifton Ings and Bishop Fields for several weeks before they were dispersed. The campaign against the Sots was unsuccessful and it was from the deanery at York, on 24 September, that the great council of Peers arranged a truce with the Scots and set on foot the process for the historic calling of Parliament in London. Charles was back in 1641, when the stocks laid in for 'the king's week' included 2000 oysters, a great salmon, four fat turkeys, eight chickens, 45 partridges, 36 teal, a dozen each of mallard and snipe, 24 plovers, six pheasants and 360 pheasants' eggs. Charles' reasons for his frequent visits at this date had more to do with the problems of the state than with the delights of the city, whose history in the previous four decades had witnessed visitation of plague, acrimonious divisions over religion, and the stress of political uncertainty. Despite this the city had endured and some of its citizens had even prospered, but the structural defects of the Stuart state were shortly to collapse into Civil Wars during which, in the summers of 1642 and 1644, York was to find itself in the eye of the storm.

Civil Wars and Interregnum

When Charles I arrived in York with his court in March 1642 it was not as the commander of an army but as a refugee from his capital, where the London mob, encouraged by Parliament, had made life too dangerous for him and his family. In such circumstances the royal arrival in the city was not universally welcome, and, although 'the streets were embroidered with people on both sides' to welcome the king, others in the city were not so pleased. On the day of his arrival, 17 March, Samuel Wintour, rector of St Michael Spurriergate, preached a sermon extolling Parliament as the assembly of God, and an anonymous inflammatory pamphlet, purporting to be a petition to the King asking him to 'reconcile the displeasures conceived against your Loyall subjectes', was circulating in the city, much to the embarrassment of the corporation. However, even among that body, the puritan members were unhappy at the turn of events, and many of them stayed away from council meetings. This was not an auspicious start to the six months in which the city became, in effect, the capital of the kingdom. Charles brought his family with him, and his court, and several ambassadors and members of the nobility were drawn to the city in these months. The King lived in Sir Arthur Ingram's house, and set up his printing press in St William's College, thus making the Minster Yard the royalist headquarters. From here the royalist propaganda campaign, produced by the king's printers Robert Barker and Stephen Bulkeley, sent pamphlets to London and throughout the country. As matters drifted towards war the city council tried to steer a cautious path between the two parties and, though visiting gentry 'ran foul of each other in the streets of York, with rough words and rough handling' and the house of Alderman Vaux, said to be the leading member of the puritan faction in the city, was attacked and pillaged by 600 soldiers, there was surprisingly little evidence of fighting in the city despite the increasing presence of soldiers and militia. Charles summoned two great musters of the county gentry, the first at the castle on 12 May and a larger one on Heworth Moor on 3 June at which Sir Thomas Fairfax was struck from his horse, thus starting one of the most famous legends of the civil war. At this date however the Fairfaxes, who played an influential part in York's political life and kept a substantial house in the city, were still keen on a negotiated settlement.

Although the message emanating from the city's pulpits continued to place a large measure of responsibility with the king, the council shared the hopes for a peaceful settlement. It agreed to put the militia at the king's disposal but the mayor asked that it not be called away from the city to fight. In the meantime, as July wore on, the council set about securing the defences, repairs were undertaken to the walls, sentry boxes were established, and the trained bands kept a close watch on the city's magazine. At the end of the month Charles launched an unsuccessful raid on Beverley and it became clear that hostilities were now inevitable. The king left York on 16 August, six days before he raised his standard at Nottingham.

At the formal outbreak of hostilities York occupied an important strategic location as a fortified stronghold on the main north-south route, and between strongly royalist countryside to the north and the Parliamentary forces of the West Riding. Charles had left a royalist stronghold there and the city had a succession of governors, with whom the corporation had to deal. Relations were not easy, not simply because a number of aldermen were inclined to the puritan side but also because of the financial burdens of an army in residence. In September the council refused an offer of protection by a group of royalist gentry, and at the end of the year asked that the supreme commander, the Marquis of Newcastle, organise a satisfactory means of paying the soldiery so that they did not have to be given free billets, but the cost of the army continued to be troublesome. The corporation refused to supply any more ammunition for the magazine until it was paid, and in March 1643 it petitioned against any further billeting of troops. Although York saw no action itself at this time the consequences of skirmishes nearby were felt by the city which set up accommodation for wounded soldiers in the Merchant Taylors' Hall and paid for surgeons to treat them. Where these efforts proved to no avail, the corporation paid for the burial of the dead. By 1643 some members of the council, such as Thomas Hoyle, John Vaux, and William Allanson, had left the city and defected to the parliamentarian cause, and the authority of that body was further diminished in January 1643 by the interference of

194

Newcastle in its affairs when he insisted that the royalist Edmund Cowper be re-elected as mayor. This high-handed action even aroused the opposition of those councillors sympathetic to the King, and they assembled on 15 January to elect another candidate only to find the Guildhall cordoned off by troops. The election was aborted and Cowper remained as mayor. This incident demonstrated how powerless the merchants were in the face of military threat, but for some it was the last straw, three members of the Twenty-Four signalled their opposition by refusing to attend any further meetings of that body, and the two sheriffs, including the puritan Samuel Brearey, pleaded sickness in order to avoid greeting Queen Henrietta Maria when she passed through York in February with munitions secured in Holland for the King's cause. Resistance to royalist pressure was demonstrated again in May when the council confirmed its earlier decision to refuse the nomination of the king's chaplain, William Dalbie, to their parish at All Saints Pavement, which they were keeping vacant for the famous puritan preacher John Shawe, who was a chaplain with Fairfax's army at that time.

The rest of 1643 passed uneventfully in the city though, at the end of the year, the puritan party lost one of their more important figures with the death of Alderman Vaux in Hull. He was replaced by a royalist, John Myers, and 1644 began with a renewed struggle over the mayoralty, Newcastle's letter beginning ominously 'I confess I have a motion to make to you which is contrary to the usual course of your city...', asking that Cowper be elected yet again, much to the disgust of the corporation. By this time the military campaign was getting closer to the city, where the royalist garrison under John Bellasis numbered about 4,000. The Scots army had crossed the border and were threatening Durham, and the army in the West Riding under Fairfax had grown to 5,000 strong. Matters came to a head on 11 April when the York garrison, having marched south to face Fairfax's army, suffered a heavy defeat at Selby, losing, it was said, 100 officers and 2,000 other ranks. This completely altered the balance of power in the north and Newcastle immediately withdrew from Durham, where he had been facing the Scots army, in an attempt to restore the depleted garrison at York. He arrived at York on 16 April, pursued by the Scots who detoured to Wetherby where, on 18 April, their commander, Lord Leven, met up with Fairfax. The two parliamentary armies, about 20,000 strong, joined forces at Tadcaster and advanced on York, taking up siege positions on both sides of the Ouse and within a mile of the city walls on 23 April. For the next ten weeks the city was at the heart of the national conflict.

Newcastle had a garrison of 4,000 at his disposal and had sent away most of his cavalry so that the forage in the city could go further. In the early days of the siege the northern countryside, where the garrison customarily pastured cattle, was still open and one observer recorded that 'Souldiers and Citizens were well contented, and Couragious, having no want of salt Meat, nor of any sort of Graine ... of Wine, Beer and Ale there was plenty', but Newcastle quickly rationed food, billeted the soldiers on even the wealthiest of the citizens, and imposed an oath on everyone which included a promise from each 'to the utmost of mine abilitie with the hazard of my life, and fortunes, assist his Majestie ... in resistinge, opposing and pursuing such Scots, in a hostile way, as rebells, and traytors against his majesty and enemies to the Crowne of England.' Thus the traditional distrust of York citizens for the Scots was employed once again.

The impact of the siege on the citizens can be glimpsed from the constables' accounts for Holy Trinity, Goodramgate, which survive for that year. Payments were made on 24 April for straw and for bread and drink for a troop of dragoons, and later entries record sums paid to injured soldiers, for musket shot, for 14 soldiers guarding the Minster, to the bakers that ground corn for General King's regiment, for the cost of a horse to run the mill wheel, and for the watch in Monk Ward. The costs to this parish alone amounted to over £30 in the first six months of 1644; the burden of supporting a garrison of 4,000 must have weighed heavily on a population of only 12,000 people. For the first month of the siege the Parliamentary armies were content to remain at some distance from the walls and made no serious attempt on the defences, though a skirmish outside Walmgate led to the capture of a few prisoners in the church of either St Lawrence or St Nicholas. Other skirmishes took place in the surrounding countryside, but it was only with the arrival of the earl of Manchester and the army of the Eastern Association on 3 June that the siege began in earnest.

On 5 June Fairfax raised a battery on Lamel Hill to the east of the city at the entrance to Walmgate stray beside the present Fairfax House on Heslington Road. From there they pounded the Walmgate area, destroying St Nicholas' church and even reaching into the centre of the city and striking St Sampson's. Walmgate Bar still bears the marks of this action, which forced the defenders to withdraw inside the walls and to fire the suburbs to the east. This took place on 8 June, by which time the Scots had attacked three gun emplacements on the west bank of the Ouse and captured two of them. On 8 June Fairfax began to mine Walmgate Bar, but the plan was uncovered, water poured over the mine, and a defensive mound built within the walls across Walmgate. This was a decisive week in which most of the suburbs were burnt down, and the bridges over the Foss at Monkgate and Layerthorpe destroyed. It left the parliamentary forces in control, and one of their chaplains, Simeon Ashe, has left a record of the 'remarkable providences of God' which the army enjoyed in these days. The best, and possibly only hope, of the defenders lay in the anticipated arrival of Prince Rupert's army, and so Newcastle began to play for time. The week following 8 June was marked by a series of negotiations, ending on 15th of June with the besiegers producing 'Propositions to be tendred to the Enemy' calling for the surrender of the city, in which they offered Newcastle's army safe passage, and promised 'no violation to the Cathedrall Church'. Newcastle refused the offer and on the following day, Trinity Sunday, the corner tower of St Mary's Abbey, at the junction of Marygate and Bootham, was mined by Manchester's army. The mine was set prematurely and in the resulting fall out from the tower several soldiers were killed. A bloody skirmish took place on the bowling green within the former abbey grounds in which many of the besiegers were slain, numbers of dead varying between 40 and 200 according to contemporary accounts, and more taken prisoner. The royalists also suffered heavy casualties, including some officers, but the assault was eventually repulsed. This was a severe blow to the morale of the Parliamentary forces, who spent the next day digging out the dead and wounded from the debris, and on the Thursday following a truce was arranged to enable the dead to be buried, and the names of many of these and other soldiers killed in these weeks are recorded in the registers of the parish churches, with most of the Royalist officers, including two colonels killed on the bowling green, being buried in the Minster. As ever in such conflicts, the names of some of the rank and file remained unknown, being recorded simply as 'soldier'.

With the besiegers demoralised and the defenders trapped, the situation reached stalemate until the arrival of Prince Rupert at Skip bridge, four miles west of the city, on 30 June. This caused the parliamentarians to lift the siege, with Manchester's army crossing the Ouse on a bridge of boats near Clifton Ings and Fairfax's doing likewise at Fulford. In a brilliant manoeuvre Rupert's army cut north to avoid the enemy and, using Manchester's bridge, he entered the relieved city sometime during the night of 1 July or the following morning. Relief was short-lived, however, for later that morning, Rupert led his army from the city to pursue the enemy, meeting them at Marston Moor, where the royalists were defeated in one of the decisive battles of the first Civil War.

The night that followed was one of anxiety for the people of York, soldiers returning from the battlefield clamoured outside Micklegate Bar for access to the city, and the defeated army were admitted the following morning amidst acrimony between their commanders, Newcastle and Rupert. On 4 July the siege was resumed and with 'not 500 fighting men left in the town' the situation was parlous. The besiegers were ready to storm the city on 11 July, whereupon the remaining garrison sought negotiations. Emissaries were sent into the town by Fairfax and, having secured the approval of their chaplains that it was a proper thing to do, serious discussions took place on Sunday 14 July, continuing through until noon the next day. It seems that, in these discussions, Fairfax's reputation and long standing connection with the city played an important role, and a meeting of the common council and best citizens was called in which articles of surrender were agreed. On 16 July Fairfax was named as governor of the city, and nine days later was presented with 'sack and french wine' by a grateful city, which escaped severe reprisals to both person and fabric in the ensuing months. The defeated garrison was allowed to leave, and the victorious army gave thanks at a service in the Minster. From this time onwards York became a parliamentary stronghold.

The puritan party petitioned parliament to send them godly preachers and, later in the year the royalist mayor, Cowper, was replaced, after long debate, by Thomas Hoyle. Soon afterwards the 'best citizens' were required to take the National Covenant advocating a Presbyterian form of church which the Scots had required of Parliament in return for their support. On 1 January 1645 Parliament ordered the removal of the six leading royalist aldermen and they were replaced by committed parliamentarians. The Council in the North was abolished, to be replaced by a County Committee working from the city, and thereafter a more thorough approach to the consolidation of puritan power in the city can be detected. Taking the Covenant was now a necessary qualification for office, even for the city surgeon, and the estates of the Minster chapter were given over to the maintenance of four Presbyterian preachers in the cathedral and other city churches. Fonts, organs, and other 'superstitious pictures' were removed from the parish churches, but not their stained glass, which Fairfax saved in the Minster and which remains one of the city's glories to this date. Social activities associated with religious rites were frowned upon, wakes and funeral feasts were banned and bell ringing at weddings strictly controlled, as was observance of the Sabbath. Another godly venture at this date was to revive an earlier attempt to establish a university in the city as a means of combating the strength of Catholicism in the north and bring true religion to the region, but this proved abortive and York did not get its university for another three hundred years.

National affairs still intruded on the city, and it was in the inner council chamber behind the Guildhall that the £200,000 ransom money demanded by the Scots for the return of the person of the King was counted out at the end of 1646. Alderman Thomas Hoyle was the leading proponent of the puritan reforms; an intensely religious man and Member of Parliament for the city, he was subject to bouts of depression which led his troubled conscience to commit suicide in 1650 on the first anniversary of the King's execution, a coincidence which the royalists made much of. By the end of the wars the city had taken on the guise of a godly commonwealth in which, before all civic events of importance, such as the admittance of new aldermen, the preachers reminded its leadership of their duties before God. In this role the person of Edward Bowles was pre-eminent. Bowles arrived in York with the army of the Eastern Association as chaplain to the earl of Manchester and, after the surrender of the city, was appointed one of the four civic preachers. He was a renowned preacher who even attracted the royalists to his sermons, and even to his house where, after the great public sermon on Sundays or market days, he expounded the text to groups of prominent citizens. His former connections with the army also gave him access to central government and he was used by the city in negotiations with the Cromwellian regime. He played a leading role at the Restoration, and accompanied Lord Fairfax to Breda as part of the deputation which invited the Prince of Wales to return as Charles II. His reputation for fair dealing and his great preaching abilities, he was 'the mouth of the city and country ministers at their quarterly meetings', contributed greatly to the settled nature of York politics after the upheavals of the war, and he was generally considered to be 'the spring that moved all wheels in the city'.

Under the godly direction of Bowles and the aldermen York's politics returned to something approaching normality in the 1650s, and national issues largely passed the city by. In local affairs the aldermen strengthened their control, even securing authority over the city militia and the castle, as well as over the city's religious life. Much energy was spent on repairing the damage caused by the siege, though John Evelyn, on a visit to the city in 1654, was one of the first in a long line of tourists to note that the streets were 'ill pav'd'! He also said that the shops were 'like London', perhaps reflecting a degree of economic recovery after the difficulties of the previous decade. Some consequences of the conflicts of the 1640s remained, a fund for the relief of lame soldiers was doubled in 1649 because of the numbers seeking support in the city, and the radicalism of the Parliamentary garrison may have contributed to the growth of Quakerism in the city, after the ejection of George Fox from the Minster in 1651 first brought the attention of the authorities to the sect. Despite their strongly held views, an early Quaker, Thomas Aldam, thought the city a den of 'vanitie ... pride, tyranie, fulnes of bread, and abundance of idleness', there is no evidence of harsh dealings with the sect, its local members at least, and relations between them and the rest of the citizenry cut across denominational lines. Outsiders, however, were treated more severely, and a number of Quakers were imprisoned in the Castle for interrupting church services during these years. Other developments continued the civic initiatives which had begun before the Civil Wars. Some leading citizens were mindful of their duties to their less fortunate neighbours and, in 1655, as a result of a substantial bequest to the corporation by Ann Middleton, an almshouse for twenty widows of York freemen was established in Skeldergate in 1659.

By that date the problems of finding a political settlement in the nation following the death of Oliver Cromwell had also begun to reverberate in the city's government. Some of the common council refused to take the oath to Richard Cromwell in 1658, and a rift occurred between common councillors and aldermen in the following year. The aldermen were deeply committed to the godly cause and were keen to keep in with the Rump Parliament and the army, but others in the city had a more pragmatic view, and were inclined to the return of the monarchy. The Yorkshire Rising, led by Thomas Fairfax, gave the pragmatists their opportunity to commit the city to the royalist cause. The Common Council prevented the army commander, Lilburne, from seizing the city magazine, and they invited Fairfax to 'liberate' the city, which he did on New Year's day 1660. On 11 January General Monck arrived in the city on his march south, leaving a strong detachment there under the command of Charles Fairfax.

201

Armorial Window in the Merchant Taylors' Hall

On 10 February Fairfax and his supporters held a great meeting in the city in support of Monck calling for a free parliament and the return of those excluded from the Rump. The common council gave it their support but the aldermen remained undecided. Once the Restoration was assured the aldermen quickly gave their support to the new regime, and elected two well-known royalists to the convention Parliament in March. The royal arms were set up in the Guildhall on 9 May and two days later the man who, twenty year's earlier had accompanied his troubled and ill-fated father to York as Prince of Wales, was declared King 'with the greatest expression of Joy that could be imagined'. A new regime in

London, and a new phase in York's history, was about to begin.

A New monarch and a New Role

Like many beginnings, that following 1660 was fraught with difficulties and troubles. In the years immediately after the Restoration the dominant issue in civic politics was the composition of the magistracy, with the mayor refusing to give way to a royal letter of February 1661 asking that disaffected, that is to say puritan, aldermen be removed from office. On the other hand the local royalist gentry, who had suffered financial loss during the wars, were orchestrating a campaign to have these men removed and gained some support in the city. Matters came to a head in April when, despite the corporation's support for Thomas Widdrington, who had served as MP in the Interregnum, two royalists were elected to represent the city. This was a set back for the godly aldermen and a group of citizens petitioned the king for their removal. This interference in the city's privileges united the city's officials in defence of their charter, despite the opposition of both MPs, and the proceedings came to nought. The victory, however, was a short-lived one and in 1662, supported by the Cavalier Parliament, the Commission for Regulating Corporations, removed from office most of the Common Council and five of the aldermen, including the three survivors of those who had been installed by the victorious Parliamentarians in 1645. This change in personnel did not bring a massive change in policy as, so ingrained had godly values become in the civic consciousness, that many of the new men shared a broadly similar outlook to that of the men they replaced, though perhaps it was not so strongly held.

Upheavals in politics were accompanied by upheavals in religion and the Minster was restored to its former self, with a new archbishop and canons; the four civic preachers were dismissed, though the corporation tried for a time to sustain them by voluntary contributions. The reintroduction of the Anglican liturgy in cathedral and parish church, and the requirement for all clergy to subscribe to those forms in 1662, meant that the three surviving preachers left the Established Church, as did the rector of St

Michael Spurriergate. The upheavals of the Interregnum, which had put civic religion before parochial religion, resulted in neglect both of the parish churches and by the parochial officers, and many deficiencies were reported in 1663, including the failure of the ministers at St Mary Bishophill Junior to maintain the vicarage house and its orchard. The Minster too had suffered, and matters were not helped by a great storm in December 1660 which damaged the south-west tower and roof. By 1662 the restored chapter had spent over £1000 on repairs to the building and its glass. By May 1663 Anglican worship had been effectively restored in the Minster, and by 1667 it seems that the parish churches had been refurbished with the books and equipment necessary for the conduct of services and that most of the faults in church fabric had been made good. The diocesan officials also noted at that date, however, that householders in several parishes were withholding payment of the rates designed for the upkeep of their churches, a fact which suggests that not all citizens went along with the religious changes of the Restoration, and points to a new element in York's life, and one which was to be very important in succeeding centuries, the emergence of dissent.

Some of the clergy who refused the subscription in 1662 continued to minister to their congregations, and other nonconformists, such as the celebrated West Riding Presbyterian Oliver Heywood, preached occasionally in the city to congregations which included civic dignitaries such as Sir John and Lady Hewley, later to establish an almshouse in Saviourgate, and an ex-alderman, Brian Dawson. When dissenters were allowed, briefly, to license places of worship in 1672, congregations of Presbyterians, Independents and Baptists took the opportunity to do so. The Quakers had also grown in numbers and importance at this time, especially in the area of Castlegate near the prison, where many of their co-religionists from throughout Yorkshire were incarcerated for refusing to pay tithes. In addition to these new elements in York's religious life the Roman Catholic community, concentrated mostly in St George's parish and sustained by the support of county families like the Vavasour's, Palmes' and a branch of the Fairfaxes, remained steady at about sixty persons and continued to enjoy the services of its priests.

With the known Catholic sympathies of the Duke of York, heir to the throne, and the legacy of puritanism left by the Civil War, religion and politics could not be kept apart in these years, and the so called Popish Plot and Exclusion Crisis which convulsed national affairs in the late 1670s and 80s reverberated in local politics. One result of the Plot was renewed persecution of Catholics, with the gallows at Tyburn on the Knavesmire in use again, including for the execution of Oliver Postgate, a priest in his eighties who had been active in Yorkshire since the 1630s, for much of the time among the farming communities of the North York Moors. By the 1680s, despite royal interference in the magistracy after 1660, the radical party had again seized control of city government. The city had offended Charles by giving a 'cold' reception to James, Duke of York, in 1679, and the balance of power in the city supported the exclusion of the catholic duke from the succession. So strong were opinions that, in 1683, a charge of seditious language was brought against the lord mayor, Edward Thompson, and a group of Tory gentry from the area sought to interfere in civic affairs. The garrison was still in the city and its governor Sir John Reresby, thought it dangerous to remove it and hand over control of the city to so ill affected a corporation. On one occasion in 1686 political differences were so strongly felt that fighting broke out between citizens and soldiers at a funeral. One of Reresby's correspondents at this time referred to the 'formerly loyal city of York', so open was its opposition to royal policy. The divisions in the corporation were sharpened by the accession of the catholic James II who soon alienated even his supporters. In October 1688 the freeholders and gentry of the county met in York to petition for a free Parliament, and on 22 November the supporters of William and Mary in the city overpowered the garrison and seized the magazine, and early in 1689 the corporation sent a message of congratulation to William on his acceptance of the throne. A consequence of these political and religious upheavals was some modest changes to the city's appearance; in 1674 the Quakers adapted some tenements in Friargate for use as a meeting house, and in 1686 a community of catholic nuns founded by Mary Ward, a York woman, moved into a house and garden on the corner of Blossom Street and Nunnery Lane, which they adapted for use as a school. Both of these buildings were replaced in subsequent centuries, but the first purpose built place of worship for nonconformists was opened in Saviourgate in 1693 for use by a congregation of both Independents and Presbyterians, and the brick built cruciform chapel remains in use to this day by the Unitarians.

The Restoration of 1660 not only led to changes in York's political and religious history, but also in its economic and social life. The failure to revive the Council in the North, despite the wishes of the corporation, meant that the city was no longer such an important centre for government administration and the law, and the consequent drop in business threatened the livelihood of many shopkeepers and craftsmen. Furthermore, rivalry with the Dutch over overseas trade disrupted the mercantile community. Fortunately, not all change was for the worse. There were no further outbreaks of plague like that which began the century, and York escaped the more serious effects of the great plague of 1665, so that one of the darker clouds which hovered over the city had disappeared, though nobody living at the time would have known that. Life remained hard for many citizens and specially for those who lived in the poorer parishes of Walmgate ward, where about forty percent of the households were considered to be too poor to pay the hearth tax in 1672. For the better off and the freemen, who mostly lived in their shops in the central parishes around Coney Street, Ousebridge and Stonegate / Petergate, conditions certainly improved and they were able to share in the increasing wealth of the nation at large as trade with the colonies brought new prosperity to the propertied classes. Many chose to spend that wealth on refurbishing and extending their houses, or on the new commodities from abroad. Craftsmen to carry out the first, and shopkeepers to provide the second, were in abundance at York and they were happy to cater for the needs of the aspiring gentry and the newly leisured classes which lived in the countryside around and who began to see the city as a convenient and pleasant social space. And not only for the countryside around. Plasterers from

York were employed in the royal apartments in Edinburgh castle, as well as in properties in York, such as those presently to be found in Oliver Sheldon House: York silversmiths not only furnished the tables of the landed gentry but also provided chalices and cups for churches throughout the north, keen to restore their plate after the ravages of mid century, and visitors to these churches can still see the work of engravers and carvers like Andrew Kearne and Samuel Carpenter, though it was not until the early eighteenth century that city churches like St Martin cum Gregory in Micklegate were to show the full range of craftsmanship available in the city.

Perhaps the best way to illustrate the quality of workmanship for which York was celebrated is to consider the career of one craftsman, the glasspainter Henry Gyles. Gyles was born in 1645, and was the third generation of the family to work with glass, his father Edmund having worked on the Minster as a lead glazier. Henry would have been taught the practical skills of his trade in his father's workshop, but it is not known where, or from whom, he acquired his artistic training, though it is clear that he developed wide antiquarian and scientific interests. His earliest surviving work is an armorial panel in the Merchant Taylors' Hall, commissioned following the grant of their charter in 1662, and he also painted the royal arms for a window in Acomb church in 1663. Thereafter examples of his work can be seen in Ripon Minster (1664), Farnley Church (1665), Nun Appleton Hall (1670), University College, Oxford (1682-87), York Guildhall (1684), and churches throughout the northern counties. Other work has been lost, including a panel commissioned for his house in Leeds by the great antiquary Ralph Thoresby. Thoresby's extensive correspondence provides us with a window into provincial intellectual life at the end of the seventeenth-century, and Gyles was a key figure in York, where a group of like-minded virtuosi met at his house in Micklegate from the 1680s onwards. In addition to Thoresby, they included George Kirke, who established a museum in his house at Cookridge near Leeds. Kirke's interests included mathematics, and another friend with a scientific reputation was the York doctor and zoologist Martin Lister, who had been made an FRS in 1671. To these can be added two fellow artists, William Lodge, who had accompanied Lord Fauconberg to Venice and translated works on painting from Italian, and Francis Place, who was probably Gyles's closest friend, he called him 'brother of the brush', and who settled permanently in York in 1692, living at King's Manor. A group such as these could not have been imagined in early seventeenth-century York. At that date intellectual interests were focussed almost exclusively on the clergy and on matters of religion, but the later half of the century brought a widening of the cultural life of the city which engaged both town and country. Among Gyles's visitors there were members of the local landed gentry with antiquarian interests, such as John Lambert, son of the Cromwellian major-general, who had an estate at Calton, and Pierce Tempest of Tong Hall near Bradford, as well as a number of clergymen serving rural livings. At the end of the century the virtuosi were joined by the exiled French Huguenot, Jaques Parmentier, who painted Gyles's portrait as well as altar pieces for the principal churches in Hull and Leeds. By the end of the century York had become the cultural capital of the north, and the centre of social life for the gentry of the region, for whom London was too expensive and too distant. The King's Manor was turned into multiple occupancy now that it was no longer needed by the Crown, but part of the building was converted for use as an assembly rooms for visiting gentry attending York races, then still held on Clifton Ings, and for the public entertainments organised by the High Sheriff of the county during the assize week.

To provide the gentry and their families with the skills needed to take advantage of these social opportunities music teachers and dancing masters arrived in the city, as did wigmakers, dressmakers, and larger numbers of barbers; when the excitement got too much the revellers could seek the services of the apothecaries and physicians who were now to be found in the city in greater numbers. Fashion was all, and to keep up with the latest trends in the capital, booksellers kept in stock the latest literature, some of which came from the pens of local scholars such as Thomas Comber, precentor of the Minster, and the physician Martin Lister. Local printers and booksellers congregated around

Minster Yard and Stonegate, where visitors can still see the printer's devil adorning the shop front, publishing from there large numbers of sermons and theological works and, in 1664, an anonymous history of the city, later attributed to the lawyer Christopher Hildyard. A more substantial history had been compiled by the recorder Sir Thomas Widdrington in 1662, but the corporation would not underwrite the costs of printing it. There was no shortage of news in the later Stuart city, and events in London and elsewhere could be discussed by the better off from town and country in the great inns, such as the George in Coney Street or the Star, still to be found in Stonegate, and in the increasing numbers of coffee houses which served as centres of exchange for both goods and ideas. Goods from all over the known world could be found in the shops of the wealthier drapers and grocers, who stood at the apex of the city's shopocracy. Silks and rugs from the east, wines from France and Spain, coffee, tea and spices from the New World were all available from York shops, from where goods were also distributed to other merchants throughout the north. The concentration of craftsmen in the city also made it a centre for manufactured luxury goods, quality furnishings, mirrors, watches and clocks, silverware and jewellery were all to be found in the city, which also had a royal mint set up in 1696, two years after the Bank of England was founded, to deal with a shortage of coin. Much of the first half of the century was characterised by competition between corporation and Minster, but in the years after 1660 the presence of senior ecclesiastics, with their learned interests and their links to the landowning classes, became of increasing importance to the city's prosperity, even if political disagreements still disturbed local affairs from time to time.

By the last decades of the century York had adapted to changes in society at large. It had survived the ravages of civil war and armed conflict and had cast off its role as a centre of government administration and replaced it with that of being a provider of the goods and services for the newly leisured classes of both town and country. Walking through the streets of York in the 1680s the visitor would see shops selling goods not known in York

209

in 1600 and would pass by men and women wearing clothes unrecognisable to their grandparents, but much else would have been familiar. The shopkeepers and craftsmen still lived in their workplaces, one's senses could still be suddenly assaulted by the smell of rotting rubbish or of a tannery, and though the city had its richer and it poorer parts, within them rich and poor continued to live in close proximity. Much of the evidence for the improvement in quality of life for the better off was found behind the front door: rooms were re-appointed to provide more privacy to partners, work space and living space was more clearly demarcated, and furnishings and fittings improved standards of comfort. Visitors today who wish to get some sense of this can do worse than visit the Black Swan public house on Peasholme Green, then lived in by Henry Thompson, Lord Mayor in 1663 and 1672, who extended and refurbished the house. *[monochrome plate 11B]* The entrance passage with its doorcases and the fine staircase with its large newel posts and bulbous balusters display the solidity expected of an alderman, whilst the front room to the left of the entrance, with its panelling and moulded fireplace beneath a painted overmantel is precisely the scene in which deals could be struck and business transacted, whether filled with tobacco smoke or not. The upper room was also panelled with trompe l'oeil decorations carried out by local craftsmen.

Perhaps because the city did not suffer from fire damage, apart from those which gutted Clifford's Tower in 1684 and destroyed part of Upper Ousegate ten years later, there was no great rebuilding in York at this time, making the city look rather backward compared to the rebuilt London, and other provincial centres which followed the capital's lead. The developments which have been traced in the years following 1660 were eventually to transform the physical aspect of the city, but that was not to come until the next century and its story forms the subject of the next chapter. When Celia Fiennes visited the city in 1697 she found it disappointing; for the seat of an archbishop 'it makes but a meane appearance, the streetes are narrow and not of any length, save one which you enter of from the bridge ... the houses are very low and as indifferent as in any Country town, and the narrowness of the streetes makes it appear very mean. ...it looks better att the approach, ... the buildings look no better than the outskirts of London Wappen [Wapping].' This negative description from a southern gentlewoman should not, however, stand as the final word on the city's history in this period, for it misses the significant changes which lay beneath the surface and were invisible to the casual visitor. Perhaps we should leave the last word with another visitor, whose observations picked up an enduring feature of York's character and still have resonance today. When Thomas Fuller, the historian and royal chaplain, visited the city in about 1660 he remarked on the range of goods available and the hospitality of their providers, remarking that 'such persons, who in their eating consult both their purse and their palate, would choose this city as the staple of good cheer'.

YORK IN THE EIGHTEENTH CENTURY

Alison Sinclair

Age of Elegance and Enterprise

   With the departure of James II for France in 1688, William of Orange and Queen Mary, James' daughter, were free to accept the invitation of English protestants to accede to the English throne. The Act of Settlement of 1701 secured the protestant succession by ensuring it would be offered to the House of Hanover, after the deaths of William and Mary, and of Anne, Mary's sister, if they died without children. In 1707, the process of uniting England and Scotland under a single protestant parliament was completed by the Act of Union, and the United Kingdom of Great Britain was created.

   In accordance with the Act of Settlement, Queen Anne came to the throne in 1702 and was succeeded in 1714 by the first Hanoverian king, George I. The following year, the first attempt by the Stuart supporters to restore the throne to James II's son failed to gain support. Both George I and his son, who succeeded in 1727, spent a great deal of time in Europe, fighting what the English thought of as foreign wars, and left the management of affairs at home to government ministers. Sir Robert Walpole served both monarchs between 1721 and 1742, coming to power the year after the South Sea Bubble brought financial ruin to many investors in the South Sea Company. Walpole's policies fostered prosperity with the object of discouraging support for the Stuart cause. In 1745, with British troops absent once again in Europe, the second Jacobite uprising was launched but quickly terminated in 1746 with the Battle of Culloden. In 1757, William Pitt the Elder became Prime Minister. In the same year the Militia Act was passed putting into place arrangements for dealing with threats of a French invasion and raising the taxes necessary to implement them.

George III succeeded to the throne in 1760, taking more direct control of government than his predecessors. From this time on, agricultural and industrial improvements gathered pace, encouraged later by enforced reliance on home-grown food and raw materials. The Gordon Riots of 1780 demonstrated the continuing antipathy of the English mob towards Roman Catholics. In 1784, with the loss of the American colonies at the end of the American War of Independence, Pitt the Younger became Prime Minister. With one interruption of 3 years between 1801-04, he remained in post until his death in 1805, and through his tax raising initiatives saved the country from bankruptcy and restored its prosperity. 1789 saw the start of the French Revolution and in 1793 the British were once again at war with the French. Renewed fears of invasion and of subversive foreign influences provoked strong counter measures financed, among other means, by the introduction in 1798 of income tax. The Peace of Amiens of 1801 lead to a brief respite in war but hostilities were renewed in 1803, with fortifications installed along the south coast of England and volunteers enrolled into the army. George III remained on the throne until 1820 although his illness led to the creation of the Regency in 1811. He was succeeded by his son the Prince Regent who ruled as George IV until 1830.

Between 1689 and 1815, Britain was often at war, usually against the French and frequently in alliance with, or in opposition to, one or other European power. Earlier in the century, hostilities were conducted largely on the continent, and often to safeguard the protestant succession against the threat of a Stuart restoration supported by the Catholic French. By the 1750s, warfare extended across the world, wherever either combatant had colonial or trade interests. Later in the century, wars were fought as much to protect

213

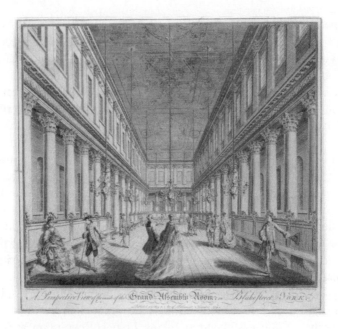

Grand Assembly Room

A Perspective View of York Castle

these interests as for any other reason. The end came only after Nelson defeated the French fleet at the Battle of Trafalgar, and Wellington met Napoleon at Waterloo. The victories of 1805 and 1815 finally brought to an end a century of conflict between two world powers competing for imperial dominance and influence, in the course of which the British navy had grown in size and efficiency greatly enhancing the country's status as a major sea power.

Dependence on trade for its wealth creating potential not only required the defence of trade routes but also the expansion of overseas territories and interests. Although Britain lost the American colonies in 1784, during the course of the century she gained territories in all parts of the globe, either by conquest or by treaty, culminating in Captain James Cook's claim to Australia in 1771. Such lands were annexed or taken under British administration so providing new opportunities for colonial influence and development. Trade in luxury goods like tea, coffee, sugar, chocolate, silk, spices and much else was carried on with China, India, and the Caribbean islands, and the slave trade with lands on the coast of West Africa.

At home, in the latter part of the century, agricultural and industrial developments leading to parallel technological revolutions gathered momentum. Progress was assisted by improvements in transport and by the movement for the enclosure of agricultural land. Britain's wealth depended upon extensive foreign trade but it was new developments in agriculture and industry which made possible the adequate supply of provisions to a growing population and munitions for the armed forces in support of it.

The Changing Role of the City

By the beginning of the eighteenth century York no longer occupied the position of national prominence it had enjoyed until the Civil War. With the abolition of The King's Council in the North in 1641, the City lost its role as the seat of government in the North of England and the occasional residence of the Court. With this loss went some of the advantages to the City associated with the rich and powerful in the way of influential employment and opportunities for advancement and business. The loss was recognised by the Corporation who petitioned for the Council's re-establishment, without success.

Nevertheless the institutions which had supported the City from earliest times remained in place. It was still the seat of the Archbishop, Primate of the North, and his apparatus of ecclesiastical government. If it had lost its status as an alternative political capital, it remained the county town of Yorkshire providing the machinery of national government administered through the county. Despite the lack of a standing army for most of the century, the tradition of a military presence survived long enough for the Cavalry Barracks to be built. And finally the well-established custom of the northern aristocracy to assemble in the City for business and pleasure continued, to the benefit of the citizenry as a whole.

It was on the foundation of this continuing framework that the role of the City changed.

Religious Affairs

The City continued to benefit from the presence of the Archbishop and the administration of the Anglican Church in the north. Congregations were generally small and during most of the century, only the east end of the Minster was in regular use for services as the nave and transepts had been stripped of their fittings. Matins and Evensong were said or sung in the choir daily and sermons given on Sundays and holy days, the old pulpit having been brought back into use so that preaching might be more easily heard. Communion was celebrated weekly until 1825 when it was changed to monthly because attendance had become so poor that sometimes there were no communicants. In the south transept three former chapels on the east side had been combined to provide a space in which morning prayers were said and the Ecclesiastical Courts held. Cathedral clergy was generally Whig in sympathy, and some like Thomas Herring politically active. Archbishop

216

Herring was responsible for rousing the County to the dangers of a Jacobite invasion in 1745.

Throughout the century there were 23 or 24 parish churches in use, most of which had a resident incumbent and most of which held services every Sunday. Livings in York parishes were poor which at least made for continuity since clergy seeking advancement were not generally attracted to them. Five held daily services and in five others, prayers were said two or three times a week. Communion was less frequent, some only celebrating four or five times a year, and several only once a month. Even so, the clergy at St Denys, Walmgate, complained that parishioners were careless of attending communion.

Catholicism had never entirely died out in York during the previous century. In 1686, the Bar Convent was founded and the following year an attempt was made to open a seminary in the King's Manor. The seminary was quickly closed down but the Convent remained, harassed from time to time, their chapel used by Catholics from all over the City. In 1743, a year after the Yorkshire Mission was founded, there were some 70 Catholic families in the City. By 1764, the number had increased to about 82, by which time Mass was being said at the Mission chapel in Little Blake Street, opened in 1760, as well as in a meeting house in the parish of Holy Trinity, Micklegate. From this time, the chapel in Little Blake Street remained the main place of Catholic worship until 1802 when a new chapel was built on the opposite side of the street, on the site of the present St Wilfrid's church. This was large enough to accommodate 700 people and had a presbytery attached. From this date onwards, numbers began to increase.

In the middle of the century, about the same number of Nonconformists as Roman Catholics were recorded, divided between Quakers, Presbyterians and Methodists.

Numbers of Quakers had increased at the beginning of the century and in 1718 a larger meeting house was built in Far Water Lane (Friargate), again rebuilt and enlarged in 1816. A description of this building was published in a volume of designs for new meeting houses produced by the Quaker bookseller and publisher

William Alexander at his premises in Castlegate. As Nonconformists, Quakers were denied membership of the Guilds and instead turned their energies to business in which they were notably successful. Presbyterians included Unitarians, who built a chapel on the Greek Cross plan in St Saviourgate in 1693; Rev. Charles Wellbeloved was Minister from 1792-1858 and from 1803 Principal of the nonconformist Manchester Academy in Monkgate. There was a congregation of the Countess of Huntingdon's Connexion from about 1750, with a chapel in College Street, described as severely plain and presenting the appearance of a warehouse. Methodism was brought to York about 1744 and John Wesley preached numerous times in the second half of the century, often in a room in the building on the corner of Patrick Pool and Newgate Market. He refused an invitation to preach in the Minster, though Charles Wesley did, in 1756. During the century, the number of Methodists remained quite small and only increased in the early years of the next century.

Administrative Role

The City continued to be the seat of County administration and various crown tax collecting offices were based at the Castle. Stamp Duty collectors for York and the West Riding were there, the Collector of Excise Duties for York and the East Riding, and the issuer of hawkers' and pedlars' licences.

The Castle continued to be the site of County justice under the jurisdiction of the County Sheriff, and both the County court and County gaol were located in Castle Yard (see illustration p.214). At the beginning of the century, justice was administered from the Sessions House of 1675 and Grand Jury House of 1668. The County Gaol was rebuilt between 1701-5 on innovative new lines, its design often attributed to the architect William Wakefield but never convincingly substantiated. Built for the incarceration of felons and debtors, it became known as the Debtors' Prison though the notorious highwayman Dick Turpin was imprisoned there before his execution in 1739. During both Stuart uprisings of 1715 and 1745, rebel prisoners were held in the gaol before trial or relocation elsewhere.

The old fashioned Grand Jury House was replaced between 1773-77 by John Carr's beautiful Assize Courthouse, followed shortly afterwards by the rebuilding of the Sessions House as the Female Prison, by Thomas Wilkinson and John Prince. As the mirror image of the Assize Courts it was clearly designed to be seen in conjunction with the two existing buildings and to form a grand architectural setpiece. The space around which it was set was laid out with a circular lawn to become known as the 'Eye of the Ridings'. This composition survived the passage of the 1824 Gaol Act which led to the construction of a new prison in Castle Yard, in the course of which the old Debtors' Prison was converted into accommodation for the prison warders.

It was because of its County status that Archbishop Thomas Herring used the Castle Yard as the meeting place in which to rouse the County nobility, gentry and clergy to action against the second Jacobite uprising in 1745. The old castle bailey had long been used for proclamations of the accession of monarchs, for announcements of war or peace, and elections of County Members of Parliament.

When he returned from his Grand Tour, the Marquis of Rockingham embarked upon a political career which was to take him to the leadership of the Whig party and to the office of Prime Minister twice, in 1765-6 and 1782. As a leading member of the local aristocracy with an estate in Malton, York as the centre of County society was the obvious place from which to promote his cause. He was supported in this by the Rockingham Club formed in 1753 by more than a hundred influential York citizens and gentry. They were to be instrumental in ensuring the election of Rockingham supporters to Parliament as Members for the City and the County throughout Rockingham's political career.

From 1779, the Yorkshire Association for Parliamentary Reform began campaigning across the county from York. An organisation with Whig sympathies, it was set up to enlist independent political opinion outside the influence of the aristocracy and gentry and was something of a challenge to the Rockingham Whigs. In 1784, William Wilberforce was elected MP for Hull and often addressed electors in Castle Yard on the abolition of slavery. The Yard continued to perform its political role, little changed, until 1831.

Military Matters

With the accession of William of Orange, the Governor of York was withdrawn, and Sir John Reresby handed over the keys of the City to the Lord Mayor. In November 1688, Lord Danby secured the City for the new King by seizing the City gates and the Castle. The day after, an anti-Catholic riot took place in St Saviourgate during which several houses were ransacked and a chapel in Mint Yard was destroyed. By the turn of the century, the garrison had been withdrawn.

The 1715 Jacobite invasion had little impact on the City although a number of prominent rebels were imprisoned in York Castle, several of whom escaped. A certain amount of alarm was generated amongst Whig wives whose husbands had gone to London, and Lady Mary Wortley Montagu wrote that she was going to join the ladies at Castle Howard rather than remain alone at Middlethorpe so close to the Archbishop's Palace. In 1745, the City took more serious measures to counter possible invasion by supporters of Charles Edward Stuart, the Young Pretender. In September, Archbishop Thomas Herring preached a sermon in the Minster against the rebels, following this up with a public meeting in Castle Yard for the nobility, gentry and clergy of the three Ridings. As a result, a regiment of volunteers was raised from the County at large, known as the Yorkshire Association. At the same time, the City Council started a fund with which the ancient walls were to be surveyed and repaired, and four volunteer companies recruited, each of 69 officers and men, dubbed the Blues. A second regiment was raised in the City, from gentlemen and prominent citizens, who called themselves the Independents. In the event, neither City regiment saw action and the Blues were disbanded in January 1746. The Independents lasted until July, and mounted guard on prisoners in the Castle and provided escorts for prisoners being transferred elsewhere. One other regiment was raised amongst local gentry, the Royal Regiment of Hunters, formed by a group of fox-hunting squires. This was the only one to see action when they engaged in a skirmish with the retreating rebel rearguard near Penrith.

The Duke of Cumberland passed through York following Culloden in 1746, to receive the Freedom of the City according to custom. This was presented to him in the traditional gold box during a private visit to Archbishop Herring, when he was entertained to dinner at the house of the Precentor, Dr Jaques Sterne. A last use for the City's defences was for the display of the heads of two of the 1745 rebels which were spiked on Micklegate Bar until being removed illegally on a night in January 1754.

During the crisis various regiments of the regular army passed through York from time to time, and for a brief period in 1756 a regiment of Foot was quartered in the City. It is likely military quarters had been re-established in 1720, the normal practice being for men to be billeted in inns around the City. A regiment of Dragoons was rewarded by the City in 1772 for helping to fight a fire but it was not until 1796 that cavalry barracks were constructed as part of William Pitt the Younger's national barrack-building programme.

In 1779, the 95th was recruited in York by Major Francis Peirson whose family lived in the City, and sent to Jersey to help defend the Channel Islands against invasion by the French. They took part in the Battle of Jersey in 1781 when Major Peirson was killed. The regiment stayed in Jersey until the end of the war in 1783 when it returned to York and disbanded. Two years before the recruitment of the 95th, a press gang had arrived in York and set up for business on King's Staith.

Defence at home was the responsibility of the militia, locally raised regiments, chosen by lot and with local gentry as officers, amongst whose duties were the pursuit of smugglers and the repression of riots. In 1757 under the Militia Act, they were put on a more regular footing, required to train regularly and to be mobilised and paid as regular soldiers when an emergency arose. The introduction of a Militia Tax to finance the new arrangement was met with widespread resistance and riots in which William

First Water Lane, 1813

Todd's Book and Print Warehouse, 1797

Bowes' house in Bootham was 'stripped and gutted in the most shocking manner'. The West Riding Militia included men from York and the Ainsty and was sent to the Lancashire Cotton Towns and to the Gordon Riots. From 1793, when a French invasion was a constant threat, the West York Militia Corps was mobilised until 1816 when they were disbanded in York.

By the end of the century, the City's importance as a garrison town had to a large extent been restored.

City Government and Politics

Throughout the century, the City returned two Members to Parliament, more often than not Whigs, though on occasions one each of both the Whig and Tory party was elected. While the Rockingham Club existed both were generally Rockingham supporters, even close associates, like Charles Turner of Kirkleatham and Lord John Cavendish, Chancellor of the Exchequer in Rockingham's second administration in 1782.

The City's affairs continued to be administered in the old way, by the Lord Mayor and Corporation consisting of 12 Aldermen and Councillors. The status of the Lord Mayor was such that not infrequently the office was filled by the sitting Member of Parliament as in the cases of Sir William Robinson of Baldersby, MP from 1697-1722, Lord Mayor in 1700, and George Fox, MP from 1742-61, Lord Mayor in 1757. Other Lord Mayors came from a wide range of backgrounds like Alderman William Cornwell, tanner and brewer and Lord Mayor in 1712; John Carr, the noted architect, Lord Mayor in 1770 and again in 1785; and James Woodhouse, a comb-maker, Lord Mayor in 1785. The Corporation maintained their tight grip on the City's trade through the Guilds and the Freeman system, failing to recognise the detrimental effect such controls had on the economy. Contemporary commentators remarked on the difficulty of becoming a Freeman and the disincentive this was to "persons of enterprising genius".

In 1724, the Corporation decided it needed a special building in which the Lord Mayor could perform his duties in the manner considered appropriate to the City's dignity. One of his most important duties was the entertainment of prominent visitors to the City and of the citizens, for whom he was expected to set aside at first one, and later two, public dining- days a week. Having failed to buy Sir William Robinson's new Red House from him in 1724, a decision was taken to build the City House on the site of the gatehouse to the Guildhall to serve this purpose and to act as well as a repository for the City's records. Work began on the Mansion House in 1725, and sufficient progress had been made for Samuel Clarke's Lady Mayoress to hold the first great public dining-day in 1726. The first resident Lord Mayor was John Stainforth, a vintner, in 1730, though decoration of the magnificent State Room [colour plate 11] was not completed until 1733.

The architect of the Mansion House has never been discovered with any certainty, but it is a most important building in the history of the City. It is a building which encapsulates many of the characteristics which distinguished life in Georgian York. It was at the height of fashion, built in the new Palladian style advocated by Lord Burlington, arbiter of York taste. It was designed principally for a social purpose and its interior is planned according to Palladian principles well suited for that purpose. An elegant formal route leads from the entrance, through a pilastered arch to the grand staircase and upwards to the ceremonial splendour of the State Room. Here the decoration is carried out in the richest of the classical orders designed to impress visitors and display civic wealth and pride. It typifies arrangements which became the norm in many of the City's finest Georgian townhouses.

The Mansion House in York was the first civic residence to be built in England. Its continued use as the residence of the Lord Mayor during his or her year of office makes it an important legacy of its time.

Contemporary Comment

When Celia Fiennes visited York in 1697 she was not impressed and considered it to be "of mean appearance" with

224

narrow streets and "low and indifferent" houses. She did concede however that "it looks better at the approach because you see the towers of the gates and several churches encompassing the Minster". When Daniel Defoe came in the 1720s he agreed with her that from the approach the City was "pleasant and beautiful" and observed that York was full of "gentry and persons of distinction ... who have houses proportioned to their quality". The presence of the persons of distinction was because of the company as well as the cheap living and he concluded that "here is no trade ... except such as depends upon the confluence of the gentry."

Defoe's conclusion was shared by the City's eighteenth century historian Francis Drake, Surgeon to the City until he lost his post in 1745 because of his political sympathies. In 1736 he had written his great work, *Eboracum: or the History and Antiquities of the City of York*, because, he said, he was more interested in history and antiquities than medicine. Of the city he says: "What has been, and is, the chief support of the city, at present, is the resort to and residence of several country gentlemen with their families in it". Like Defoe he recognised that the nobility and gentry came to York to enjoy themselves and that their presence provided the opportunity for employment and prosperity for a large proportion of the remaining population.

One other publication attests to the City's social importance at this time, reflecting the same response as Defoe's to the impressiveness of the houses of the persons of quality. About the same time Defoe came to York, a surveyor named John Cossins produced a 'New and Exact Plan of the City of York' which included in its borders illustrations of fashionable town houses newly built by some of the prominent subscribers to his map. The map was revised and reprinted in 1748 when three more important buildings were added to the selection *[monochrome plate 12]*. Subscribers to his map in 1726 included persons like the Duke of Rutland, the Earl of Carlisle, and Lord Irwin of the nobility, Sir John Lister Kaye and Matthew St Quintin of the gentry, The Lord Mayor of York, Samuel Clarke, and of City worthies, Richard Manklin, Stationer and Bookbinder, Francis Hildyard, bookseller of Stonegate, and William Dobson, Apothecary and former Sheriff of

York. The map was dedicated to the City's MPs Sir William Milner and Edward Thompson.

Many of the subscribers to John Cossins' map were subscribers to Drake's *Eboracum* and to the Assembly Rooms, the building which perhaps more than any other symbolises the evolution of York into the social capital of the north. It was through their activities that this came about.

Nobility and Gentry

Both Defoe and Drake comment on the assemblies held in York on Mondays from early in the century at the King's Manor and in Lord Irwin's mansion. The man to whom Drake dedicated *Eboracum* was one of the most influential people in making the assembly the height of York fashionable society.

This man was Richard Boyle, 3rd Earl of Burlington, of Londesborough Hall near Bridlington *[colour plate 12]* whose architectural reputation was already established when he received an invitation from a group of Yorkshire aristocracy and gentry to design for them a building in which they could meet and enjoy company. The brief was for a large room for dancing, a smaller one for cards and gaming, somewhere for refreshments and a place in which to make tea. Burlington's response was to reproduce an Egyptian Hall, a building of Roman antiquity known from sixteenth century engravings by the Italian architect Palladio who described it as suitable for festivals and entertainments. This extraordinary notion resulted in the Assembly Rooms which were to become the model for similar formal reception rooms in English country houses for the rest of the century. The Duchess of Marlborough nonetheless dismissed them as exceeding "all the nonsense and madness" she had ever seen, complaining that she could not easily manoeuvre her hooped skirts between the columns (see illustration p.214)!

The second member of the aristocracy influential in promoting the social importance of York was the Marquis of Rockingham. Rockingham's political career began amongst his fashionable peers in York when he took a leading part in plans to erect a viewing stand at the race course in the early 1750s. Racing had been conducted since 1731 on the Knavesmire, to which it had been removed because of flooding on Clifton Ings. A design by the up and coming architect John Carr was chosen for the proposed 'standhouse', completed in 1755. Many of those subscribing to the viewing stand, including Sir George Savile and Sir Rowland Wynne, were to become Rockingham's most loyal political supporters.

Burlington's Assembly Rooms were first used during Race Week in August, 1732, the meeting which survives today as Ebor Week. Drake tells us it was the Assizes which had first brought the northern nobility and gentry to York in order "to partake of the diversions that were usually set up in the city for that time". Attending the assizes was undoubtedly a form of entertainment, especially if, for example, the trial of Dick Turpin was taking place, as it did in 1739. Until 1773, the public had only the old-fashioned Grand Jury House and Court of Justice (see illustration p.214) in which to follow high profile trials. In that year, the new Assize Courts were built, now the Crown Court, to designs by John Carr. Their interiors are truly theatrical with public galleries high above the well of the court where the drama of the trial unfolds.

A more conventional form of theatre had been available since 1734 when stage performances had been given in the old tennis court at Lord Irwin's mansion. Premises on the present site were occupied in 1744 and enlarged in 1764; parts survive in the house in Duncombe Place which originally gave access to the theatre. In 1766, the management was taken over by Tate Wilkinson who applied for the Royal Patent in 1769, and under whose direction it enjoyed great success. Actors like Mrs Siddons and John Philip Kemble appeared regularly, and performances such as Canon Mason's dramatic poems *Caractacus* and *Elfrida*, set to music by Thomas Arne, were given. As well as the Theatre Royal, there was in the middle of the century a dramatic company at the Cock Pit outside Bootham Bar, managed by Mr Keregan, where amongst other things the *Beggar's Opera* was performed.

Celia Fiennes had remarked in 1697 that "people of fashion" used the Minster to walk in and it was a pity they didn't keep it cleaner! Lord Harley visiting in 1725 offered the explanation that "the gentlemen and ladies walk after the evening service in the summertime, for want of a convenience of a park or gardens". By that time in fact, Lord Mayors Walk, previously Goose Lane, had already been improved as a promenade by the planting of new elm trees in 1718. Matters were to be improved again in 1730 by two further developments. Firstly, a new floor was laid in the Minster to a design by Lord Burlington consisting of a Greek key motif in blue marble set into white stone. Secondly, the first stretch of the New Walk was laid out from Tower Place to Blue Bridge, to be extended three years later almost as far as the village of Fulford. It was the custom also for the gentry to promenade in Castle Yard, maybe calling on an over-extended friend taking the air at the same time in the prisoners' exercise yard at the front of the Debtors Prison (see illustration p.214).

Fashionable society met in private as well as in public and many of the families who enjoyed the season in York occupied newly built or refurbished town houses during their stay. There are many fine examples of these houses, beautifully fitted out and designed to impress, with grand staircases and panelled reception rooms on the first floor. One of the earliest, opposite the Judges Lodgings and built about 1714, was occupied by Sir William Wentworth in the 1730s. In the 1760s, Fairfax House in Castlegate was refurbished by John Carr for Viscount Fairfax, who gave a ball for 200 people in 1763 for his daughter whose future he was anxious to secure. Sir John Bourchier of Beningbrough Hall also had a daughter, and his town residence, Micklegate House, was rebuilt about 1750 on a site already belonging to the family. Paintings of their dogs, Rover and Dick, executed by the glass painter William Peckitt, are still in place in the window of the former Library.

Those living in York or coming for the season because of the company comprised the cream of northern society, including the Duke of Rutland and Lord Carlisle, Lord Irwin, the St Quintins of Scampston and Lord Burlington himself. These were the persons of distinction from whom the City's reputation as the social capital of the north was derived.

Merchants, Ministers and Professional Men

Building a grand residence was not an activity restricted to members of the aristocracy and landed gentry, and indeed the house in Lendal occupied by Sir William Wentworth had been built as one of a pair about 1714 by Alderman Henry Baines, who lived next door himself.

Alderman Baines was a 'toyman' or maker of trifles and trinkets, and Lord Mayor in 1717. A little earlier, about 1710, Alderman William Cornwell, tanner and brewer, and Lord Mayor in 1712 and 1725, built himself a splendid new house, with cellars below and conveniently located on Kings Staith to handle his raw materials. Known now as Cumberland House, it is supposed to have been occupied briefly by the Duke of Cumberland in 1746. Others in this category include those wealthy individuals who initiated York's banks in the second half of the century. These were men like Francis Willoughby of the Middleton family of Birdsall, a partner in the Willoughby, Raper, Clough and Swann bank founded in 1771; and the Ewbank family, chemists, who occupied a site in Castlegate from the 1730s to the 1790s. In 1766 George Ewbank built a handsome new house, marking the occasion by stamping his initials and the date on the rainwater head, and eventually expanded into the adjoining property for use as a warehouse. In 1771, he was a partner in a bank which opened at the corner of the newly built New Street. Messrs Oldfield, Wilson, Smith, Hartley and Tweedy opened for business in 1792, in Thomas Wilson's grandly pilastered house at 14 High Ousegate, from where he also sold books. Some of the founding partners of these banks were receivers of official funds needing somewhere to deposit them before remitting them to central government. The Clough of the Willoughby bank was Collector of Stamp Duties for York and the West Riding, as well as being Registrar of the Deanery and Dean and Chapter's Court, and Proctor of the Ecclesiastical Court. Others like Joshua Oldfield, the York Postmaster, held an official position but also derived their wealth from successful trading activities. His family had been established as wine merchants in the vaults behind today's Post Office from the middle of the seventeenth century.

Daniel Defoe had been impressed by the houses of the Minster clergy which he described as very good, or little palaces. He may have been thinking of the house occupied by Canon William Mason after he became Precentor in 1756 but built in the early years of the century. William Mason was very much part of fashionable society, moving in the highest social and political circles, supporter of Lord Rockingham, friend of Lord John Cavendish, and correspondent of Horace Walpole. A man of many parts he was a highly regarded poet and biographer of his friend Thomas Gray. His predecessor as Precentor was Jaques Sterne who lived in part of the old Treasurer's House and improved his residence to such an extent it was considered fit for the entertainment of the Duke of Cumberland when he collected the Freedom of the City after Culloden. Jaques Sterne was the uncle of Laurence Sterne, author of *Tristram Shandy*, the first two volumes of which were published in York, in 1759.

Like his uncle Laurence Sterne was a clergyman, but well acquainted with York society. The character of Dr Slop in *Tristram Shandy* was based upon that of Dr John Burton, Chief Physician to the County Hospital and eminent obstetrician, who lived in The Red House after 1740. Dr Burton was a staunch Jacobite but fell foul of the City authorities when he inadvisedly left York during the advance of Charles Edward Stuart in 1745 and met up with him in Lancaster. Despite Burton's claim that he was inspecting properties he owned in the area, he was questioned by Archbishop Herring and subsequently imprisoned in York Castle. This was due in no small part to the actions of Precentor Jaques Sterne, a Magistrate and fanatical Whig, and the avowed enemy of Burton. Francis Drake himself was another medical man penalised for his political sympathies. Like Burton, he was a Jacobite supporter and lost his post as City Surgeon for his views. Unlike Burton who was the tenant of a fine house, Francis Drake lodged in Coney Street, with Caesar Ward, the newspaper publisher. Dr Clifton Wintringham, on the other hand, had built himself an impressive residence soon after his arrival in York around 1711, which was included in the border of Cossins' map *[monochrome plate 12]*. Now the Judges' Lodgings, following its acquisition for that purpose in 1806, it is as richly finished inside as any built by his social superiors.

Lawyers were well represented, including Thomas Place, Recorder of York during the 1745 troubles and subscriber to the Assembly. His successor was Peter Johnson, appointed in 1759, who built for himself, between 1760-62, one of the best houses designed by John Carr (see illustration p.241). William Bowes whose house in Bootham was damaged by anti-Militia riots in 1757 was an attorney. Another Proctor of the Ecclesiastical Court, and predecessor to Mr Banker Clough, was John Shaw who occupied another fine house close to Minster Yard erected about 1725 on part of the site of the old Talbot Inn. Considerably extended later when it became York College for Girls, it was occupied from the latter part of the century by a succession of physicians.

Associating with these men for business and pleasure were the master artists and craftsmen. William Wakefield was described in Cossins' list of subscribers as 'gentleman architect' and was a subscriber to the Assembly. William Etty, noted by Cossins as Joiner and Carpenter, worked at Castle Howard and may have been the architect of the Mansion House: he was City Husband in 1709 and Chamberlain in 1716. John Carr, a founder member of the Society of Architects, subscribed to his own 'standhouse' on the Knavesmire, and was a member of the Rockingham Club. And John Fisher, carver and sculptor, worked closely with Carr and like him was a member of the Rockingham Club.

There is a monument in the Minster which combines the endeavours of several of these men. The physician Dr John Dealtry took up residence in Dr Wintringham's house after his death in 1748, and died himself in 1773. The exquisite figure of Hygeia forming his monument in the Minster *[monochrome plate 13]* was carved by John Fisher and includes an inscription extolling the doctor's skill and humanity composed by the poet and cleric, William Mason.

Butchers, Bakers and Comb-makers

Both Defoe and Drake commented upon the abundance and variety of provisions in the York markets, and on their cheapness and value for money. Drake offered this as a reason for the continuing popularity of the City as a place of resort. Set as it was in a fertile hinterland, a port on a still navigable river it remained a regional warehouse for all kinds of luxury goods until the railways made communication with the capital a viable alternative. Merchants like the Quaker Tuke family flourished as grocers and importers of tea, coffee and chocolate in premises on the corner of Castlegate and High Ousegate from 1733. They held the only licence in the north of England for processing coffee beans and distributed roasted coffee, tea and chocolate across the north. This was the business which was to form the basis of the Rowntree Cocoa Works more than a century later. In 1767, a confectionary and grocery business was started which, after a move in 1824 to St Helen's Square, was to become Terry's of York.

Drake tells us that apart from a "few wine merchants, the export of butter and some trifles not worth mentioning, there is no other trade carried on in the city of York" in his time. Wine was imported in increasing quantities to supply the needs of fashionable society by merchants like the Oldfields and new-built town houses generally included a wine cellar. The wholesale export of butter grew into a major trade, conducted from a Butter Stand in the churchyard of St Martin's church in Micklegate, for which the Corporation obtained an Act of Parliament in 1722 to bring it under closer control. Its long-standing importance was recognised in the Preamble which noted that butter was "one of the chief commodities of the product of the county of York ... and great quantities thereof are brought into the city of York, from thence to be transported beyond the seas." That it was a lucrative trade is evidenced by the founding partners of two York banks, both members of the Swann family of butter factors. The trifles to which Drake refers were supplied by merchants like Alderman Baines of Lendal, whose business produced 'toys', or frivolous trinkets and trifles, appealing only to those who could afford

232

objects of limited practical use. James Doughty of the Fish and Fly in Minster Gates made snuff boxes and backgammon pieces from ivory and bone, and James Northrop had a shop in Feasegate from which he sold tea boards and combs. Combs were manufactured from horn, ivory and tortoiseshell and when fashion dictated more elaborate hair styles towards the end of the century, demand rose dramatically. The number of people employed increased and production grew to such an extent that combs were exported from York to London and other centres of fashion. About 1800, S and J Nutt took over premises in Trinity Lane previously used for soap-boiling and made combs there until after 1851.

Other services available to the fashionable included dancing classes offered by Edward Allen at the Sycamore Tree in Minster Yard and musical instruments made by Thomas Haxby who had his workshop in Blake Street conveniently close to the Assembly Rooms. Shopping developed into a fashionable pastime by the end of the century and warehouses like Thomas Brooks' in Low Petergate supplied dressmaking requirements. Book-selling and printing maintained their historic importance, especially around Stonegate, including Todd's Warehouse (see illustration p.222) and John Wolstenholme's stationers' shop which also sold prints. His splendid shop sign (repainted) still advertises his business at the corner of Petergate and Minster Gates. Many booksellers were also publishers and it was John Hinxman at the 'Sign of the Bible' who published the first two volumes of Laurence Sterne's *Life and Opinions of Tristram Shandy* in 1759.

Tristram Shandy was printed at Caesar Ward's printing house in Coney Street. During the course of the century, thirteen printers were in operation, including Thomas Gent in Low Petergate and John Jackson whose business came eventually to the Sessions family. Printing houses often doubled as newspaper printers like Caesar Ward who published the *York Courant*, established in 1725 by John White, son of Grace White, the founder of the *York Mercury* in 1719. The *York Journal* was started in 1740 to provide Whig competition to the Tory *Courant* but survived only until 1753. In 1790 the *York Herald and County Advertiser* was produced from Thomas Wilson's premises at

14 High Ousegate.

Newspapers were available at coffee houses, many of which were conveniently located around Stonegate. Coffee houses arrived in York in 1669 and in his diary written between 1688 and 1690, John Webster, a young lawyer, mentions three in which he regularly met friends and associates. Sunton's in Coney Street was frequented by Laurence Sterne and musical citizens and when Dr Burton was arrested in 1745 for consorting with Charles Edward Stuart, the Recorder of York went round the coffee houses until he could find enough gentlemen to hear Dr Burton's case. Alcohol and food as well as coffee were served in coffee houses so it is not surprising that in the early 1800s many were converted to public houses, like Brigg's Coffee House on the corner of Stonegate and Coffee Yard. Inn-keeping was an essential occupation, becoming more so as transport improvements during the course of the century increased people's mobility and their need for temporary lodgings. It was in 1733 that the famous sign for the Star in Stonegate was first erected across the street.

Meanwhile, the old trades continued in the traditional way. In 1784, there were 16 common brewhouses, reduced through amalgamation and acquisition to 8 by 1825. One of the earliest breweries was Hothams, established in George Street in 1716, now part of the Bass group. Freeman butchers sold their wares from their own shops in The Shambles and country butchers brought their meat to Thursday Market. Both Thursday Market and Pavement Market were general markets and from 1705, Thursday Market had a cross with a clock from which dairy produce was sold. A herb market was set up in High Ousegate in 1729, with vegetables included from 1735, the whole moved to Pavement after 1782. Grain and cereals were sold from Pavement market and corn ground at any number of windmills around the city. Castle Mills was the only water-powered corn mill until it was converted to steam in 1787 by the Tukes. Bread was baked either at home or taken to a baker's shop, from where it could be purchased if preferred. Traditional food guilds provided three services; cooking for general sale, catering for private customers, or cooking customers' own dishes. Often they doubled as pastrycooks to whom homemade pies could be taken for baking and in 1830 Joseph Terry was in business as both baker and pastrycook as well as confectioner and importer of luxury foodstuffs.

A large number of Freemen in 1784 was engaged in the manufacture of clothing and shoes. There were 46 cobblers, 3 glove and 4 stocking workshops, and silk and lace-making manufactories. Tanning was carried on widely, generally on riverside sites outside the City walls. Thomas Griffiths, the York Castle gaoler in 1745, was a tanner by trade and operated 72 soaking pits and a horse mill at his tannery at the bottom of Marygate. By-products of the process included soap- and candle-making, glue and horn-breaking.

All these activities were labour-intensive and provided employment for nearly half the working population of the city. Throughout the century there continued to be no major industrial enterprise although shipbuilding enjoyed a small resurgence from 1770, when a fleet of brigantines was needed for the butter trade. A glassworks was established in Fishergate in 1797, and in the early years of the next century, a steam-powered flax mill in Lawrence Street. But it was upon the enterprise of the small businessman that much of the prosperity of the City depended and enabled the support and supply of fashionable society.

Widows, Spinsters and Orphans

At the end of the seventeenth century the population of the City was about 12,000. By the beginning of the nineteenth century, it had risen to around 17,000. If one third of the population of the City formed the wealthiest level of society, and a half was engaged in supplying goods and services to them, there remained a sizeable minority which existed in poverty.

Throughout the century the Corporation continued to initiate and support attempts to provide poor relief either in the form of work or by the supply of basic essentials like clothing, coal and candles. Some were paid a subsistence allowance and during the 1720s about 500 people were granted relief from taxes each year. Later in the century, one half of the fines collected for offences against the butter regulations was paid by law to the poor of the parish in which the offence was committed. In 1784 after a big freeze followed by floods had interrupted the supply of essential goods to the City, a fund was set up to provide coal and bread to the poor.

Manufactories were set up in residential schools supported by private charities and in parish organised workhouse schemes. The residential schools were the Bluecoat School in St Anthony's Hall for 40 poor boys, and the Greycoat School in Marygate for 20 poor girls. A disused cotton manufactory was taken over by 18 parishes in 1768, for use as a Union workhouse for 150 paupers, some of whom were employed making woollen goods from worsted yarn spun by children and persons unfit for hard labour. About the same time, the Corporation initiated a scheme to train boys and girls in spinning and weaving, successful enough to be adopted by each ward in the City and maintained for several years. By the end of the century, spinning and weaving were replaced by knitting and sewing.

A number of almshouses were founded through charitable bequests often recognised in an inscription on a datestone. In 1700, Dame Sarah Hewley left an endowment for the foundation of a hospital for the poor in Tanner Row, which moved in 1840 to its present position in St Saviourgate. When she died in 1726, Mary Wandesford left a bequest "for the use of 10 poor gentlewomen who were never married" with which Wandesford House was built in Bootham and dated on the rainwater head 1739. Beside Fossbridge is another almshouse, built by Dorothy Wilson's Charity in 1765 in accordance with a legacy of land for the maintenance of 10 women, combined, oddly, with a school for 20 boys, both groups to benefit from the twice daily reading of prayers by the schoolmaster. There was another in Walmgate, Winterscale's Hospital, founded in the early part of the century, now demolished.

Meanwhile those who failed to qualify for these provisions congregated in old and decrepit buildings around Walmgate, Gillygate, Monkgate and the Water Lanes (see illustration p.222). The wealthier parishes were in the city centre and Micklegate.

236

Buildings

Evolving activities and occupations had their effect on the appearance of the city.

Buildings changed by adaptation, conversion or extension. Four great medieval buildings, the King's Manor, Treasurer's House, St Williams College and Lord Irwin's mansion were sold off, sub-divided and let out to a variety of tenants. Lord Irwin's mansion, begun by his ancestor Sir Arthur Ingram in 1616 and incorporating remains of the original Archbishops' Palace, stood on the site of the present Purey Cust hospital and was demolished between 1814-21.

Minor medieval houses underwent a similar process of change. The Garrick Head Coffee House in Petergate was converted from a fifteenth century house, doubled in size by an extension at the back and given a new staircase and sash windows. John Todd's bookshop (see illustration p.222) was enlarged by extending into, and roofing over, the backyard, a less costly and much quicker expedient. At the turn of the century, John Wolstenholme's shop at the corner of Minster Gates was modernised by cutting back its medieval jetties, refronting and installing newly developed shop windows to increase the visibility of goods for sale inside.

New Types of Building

Buildings changed through the need for modification to accommodate established activities requiring improved facilities. Almshouses fall within this category, although the inclusion of a school in Dorothy Wilson's was not an orthodox arrangement. Schools usually were housed in old buildings, like Mr Lumley's Boarding School for Young Ladies at The King's Manor, or in buildings intended for another purpose like Robert Sowerby's in the upper room of the Pavement Market Cross. St Peter's School at this time was housed in the derelict St Andrew's Church. Occasionally accommodation was purpose built as with the Greycoat School in Marygate, the enlarged facilities provided at the Bar Convent in the 1780s and 90s or the schoolmaster's house and schoolroom added to Dorothy Wilson's in 1805. Such buildings were domestic in character and purpose-designed accommodation had to await the establishment of a National School at The King's Manor in 1812.

The first infirmary for the poor came with the founding of the York County Hospital in 1740, the only purpose-built hospital in the north of England and illustrated on the second edition of Cossins' map. John Carr designed the York Lunatic Asylum for 54 patients in 1777, when it was one of only four in the country. By the 1790s, its reputation for inhumane treatment of patients was so bad that The Retreat was opened by the Society of Friends as a model establishment for the care of the insane.

Architectural Style

The accession of a Dutch monarch to the throne in 1690 brought new architectural ideas to Britain, though they reached York only early in the next century. Two buildings in High Ousegate reflected the architectural style of the 1630s when they were rebuilt a few years after the fire of 1694: one was to become Thomas Wilson's bank and bookshop at no.14 a century later. Houses like Sir William Robinson's Red House in Little Blake Street, built about 1710, with its orderly appearance and high hipped roof exemplify the new influences. In 1726, the Mansion House was built in the style known as 'Palladian' after the Italian architect Andrea Palladio because it is based on his principles of architectural design. Developing from the Palladian came the Georgian townhouse, of which Castlegate House (see illustration p.241) of 1762 by John Carr, is one example of many. Used individually as here, or joined together in a row or terrace, the type is characterised by elegant proportions, symmetry and an almost invisible roof. With interior arrangements as in the Mansion House, the tall sash windows on the first floor reflect the social importance of the grand first floor reception room.

The Suburbs

Celia Fiennes and Daniel Defoe both admired the open view of York as they approached from a distance. Defoe recognised this was the result of the clearance of the City's Civil War fortifications, which had replaced timber framed medieval houses demolished for the purpose. So it was that when increasing wealth and changing life styles demanded new houses equipped with the latest amenities, they were built either on the site of a previous residence, or outside the City walls, along Bootham, Monkgate and Blossom Street. In this way the suburbs began to spread out, firstly as handsome townhouses with spacious gardens, later extended in the 1820s by the first terraces of artisan houses.

Infrastructure Improvements

All this building and social activity brought the familiar problems of traffic congestion. Attempts at improvements were introduced at various times, from the demolition of houses on street corners to the creation of New Street in 1746. Footways were inserted through all four of the City's Bars between 1753 and 1825, and between 1810 and 1820 Ouse Bridge was rebuilt and widened. Foss Bridge was rebuilt about the same time, to improve passage down Fossgate and Walmgate, still the main easterly route out of the City.

A single Act of Parliament in 1763 was a comprehensive attempt to address several conditions causing offence to 'Persons of Distinction and Fortune' who frequented the City. Its title an 'Act for the Better Cleaning and Enlightening the Streets, Lanes and Publick Ways of the City of York and the Suburbs thereof ..: and for keeping the same in Repair and Free from Annoyance; and for regulating the Hackney Coachmen and Chairmen, Carmen and Draymen' clearly indicates the areas of offence. As a result of the Act, sometimes elaborate rainwater goods began to be installed on all domestic premises; the Watch strengthened by the employment of younger men; the penalty to householders who failed in their responsibility to maintain the street outside their house was increased; and operators of public transport were to be licensed.

By the end of the century York presented a less crowded and more spacious appearance and was cleaner, lighter and more orderly than ever before in its history.

High Roads

Underpinning these changes and fundamental to their achievement were the transport improvements which took place over the century.

Between 1745 and 1771, the network of ancient roads linking York to its hinterland and beyond was brought under the management of a number of turnpike trusts. Seven trusts were set up covering routes to Tadcaster, Boroughbridge, Scarborough, Northallerton, Kexby (for Hull), Garrowby Hill (for Bridlington), Oswaldkirk Bank (for Helmsley) and Collingham. Finance for trusts came from local landowners, the gentry and country clergymen, and any others possessing the necessary funds who would benefit from better roads. Trusts had the power to levy tolls on different categories of user for the purpose of improving the roads and providing for their regular repair and maintenance. The road to Helmsley north of Oswaldkirk Bank was funded by local landowners, amongst whom were the Duncombes, hopeful of travelling more easily to York for the races and assemblies. Country carters too benefitted from road improvements making it quicker and easier to bring their produce to market.

The steady increase in turnpiked roads progressively reduced the journey time from York to London, from 4 days early in the century to under 36 hours by the early 1790s. By 1796 three daily coaches ran between York and London, two daily coaches operated to Leeds with connections to Sheffield and Birmingham and a daily Royal Mail coach ran to Liverpool via Leeds. London stage coaches departed either from the Black Swan in Coney Street, or the York Tavern in St Helen's Square; ongoing services to the north left via Blake Street, Little Blake Street, Petergate and Bootham Bar. Coaches for the east coast and Hull used the White

A Staith or Wormalds Cut

Castlegate House

Swan in Pavement and left the city down Fossgate and Walmgate, those to Scarborough departing from the Black Swan. The George in Coney Street served the mail coaches and Etteridge's Hotel on the corner next to the Assembly Rooms supplied horses for the private traveller.

Navigation Improvements

Long standing efforts to improve the navigability of the River Ouse and the viability of the City's port continued. In 1727, a Navigation Trust was established to investigate the possibilities of canalising the river. A lock and weir were constructed at Naburn in 1757 with the object of raising water levels upstream. Conditions improved to such an extent that a passenger service by steam packet between Hull and York was instituted in 1816, and extended two years later to Selby and Leeds. In 1823, the Trustees built themselves a handsome little Banqueting House at Naburn, to which they could retire for meetings and feasting.

An Act was obtained in 1793 for the canalisation of the River Foss from its confluence with the Ouse to Stillington mill. The first installation was Castle Mills lock, in operation by 1794 and six more were completed before the Trustees ran out of money, one still detectable upriver from Monk Bridge. In the event canalisation reached only to Sheriff Hutton, in 1801. One successful improvement of the scheme was Wormalds Cut (see illustration p.241), built to serve Samuel Wormald's brewing, shipping and timber interests by providing water-borne access to the rear of his Walmgate yard.

Canalisation further afield, including improvements to the River Derwent in 1719, encouraged river-borne trading and revitalised the old trading link with Hull. Kings Staith, used for the shipment of corn and wheat, flour, salt, lime and coal, was rebuilt as part of the Ouse Bridge widening project, 1810-20. Queen's Staith, used by the butter trade conducted from St Martin's churchyard, was likewise improved in the early nineteenth century. The merchant who operated a steam flour mill in North Street was permitted to own a private staith near his warehouse. A new staith

9. Distant View of York by Alexander Keirincx, 1639-40.

10. Doorway and Royal Monograms, King's Manor.

11. State Room in the Mansion House, York.

12. Lord Burlington by Knapton.

13. Clifford St, 1905.

14. The Yorkshire Museum.

15. Council Housing on Hull Road.

16. York's First New Citizen of the Millennium.

was constructed at Lendal for the delivery of goods to the Bootham area and coal was unloaded at Old Crane Wharf and Marygate. The Old Crane near Skeldergate Postern was replaced by a New Crane around 1770.

Without these road and river improvements, the City's reputation as a regional supplier of quality merchandise would have been difficult to maintain and its attractiveness to society as a place where the living was good value would have been significantly impaired.

Conclusion

The City's role was defined in the Preamble to the Cleaning and Lighting Act of 1763 as the "Capital City of the Northern Parts of England, and a place of great Resort, and much frequented by Persons of Distinction and Fortune". Only a few years later, however, the brilliance ascribed by Drake to the Assembly Rooms had dimmed and Arthur Young, visiting in 1771, could only deplore their lack of lustre and enumerate their shortcomings. By the 1790s, there were still 59 gentry families listed in Directories, but the City had outlived its reputation as a centre of fashionable society. With the continuing absence of an industrial enterprise of any magnitude, the economy was becoming stagnant. The small enterprises which had sustained the elegant society nevertheless survived and continued to provide opportunities for employment into the early nineteenth century. Those institutions upon which the City's role had depended historically were intact, though challenged and changing. The legacy left by the changes wrought during this age of elegance and enterprise is seen not only in the continuation of these traditional institutions but also in the humane environment of the present-day city. Its human scale, its well proportioned streets and buildings, the Mansion House, visible symbol of civic dignity, are all part of that legacy. Most valuable of all, perhaps, it bequeathed the habit of visiting York for enjoyment and pleasure so that, once again, the City is a place of resort and a desirable place in which to live.

8

YORK IN THE NINETEENTH CENTURY

A City Transformed

Edward Royle

Introduction

At the beginning of the nineteenth century, York was the sixteenth largest city in England, surpassed in Yorkshire only by Leeds, Sheffield and Hull. By 1901 it ranked forty-first and in Yorkshire had been overtaken by Bradford, Middlesbrough, Halifax and Huddersfield. At a time of rapid industrialisation and urbanisation, nineteenth-century York seemed a backwater. A French visitor in 1828 commented how, 'While commercial towns in England have grown enormously in recent years, market towns in agricultural areas have remained unchanged or even been reduced in size. York, which was once the second largest city in England, now has only twenty thousand inhabitants and has not grown at all.' Appearances were deceptive and this observation was no more true than his next, that 'The cathedral is the only historic building of note', but the impression is useful.

York was a city of contrasts, ancient and modern. Between 1801 and 1901 it grew more slowly than the great industrial cities and ports, but faster than comparable cities such as Norwich, Bath or Exeter. It became a manufacturing and communications centre but remained a market town, with cattle and sheep still driven through the streets to the livestock market just outside the city walls. York's medieval pomp and display with its cathedral, Lord Mayor and assize courts sat next to a depth of urban poverty to equal that of any large town in England.

If at the end of the nineteenth century a party of visitors had returned to York after a hundred years away they would have noticed some similarities with the city of 1800 but also many differences. The city sky line was still dominated by the Minster and the castle, and punctuated by the spires of All Saints, North Street and St Mary, Castlegate and the lantern of All Saints, Pavement - though the Minster had twice been restored after fires in 1829 and 1840 and the lantern of All Saints had been rebuilt in 1837. The medieval city was still surrounded by its walls, despite several attempts in the 1820s to demolish them. Medieval houses still clustered in central streets like Low Petergate, Goodramgate and the Shambles and splendid Georgian houses still graced the main thoroughfares and approaches to the city, but the more the visitors looked the more they would have realised that York was a city transformed. Despite superficial similarities with the medieval city whose past the citizens were learning to cultivate and recreate, York had become during the course of the nineteenth century a thoroughly modern city, transformed in almost every aspect of its appearance as well as in its political, social and economic life.

A Medieval City Transformed

Even the city walls in 1900 were not what they had been a century earlier. For a start, they were generally in a better state of repair, but Monk, Micklegate and Bootham bars had all lost their barbicans (in 1825, 1826 and 1835 respectively), Fishergate Bar, bricked up in the late fifteenth century, was reopened in 1834 to give better access to the cattle market, and a new entry off Nunnery Lane called Victoria Bar was created on the site of an old gate in 1838. One section of city wall to the south-west of Bootham bar was demolished to make way for a new road, St Leonard's Place (1831-5), and new arches were cut into the walls at Monk (1861), Walmgate (1861) and Micklegate (1863) bars. Of the various minor entrances to the city, most were demolished or transformed during the century, Fishergate postern alone remaining relatively unscathed. The postern at the approach to Skeldergate at the foot of the Old Baile hill was pulled down in 1807; Layerthorpe postern was demolished in 1829 when a new bridge was built over the river Foss to carry the road from Heworth; North Street postern was widened in 1840 to allow access to the North Eastern Railway's coal yard; and Castlegate postern on the river Ouse side of the Castle was demolished in 1826 to make way for the enlarged York Castle gaol.

Visitors to York in about 1820 would have arrived at the York Tavern, St Helen's Square, by one of over thirty coaches running daily from all parts of the country. Entering the city along the traditional route from Leeds or London along the Mount and Blossom Street, the visitor returning in 1900 would have noticed many fine houses, most of them erected during the nineteenth century and indicating the presence of an opulent middle class. Entry through the bar into Micklegate with its familiar medieval and Georgian town houses, would also have presented unfamiliar sights. On the right the old archway which marked the entrance to the gardens of Holy Trinity priory had given way to a new street, Priory Street, filled with Nonconformist chapels. The biggest shock, though, would have been the disappearance of the old Ouse bridge, with its medieval chapel and council chamber and famous single arch of 1566, replaced by a utilitarian, three-arch bridge of 1820.

After 1839 visitors were more likely to arrive by train. A temporary station was opened outside the city walls in Queen Street while the first station proper was constructed within the walls in Tanner Row, opened in 1841, with the lines penetrating the defences of the city through two arches, cut in 1839 and 1845. 'The erection of this station', observed one contemporary, 'has transformed a remote and retired part of the City into a scene of vitality and commercial activity.' *[Illustration p.260]* A new street named after the chairman of the railway company, George Hudson, was built to connect the station with Ouse Bridge in 1843, and after years of argument a new bridge was built over the Ouse at Lendal in 1863 to connect the station directly to the most fashionable part of the city. Subsequently, in 1877, a new station was opened outside the walls to avoid trains having to enter and then reverse out of the old terminus. Two road arches were built through the walls in 1874 and 1876 to afford access from the new station to Lendal bridge, which was freed from tolls only in 1894. Further investigation would bring other surprises. Though many streets with medieval houses still survived, dirty and dilapidated, the church of St Crux at the bottom of the Shambles was gone, demolished in 1887. By contrast, Holy Trinity, commonly known as Christchurch, at the top of the Shambles in King's Court externally looked much smarter and more 'medieval' than it had at the start of the nineteenth century, thanks to an extensive 'restoration' in 1861 employing the Decorated style. A glance inside, though, would have found it already disused with evidence that the parishioners were keeping sheep in it.

To the south of the city, the castle looked quite different, for Clifford's Tower and the eighteenth-century prison and court buildings were now enclosed within a huge new boundary wall, 32 feet (9.75 metres) high with pierced battlements and a new recessed gateway with projecting towers. These works, begun in 1826, were completed ten years later at a cost of over £203,000. Within the walls, between Clifford's Tower and the river Foss, stood the new county gaol, though from 1900 it was used only as a military prison.

One of the greatest of nineteenth-century street improvements in central York was the rebuilding of the market in 1836 through the wholesale clearance of what a contemporary called 'a dense mass of old buildings' between the Thursday Market (renamed St Sampson's Square) and Pavement to create Parliament Street. *[Illustration p.260]* In 1911-14 a further road was made from the bottom of Parliament Street through the medieval buildings which had once housed the offices of the *York Herald* newspaper, over a new bridge across the river Foss to join Piccadilly, itself a medieval street widened and renamed after the London street in 1840, which led out of the city at the Fishergate postern.

A second area of improvement was around the Minster. In 1839, Minster Yard was widened with the removal of several

247

buildings in the vicinity of the west front of the Minster and St Michael-le-Belfrey church; then in 1860 property in Little Blake Street or Lop Lane to the west of the Minster was acquired and demolished at the instigation of the new Dean, Augustus William Duncombe, to create in Duncombe Place an open space affording a fine prospect of the fifteenth century west front of his Cathedral. Finally, in 1903, a link road known as Deangate was opened between Goodramgate and Minster Yard to improve access from Monk Bar to the railway station. These measures made the cathedral more accessible but were also to expose it to increasing volumes of traffic in the twentieth century.

The third area of nineteenth-century road construction was Clifford Street, constructed in 1881 in association with a third bridge over the River Ouse, Skeldergate Bridge, on which tolls were charged until 1914. The Clifford Street project was in the true spirit of Victorian improvement. Not only did it sweep away the notorious slums of the Water Lanes which reached from Castlegate down to the Ouse, but it proclaimed through its new public buildings the spirit of the age. On the west side stood the premises for the York Institute of Art, Science and Literature, the Liberal Club and the new magistrates' court and police and fire station; and on the Castlegate side the School Board offices, the Friendly Societies' Dispensary and new premises for the Society of Friends (the Quakers). This street more than any other in York proclaims its Victorian identity. *[colour plate 13]*

Population

The population living within the original area of the borough of York more than trebled between 1801 and 1901, from 16,846 to 54,742 *[Table 1]*. The decade of fastest growth was the 1840s when the population went up by a quarter. But this tells only part of the story, for by 1881 several suburban villages had become part of York and these held as many people as the whole of York at the beginning of the century. If this 'greater York' is considered, the city's population more than quadrupled, from 19,325 in 1801 to 83,058 in 1901. The decade of greatest growth in the suburbs was the 1870s, when their population increased by two-thirds - a fact recognised by boundary extensions to the city in 1884 and again in 1893. By contrast, the population of rural villages in the Ainsty to the west of York actually fell during the second half of the century and was very little different in 1901 from 1801. This suggests that a major source of the city's population growth in the nineteenth century was in-migration from the surrounding countryside.

The 1851 census shows that, whereas almost a third of the adult population of York had been born in the city, nearly a half came from elsewhere in Yorkshire. The remainder were evenly divided between other northern counties, the rest of England and Wales, and Ireland: the Irish-born population in York in 1841 was 429 but had risen to 1,928 by 1851.

City and suburbs

The effects of this population expansion are spelt out on the map of the city's housing development. At the beginning of the nineteenth century the built-up part of the city scarcely extended beyond the walls and there were many open spaces even within the walls. Only on the major thoroughfares out of York was there a little ribbon development, particularly along Bootham, Monkgate and Blossom Street. Within the walls much of the Micklegate district beyond the main street and riverside remained open gardens. Toft Green was the site for the new House of Correction from 1814 until 1838 when it was demolished to make way for the railway station. *[map p.251]* The rest of the upper part of Bishophill beyond Trinity Gardens was occupied by the City gaol, erected in 1802-7 and demolished in 1878 as the area was developed for housing. Similarly in the Walmgate district the main buildings were in Walmgate itself and courts running from it. Much of St George's parish as far as Fishergate postern was still gardens. The most densely populated part of the city lay to the east of the Ouse and north of the Foss, stretching from the Castle to the Minster, but even here much low-lying land near the Foss in Pound Garth beyond Hungate lay undeveloped, not least because of its

Table 1:

Population of the York area within constant boundaries, 1801-1901

Population of York municipal borough

	1801	1811	1821	1831	1841	1851	1861	1871	1881	1891	1901
	16,846	19,099	21,711	26,260	28,928	36,303	40,661	43,796	49,530	51,105	54,742
% change		13.37	13.68	20.95	10.16	25.49	12.00	7.71	13.09	3.18	7.12

Population of suburban townships and villages (Acomb, Dringhouses and Holgate (W. Riding), Gate Fulford (E. Riding) and Clifton, Marygate and Heworth (N. Riding)

	1801	1811	1821	1831	1841	1851	1861	1871	1881	1891	1901
	2,429	2,842	3,065	3,566	4,787	6,628	7,951	10,225	17,116	21,015	28,316
% change		17.0	7.85	16.35	34.24	38.46	19.96	28.60	67.39	22.78	34.74

Population of York municipal borough, suburban townships and villages

	1801	1811	1821	1831	1841	1851	1861	1871	1881	1891	1901
	19,325	21,941	24,776	29,826	33,715	42,931	48,612	54,021	66,646	72,120	83,058
% change		13.54	12.92	20.38	13.04	27.34	13.23	11.13	23.37	8.21	15.17

Population of Ainsty villages (omitting Acomb, Dringhouses, Holgate and Tadcaster E.)

	1801	1811	1821	1831	1841	1851	1861	1871	1881	1891	1901
	6,120	6,725	7,149	7,312	7,305	7,415	7,302	6,922	6,837	6,429	6,461
% change		9.89	6.30	2.28	-0.10	1.51	-1.52	-5.20	-1.23	-5.97	0.50

Source: Calculated from G. Minchin, 'Table of Population, 1801-1901' in W. Page, ed. *The Victoria History of the County of York*, volume 3 (London 1913) pp. 487-548.

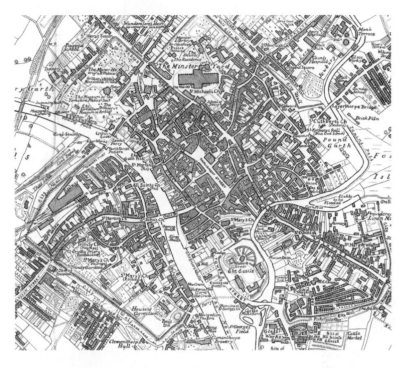

York 1849 Ordnance Survey Map

liability to flood.

    A glance at a map of York at the beginning of the twentieth century tells a very different story. *[Monochrome Plate 15]* Apart from disused parochial graveyards, the only green areas within the city walls lay to the north side of the Minster in what is now Dean's Park, and an acre (0.4 hectares) within the Castle walls in Castle Yard. Streets of terraced housing interspersed with industrial premises now filled former open spaces, while many town-house gardens had been built over with back streets and courts during the course of the century. Outside the city walls also there were now large areas of terraced housing, filling in the fields between the major roads and reaching out

Yorkshire Insurance Company Fire Station, 1845

Duncombe Place 1910

252

towards the villages of Clifton to the north west, Heworth to the north east, Fulford to the south east, Holgate and Acomb to the west and the Scarcroft and South Bank districts to the south west. While, generally speaking, inner city parishes experienced an initial increase in population followed by a decrease as commercial development took place, suburban areas saw steady growth.

The population figures for selected parishes illustrate this process. The combined population for the four parishes on the Walmgate side of the river Foss, an area of 48 acres (19.42 hectares), rose from 1,457 in 1801 to 5,248 in 1901. The peak came in 1881, with 6,344 people living at a density of 132 per acre (53 per hectare). In the most densely packed parish, St George's, the population density was 195 per acre (79 per hectare). This was a major area of Irish settlement. Over forty per cent of the population of Walmgate in both 1841 and 1851 was Irish by birth or parentage. In the 1840s, St George's parish doubled in size, from 1,024 to 2,095. In 1851, a fifth of the population of the parish was Irish born. Other important areas of Irish settlement were Bedern, close by the east end of the Minster, and the Water Lanes in the parish of St Mary, Castlegate.

The story of parishes which reached beyond the city walls is very different. Though their intra-mural parts were similar to small inner city parishes, their extra-mural suburbs were capable of accommodating far larger populations at much lower densities. In St Maurice, a parish of 98 acres (39.66 hectares) just outside Monk Bar where an extensive housing district was built in the Groves in the mid-century, the population, which had been 567 in 1801, rose to 1,477 in 1841 and 4,327 in 1861, before settling to a steadier rate of growth and reaching 5,941 in 1901. On the Micklegate side of the river St Mary, Bishophill Senior, an area of 212 acres (85.8 hectares), held just 397 people in 1801, mainly within the walls. The population grew steadily to 1,227 in 1851 and then doubled in each of the next two decades, so by 1901 it stood at 8,395. These patterns of urban and suburban development were to have a profound effect on the institutions and lives of the people of York during the nineteenth century.

Economic Development before the Railways

At the beginning of the nineteenth century, York was principally a market town and administrative centre. Most of its industries were based on agriculture or to serve the needs of a regional capital. There was little of that large-scale industry which was beginning to reshape the economy of the West Riding or a major modern port such as Hull. Baines's *Directory* of 1823 lists York's manufactures as 'carpets, linens, stuff, flax, cordage, agricultural implements, combs, gloves, paper hangings, articles in chemistry, musical instruments, and jewellery'. These were the products of small-scale artisan trades. In 1841, there were thirty-eight firms engaged as chemists or druggists, employing a total of seventy-six people; and the six iron works employed only twenty-five people. One of the few industries to develop was Prince and Prest's glass manufactory, founded outside the walls in Fishergate in 1797, but in 1814 this and two other glass works employed only fifty-four people between them. The total percentage of the workforce employed in manufacturing in 1841 was well below the national average.

Where York did exceed national averages by significant amounts was in small-scale handicraft industries and shop-keeping for men, and domestic service for women. This is what one would expect of a pre-industrial regional capital, servicing the vale of York, the county gentry and the Church of England. It was reflected in the traditional way the city was governed. Only freemen could set up businesses as master craftsmen in the city, which meant they had to be the sons or daughters of freemen, have served apprenticeships under such, or paid the corporation an entry fee of £25 each. Until 1827, it was believed that only a member of the Merchant Adventurers' Company could trade in imported goods: as Baines observed in 1823, it had 'outlived the commerce of the city'. Economic life was still organised in the traditional way, around markets and fairs. There was a wool fleece market held in Peasholme Green between March and September at which farmers could sell their fleeces to West Riding manufacturers. In 1815 a quarterly leather fair was established but by the 1850s this had been moved to Leeds. There were seven fairs a year for the sale of flax, and three major and several minor horse and cattle fairs. The prosperity of the cattle trade led the corporation to open a new site for a fortnightly cattle market outside Walmgate Bar in 1827, though the weekly pig market continued to be held within the walls near Foss Bridge.

Retail markets were also held at various points in the city. The Corn Market was outside the east end of All Saints' Church, Pavement, and the Butchers' Market in St Sampson's Square (the two locations being joined by Parliament Street in 1836); the Hay Market moved from King's Square to Peasholme Green in 1827 and the Fish Market was held in a building erected outside the west end of St Sampson's Church, and later - because of the smell - in St Sampson's Square.

The agricultural nature of York was reinforced by the influx of Irish in the 1840s. The 1851 census recorded a third of all occupied Irish men and women as agricultural labourers, twice as many as were general labourers. Contemporaries observed the extent to which the Irish were identified with chicory cultivation in the villages around York, an industry that was expanding rapidly in the 1840s. The Walmgate district, with its Irish agricultural workers and livestock markets must have resembled as much an extension of the countryside as a district of the city

The commercial side of the city's economy saw an increase in banking and other financial institutions during the first half of the century. Although the newest of three private commercial banks failed in the national banking crisis of 1825, three of the four public banks opened in the 1830s prospered - the City and County Bank (1830), the York Union Bank (1833) and the Yorkshire District Bank (1834), taken over by the Yorkshire Banking Company in 1843. There was also a York Saving Bank, established in New Street in 1816 to encourage servants not to spend all their money at once. It moved into new premises designed by the York architect, J. P. Pritchett, in St Helen's Square in 1829. The only failure was the Agricultural and Commercial Bank which collapsed in the depression of 1842. There were also two major insurance companies formed at this time - the Yorkshire

Fire and Life Insurance Office (1824) and the York and North of England Insurance Company (1834). York also gained another newspaper, the *Yorkshire Gazette* (1819). Its editorial policy was Evangelical and Tory, and in 1839 it merged with the more moderately Tory *York Chronicle*. A fifth paper, the *Yorkshireman,* appeared in 1834, but it amalgamated with the Whig *York Herald* in 1858. Since the *Herald* had also taken over the oldest of the York papers, the *Courant*, in 1848, for most of the Victorian period York opinion was represented by two major papers, the Whig-Liberal *Herald* and the Tory-Conservative *Gazette.*

One man who might typify the York economy in these years was James Meek (1790-1862) who was born at Brompton, Northallerton, the son of a linen manufacturer. At the age of 14 he came to York to be apprenticed to Joseph Agar, a currier and leading Wesleyan. He subsequently became a master currier himself with premises in Goodramgate, as well as a leading member of New Street Wesleyan Chapel. He was a member of both the old and new corporations, serving his turn as Sheriff in 1827, alderman in 1835 and Lord Mayor in 1836-7, 1848-9 and 1850-1. Thus far he was part of the old economy of York but, as a partner in the glass works from 1837, chairman of the York City and County Banking Company, vice-Chairman of the Yorkshire Fire and Life Insurance Office, trustee and manager of York Savings Bank, vice-Chairman of the York and North Midland Railway (until he resigned over Sunday travel) and a director of the Great Northern Railway, he was also to be part of the new economy.

The Transport Revolution

York had good mail and passenger communications along the main coach routes of the county and with London and Newcastle. In the mid-1830s some 93,760 passengers travelled on the coaches from York to Leeds, Hull, Selby and London, and a further 20,800 went by river to Selby and Hull. Goods were mainly reliant upon water transport and here Leeds gained an advantage over York, particularly with the opening of the Aire and

Calder Navigation's canal to Goole in 1826. Boats of 150 tons regularly used the lower Ouse from York, while smaller boats distributed goods as far north as Ripon and Boroughbridge. Coal was brought in by barge from the West Riding, but at a premium of 5-6 shillings (25-30p.) a ton in canal and lock charges.

Contemporaries were aware of how important the transport revolution was for York: 'The formation of railways to open a better communication with the West of Yorkshire and the North and South of England, are in progress,' observed White's *Directory* of 1840, adding, 'and with these improved modes of transit for goods, it is to be hoped that the trade of York will improve.' A meeting was called in York in 1833 to discuss the need for a railway connection to York, but it was 1839 before the first line linked the city with the Leeds to Selby at South Milford. This had little effect on passenger transport to Selby, for which the river continued to be more convenient, but the link with Leeds had an immediate effect on coal traffic, cutting the number of river vessels from an average of 873 in the 1830s to only 203 in 1844. By 1850, toll receipts on the Ouse were only about a third of what they had been in 1839. Nevertheless, river traffic on the Ouse did continue to play an important though diminishing part in the commercial life of York for the rest of the century *[Monochrome Plate 14]* but the Foss Navigation, opened in 1801 and never very successful, was driven out of business and taken over by the Corporation in 1853. In 1879, a railway branch line was built to the Foss Islands side of the city to connect the cattle market and gas works to the main network.

The impact of the railways on passenger transport was immediate, once the line from South Milford had been extended to Normanton in 1840 to connect with the North Midland to Derby and thence to London. The following year the Great North of England Railway took the line from York to Darlington to meet the line from Newcastle. Further lines and amalgamations of companies followed in the next few years, orchestrated by George Hudson as chairman of the York and North Midland, with lines to Scarborough (1845), Market Weighton (1847), Knaresborough (1848) and a more direct line to London through Burton Salmon and Knottingley to Doncaster in 1850.

This last line, reluctantly accepted by Hudson, marked the end of fifteen years during which his personal influence shaped the development of the network throughout much of the east of England, centred on York. Though his financial dealings, even in a world in which the rules of the game were ill-defined, were less than honest and his political enemies were quick to rejoice at his downfall in 1849, his legacy to York was both permanent and positive: in 1854, when several companies amalgamated to form the North Eastern Railway, York was chosen for its headquarters.

The first direct train from York reached London by way of Derby on 11 May 1840, after a journey lasting all day, but this compared favourably with the fastest coach which took 20 hours. In 1842, the last mail coach ran from London through York to Edinburgh and, whereas the stage coaches had carried around 23,000 passengers a year between York and London, by the 1850s thirteen trains a day were carrying 341,000 passengers annually. Journey times by the Midland Railway were down to under six hours and when the direct Great Northern line through Selby to Doncaster and London was opened in 1871, it was possible to cover the distance in under five.

As a measure of the expansion in traffic, the seventy-six trains a day in 1854 had doubled by the opening of the new railway station in 1877 and thirty years later the daily number of trains was up to over 350. This stimulated the local economy. Whereas in 1843 the trade directories recorded sixty-seven carriers operating from twenty-six inns and serving seventy-three villages, 107 carriers were operating from twenty-nine inns and serving some ninety-one villages in 1855. The census in 1831 recorded thirty-three people as carriers; in 1861 the number was ninety-three. As anticipated, the price of coal fell from around fifteen shillings (75p.) to no more than nine shillings (45p.) a ton but this did not give York any economic advantage over Leeds. Although with six main line companies running their trains through York the railways promoted the construction industry, tourism and local transport, there was no major influx of new industries.

The Railway Industry

The railway was an important direct employer of labour and this was its most obvious impact on York. In 1839 a small repair shop was opened in Queen Street but of 306 workers in transport in 1841, only forty-one were employed by the railways. This number grew rapidly in the 1840s, with the increase in traffic and the opening of an engine repair workshop in 1842. By 1851 there were 513 railway workers, employed as footplate men, guards, porters, station officials, labourers, office workers, employees in hotels associated with the railway, and at the railway works. The latter expanded rapidly, undertaking repairs to engines worth £15,000 a year in 1849. Though locomotive work was initially important, some repair work was transferred to Darlington in 1885 and then the whole works was moved there in 1905. York's main industry was the wagon and carriage works. The former was extended in 1864 giving a capacity to produce a hundred wagons a week; and in the 1870s a new site was acquired in Holgate where the works built in the 1880s had grown to cover 45 acres (18.21 hectares) by 1910.

This made the North Eastern Railway Company York's largest employer and gave the city its first really 'modern' industry. In 1855 it was calculated that the total workforce was around 1,200, earning £1,350 a week for the local economy. Many of these employees were skilled craftsmen or clerical workers for whom streets of terraced housing were built, first off Nunnery Lane near the Queen Street site and then down Leeman Road after the opening of the new station and the development of the Holgate site. By the end of the century there were around 5,500 railway employees, half of whom were in the wagon and carriage works.

Manufacturing

In most other respects, York industry continued much as before, no doubt helped by the railways and the purchasing potential generated by them, but without any dramatic changes. Some of York's traditional industries, such as leather

An early twentieth century view of the old railway station built 1841

The market in Parliament Street, 1889

working, clothing and comb making failed during the course of the century. Others continued as before, or gradually expanded with the city. At the end of the nineteenth century about 500 people were employed in various printing works, the largest of which developed from the bookselling and printing business of the Quaker, William Alexander, founded in 1811. After several changes of ownership, the premises in Low Ousegate were purchased in 1865 by William Sessions, another Quaker.

Chemical and drug manufacturing also remained important, with firms such as Bleasdale's wholesale chemists, founded in 1780 with premises behind Colliergate; Raimes and Company, wholesale druggists, founded in 1818 with premises in Micklegate; and Henry Richardson and Company, fertilizer manufacturers, founded in 1824 with premises outside Skeldergate Postern in Clementhorpe. But they were scarcely expanding, with a total workforce in 1901 of only about 150. There was a similar story at the Fishergate glass works, which was in difficulties in 1837 when taken over by Joseph Spence, a Quaker analytical chemist, James Meek, and Thomas Price. Together they made the York Flint Glass Company a successful company, employing 223 men in 1851 but there was little further expansion during the rest of the century.

Some new firms succeeded because they offered highly specialised products. Thomas Cooke, an optician, began manufacturing sundials, microscopes and telescopes in 1837, moving to new premises in the Buckingham Works on Bishophill in 1856. After his death in 1868 the business continued to prosper under his sons and at the end of the century they were employing approaching five hundred workers and had diversified into the manufacture of public clocks. Another firm to acquire a national reputation was John Walker, iron founders, started at the beginning of the century to manufacture gates and railings for the gentry and aristocracy. National approval was won in 1847 when the Queen gave her royal warrant. In 1850 they won the contract for the railings outside the British Museum and the firm later supplied ironwork to Sandringham. In 1851 Walker's was employing

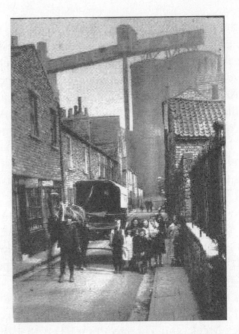

Garden Place, off Hungate, with Leetham's Mill, 1904

fifty-two men.

A major development towards the end of the century came in flour milling, a traditional agriculture-based industry, using river transport. Older steam mills, such as the Castle Mills and L. & J. Simpson of North Street, both closed in the 1850s but others replaced them. The most important was Henry Leetham & Sons. Leetham started milling in Hungate on the banks of the Foss in 1850, but the real advance came in the 1880s when he introduced steel rollers for milling the corn: whereas in 1891 fewer than a hundred workers in milling were recorded in the census, by 1911 there were around six hundred. The trade in grain gave new life to the river navigation and in 1888 Leetham used the threat of moving to Hull to persuade the corporation to enlarge the lock at the entry to the Foss. Grain replaced coal as the most important river cargo, and in 1895-6 Leetham built on Wormald's Cut a new warehouse with five-storeys and a nine-storeyed castellated water tower, linked to the Hungate mill by bridges over the Foss. Old photographs show how the mill dominated the narrow streets off Hungate at the end of the nineteenth century. *[Illustration p.262]*

Confectionary and Cocoa

The most remarkable development in York's economy in the nineteenth century was again in a traditional, food-based industry - confectionary and cocoa processing. Among the twenty-one 'confectioners, pastry-cooks, &c' listed in Baines's *Directory* in 1823 was Robert Berry of St Helen's Square. He was joined by Joseph Terry shortly after this and by 1838 the firm had become Joseph Terry and Company. At this time Terry's was noted chiefly for confectionary but following Joseph Terry senior's death in 1850 they branched out into candied peel. A new factory was built in Clementhorpe in 1864 and here in 1886 cocoa and chocolate production was started. By the time of the death of Joseph Terry junior in 1898 the firm was employing about three hundred workers and was exporting its products all over the world. By contrast another of York's confectionary firms, run by Thomas Craven and then from 1862 by his widow, Mary Ann, remained in the sugar confectionary trade throughout the century, growing to a work force of over two hundred.

York's third and largest confectionary business, Rowntree & Co., had different roots. Among the thirty-one tea dealers in York in 1823 was Samuel Tuke & Co. of Castlegate. This Quaker firm had also begun to trade in coffee and cocoa in the eighteenth century but after the ending of the East India Company's monopoly on the tea trade in 1834, Tuke & Co expanded outside York, to Liverpool, Bristol, Hull and London. In 1862 the Castlegate firm was acquired by its manager, Henry Isaac Rowntree, a fellow Quaker whose father Joseph owned a grocery shop at 28 Pavement. Henry was soon joined by his older brother, also Joseph, and they opened a factory in some old buildings in Tanner's Moat in which to grind cocoa beans. At this stage they employed about a dozen men.

The transformation of the business was begun by Joseph

Rowntree junior in the 1870s when he introduced hydraulic presses for squeezing the roasted beans. It was now possible to produce a less fatty and more palatable cocoa for drinking, and the by-product, cocoa butter, could be used for the manufacture of chocolate. An added venture in 1881 was the manufacture of gums and pastilles, hitherto a French speciality, in the former flour mill in North Street. The latter was converted and added to, and so the company expanded rapidly. In 1879, there were about a hundred employees. By 1894 there were 893 and ten years later nearly 3,000. The staple produce was Rowntree's 'Elect' cocoa, first marketed in 1887 - the word 'elect' being taken from the druggists' trade where it signified quality. Marketed as 'more than a drink, a food', it challenged the idea that beer was essential to the manual worker because it gave him sustenance as well as refreshment. Quaker cocoa was a temperance drink. Ironically, as a younger man, Joseph had been hostile to sweets because he thought they indulged the appetite and so were anti-temperance! So rapid was the expansion of the firm as the falling cost of living after 1886 put new spending power into the pockets of ordinary people, that by 1890 Rowntree was looking to expand his works on a new site outside the city. He acquired land on the Haxby Road and by 1908 all manufacturing had been transferred to his new factory there. The manufacturers of cocoa and related products were now second only to the railways as employers in York. Moreover, unlike the railways, they offered a major source of employment for young women.

Municipal Government

The way York was run in the nineteenth century was transformed by population growth and economic development. Already, before the Municipal Corporations Act of 1835, the old corporation was proving inadequate to its task. It was a self-elected body dominated by the Whigs: council men retained office until death, removal or resignation. The main business of the corporation was the administration of justice, regulation of the city's markets and trade, maintenance of certain roads and buildings, including the walls, bridges, city gaol and house of correction, the administration of several local charities and, by a local act of 1727, the Ouse Navigation. Much else was done by the parishes, which were responsible for the poor law, and private companies, such as those that provided York with water and gas.

Other matters remained undone. To remedy this defect, the York Police Act of 1825 set up a board of forty-four Improvement Commissioners who, together with the city magistrates, were responsible 'for paving, lighting, watching and improving the city and suburbs, and the Liberty of St Peter therein'. The latter until 1838 was an independent jurisdiction within the city, responsible for the Minster Yard and Bedern. Unlike the corporation, the commissioners were elected for three years by all male householders with property worth £10 a year.

Also unlike the old corporation, the commission was open to non-Anglicans and Tories. Though this initially led to some friction with the corporation, the repeal of the Test and Corporation Acts in 1828 began that process of opening up local government which culminated in the reform of the corporation itself in 1835. The Quaker, William Alexander, chaired alternate meetings of the commission from 1825, but in 1830 the corporation itself had a Quaker sheriff and a Catholic Lord Mayor.

The 1835 Act replaced the four ancient wards of the city with six, Guildhall and Castlegate being added to Walmgate, Monk, Bootham and Micklegate. Each elected six councillors, two of whom were to seek election each year, and the councillors elected two aldermen for each ward, making a total corporation of forty-eight members, all of whom sat in a single chamber. Their responsibilities were different from those of the old corporation, as they no longer administered justice, which passed to the Commission of the Peace, or local charities, or the strays which were administered by the pasture masters on behalf of the freemen who were the legal owners of the city's open land. The Municipal Corporations Act of 1835 made each corporation responsible for its own police force under a watch committee.

Until 1835, York was policed by three separate authorities: the city peace officer and two constables, responsible to the

Corporation; the constables appointed for each civil parish - a force of fifty-four men, but not police in the modern sense; and the Night Watch comprising a captain and four constables appointed by the Improvement Commissioners. The 1835 Act neither superseded the parishes nor abolished the commissioners, and the attempt to create a unified police force was fraught with political and financial difficulties. The recommended level of policing was twenty constables and three sergeants; the actual number finally approved in 1836 was only twelve. Though this was subsequently increased to twenty-nine by 1855, York remained inadequately policed until after the County and Borough Police Act of 1856 provided treasury grants to 'efficient' local forces. Numbers then gradually increased, a new police office was opened in Clifford Street in 1892, and by the end of the century the force stood at seventy-two.

The reluctance of the corporation to spend money resulted from its parlous financial situation. The old corporation had depended largely on its income from rents and the entry fees paid by freemen, which ranged from £25 in the case of an ordinary person wishing to purchase his freedom for the purposes of trade to £150 in the case of one of the city's MPs. There was also a regular income from fines paid by those refusing public office, ranging from £10 for the chamberlain to £500 for the Lord Mayor. The latter also had to pay £500 if, having accepted office, he did not wish to reside in the Mansion House. This money was scarcely adequate to meet the corporation's expenses and in the first decade of the nineteenth century the accumulated deficit was £10,720. Though this had been turned into a surplus of £3,070 by 1820, thanks largely to retrenchment and increased rental income, continued heavy capital expenditure led to further borrowing. Between 1811 and 1833, total extraordinary capital expenditure of this nature was £28,855, including £10,500 on the new cattle ground, £9,670 on the Ouse, Foss and Layerthorpe bridges, and £4,550 on new council offices attached to the Guildhall. Though a county rate could be levied on the city and Ainsty to pay for expenditure on the gaol and house of correction, the corporation could not itself levy rates to meet its other expenses. This was not true of the Improvement Commission which did levy on each parish a rate of a shilling (5p.) in the pound of rateable value.

The new corporation inherited a debt of £21,500, secured on corporation bonds at four per cent, hence the reluctance to spend an extra £1,000 a year on bringing the police force up to strength. Sensitive to the new ratepayer voters, the political parties aimed to spend as little as possible. The sale of the House of Correction in 1838 can be seen as an economy measure. Gradually, though, the demands of the expanding city and of national legislation reshaped the work of the corporation along more recognisably modern lines. The 1848 Public Health Act resulted in the creation of a local board of health which replaced the Improvement Commissioners. Under the Public Health Act of 1872 the work of this body was then taken over by the corporation, together with a debt of over £11,000.

Despite this consolidation of local government in the hands of the corporation, basic services remained in private hands. The commissioners attempted to buy out the water company, formed in 1799, but could not raise the necessary finance and so a new private company was formed in 1846 to take over from the old. In 1850 it was supplying 5,861 houses and by 1900 three times that number. York had two gas companies. The York Gas Company with a site between the river Foss and Monkgate, was founded in 1823. The prices charged by this monopoly were considered too high. Indeed, in 1828 the commissioners refused to renew their contract for gas street lighting, installed by the company in 1824, and reverted to oil lamps until the company reduced the annual charge by a third. The gas monopoly was then challenged in 1837 by the York Union Gas Light Company, with a site in Hungate, but the two companies amalgamated in 1844 with the result that gas prices remained high. An attempt by the corporation in 1871 to buy the company out failed through lack of finance. The fire brigade, though, which had been run for the city by the Yorkshire Insurance Company since 1830, was taken back into corporation hands in 1875, and in 1897 the corporation decided that electricity supply should be a municipal undertaking and a generating station was opened on Foss Islands Road in 1900.

In 1901 there were just 180 consumers.

Transport by contrast was largely in public hands. The corporation was responsible, as trustees, for the Ouse Navigation, though they were somewhat negligent in their duties. The Royal Commission on Municipal Corporations report in 1835 criticised their decision in 1823 to build a banqueting house at Naburn lock for the corporation's own use at a cost of £2,742 at a time when the lock itself was neglected and the river badly needed dredging. A report commissioned in 1833 led to improvements and the purchase of a steam dredger - and a debt of £16,000 which was inherited by the new corporation in 1835. There then followed a further period of neglect and declining trade in competition with the railways. In 1853 the corporation took over the bankrupt Foss Navigation, more for reasons of public health than transportation, and the attempt to keep the river open beyond the city boundaries was abandoned in 1859. Towards the end of the nineteenth century the commercial prospects of both began to improve. In 1877 Naburn lock was rebuilt to take boats of up to 400 tons - over a decade after this had first been recommended - and in 1879 the corporation bought a steam tug and a new dredger. The lower reaches of the Foss were improved in connection with the Leetham's mill development in 1888. As early photographs show, despite its railways York was still a busy river port at the end of the nineteenth century. *[Monochrome Plate 14]*

The corporation was also instrumental in promoting the York Tramways Company in 1879, which opened a horse tram line from Castle Mills bridge to Fulford in 1880 and ran horse buses within the city. Further lines were then laid through the city over Ouse Bridge to the Mount and the railway station. In 1886 the corporation took over the company and in 1909 began to electrify and further extend the lines.

One public responsibility imposed on all localities by Act of Parliament was the support of the poor. Before 1834, each parish was responsible for its own poor, though in York most of the parishes shared a common workhouse in Marygate, built in the 1760s. This was run by a rope-maker who used pauper labour in his business. The weekly cost to the parishes was an average of

268

3s.2d per head, compared with a rate of relief to paupers in their own homes of 2s. 6d. and half that for children. It is no surprise, therefore, to find that most paupers were relieved in their own homes. Though the workhouse was said to hold up to 150, it was only about a third full. A major cause of pauperism in York by the early 1830s was, according to J. D. Tweedy who was reporting on the situation for the Royal Commission on the Poor Laws, 'a redundancy of population as compared with the quantity of labour' - that is, unemployment. However, Tweedy was convinced that if relief were not so easy to come by there would be less demand for it. His conclusion was that 'The increase in pauperism is greater than the increase of population; and the evil is increasing, not merely in the amount of taxation, but in its effects on the morals and habits of the working classes.'

The solution proposed nationally was to combine parishes into unions, in which the poor law would be administered by 'guardians' elected by ratepayers, subject to a central Poor Law Commission in London. The new unions would each provide a workhouse, the threat of which would deter all but the most desperate from applying for relief. Unlike in the old workhouse, where married couples were permitted to share a bedroom, there would be strict segregation of the sexes, not least to prevent the poor from having any more children.

The York Poor Law Union was formed in 1837. Covering 103 square miles (266.7 square kilometres), it included thirty-two urban and forty-eight rural parishes situated mainly between the Ouse and Derwent rivers. A combination of historical localism in the city and rural reluctance in the villages to spend money on urban paupers ensured that the new measure was at first resisted and then imposed half-heartedly. Under the new, segregated scheme, the Poor Law Commission restricted the capacity of the workhouse to ninety, at a time when there were about two thousand paupers in the city, yet the Guardians refused to levy a rate to build a new workhouse until the further rise in population in the 1840s and the influx of poor Irish brought the guardians in 1847 to resolve to build a new workhouse to house three hundred. This was opened outside the city in Huntington Road in 1849.

Politics

The politics of the corporation, which had been solidly Whig before 1835, remained so until November 1837 when the Tories won a majority of 25 to 23. The Tory George Hudson succeeded the Liberal James Meek as Lord Mayor. This was the beginning of Hudson's political ascendancy in York and the Liberals were not to recapture the corporation until after his fall in 1849. For a decade and a half Hudson was dominant. He got himself re-elected Lord Mayor in 1838, an act declared illegal only after his second-term was completed. This did not stop his appointment for a third time in November 1846. Hudson exercised the power of money and personality not only through the corporation, but also through many sinews of city life including the *Yorkshire Gazette*, the Union Bank and the Union Gas Company. His opponents, the Wesleyan banker and businessman, James Meek, and the Congregational lawyer, George Leeman, bided their time. Criticisms of Hudson mounted during 1848 and that November Meek became Lord Mayor for a second time. He served a third term in 1850-1, and Leeman held the office in 1853-4, 1860-1 and 1870-1. By 1860 the Liberal representation on the corporation was 30 to the Conservatives' 18.

Liberal dominance was maintained until the later 1880s. By this time the Conservatives, now calling themselves Independents, were whittling away the Liberals' majority, to just two in 1891. Finally, in 1893, the count was 25 Independents, 22 Liberals and 1 Labour - the latter was James Desmond O'Connor, elected for Walmgate ward with support from the Irish. By 1897 there were 30 Independents and only 18 Liberals. Conservative dominance remained until 1945 and not for a hundred years were the Liberals to come close to winning control again.

Some of this political story is reflected in the history of parliamentary representation in the nineteenth century. York was, like most English boroughs at the start of the century, a two-member constituency but unlike most it remained such throughout the period. Before the franchise was reformed in 1832, the electorate comprised freemen and freeholders of the city. In that year Parliament extended the franchise to all male heads of households with property valued at £10 a year, but the effect in York was relatively small since of the 2,890 who were registered to vote after 1832, 2,345 were already freemen.

With a few exceptions when the Whigs held both seats, the representation of York was shared by the Whigs and Tories, later Liberals and Conservatives, until 1898. Such was the cost of conducting an election with York's unusually large electorate that, in nine general elections between 1802 and 1831, the city was contested only four times. Usually the two parties agreed to split the seats between them to avoid the expense of an election. The main effect of the 1832 Reform Act was to sharpen local party politics and ensure that all but one of the twenty general elections between 1832 and 1914 were contested. Representation during the century was very much a family affair, with three Dundases, two Lowthers, and three Milners. George Leeman, elected in 1867 and 1871, retired in favour of his youngest son, Joseph Johnson Leeman, in 1880. Gladstonian Liberals swept the board in 1885 and 1886 but when they lost a seat to the Conservatives in a by-election in 1898, for the first time in the century York had no sitting Liberal MP. Not until the Liberal 'landslide' election of 1906 was the balance restored.

Religion

When Edward Baines gave his account of York in 1823, he assumed that 'In manufacturing and commercial towns and districts, dissenters from the established church are generally numerous and influential; but in ancient cities, and particularly in the seats of episcopal sees, the members of the established church have a decided preponderance.' This seemed true of York. The city was served by twenty-three churches belonging to the Church of England, not counting the Cathedral Church of St Peter - the Minster. All but three of these churches were within the city walls. By contrast the various denominations outside the Established Church were only just becoming visible. The oldest Nonconformist chapel was English Presbyterian - now Unitarian -

271

in St Saviourgate, built in 1692-3. The Catholics replaced their mass house with a new church in Lop Lane, next to the theatre, in 1802, in the ancient parish of St Wilfrid to whom the church was dedicated. The Quakers built a new meeting house, large enough for the Yorkshire Quarterly Meeting, in Far Water Lane off Castlegate in 1817. The architect of this, J. P. Pritchett, was a leading member of the Independents (later known as Congregationalists) whose cause he revitalised in York, designing a new chapel in Lendal to which they moved from Jubbergate in 1816. So successful was this chapel under the ministry of James Parsons that, despite enlargements, it could not accommodate its congregations and so Pritchett designed a second chapel, Salem, built in St Saviour's Place in 1839. There were only a few Baptists in York at this time: the Unitarian Baptists met in the Jubbergate chapel from 1816 to until its demolition in 1834 with the building of Parliament Street, and a small group of Particular Baptists met in a chapel in Grape Lane between 1806 and 1820.

The largest group outside the Church of England were the Methodists. By the beginning of the nineteenth century their chapel in Aldwark (opened 1759) was proving too small, so they built again in New Street in 1805, with seating for at least 1,500 people. They followed this in 1816 with a second chapel in Albion Street on the Micklegate side of the river and a third, smaller chapel off Walmgate in St George's parish in 1826. This was replaced in 1840 with Centenary Chapel in St Saviourgate. Known as 'the cathedral of Methodism', it held 1,500 people and cost nearly £8,000. St Saviourgate in 1840 sums up the history of religion in early nineteenth-century York, with its two parish churches, St Crux at one end and St Saviour's part-way along (newly restored in 1844), the seventeenth-century St Saviourgate chapel, and two very large modern chapels which, with their Ionic porticoes, might have been mistaken for Greek temples - Salem looking down the street from one end and Centenary looking across the street from the other.

A Skeldergate Wesleyan Mission Service in Beedham's Court, c.1900

Harvest Festival at the Primitive Methodist Duke of York Street Mission

With six new major Nonconformist places of worship in 35 years and no comparable work for the Church of England, the balance assumed by Baines in 1823 was rapidly shifting. When the Manchester Statistical Society conducted a survey of numbers attending worship in York in 1837, they found that only 38 per cent of attendances were Church of England compared with 56 per cent Protestant Nonconformist and 6 per cent Catholic. Most parish churches were open for only one service on a Sunday, either morning or afternoon, a reflection of the poverty of the livings which meant that many clergy had to take on two or even three churches in order to get a decent income. The parish churches were small, dark, dank and unappealing when compared with new, gas-lit Nonconformist chapels.

By 30 March 1851, when a national census of worship was conducted, the position of the Church of England had begun to improve, not least because the number of services, especially those held in the evening, had increased and the rebuilding and repewing of some of the ancient parish churches had begun - starting with St Saviour's and St Sampson's. Church and Nonconformity now shared the honours, with 45 per cent of attendances each, the Catholics having risen to 10 per cent thanks to the Irish influx. York in 1851 was no longer dominated by the Established Church.

The growth of Wesleyanism was temporarily halted in 1851 when a row over the powers of the central Wesleyan Methodist Conference split the church across the country. York was particularly badly hit as a third of all members declared themselves Reformers and left or were expelled. Even so, in 1856 Wesley chapel was opened in Priory Street to replace the unfashionably-located Albion Street chapel. In addition the split led to an expansion in other forms of Methodism. The Primitive Methodists were strongest in the villages to the east of York, but in 1820 they had moved into the vacant Grape Lane chapel where they grew only slowly until 1851. Then they acquired a site for a new Pritchett-designed chapel in Little Stonegate, known as Ebenezer. The Methodist New Connexion, which had briefly maintained a cause at Grape Lane between 1798 and 1801, built Trinity Chapel in Peckitt Street, just beyond the Water Lanes near the castle entrance, in 1856. And the Wesleyan Methodist Association, whose chapel in Lady Peckett's Yard off Pavement dated from 1830, united with the Wesleyan Reformers in 1858 to open the United Methodist Free Churches chapel just inside Monk Bar, which was built when that part of Goodramgate was widened.

So four new chapels were opened in a decade, reflecting in part the rapid population growth of the 1840s. More were to follow, as first the Baptists (1862) and then the Scottish Presbyterians (1873) founded churches to meet the requirements of immigrants to the city - Scottish regiments and railway workers in the case of the Presbyterians. The new Priory Street began to assume the symbolic role held by St Saviourgate earlier in the century. At the Micklegate end sat Holy Trinity Priory Church and at the other, St Mary, Bishophill Junior. The Wesleyans acquired the whole site between the two in 1856 for their new Wesley chapel and an accompanying school. Across the road the Baptists built their chapel in 1868, complete with spire and looking like a modern gothic parish church; and at the Bishophill end in 1879 the Presbyterians opened their new chapel. Just further down the road inside Victoria Bar the Primitive Methodists opened their second city chapel in 1880.

Despite their new buildings, however, the Nonconformists were only keeping pace with population growth. In relative terms, the Catholics were gaining on both Church and Nonconformity. Plans to replace St Wilfrid's were shelved in the late 1840s when the need was greater to build a new church for the Irish immigrants. So on 4 September 1850 St George's Catholic church was opened off Walmgate, built in a quietly unostentatious late thirteenth-century style to a design by the York Catholic architect, Joseph Hansom. Three weeks later the restoration of the Catholic bishoprics was proclaimed in Rome and York became the centre for the see of 'Beverley' - the Church of England having the legal claim to 'York'. St George's became the pro-Cathedral until more money could be raised to rebuild St Wilfrid's in an appropriately grand style. This was effected, in French gothic, in 1864. The tower of St Wilfrid's is constructed so as to give the impression as one crosses Lendal bridge (opened in 1863) and looks down Dean

Duncombe's new street towards the west front of the Minster that the latter is actually the smaller of the two cathedrals. *[Illustration p.252]* As if to make the point, at the opening Cardinal Wiseman preached on the text, 'Thou art Peter'.

Despite this, relations between Protestants and Catholics in York were generally good. St Wilfrid's was in its origins an English gentry church and there was little prejudice against Catholics. Local historian and newspaper proprietor, William Hargrove, praised the nuns of the Convent outside Micklegate Bar as 'extremely beneficial' in 1818. The low point was reached in 1850 when the opening of St George's coincided with the restoration of the Catholic hierarchy, prompting the Tory-Evangelical *Yorkshire Gazette* to fulminate against 'The arrogant pretensions of the Pope' and the Wesleyan Lord Mayor, James Meek, called a meeting in the Guild Hall to affirm 'their bounden duty as Protestants, to protect our Protestant Queen, to stand by our Protestant institutions, and to prevent any foreign potentate from stretching his mantle over this decidedly Protestant country'.

In 1828 the Bar Convent chapel was closed to public worship and the Micklegate side of the city was served from St Wilfrid's but in 1878 the diocese of Beverley was dissolved and York was divided along the river Ouse between the new dioceses of Leeds and Middlesbrough. Both St Wilfrid's and St George's were in Middlesbrough and so a new church of the English Martyrs was begun in St Mary's Court, Blossom Street. With this exception, Catholic policy in the nineteenth century was to focus worship within the city and not to extend into the suburbs. If more capacity were needed, that could more easily be catered for with additional services rather than additional buildings.

This was in contrast to the policy of the Protestant churches which responded to the growth of the extra-mural districts with new buildings and parishes. So far as the Church of England was concerned, this policy proved to be short-sighted. The Church had a three-pronged approach to the changing needs of the enlarged city. First, medieval churches were rebuilt and improved, as with St Mary, Castlegate, 'restored' with £4,000 from Dean Duncombe by the gothic revival architect, William

Butterfield, in 1868-70. Other churches were demolished and replaced, as with St Maurice outside Monk Bar (1878) and St Lawrence, outside Walmgate Bar (1883), or simply demolished, as happened to St Crux in 1887. The outcry which greeted this latter gave new impetus to the movement to conserve York's historic buildings. Thirdly, new churches were built for the growing suburbs, beginning with St Paul's, Holgate (1851) and St Thomas in the Groves (1855). In most cases, this led to the creation of new suburban parishes and the impoverishment of the original parish within the city walls. Thus yet more small, non-viable inner city parishes were created. In only one instance was this mistake avoided. St Clement's was built outside the walls in St Mary, Bishophill Senior parish in 1874. Two years later it replaced St Mary's as the parish church and in 1885 the intra-mural part of the parish was transferred to St Mary, Bishophill Junior. The rector of St Clement's, George Argles, would not permit his parish to be further divided, and as its population grew in Clementhorpe and along the South Bank, he served it with mission halls and a team of curates based on the parish church. This proved to be the most successful of all York's Victorian parishes.

This method of proceeding was built into the Methodist circuit system, whereby a strong central church was responsible through satellite churches for an entire district. The three large Wesleyan chapels each headed its own circuit: New Street (1805), Wesley (1867) and Centenary (1884). From each, mission chapels with Sunday schools were set up in the suburbs, leading to the establishment of larger chapels where the cause was successful. Thus Melbourne Terrace chapel was opened in 1877 to serve New Fulford outside Walmgate bar; the Groves chapel was opened in 1884 following a successful school-chapel in Brook Street (1867); Southlands chapel was built to serve the South Bank in 1887; and in Clifton a small chapel of 1884 was replaced by a large gothic church in 1909. In some suburbs based on earlier villages, the Wesleyans were already present when the new parish church arrived. Thus in Heworth, Holy Trinity (1869) was preceded by Heworth Wesleyan chapel of 1826. In 1894 the vicar of Heworth complained that 'three quarters of the population belong to the

Wesleyan or other non-conformist denominations'.

So despite all its efforts, the Church of England in York was not able to improve upon the market share of church attendances that it had achieved in 1851, and while the Wesleyans did succeeded they no more than made up for the deficiencies of other branches of Nonconformity. As the practice of attending church twice on a Sunday, or perhaps of attending at all, declined only the Catholics increased their absolute numbers between 1851 and the census of attendance conducted by Seebohm Rowntree in March 1901.

Rowntree's survey was the only one to attempt both a division of church attendances into men and women and a rough estimate of social class. For the latter he estimated that two-thirds of congregations were 'working' class, about the same percentage as he would have expected in the total population. This contradicts the impression formed by many Church of England clergy from inner-city parishes but perhaps reflects success with the better-off workers of the suburbs. So far as women were concerned, 65 per cent of Church of England attendances were made by women and 59 per cent of Catholic attendances. Only the Nonconformists, with 51 per cent women, came close to equality in attracting the sexes. At their morning services, a clear majority of worshippers were men - perhaps an indication of the numbers of Nonconformist female servants and other Sunday-dinner cooks who were free to attend chapel only at the evening service.

What went on inside the various churches and chapels changed considerably during the nineteenth century. The interior lay out of most churches - other than Holy Trinity, Goodramgate - was also transformed, and the latter survived only because it shared its parish with St Maurice. Elsewhere by 1900 gone were the box-pews of 1800, covered with dirty green baize and clustered round the pulpit like sheep pens at the market in front of the auctioneer's gaze. Neat benches, all facing eastwards, now had a clear view of the altar table, sitting in an elevated chancel and decorated with candle sticks and a cross, instead of being hidden behind the pulpit on the same level as the main body of the church and decorated only with boards containing the words of the Ten

Commandments and the Lord's Prayer. The central ministry of the word had been set aside in favour of an increased emphasis on the sacraments. Communion, instead of being offered between four and twelve times a year was now said weekly and sometimes more frequently. At the Minster, full choral celebrations were introduced in 1874, but more communion services did not necessarily mean more communicants: the average numbers attending any one service at the Minster throughout the later nineteenth century remained constant at just under fifty.

Nonconformist worship was similarly changing during the nineteenth century, although the lack of formal liturgy and a readiness to experiment with hymns had long made their services more attractive and open to casual attenders. But whereas in 1800 most chapels - and, indeed, most parish churches - would not have had an organ but relied instead upon a string band, by the 1840s organs were being introduced - Centenary chapel had one from the start - and by 1900 where an organ loft could not be added or built a harmonium was used to lead the singing. The nature of the hymns also changed during the century, with more informal choruses and simple revivalist words. The famous American revivalists, Moody and Sankey, started their first English mission at Priory Street Baptist chapel in 1873 and the Salvation Army, with its popular brass bands, opened its barracks in Gillygate in 1883.

Mission services, and mission rooms became a regular feature of the outreach of the churches. The Established Church was hampered by legislation prohibiting services in mission halls until 1855, but there are few examples of regular mission services in York even after this date. In 1863, the Dean of York organised special Minster nave services for 'working men', which attracted congregations of over two thousand, but local parochial clergymen felt this undermined their own efforts which consisted largely of house-to-house visitation, whether undertaken informally by clergy and lay volunteers, or by the Anglican Scripture Readers' Society, or by members of the interdenominational Tract Society or City Mission. This last organisation grew out of the Ragged School founded under Wesleyan leadership in Bedern in 1846. It

279

appointed missionaries to work full-time in the worst areas of the city - Bedern, Walmgate, the Water Lanes and Hungate. The chief work was to distribute tracts and bibles and seek to save drunkards and prostitutes from themselves and for God. Their annual successes rarely reached double figures and like similar missions in the city and elsewhere their chief importance lay in their secondary work of social relief. Arising out of the City Mission in 1902 was the special Race Course Mission, aimed at preventing the worst excesses of drinking and gambling during race weeks.

The Nonconformist strategy was to opening mission halls in various parts of the inner city. The most important of these were the Hungate Mission (1861), run from the former Wesleyan schoolroom in Garden Place; the North Street Mission, begun by Wesley chapel on the riverside in 1868; and two missions organised in Layerthorpe by the Primitives in Duke of York Street (1877) *[Illustration p.273]* and the Wesleyans (1888). Other mission chapels were started by the Wesleyans and Primitives respectively in the vicinity of the railway workshops in Holgate (1872) and Leeman Road (1884). Thus the spreading suburban geography of the city can be traced in the planting of churches, chapels and mission halls to reach out to, and perhaps meet, some of the needs of the people.

Education

Education and religion were closely connected in York through much of the nineteenth century. Sunday schools were a major activity. In view of the smallness of the city parishes, the Church of England Sunday schools were organised on a city-wide basis by the Sunday School Committee, founded in 1788. This was unpopular with some parish clergy, partly because it deprived them of the means of bringing up the children of their own parishes with an attachment to their parish church, and partly because the Committee was dominated by Evangelical interests. Gradually, as the city expanded beyond the walls, the Committee's monopoly was challenged. St Lawrence's was organising its own schools in 1868 and St Mary, Bishophill Senior / St Clement's in 1872. The

Nonconformists also had their Sunday schools, closely linked with chapel life. To begin with the Wesleyans had one school each for boys and girls, located off Hungate, but others were started later in connection with Albion Street and St George's chapels.

When the Manchester Statistical Society surveyed the state of education in York in 1836, they found fifteen Church of England Sunday Schools, four Wesleyan, two Independent, and one each for the Protestant Methodists in Lady Peckett's Yard, the Primitive Methodists in Grape Lane and the Unitarians in St Saviourgate, the last two being very small. With 3,363 scholars on the books and an average attendance of two-thirds, just over half the pupils were in Church of England schools, about a quarter were Wesleyan and a seventh were in the Independent schools at Lendal and Salem. Most taught only reading, religion and morals for between two and three hours a week, and most pupils were aged between five and fifteen. Only the Protestant Methodists taught writing on a Sunday. Two-thirds of the schools had lending libraries.

Where York differed from most of the industrial towns further west, was that it did not rely upon Sunday schools to provide the majority of its children with a basic education. Partly because of the number of educational endowments for schools in the city and partly because there was little opportunity for childhood employment until the age of apprenticeship and domestic service at fourteen, day-school education was widely available in York. In 1836, about two thirds of all children between the ages of five and fifteen were in receipt of education, 85 per cent of them attending some form of day school. These ranged from dame schools and common day schools to 'superior private and boarding' schools, but over half the pupils were in what were called 'charity schools and schools attached to public institutions'. The dame schools taught chiefly reading and needlework, and the common day schools were only a little better with writing and arithmetic for boys and perhaps some writing for girls, while the charity schools offered reading, writing and arithmetic, together with some needlework, grammar, geography and history.

In 1836 the largest charity schools, dating from the eighteenth century, were the Blue Coat (64 boys) and Grey Coat (43 girls) schools, Wilson's Green Coat on Foss Bridge (40 boys), the Spinning School in St Andrewgate (46 girls) and Catholic schools at the Nunnery (50 girls) and near Monk Bar (85 boys). The major new additions in the nineteenth century were denominational schools associated with the National Society, the British Society, the Wesleyans and the Catholics.

The first schools set up in association with the National Society for Promoting the Education of the Poor in the Principles of the Established Church (founded 1811) were at the King's Manor, for boys, in 1812 and in the Merchant Taylors' Hall in Aldwark, for girls, the following year. By 1836 these had 220 and 190 pupils respectively. A second National School for boys was opened just outside Micklegate Bar in 1835 and a school for both boys and girls was opened in St Margaret's parish, Walmgate, in 1842. Other schools were started in association with specific parishes, notably St Cuthbert's where the rector's wealthy wife built girls' (1826) and boys' (1832) schools in Layerthorpe to meet the needs of the working classes in that rapidly expanding part of the parish. These schools were later associated with the National Society.

The first school in association with the largely Nonconformist British and Foreign Schools Society (1814) was a girls' school started by Quakers in 1813 in the centre of York, but moved to better premises built on the former Friends' burial ground on Bishophill Senior in 1829. A parallel boys' school was started in Hope Street, Walmgate, in 1827. At first the Wesleyans ran only an infant school, begun in 1830 at their Sunday school in Garden Place, off Hungate, but in 1840 they started a boys' school at Albion Street which in 1857 was moved to premises next to Wesley Chapel in Priory Street where schools were built for both boys and girls. There were also schools for boys and girls in the former St George's chapel, begun in 1847. Catholic schools for boys and girls were opened in the same area in association with St George's Catholic church in 1850.

The presence of these and many more, smaller schools in

York meant that the Education Act of 1870 was not applied. This Act stated that a School Board should be elected to raise a rate to build and run new schools on non-denominational lines where the existing provision was inadequate. Churches were given six months to make up any leeway before the Act could be applied. There immediately followed a flurry of activity as schools were opened by the Church of England to keep a School Board at bay: St Dennis's (1870), St Lawrence's (1872), St Clement's (1872), Bedern (1872-3), Heworth (1873), St Paul's (1877). In providing for city centre and suburbs alike, a School Board was put off. Instead, following legislation in 1876, a School Attendance Committee of the city corporation oversaw education in the city but had no responsibility for running schools. This remained the case until 1889 when a School Board became necessary.

Once elected, despite sectarian wrangling the Board planned and began to build six fine new schools which added to the architectural as well as educational legacy of nineteenth century York. The winning design, chosen in open competition, was provided by the York architect, W. H. Brierley. Though the first building, Shipton Street (1890), was single storey at the Board's insistence, thereafter he designed tall buildings with a high central hall: Fishergate (1894-5), Park Grove (1895) and Scarcroft (1896). *[Illustration p.284]* The final two schools, Poppleton Road and Haxby Road, followed in 1904. There were now places for some 12,000 pupils, twice the number in 1869.

More advanced education for the middle classes was provided in quite different schools, three of which were inherited from earlier centuries. The oldest, Archbishop Holgate's school (1546) in Ogleforth, close by the Minster, had eleven pupils in 1836, only one of whom was above fifteen, and one master teaching reading, writing, arithmetic, grammar, geography, history, languages, mensuration and mathematics. St Peter's school (1557) formerly held in the disused St Andrew's church, was in a slightly better condition, with twenty-five boys, six of whom were over fifteen, but in addition the master was taking in fifty-five fee-paying pupils of whom fourteen were over fifteen. The reason for this growth was the acquisition of new premises - again the work

Scarcroft School, built 1896

of Pritchett - in 1833, built on the site of the old deanery to the south of the Minster with proceeds from the increased rents received from the lands with which the school had been endowed in the 1550s. But in 1838, with the opening of a new proprietary school in Clifton, St Peter's rapidly lost pupils and by 1843 was in danger of closing. St Peter's now had few pupils but Clifton had little money. At this point a union was effected between the two, and the Clifton school continued with St Peter's name and endowments. In 1868, there were 105 boarders and 91 day-pupils, and boarding fees averaged £56 a year, with a further ten or twelve guineas (£10.50 - £12.60) for tuition fees. Most parents were from a professional, military or clerical background. Archbishop Holgate's school was less fortunate in its endowments. It struggled on until 1858 when it was amalgamated with the Yeoman School, built in Lord Mayor's Walk alongside the Diocesan Training College in 1845 as its practising school. But the natural clientele for the school were farmers who needed a good English education, whereas the grammar school persisted as a Classical school inferior to St

Peter's. Like many local grammar schools it fell between the two stools and by the 1890s was again in difficulties as it strove to find a new role in the city's educational provision.

The Diocesan Training College, later known as St John's College, was opened in the former premises of Manchester College (see below) in May 1841 with no pupils; numbers had built up to four by the end of the year. The aim was to supply teachers for Church of England elementary schools throughout the diocese. In 1842, the college was put under the joint management of the dioceses of York and Ripon and a nearby house was taken in Monkgate in which to begin training female teachers. In 1846 when the male students moved out to the new College being built in Lord Mayor's Walk to designs by Hudson's architect, G. T. Andrews, the female students moved into the former male premises and remained there until a new college was opened in Ripon in 1862. By 1913, what was now informally being called 'St John's College' had 120 pupils, but very few of them aspired to matriculate from the college to take a London university qualification: they were there simply to learn how to become elementary school teachers.

The earliest non-Church of England school in York was that provided for girls by the sisters at the Bar Convent since 1686. Described in 1857 as being for 'the daughters of the Catholic nobility, gentry, and respectable classes', its numbers grew in the first half of the nineteenth century from around fifty to over eighty. There was no equivalent Catholic school for boys, that being provided for the county from 1802 by the monks of Ampleforth. The Quakers also had their own schools. What became Bootham School was begun in 1822 when the York Quarterly Meeting bought a house from the Retreat asylum outside Walmgate Bar and let it to William Simpson as a boy's boarding school. When he retired in 1828 the Quarterly Meeting took over the school and put John Ford in as head master. This was to be a school providing a liberal education for the sons of middle and upper class Quaker families (the poorer boys went to Ackworth near Pontefract). In 1846 the school moved to a house in Bootham. The Schools Enquiry Commission (1868) found fifty-six boarders and five day-pupils. The purpose of the school was 'To afford a religious, guarded, and good literary education, on moderate terms' to Yorkshire Quakers. The average fee was £63 and the parents were mainly shopkeepers, farmers, manufacturers and professional men. Unlike at St Peter's, there was no corporal punishment. The equivalent Quaker school for girls was established in Castlegate, near the Friends' Meeting House, in 1831, moving to a house on The Mount in 1857. In 1869 there were forty-two boarders and one day-pupil. The curriculum was very wide and though the subject which commanded most hours a week was needlework (five hours), one hour a week was devoted to physics, natural history and chemistry.

A considerable addition to the intellectual life of York came in 1803 when Manchester College, the leading Unitarian Academy, chose Charles Wellbeloved as its principal. Wellbeloved had ministered at the St Saviourgate Chapel since 1792 and he brought the College from Manchester to York. At first it was accommodated in Wellbeloved's own house in Monkgate but later moved to its own premises in the same street where it remained until 1840. The principal purpose of the College was to train students in Divinity for the ministry and, although open to all without creedal test, this in practice restricted it to Unitarians. Lay students were also admitted on payment of a fee of a hundred guineas (£105) a year. There were about twenty students in 1819. The educational importance of the College, though, goes beyond this and is impossible to separate from the presence in York of Wellbeloved himself and his son-in-law, the classics tutor John Kenrick. Among the other ventures with which Wellbeloved was concerned were the Subscription Library (1794), the Yorkshire Philosophical Society (1823) and the Mechanics Institute (1827).

The first of these was primarily for the educated middle classes. In 1823 the entry fee was ten guineas (£10.50) and the annual subscription 26 shillings (£1.30): there were 477 subscribers. The Library was moved in 1812 from Minster Gates to St Helen's Square, across the road from the Mansion House;

then in 1836 elegant modern premises were taken at the end of the new terrace built in St Leonard's Place, where it remained for the rest of the century. The existence of such a library was probably one reason why the ratepayers of York did not feel it necessary to levy a penny rate under the 1851 Public Libraries Act to fund a free public library for the people of York.

For those lower down the social scale there was the Mechanics Institute, or Institute of Popular Science and Literature, which moved to new premises in St Saviourgate in 1846. Here there were a news room, a library, a lecture hall where lectures could be heard on various aspects of science and literature, and class rooms for more elementary subjects. In 1857 there were 468 members, and youths under eighteen paid as little as sixpence (2½p.) a month. Ladies were admitted for ten shillings (50p.) a year. New premises were built in Clifford Street in 1885 and the former building became the Masonic Lodge. Then in 1891 the city corporation bought the Institute as a Technical School and in 1893 its library became the first public library in York.

Closely associated with these developments was the School of Design which began in 1842 with accommodation in Lop Lane. It then moved into the premises vacated by St Peter's School (now the Minster Choir School) where it remained until 1890 when it was relocated in the north gallery of the Exhibition Building which also housed the Art Gallery. This building was taken over by the Corporation in 1891. Then, in 1905, the School of Design was merged with the School of Art which had previously been part of the Technical School. By the beginning of the twentieth century, therefore, the Corporation had acquired responsibility by various Acts of Parliament for the School Board's schools, the York Institute and the Design School, and was also running both the Art Gallery and the Public Library.

York as the county town also attracted schools to serve the county and region. One such was the Yorkshire School for the Blind, founded as a boarding school in part of the King's Manor in 1835 in memory of William Wilberforce to educate sixty blind boys and girls. In 1870 there were seventy-four boys and twenty-six girls and in 1886 an out-pupils department was added. As well as receiving an elementary education the pupils learnt music and craft skills. Another institution with regional appeal was Elmfield College, established on the outskirts of York in Heworth in 1864 by the Primitive Methodists to provide a classical education up to university matriculation for middle-class boys. One purpose of the school was to educate the sons of ministers and those aspiring to become ministers in the Primitive Methodist connexion. Towards the end of the century there were financial problems as numbers fell and the College temporarily closed in 1906.

The late nineteenth century saw the beginning of day-schooling for middle-class girls in York. In 1880 the Girls Public Day School Company opened York High School for Girls in Fishergate House; and in 1891 the Church Schools Company began York Church High School in Low Petergate. Evidently there was not room for both, and in 1900 the Church High School closed. With over a hundred pupils, the York High School then moved into the Low Petergate premises vacated by its rival but in 1906 these premises proved inadequate and the school closed. The Church Schools Company then moved back and started York College for Girls which survived for nearly a hundred years.

For most children of both sexes in nineteenth century York, the story was one of developing the provision of basic, elementary education to fit them for work by the age of fourteen. Not until after the Education Act of 1902 was it thought appropriate for public money to be spent on a secondary education leading, for those who wanted it, to university entrance.

Poverty and Health

It is easy when considering the industrial, artistic and commercial achievements of nineteenth century York to forget that most people were relatively poor. As James Smith observed in a report prepared for the Health of Towns Commission in 1845, 'The aspect of York, as seen in the principal streets, is tidy and pleasing, and the streets, though narrow, are well kept; not so, however, the

288

more retired and densely crowded parts, which have the same damp and filthy character as all the other towns.' The basic problems were poor drainage, inadequate arrangements for the removal of refuse, and a polluted water supply.

Dr Thomas Laycock, house surgeon at the County Hospital and physician to the Dispensary, prepared a full report for the Commission in 1844. He subscribed to the common theory that disease was spread through bad air, detectable in bad smells, but in his careful analysis of living conditions and patterns of disease he came close to understanding the connection between polluted water and the spread of disease. In the courts and alleys inhabited by the poorer classes, 'night soil' was left to accumulate until there was sufficient to take away. This was then barrowed into the streets where it was collected and taken to huge dung hills within the city. Major piles of dung were stored alongside the river Foss at Layerthorpe Bridge but there was another at the back of St Margaret's church, Walmgate. To this human excrement were added piles of manure from the numerous pigsties, cowhouses and stables that filled the city.

One of the worst parts of York was Bedern where former mansions of the rich and their outhouses were let as tenements for the poor. Of 98 families living there in 1844, 67 each inhabited only one room. In one house with sixteen families there were only two privies. Water from dung hills seeped back into the houses. In the parish of St Dennis, a quarter of families each lived in one room. The state of the parish burial grounds was an added cause of concern, many of them filled to overflowing. Laycock calculated the correspondences between mean age at death, the social make-up of a parish, and its height above sea level. He concluded that those parishes which were low lying, which were also where the poor tended to live, had a far lower mean age at death than more fortunate, elevated, middle-class parishes. For example, in All Saints, North Street, down by the river Ouse where nearly four out of every five inhabitants were of the labouring class, the mean age at death was under twenty. Further up Micklegate in Holy Trinity parish, the mean age at death was nearly forty-three. St Cuthbert's parish by the Layerthorpe dung piles was only thirteen feet (3.96

metres) above sea level and the mean age at death was just over twenty-two. Furthermore, with increased overcrowding things were getting worse. In 1816-21, when the population of St Cuthbert's parish (including its suburban parts) was 820, the mean age at death was thirty-four; in 1839-41 when the population was 1,995, the mean age at death was twenty-nine. Moreover, the most significant change affecting the mean was deaths of those under five years of age, which rose from 36 per cent to 54 per cent. In minute detail, Laycock built up an impressive array of statistics, all of which pointed to the necessity of improving the environmental health of the poorest districts of the city.

The water supply to York came partly from deep and shallow wells and partly from the Ouse. The shallow wells in particular were badly contaminated by the accumulated rubbish of centuries, while the water pumped from the Ouse was both in short supply and 'usually so dirty and turbid as scarcely to be fit for washing, and still less for cooking, or for being drunk'. All but 1,500 families were dependent on water carriers and wells for their water, or fetched it themselves from the river. The whole of the eastern side of the city, which drained into the Foss, suffered from the fact that the river was kept at seven feet (2.13 metres) above its natural level by the lock at the confluence with the Ouse. Houses and courts off Walmgate and Hungate in effect had a stagnant open sewer at their doors. Similar places along the Ouse received the discharges from the rudimentary drains of the better-off houses on the higher land where the introduction of water closets simply made matters worse. Between 1825 and 1844 the Improvement Commissioners spent £2,000 on 6,000 yards (5,486 metres) of drains, but this was nowhere near enough.

The main causes of death were pulmonary diseases, including tuberculosis and pneumonia, and epidemic and endemic diseases such as diarrhoea, dysentery, typhoid, typhus, measles and diphtheria. These were all regular occurrences but the spasmodic cholera, more spectacular because more unfamiliar, produced a reaction out of all proportion to the numbers it actually killed. York suffered two major outbreaks, in 1832 and 1849. An order of the Privy Council in October 1831 recommended towns to set up boards of health to take remedies against the disease, and one was formed for York the following month but it had no powers to raise money to make improvements before the disease actually arrived. A public subscription was raised which enabled the Board to rent a house near Fishergate Bar as a temporary hospital. After some arguments about where victims should be buried, the corporation gave a plot of land outside the city walls near the present railway station. The first death in York, in June 1832, was a man from Beedham's Court - otherwise known as 'Hagworm's Nest' - off Skeldergate, a regular source of epidemic diseases. The cholera then spread until every part of the city was affected. By the end in September there had been 450 cases and 185 deaths, or 1 in 137 of the population.

Once the disease had departed it was quickly forgotten as the reluctance of party politicians to tax ratepayers took precedence over improvement to the environment. Laycock's report in 1844 showed how little had been done to prepare for the next outbreak in 1849. The most important development, long overdue, was the creation of the York Public Cemetery Company which opened an 8-acre (3.24 hectares) burial ground beyond Walmgate Bar in 1836, with a scaled-down version of a Greek temple for a chapel, designed by J. P. Pritchett who was a member of the founding committee.

Laycock's report came as the population of York was being swelled by Irish and other immigrants. The worst typhus epidemic of the century came in 1847. Of 403 deaths, 283 occurred in the three parishes of St Dennis, St Margaret and St George - no wonder it was known as 'the Irish disease'. Unlike the cholera and typhoid, typhus is not water-borne but is spread in filthy conditions by the bite of a louse. The next cholera epidemic in the summer of 1849 also struck Walmgate hardest: of eighty-eight deaths in the city, sixty-one of them were in the Walmgate district, though Beedham's Court in Micklegate was also affected.

The combined effect of the Health of Towns movement, as represented locally by Laycock's report, the renewed onset of cholera, and national legislation in the form of the 1848 Public Health Act, led to the creation of the York Board of Health in 1850 which at last began the serious business of improving the environment in York. In 1854 the Foss Islands area was drained and a new road was built between Walmgate Bar and Layerthorpe bridge. Between 1850 and 1856, £8,519 was spent on drainage and sewerage, but the Board of Health's priorities become clear when it is realised that £4,000 of this was spent on the middle-class Mount which needed improvement least. In all, during the lifetime of the Board between 1850 and 1872, the annual average expenditure was only £1,000. The death rate in York in the 1870s was 25 per thousand compared with 24 per thousand in the 1850s. In Walmgate as late as 1888, one in three children failed to reach their fifth birthday. In 1884 water closets were still the exception rather than the rule.

The problem lay in the slums, which were growing worse with the increase in population and the age of the buildings. Under parliamentary legislation, local authorities were enabled to set standards for new housing and to demolish old ones but had no powers to replace them. The only example of widespread demolition on health grounds in York in the nineteenth century was the destruction of the Water Lanes after 1875. This may actually have made matters worse, for the poor had nowhere else to go but to similar housing elsewhere in the city. As Laycock realised in 1844, the poor were trapped in a vicious circle: 'Sickness makes them poor, therefore food and clothing are inadequate', but without good food, the poor were more liable to disease. Further, the poor could not afford high rents. Slum landlords served with improvement notices by the Board could point out that, if they brought sanitation up to standard, they would have to put up their rents, which would drive the poor into cheaper and more insanitary dwellings.

The problem with poverty and public health alike was ignorance of their causes. Just as the medical profession stumbled towards understanding the role of impure water rather than bad air as a major cause of the spread of disease, so philanthropists and poor law officials slowly came to understand why people were poor. At the beginning of the century the problem seemed simple. The 'deserving' poor, those who through illness, old age and bereavement were poor through no fault of their own, were the proper objects of the charity of the rich and the overseer of the parochial poor. The idle should be denied charity and parochial relief. In this spirit local bodies such as the York Charitable Society were set up to use local knowledge and house-to-house visitation to seek out those who deserved relief, to prevent it being 'intercepted' by undeserving street beggars. This was also the purpose of the 1834 Poor Law Amendment Act, to deter the idle from claiming relief.

York was well provided with public charities, mainly endowed in earlier centuries but augmented in the nineteenth. There were sixteen groups of almshouses or 'hospitals' for the aged poor, some of which, such as Anne Middleton's hospital in Skeldergate (1828) and Lady Hewley's hospital (1840), were rebuilt in the nineteenth century - the latter being moved from Tanner Row to St Saviourgate when the railway station was built. There were schools for poor children, such as the four Dodsworth schools, endowed by a local ironmonger in 1798-1803 to teach poor children to read and write. There were numerous parochial and municipal charities for the distribution of bread, coals and small sums of money to the poor.

The sick could obtain tickets from subscribers to the York County Hospital, rebuilt in 1851, or the York Dispensary. These eighteenth-century foundations continued to serve the deserving poor of York throughout the nineteenth century. The Dispensary moved from the Merchant Adventurers' Hall to St Andrewgate in 1808. By 1828 it was treating perhaps 12 per cent of the population. Further new premises were built in New Street in 1829, where it remained until the new dispensary was erected in Duncombe Place in 1899. By the early 1880s, the Dispensary was dealing with around 5,000 patients a year, and the same number were being treated as out-patients by the hospital.

York was also noted for its treatment of mental illness with its two eighteenth-century foundations, the York Lunatic Asylum in Bootham and the Retreat. The reputation of the former continued to be controversial. The issue of treatment of the insane was raised by Samuel Tuke, grandson of the founder of the

Retreat, in a publication of 1813 in which he advocated the 'moral' approach favoured at the Retreat. This stimulated an argument in the newspapers about conditions at the York Lunatic Asylum under its physician, Dr Best. Tuke's quest for an enquiry into the conduct of the Asylum was abetted by Godfrey Higgins, a magistrate from Doncaster who was concerned about the treatment of a patient from the West Riding. As a result of the enquiry the physician's fees were replaced by a fixed salary, a committee of management and asylum visitors were appointed, and the average number of annual admissions was reduced from ninety-four in 1777-1814 to forty-eight in 1815-33. The Retreat was a smaller institution, with about a hundred patients in 1830 growing to just under two hundred by 1914. Until 1880 annual admissions were around twenty, growing to between thirty and fifty only at the very end of the century.

Both fee-paying and pauper lunatics were admitted to the York Lunatic Asylum until 1845 when the new North and East Riding Asylum was opened at Clifton and most York paupers were sent there; but in 1861 Clifton could no longer cope with the numbers and they were again sent to Bootham. This probably saved the Asylum for the attempt to develop it solely for the middle classes was proving unsuccessful. Only in 1906 did the city open its own asylum for pauper lunatics at Naburn, when nearly three hundred patients were admitted.

Building upon eighteenth century foundations, many social needs were met in the nineteenth century through the device of institutions - schools, hospitals, workhouses and asylums - but, despite such good works in the relief of sickness and poverty, by the 1880s it was becoming increasingly clear that this was not enough, as was shown in a major survey of the city's poor undertaken in 1899 by Benjamin Seebohm Rowntree, son of Joseph Rowntree. Rowntree looked at income, diet and housing conditions. Poverty caused principally by low wages was still the fate of a considerable minority of the population and housing conditions for such people were still appalling. Much of Bedern had been cleared in 1872 to make way for a school and there were only a few tenements left in York, housing just under five hundred families, but nearly another three thousand working-class families lived in what Rowntree regarded as sub-standard housing - near slums and slums: back-to-back houses, dark, damp and decaying with inadequate water supplies and over-flowing privies. Though the extent of such housing was less than in Dr Laycock's day, Rowntree's worst examples were comparable with what had been reported in 1844.

Wealth and Leisure

Though a third of the population of York was in poverty at any one time during the century and perhaps as many again were affected by poverty at some stage in their lives, that still left some thirty per cent who comprised that class of people who could afford to keep servants. Not all were wealthy, but they were comfortable and could afford to support a life-style which permitted leisure-time pursuits. This elite would be joined from time to time by others from the middle of society whose temporary affluence in the better-built small terraces of suburban York enabled them to join in at least some of the social life of the city.

In 1828, the Assembly Rooms were given a face-lift with a Greek temple carriage portico designed by the ubiquitous J. P. Pritchett. This was an attempt to refurbish the image of York as a city for the leisured gentry, but times were changing. Assemblies were largely confined to the Assize and Race Weeks. As Whellan's *History of York* put it delicately in 1857, 'The assemblies in these rooms are now very well attended, though they were much exceeded by those of the close of the last century, when York was the metropolis of the north, and the centre of attraction.' There was also decline at the races, no longer patronised by great aristocrats such as the Fitzwilliams, yet in 1832 the races were sufficiently important to the economy and self-esteem of the city for the corporation to make a regular subscription of £200 - with a further £50 for the fox hounds. The prestige of the races continued to decline until at least 1858, while the reputation of Doncaster rose. The Theatre Royal was also passing through a lean patch. In 1813 the manager, John Wilkinson, went bankrupt and his successors did little better. The interior was redesigned in 1821-2, gas lighting was installed in 1824 and a new façade fronting St Leonard's Place was added in 1835, but not until the railway network enabled the managers to bring in London actors and even whole companies did the fortunes of the theatre begin to revive. After a further bankruptcy in 1876 the resident company was disbanded and thereafter only touring companies performed.

To concentrate on the decline of York is, however, to miss alternative points of growth. If the city could no longer rely upon the county gentry and aristocracy to maintain its social life, it could still draw upon the old professions - the church, the law, medicine and the army. York remained an assize town; it was home to large numbers of country solicitors and medical men serving the county town and its hospitals, including an enlarged military hospital from 1854; it was still the centre of the diocese and province of York with its ecclesiastical courts and increasing numbers of clerical gatherings; and its importance as a military city was growing as the barracks, opened in 1796, were expanded in the 1860s and again in 1878 when the headquarters of the North Eastern Command were moved from Manchester to York. In 1841, a company was formed to build a social venue for officers of the Yorkshire Hussars and barristers attending the York Assizes. The rooms, named after the colonel of the regiment, Earl de Grey, were opened in 1842 and were used also for balls, concerts, meetings and other public entertainments.

Symbolic of the vigorous intellectual life engendered in nineteenth century York by an elite of professional men was the foundation of the Yorkshire Philosophical Society in 1822, with its botanic garden in the grounds of St Mary's Abbey (acquired in 1827), its classically fronted museum (1830, this time by William Wilkins) *[colour plate 14]* and its observatory (built in 1833). The impetus to found the Philosophical Society came partly from the need to preserve the city's past, not least the ruins of St Mary's Abbey, and partly the stimulus given by the discovery of prehistoric bones in Kirkdale Cavern, Kirbymoorside, in 1821. The men whom the Society brought together had wide-ranging interests of a scientific nature. Their leading member and first president was William Vernon, son of the Archbishop of York, but the active membership brought in men of many intellectual and denominational backgrounds, Quakers and Unitarians, doctors, ministers of religion and solicitors: names such as Graham and Gray, Wellbeloved and Kendrick, Tuke and Ford, Atkinson and Laycock. In 1831 Lord Milton, son and heir of Earl Fitzwilliam, became second president. The British Association for the Advancement of Science chose York for its inaugural meeting in 1831.

The proliferation of learned societies in the first half of the nineteenth century, involving these and similar men, with aristocratic patronage and support, is quite remarkable. Among such might be listed the Yorkshire Central Agricultural Association (1832), patron Lord Harewood, Lord Lieutenant of the West Riding; the Yorkshire Architectural Society (1841), presidents the Earls of Carlisle and Zetland, the former being a past Lord Lieutenant of the East Riding and the latter being current Lord Lieutenant of the North Riding and, as Thomas Dundas, MP for York in 1830-4; the Yorkshire Naturalists Club (1849), president Lord Londesborough; and the Yorkshire Antiquarian Club (1849), president Charles Wellbeloved. Among more specialised institutions were the York Medical Society (1832), which established a medical school at the County Hospital between 1834 and 1858; and the York Choral Society (1833) which gave four subscription concerts a year and included among its subscribers in 1857 the Archbishop of York and Lord Wenlock as well as 'most of the gentry of the City and neighbourhood'.

Nineteenth century York saw the building of a number of places of public resort which sought to bring the arts to a wider public. Music was the most respectable form of entertainment in Victorian England but the Assembly Rooms were too intimate for more than the small orchestras and select audiences of eighteenth-century society and certainly could not accommodate the Yorkshire Music Festival. This grew out of a series of concerts, begun in 1808 with the venue rotating between Sheffield, Leeds and York. In 1823 the four-day festival included two concerts in the Minster and two in the Assembly Rooms; there were also two balls in the Assembly Rooms, William Charles Macready of Covent Garden and Drury Lane fame appeared at the Theatre, and there was a balloon ascent from Toft Green. The profit of £7,200 was shared between the York County Hospital and the infirmaries in Leeds, Sheffield and Hull. Flushed with this success, the following year the Festival Concert Room with seating for around 1,500 was built off Museum Street at the back of the Assembly Rooms. Thereafter this became the regular venue for major entertainments. The famous soprano, Jenny Lind, appeared in 1848 and 1856; Thackeray lectured on 'George III' in 1857; Dickens read his *Christmas Carol* in October 1858; and Lord Brougham lectured on political questions of the day in the same year. The British Association held some of its fiftieth anniversary meetings in the Festival Concert Room in 1881, but the opening took place in the new Exhibition Hall, illuminated by electricity. This building had been completed in 1879 to house a great exhibition on the model of the successful Fine Arts and Industrial Exhibition held in a temporary building in Bootham asylum field in 1866. The 1879 exhibition ran from May to November, during which time 548,890 people attended. On the final Saturday a special day for 'the people' attracted 14,019. The overall profit from the exhibition was £12,000. The building, in what is still known as Exhibition Square, was sold to the Corporation in 1891 for the City Art Gallery. *[Illustration p.299]*

The hub of elite social life in nineteenth-century York was the new St Leonard's Place with the Subscription Library, the De Grey Rooms, the new entrance to the Theatre and, nearby, the Yorkshire Museum, the Assembly Rooms and the Festival Concert Room, so it is not surprising that the central house on the crescent was the first location for the Yorkshire Club, established in 1835 'for the nobility and gentry of the County'. With an entrance fee of 10 guineas (£10.50) and an annual subscription of £5, there were about 250 members in 1857. When Lendal Bridge was opened in 1863, new premises were built next to the bridge with a terrace overlooking the river. It is not surprising that opposition greeted the decision of the Poor Law Guardians to move their offices to Museum Street in 1859, thus introducing vagrants into

The Exhibition Building, later Art Gallery, 1879

the fashionable heart of the city.

Between the elite and the poor, the middling section of society had increasing leisure and money in the late nineteenth century and this is reflected in an expanding provision for their needs. Many leisure time activities were associated with the various churches and chapels, but there was also the York Institute and some commercial provision. The York Swimming Bath company was formed in 1836 with both swimming and shower baths in Marygate - subscription ten shillings (50p.) a year including a fresh towel every day - but the corporation did not open their municipal baths on St George's Fields until 1879. At the end of the nineteenth century the York Institute had a gymnasium and Wesley chapel had two cricket teams and cycling and swimming clubs, while the Groves chapel had its own brass band. Indeed, brass bands were a popular means of making music and before 1914 there were several bands in the city, formed in association with churches and chapels and places of work, including Rowntree's and the Railway Works.

299

As Rowntree discovered in 1899, the most popular pastime for the bulk of the working-class population was the public house. Some had popular singing rooms attached. There was, he calculated, one on-licence for every 330 of the population, a far lower ratio than either Leeds or Bradford. The most popular sports were off-course betting (then illegal), attending the races and playing football. The latter developed slowly, the York and District Football League dating only from 1897 with the York and District Football Association three years later. The first York City Football Club was formed only in 1908, and this was on an amateur basis. Cricket was much older. York Cricket Club went back to 1784 and the York Amateurs, a rugby union team composed largely of old boys from St Peter's, was formed in 1868.

One of the most interesting social developments in the later nineteenth century were the Quaker Adult Schools - partly educational, partly religious, but increasingly also concerned with leisure, an embodiment of the Quaker belief in the whole man which had inspired Joseph Rowntree to move his cocoa works to a green-field site in the 1890s. The first school was started by John Stephenson Rowntree in 1848 at Hope Street with the aim of teaching youths 'to apply the teaching of the Bible to everyday life and the problems of society'. It moved to a room in Lady Peckett's yard, behind the Rowntree shop and house, in 1857 and from there grew and spread. A savings bank, a library and a temperance society were formed but other methods had also to be used to attract young working men and, later, women. A Friday evening social club for boys was started at Hope Street, and at the Leeman Road school there was a social club and an allotment society with 150 plots of land. By 1902, there were four schools with 729 members; in 1906 there were thirteen schools with 2,373 members. The York and District Adult School Union, formed in 1903, offered Horticultural and Fur and Feather shows and a choral competition; there were nineteen billiard tables in twelve schools, with inter-school competitions, and also cricket and fishing matches as well as reading rooms and libraries. The rapid expansion of these schools around the turn of the century suggests an unmet need for diversified leisure provision in York at this time.

One final institution characteristic of nineteenth century York is the Equitable Industrial Society - otherwise known as 'the Co-op' - a working-class institution calculated to appeal to the better-off section of that class. Founded in 1858, it struggled at first and really came into its own only during the final quarter of the nineteenth century when rising real wages expanded its market in much the same way as they increased demand for Rowntree's products. In 1888 there was just one store, in Market Street, with 438 members and sales of £3,420. Twelve years later there were twenty-one stores, 7,250 members and sales of £167,337. The dividend on purchases was 2s. 4d. (12p.) in the pound. New central buildings were opened in Railway Street in 1899 by which time local stores were a feature of many working-class districts, beginning with Holgate Road near the railway works in 1889. But the Co-op stood for far more than coal, flour, tea and 'the divi'. There was an Education Committee which arranged lectures and paid the fees for the children of members who wished to attend continuation classes run by the School Board; a penny bank with 1,700 depositors, mainly children; and a lending library. There was also a branch of the Co-operative Women's Guild which organised lectures for women. This was another face of nineteenth century York, reported in Rowntree's survey of poverty though not usually highlighted in references to that work. In it we can glimpse the life not of the slums so frequently exposed to the gaze of the social enquirer but the more private world of respectable workers who lived in those rows of suburban terraces which were such a feature of nineteenth century York.

9

A FUTURE FOR THE PAST - YORK IN THE TWENTIETH CENTURY

Patrick & Bridget Nuttgens

Introduction

The life of a man born in 1900 who lived into his ninth decade would encompass the century of greatest change in the history of this country. His childhood would be in the Golden Edwardian Age, when the British Empire was at the height of its extent and powers, and when Britain really ruled the waves. He would watch a countryside become denuded of farm labourers as hedgerows were ripped out in the early thirties and   bigger and bigger machines took over men's work on bigger and bigger fields, a landscape increasingly crossed by marching electricity pylons, telegraph wires, motorways and airport runways.   He would find cities that climbed higher and higher in towers of glum, monotonous concrete or shimmering glass, cities that bristled with lights and frenetic activity.   He would see the arrival of cars, regular train travel - even daily commuting, for instance, between York and London; and from time to time become aware of the shrinking of distances that comes with aeroplane flights and the telephone.   The entire tempo of life would change. Radio, films, television, and eventually the space race and the internet would become part of everyday life. He would grow from being a citizen of his country with power in the political process to being a global citizen; indeed he might envisage the possibility that his descendants could be citizens of space. At the start of the century quite a proportion of the population, particularly workers in the country and of course women, would not in their lifetime go further than ten miles from their birthplace. By the end the average person, even in the lower income groups, will have gone to Benidorm or Majorca or Tenerife for holidays, and many will have flown as far as the States or Australia or gone on a round- the- world trip.

He would have lived through two world wars and the press and television would have made him an intimate witness to many civil and tribal wars whose cruelty, violence and devastation would surpass the record of previous generations. In his lifetime empires, including our own, would break up with the granting of autonomy if not freedom to their colonies; new empires based on financial power, like that of the United States, would take over world domination.

He would witness the enormous social effects brought about by two world wars. At the start of the 1914-18 War over 80% of working women were employed in domestic service; afterwards there was a changed scene. The Suffragette Movement's success in extending the vote to women in 1928 was the start of a movement for women's rights which was to gather pace throughout the century, culminating in the control of their sexuality offered by the contraceptive pill and the Abortion Act in the 1960s. The Welfare State after the Second World War changed the health of the nation and successive improvements in living conditions altered the perception of 'poverty' from decade to decade. However, towards the end of the century, the emphasis on individual 'rights' would cross the Atlantic from America to produce a culture of litigation which would have deleterious effects on, in particular, medicine, architecture and political decisions. The 'Thatcher revolution' would affect everyday living, particularly in respect of the reorganisation of council houses, the 'right to buy' accorded to council tenants to buy their house at a very competitive price creating a 'property owning democracy' in the country. He would watch Britain becoming a multi-racial society. He would witness a relaxation in dress, in manners and morals, and in relationships between generations.

This chapter will chart how many of these changes took place more slowly in this northern city in the early part of the century, but accelerated rapidly in the second half. Some crucial movements scarcely affected York at all. Because of her stable economy based on the two main industries – confectionery and the railways – she did not suffer the catastrophic unemployment visited on other cities during the depression of the twenties and thirties; nor did York experience an influx of immigrants - neither as regards Jewish immigrants fleeing persecution, the Irish looking for work, the West Indians recruited into other British cities to run the transport system, or people from the Indian subcontinent, originally recruited as workers in the mills and foundries. Unlike London, the Midlands, West Yorkshire and Glasgow York has remained predominantly white and Anglo-Saxon.

Social Conditions

But in matters of poverty, York at the start of the century had no fewer   problems than any other British city. In February 1901 Seebohm Rowntree published a book which gave an unparalleled picture of the life of working people in York. It was entitled *Poverty: a Study of Town Life*. With a small team of volunteers he had in the last decade of the previous century visited 11,560 families and seen 46,785 people. It was an unprecedented description of the existence of thousands of York citizens at the turn of the century. He wrote: "The conditions of life obtaining in my native city of York were not exceptional, … and they might be taken as fairly representative of the conditions existing in many, if not most of our provincial towns".

One hundred years later, York presents a totally different face. In spite of losing most of its main sources of employment – between the seventies and the eighties the city lost for a time its status as a county burgh and became merely a district of North Yorkshire, run from Northallerton; it suffered demotion as a

304

major junction in the railway network; the railway carriage works, once a major employer, were sold; of the native confectionery industry, Rowntrees after a successful amalgamation with Mackintosh was sold to the Swiss firm of Nestles, Terry's was sold to Suchard and Craven's disappeared altogether. In spite of these changes which might have been expected to plunge York deeper into poverty and destitution, at the start of the 21st century the city presents an appearance both beautiful and prosperous. There still exists the section of the population which has 'fallen through the net' of welfare provision - the young boys with their bony greyhounds on strings who sleep in the doorways of Coney Street, and the mentally ill or drug addicted figures (discarded from hospitals under the 'care in the community' policy) who sit on the benches outside the Art Gallery in Exhibition Square – but these are a feature of all British towns at the end of the twentieth century.

Seebohm's Rowntree's book which ushered in the new century did more than carry out a social survey; he analysed the causes of poverty and divided it into two categories – primary and secondary. Primary poverty included those "whose total income was not enough to obtain the minimum necessities of life for mere physical efficiency". He vividly described what this meant in practice: "A family living on the scale allowed for this estimate must never spend a penny on a railway fare or omnibus. They must never go into the country unless they walk. They must never buy a half-penny newspaper or spend a penny to buy a ticket for a popular concert. They must write no letters to absent children, for they cannot afford to pay the postage. They must never contribute anything to their church or chapel, or give any help to a neighbour which costs them money. They cannot save, nor can they join a sick club or a trade union, because they cannot pay the necessary subscriptions. The children must have no pocket money for dolls, marbles or sweets. The father must smoke no tobacco and drink no beer. The mother must never buy any pretty clothes for herself or her children. .... Should a child fall ill, it must be attended by the parish doctor; should it die, it must be buried by the parish. Finally the wage earner must never

Seebohm Rowntree

Bootham School

be absent from his work for a single day." In 1899, 9.91% of the city's population (15.46 of all wage earners) lived *below* the standards outlined above. A third of the men who volunteered for military service between 1893 and 1902 were turned down on medical grounds, according to Theo Barker in *The Long March of Everyman*. Secondary poverty included those who would have enough money to reach the bread line if some of it were not spent on something 'wasteful'.

In the areas of primary poverty there were few houses fitted with a bath and the sewers were defective. In areas such as Walmgate and Hungate, many such dwellings were occupied by labourers whose families had come from Ireland in the 19th century, people with low wages and large families. Not surprisingly, the first Victorian Catholic Church, St George's, was built in that area.

Poverty was an instant success; it was republished in 1902 and 1903 and it became a standard work. For the purposes of this study it tells us much about the city of York. The numbers were alarming. Only about 12% of the working population were well housed. 9% of the houses in the city were back-to-back and the density – the number of people per acre - in areas like Skeldergate was 349. It was not a 'slum' city with the problem of acres of back-to-backs as was Leeds at the same time, but it had low standards and expectations.

Forty years later in 1941 Seebohm Rowntree published a new study *Poverty and Progress*. Although, the average weekly diet for a working family outlined by Rowntree, consisting largely of tea and bread and dripping, with the occasional feast of sausages or cod and chips, was still of low nutritional value, the comparison between 1899 and 1936 when the later survey was carried out was a story of social improvement. Whereas 15.46% of the working population lived in conditions of primary poverty in 1899, the proportion had been reduced to 6.8% in 1936. Wages had improved, families were smaller, and social services such as unemployment benefit and pensions had greatly improved. Many more families were accommodated in either private houses or council houses.

In this story of social improvement the firm of Rowntrees played a major role. Joseph Rowntree had spent several weeks in Ireland in the 1840s, studying poverty and starvation. In the 1860s he read papers on poverty at several conferences in England. He made significant social improvements in his own firm – wages and pensions, for example, in which Rowntrees were pioneers. Seebohm was the son of Joseph Rowntree who in 1869 joined his brothers' cocoa business in Tanner's Moat and enlarged it to become Rowntree and Co. In 1895 its new factory the Cocoa Works was built in the Haxby Road and in 1897 it became a Limited Company. The business which had started with 200 workers now had 2000 workers and went on expanding.

The social work of the Rowntree family did not only apply to the workplace. In the same year in which Seebohm published *Poverty*, Joseph purchased 123 acres of land near the village of Earswick and laid out a model village, New Earswick. In that he was following the example of Quakers like Cadbury's at Bournville and others like Reckitts in Hull and Lever in Port Sunlight.

New Earswick was to be a village of much improved standards for workers in the cocoa works and also for others. Rowntree wanted to find out "whether we can build to let at a price people can pay." He had been impressed by Ebenezer Howard's book *Tomorrow* republished in 1989 as *Garden Cities of Tomorrow*. New Earswick was the first 'garden village' designed by Barry Parker as planner and Raymond Unwin as architect. The first houses were built in 1902 at a generous density of 11 houses per acre in blocks of four houses, with the living rooms facing south, wide roads with grass verges, two fruit trees per house, three bedrooms, a bathroom upstairs and a w.c. downstairs. It was probably the first time that 'social housing' as it was later called, was planned with true consideration of the needs of tenants. Innovations included a cupboard under the stairs large enough to house the pram, and the first 'through' living rooms allowing the house type to be orientated in different ways. They were the model for thousands of middle class homes in most parts of the country. The intention was that the garden village would be an education in itself, and provide a new way of life for its tenants.

Some of the occupants of New Earswick did work in the Cocoa Works, but with the Quaker detestation of ghettoes and bigotry, Joseph Rowntree insisted that a number of houses should always be let to non-Quakers and to non-employees of Rowntree's. Indeed the largest proportion of tenants worked on the railways. The roads in the village were named after garden trees – Birch Grove, Willow Glade and Hawthorn Spinney – and the land between the village and the factory alongside the river Foss, here only a beck as it runs towards the centre of the city, was laid out a grove of cherry and almond trees, heavy with blossom in Spring and magical when frosted over in Winter.

Seebohm Rowntree noted that by 1936 there were many forms of recreation that were unknown to workers in 1899; he listed among these benefits the cinema, wireless, bicycles, cheap books, parks and public gardens, swimming baths, small private gardens attached to the houses, and a repertory theatre. He believed that providing such opportunities would ensure fewer drunken people in their homes and in the streets. A community hall for meetings and entertainment, The Folk Hall, was central to the village complex. The Rowntree Baths and Rowntree Theatre were built close to the factory and still play an active and highly prized part in the life of the city.

The story of Rowntree Village Trust involvement does not end with the building of New Earswick. In the second half of the century, other housing needs materialised due to demographic changes; these were satisfied in the shape of 'Lifetime Homes' which would provide accommodation for families from the cradle to the grave, and a village specifically for the retired and elderly, Hartrigg Oaks. From the exterior, a 'lifetime home' looks no different to a typical house on a pleasant estate. But ramps, not steps lead in at the door, passageways and corners are wide enough to make the movement of pushchairs and wheelchairs possible, electric sockets and window height are at a level for wheelchairs, planning allows for the later introduction of a wheel-in shower in the downstairs toilet, and for a stair lift, and the roomy dining alcove off the living room can be converted into a bedroom for an elderly relative. Hartrigg Oaks is a complex of one or two-bedroom houses for single retired persons or for couples, with a nursing wing for full care, and a social centre with dining room, coffee room, library, music and fitness rooms.

Local Government

The Rowntree Village Trust was, in the private charitable sector, a pioneer in what was throughout the early half of the century increasingly seen as an obligation on the local authority – to supply better housing. The change was countrywide. In York, as in all towns and cities, local government was no longer mainly concerned with drains and policemen. It was engaged in an ever-widening group of activities, affecting almost every aspect of the life of the community. Between 1875 and the end of the century, the Fire Brigade had been handed over to the Corporation by the Yorkshire Insurance Company, the city had adopted the provisions of the Libraries Act and in the last decade a technical school had been created which encompassed the School of Art. A school board had been formed in 1889, and in 1902 the Corporation took over overall responsibility for education. In 1930 it accepted responsibility for the poor. Increasingly it engaged in trading activities, for instance associated with the Ouse and Foss Navigation and the tramway system, and by the middle of the twentieth century it was one of the principal employers of labour in the city. The provision of electricity began in 1900 and increased with every year. Because of the increasing demand for water, the Severus Hill Reservoir was replaced in 1914 by a water tower; this in its turn was replaced by a bigger tower on Siward's Howe, on the hill behind Heslington, in 1957. At the end of the century the water tower is no longer used for its original purpose, and exhibits a microcosm of the changed use of many buildings in the city by storing scenery from the Theatre Royal. The York Public Cemetery Company owned 13 acres of ground by 1914, and the following year a municipal cemetery including a military section for the barracks, was

310

opened at Fulford; by 1950 it covered 20 acres. At the end of the 19th century, intercepting sewers to stop sewage emptying directly into the Ouse had been built – a move similar to that adopted in the 'great stink' of London which was to prove crucial in delivering our cities from the scourge of typhoid. Instead the sewage was pumped to sewage works near Naburn. These were extended and improved in the nineteen fifties, and a second works to serve the west side of the city was built at Middlethorpe. The use of libraries expanded. The new library was built in 1927 within the corner of the Roman wall near the Multangular Tower.

York was slow to implement the Public Health Acts of 1849 and 1872, due to endless quarrels in the Health Board of the Council over sewerage, paving, lighting and improvements in the cattle market, particularly whenever - as usually was the case - improvements would mean increases in the rates. Before the new sewage disposal scheme was passed in 1889 York's health was below the national average. As late as 1902 a vote of the Corporation blocked the implementation of the Act of 1902 which gave powers to widen streets and compel builders to install water closets.

During the first half of the 20th century, the health of the city was entrusted to a group of general hospitals - the County, the City and the fever hospital of the last century off Haxby Road at Yearsley Bridge. After the institution of the National Health Service in 1948, the hospitals came under the York and Tadcaster Hospital Management Committee. Bit by bit, the work of the County, the hospital for infectious diseases and the City Hospital and eventually the General and Maternity Hospital in Fulford, set up in 1954 in prefabricated huts that had been used for military purposes during the war, were transferred in the second half of the century to the new York District Hospital. This was designed in 1976 by Lord Llewelyn Davies on a site on Wigginton Road in a series of two- or three- storey ranges with a view to future expansion. In spite, however, of many more blocks being added as it took over the functions of the other hospitals, the accommodation has proved quite inadequate, and by the end of the century problems of parking for both patients and staff were extreme. The intention of the University to launch a medical school in association with Hull in the 21st century, will demand further decisions about accommodation. There is a possibility that the entire hospital complex may have to be moved to the extended Science Park of the University at Heslington.

York's provision for the mentally ill has been more ample – indeed, York was known colloquially as 'a city of loonies and lollies'. Bootham Park by York's most famous architect John Carr in 1777 was unusual in its time in that it was a purpose-built lunatic asylum. This classically handsome building set back in considerable grounds is still in use today for its original purpose and   retains its little chapel. Since its grounds back onto the District Hospital, nurses' hostels and other blocks virtually join up the two sites. Another hospital for the elderly and demented, Clifton Hospital at Rawcliffe, stood beside the river in even more extensive policies. It was sold off at the time of the Care in the Community policy, and there are now housing estates and a restaurant on the site. Unhappy about some of the methods of treatment in Bootham Park, a member of the Society of Friends started at the end of the 18th century to build a psychiatric hospital, known as the Retreat, off Heslington Road. It was extended throughout the 19th and 20th centuries, with some notable work by Brierley's firm and by Brierley himself.

All these were necessary improvements, but the health of the city was unlikely to improve substantially until the Local Authority assumed responsibility for housing and implemented its provision. Under the 1890 Housing of the Working Classes Act little effectively had been done. By 1901 only 88 houses in York had been declared ' unfit for human habitation', and in 1900 there were still 6,418 'midden privies' in York, even though by then they had been proved to be associated with recurrent outbreaks of typhoid. At the turn of the century, privies were shared by one fifth of York's houses, and a single water tap might be shared by as many as 25 houses in the poorer parts of Hungate and Walmgate.

Much more effective was the 1909 Housing and Town Planning Act under which slum clearance began seriously for the first time. York had still 1, 519 back-to-back houses all of which required attention. It was, however, with the passing of the 1919 Act, which made subsidies available for housing, that the corporation began to act on a substantial scale. Thus 'council housing' was born. At that time it was estimated that the city had a shortage of 560 houses; it also needed to demolish about 450 houses in the area around Walmgate. Adding those together, and adding to it also a number of other requirements, it seemed that the city needed 1,250 new houses straight away.

In 1915 the corporation had purchased the Tang Hall estate immediately to the east of the built-up area. It now began to build there, settling many of the people moved from Walmgate and other parts of the city. It was a major development, some 288 acres in extent, and it contains the earliest council houses in York. At the same time a start was made on the estate at Acomb which was, over the years, to become the major expansion area for York. However, sites were sold for development by private builders as well as by the Corporation itself.

Clearance of sub-standard housing began to speed up. More houses were demolished in Walmgate and houses in the Layerthorpe, Navigation Road and Hungate areas began to be cleared. Between 1919 and 1939 nearly 2000 houses were demolished and nearly 7000 people were rehoused. To accommodate them, nearly 5000 council houses were built. As a result only about 500 seriously inadequate slum houses, with another possible 3000 requiring treatment, remained by the beginning of the Second World War.

The second main area of activity undertaken by the Corporation was the implementation of the Town Planning Act of 1925. Under that Act, local authorities were required to carry out town planning studies for towns with populations of more than 20,000 and to prepare schemes in anticipation of future developments. In York there had been a steady rise in population; in 1901 it had been 77,914; by 1931, it was 84,813. Despite the Second World War, by 1951 it reached 105,000 and grew to about 106,000 in the next decade.

On the eve of the Second World War, York was a city not

fundamentally different in character from that of the 19th century. But it was a city that had significantly spread its boundaries, and changed, not so much in the centre, as in the housing areas surrounding the city. The built-up area, once less than 300 acres in extent, had increased to about 1,800 acres in 1882; by the end of the First World War it increased to over 6,000 acres. The big housing developments first in the Groves to the north, then in Tang Hall to the east and at Acomb in the west, had begun to give York a new character – with low-density housing, grass and trees, and two-story brick houses, many of them semi-detached.

The Town and Country Planning Act of 1947 transformed the system of development. By that time York, like most other cities, had commissioned an advisory plan. Published in 1948, it estimated the population at the end of the war as 102,340 and the area of the city as 6,450 acres. It followed the current fashion in town planning in recommending 'primary use zones' and emphasised the problem of traffic. Housing zones had already resulted from the extension of city boundaries. Provision for both traffic and zones of employment was another matter. York's historic walls, the asymmetrical street patterns and the Rivers Ouse and Foss which ran right through the city centre made planning for the motor car particularly difficult.

The city centre of York is characterized by the overlaying of one historical period upon another. The twisting irregular streets go back to the Middle Ages or in important cases to the Viking period. The characteristic buildings tend to be small in scale, juxtaposed in close packed groupings of different building types, of different periods and with mixed use. This results in irregularity, and the lack of a coherent style. There is no symmetry in the street scene, no straight axes: all groupings are informal. This even applies to the Georgian developments which in other cities such as Edinburgh, Bath and London tend to be symmetrical, formal and large-scale; in contrast, the Georgian developments of York are isolated and intermingled with buildings of other periods.

In a paper entitled *The York Aesthetic*, George Pace, the York architect, wrote of how "Minster, churches, chapels, ruins,

314

assembly rooms, Mansion House, public buildings, shops and houses are all cheek by jowl, bounded by the Bar Walls and gates..." This was particularly so along the rivers. Behind banks, and hotels – even behind churches can be found patches of trees and scrubland and yards hosting a multitude of small workshops – what Harry Teggin, later working on the Esher Plan for York in 1969, was to refer to as ' the backlands and shacklands of York' - mixed in with housing and commercial premises of all sorts.

Partly in answer to the parking and congestion problems in the centre of York there was a steady move of business premises including many of the old family firms for which York was famous, out beyond the ring road.

Employment

York has always had a strong tradition of family businesses which include all the basic trades and commercial enterprises. The building firms of Shepherd's and Birch's were long established in the city; Aneley's which came to York from Doncaster at the request of Walter Brierley, the York architect sometimes known as 'the Yorkshire Lutyens', soon became another city institution. There was Leetham's Flour Mill opposite Rowntree Wharf, Penty's animal feed mill, the York Flint Glass Works on Foss Islands Road, Ben Jonson's and Session's Printing Works and Bellerby's paint works - all had a long history of local operation. There were long established shops too, often family concerns, which like Jonathan Jo in the AA Milne poem could supply anything that was asked for 'no matter whatever the size is'. Boxes were hefted down from high shelves in Brown's the drapers, and the smallest screw was not too much trouble to rout out to the customer's satisfaction by the ironmongers in Parliament Square, or Stubbs on the Foss Bridge. Pickerings, the booksellers in the Shambles could immediately go to the tottering piles of books that dotted the shop floor and retrieve from the bottom the very thing asked for. The upper floors of Godfrey's bookshop in Stonegate were so weighed down with priceless ancient tomes which nobody wanted to buy that annual decisions had to be made at stock-taking time as to whether these goods were assets or liabilities.

In terms of the economic life of the city, increasing specialization in its workplaces lent itself to zoning as regards its two greatest industries: the confectionery business and the railways. In 1911, 3,733 people were employed in the confectionery industry, but this was still less than the number employed in the railways. The inter-war period however saw the expansion of the confectionery industry, mainly because of the expansion of Rowntree and Company. By the Second World War it dominated the employment pattern of the city, employing 12,274 people. That represented 30% of York's insured working population. The railways employed 13%. An important difference however between employment by the railways and employment in the confectionery industry, was that more than half the employees in the latter industry were women and girls. But other developments occurred at the same period. In 1907 the Corporation set up a special committee to encourage new industries and promote existing businesses. Between 1900 and 1939 the printing industry flourished; by 1929 over 1000 employees worked in that industry. The British Sugar Corporation built its factory at Acomb in 1927. There was a significant increase in the service industries and distributive trades, and in government services both national and local. This may explain why, unlike many towns of its size, York was relatively little affected by the slump between the wars; in the worst period of the Depression unemployment in York was approximately half the national level.

The major areas of employment in York in the first half of the century could be neatly tucked into the zoning plan adopted after 1947. But there was another strand to the distribution of work places in the city, crucial to the character of York, which was in direct conflict with zoning and with the bigger buildings, wider streets and new shop fronts of the modern city. The old York proved a distinct impediment to any such plans.

Many of these long-established businesses, both great and small, were eventually to be taken over or go out of business

316

Stonegate Pedestrian Street

New Earswick Folk Hall

altogether in the second half of the century. The problems of traffic and parking had started the inexorable tide of movement to the perimeter of the city, frequently followed by a second phase in which the businesses were ousted by the rapidly spreading great supermarket combines. These included the Clifton Moor and Monks Cross complexes; Tesco's at Dringhouses whose distinctive splayed roofs indicate to train passengers from London that it is time to get their bags down from the rack if they are alighting at York; and the most recent developments in the Naburn area.

This has all happened in the latter half of the century. Other than confectionary and the railway, for the first sixty years of the century, it was the small thriving business concerns that were the backbone of York's economic life. These business folk along with an important group of professional people in effect ran the cultural life of the town. Some of them could be encountered in the Yorkshire Club in its red brick fastness overlooking the Ouse by Lendal Bridge. Founded in the previous century, it still retained the essence of a gentleman's club. Its position was of historical importance, for gentlemen would ride into York from their country estates, stable their horse in Botterill's Horse Repository below the bridge (another casualty of the second half of the century), stay overnight in the Club and be in a position to take the morning train to London. It numbered among its members many of 'the great and the good', as well as some representatives of the old family businesses we have talked of. Faded members of the aristocracy like Lady Eve Fairfax would use it as a country club; deans from the Minster, circuit judges on their annual visits to the Law Courts and officers from the several army barracks round the town would dine there; at midday lawyers from old-established firms like Gray Dodsworth and Cobb in Duncome Place and specialists from the medical world would gather there for lunch. A title or an army background was certainly an asset if applying for membership. It was probably the arrival in the early sixties of the University who, having at that stage no buildings of its own, used its premises for meeting and entertaining, that opened the doors wider to a reasonably affluent section of the population. But not wide enough. When the end of a long-term lease had to be renewed in the eighties at a greatly increased rent, the Club went out of business, and now operates as a club for occasional meetings and social events but without its own premises, hiring rooms in the King's Manor, the part of the University in the city centre, for this purpose. The old Club building on Lendal Bridge is now a pizza restaurant.

Politics

The established Whig ascendancy had been broken in the previous century by the Tory George Hudson, the Railway King, heir to a fortune and a millionaire in his own right, who became the first Tory Lord Mayor, a position he held for three terms of office. There was, however, a Liberal revival in the Edwardian period. But this, as the Labour Leader of the Council Rodney Hills writing after 1971 states "merely postponed the inevitable. The party was middle class, and, as the 1906 and 1913 elections showed, its supporters were suspicious of the organised working class. The consequential failure to widen the party's class base was to be fatal. The war, the extension of the franchise and the economic travails of the interwar years accelerated the class polarisation of the electorate, and during the 1920s this was aided by the strident anti-socialism of the Conservative party."

The Liberal party never featured significantly again. The first Labour M.P. for York was F.G. Burgess, elected in 1929 with a majority of 3,300. The Labour ascendancy was, however, short lived, as the Conservatives were returned for the next three elections – L.R. Lumley in 1931 and 1935, and the Hon. C.I.C. Wood in 1937. In local election terms York after 1945 became a marginal seat. As Rod Hill observes: "Perhaps what is important about York's history is that ... the fundamental recasting of the political system was achieved at local level with the minimum of conflict".

At national level, Dr J. Corlett, the Labour candidate, was elected in 1945, but again the seat was yielded to the

Conservatives who held it for the next five elections of 1950, 1951, 1955, 1959 and 1964, three under H.B.H. (later Sir H.B.H.) Hylton-Foster, and the latter two under Charles Longbottom, sometimes with narrow majorities. In 1966 Alex Lyon took the seat for Labour and kept it throughout the four subsequent parliaments of 1970, twice in 1974, and in 1979, until, with York's typical swings in allegiance, a Conservative was returned in 1983 out of a list of five candidates. Conor Gregory retained the seat for the Tories by a tiny majority of 147 in 1987, and after that the seat again reverted to Labour with Hugh Bayley as Member in 1992, 1997 and 2001, when, in keeping with the Labour landslide of that and the previous election, he achieved a majority of 13,779 over the other six party candidates.

Religion

Religion, and particularly the established religion, had always played an important part in the life of York. It used to be said that York contained a pub for every day of the week and a church for every Sunday. At the start of the century adult attendance is given as 7453, 15.5% of the population, for the Church of England; and Wesleyans, who had a different pattern of worship from the established church, boasted an attendance of 6,153 in their 35 Sunday Schools (for both children and adults). In 1936 there were still 27 established churches operating in the city, twenty-three of them having a weekly Communion service. But these observance figures went down through subsequent years, showing a steep decline from the start of the First World War. One effect of this was that York had a great number of redundant churches, all of historic merit, and expensive in terms of upkeep, a fact which formed a serious element in the major role the city was to play in the conservation movement from the sixties onwards. After World War Two, St Saviour's, St John's Ousebridge and St Mary's Bishophill Senior were all being used for secular purposes.

There were two exceptions to the decline in religious observance. One was as regards the Catholic Church which had in previous centuries held a respected place in York's social makeup, due to Yorkshire, like Lancashire, being an area in which many of the gentry had retained their Catholic faith from penal times. This included the Fairfax family whose members were divided between the old and the new faiths. Fairfax House in Castlegate, taken over by the Civic Trust and magnificently restored by the architect Francis Johnson, under the auspices of John Shannon and the Civic Trust, has Catholic and Jacobite symbols in its handsome plasterwork ceilings. The Bar Convent in Blossom Street, which, in penal times, hid its delightful domed chapel behind its pediment on the street front, was built as a boarding school for young ladies in 1686. There was a Catholic Lord Mayor in 1830. With the influx of poor Irish immigrants to work in the new sugar beet factory, the cattle market or on the chicory farms round York in the 1840s Catholic numbers were boosted but their social status was lowered. The little mission of St Wilfrid's, founded in 1760 in Little Blake Street, disappeared when Dean Duncombe removed the Peter Port and opened up Duncombe Place to give a better view of the Minster; it was replaced in 1864 by a towered church in bi-coloured brick, very ugly, by the architect George Goldie, in conscious competition, it has been said, with the Minster towers. Nevertheless, a certain degree of ecumenical cooperation appears to have existed. All Saints, North St, whose very High Church vicar 'Fr' Patrick Shaw, was frequently asked to mediate in domestic disputes among the Roman Catholics in the new working class schemes around Walmgate. There is also a story that somewhere in mid century, the Church of England approached the Catholic Middlesborough hierarchy (in which diocese that side of the river in York was placed) and offered to give them St Michael le Belfry, if they would pull down St Wilfred's. The offer was refused. In 1914 York had only two Catholic churches – St George's and St Wilfred's; by 1981 there were 7, including, from the thirties onwards churches in the suburbs - English Martyrs on Dalton Terrace, St Aelred's in Tang hall, St Joseph's in 1939 in Water Lane - to serve the growing community of Council estates there associated with the planned ring road which was never built, and Our Lady's Church and Council school at Acomb.

The other exception to the decline in numbers of church attendees was the congregation of a charismatic evangelical priest of the Church of England, David Watson, first at St.Cuthbert's and then at St Michael le Belfry. These churches would be packed out on Sundays with an active participatory congregation (Bring on the dancing girls! some of his opponents called it) which lasted even after David Watson's early death from cancer. Several times a year, he took over the Minster for services, and packed that too.

Whatever the attendance figures, the Minster still dominated the city. The names of certain notable deans live on in the contribution they made to York. Dean Duncombe removed Little Blake Street to improve the prospect of the Minster from Lendal Bridge, and the new grand street was named after him. Dean Purey Cust gave his name to a nursing home for the middle classes, built in 1915 by Walter Brierley to the west of the Minster and adjoining the wonderful Deanery gardens which back onto the Wall. The Dean had always contended that rich and poor were amply provided with medical care in the city but that the middle classes lacked hospital provision, so the Purey Cust Nursing-home was established as a testimonial to his 25 years service as Dean. Dean Milner White, whose death was announced during a spectacular thunderstorm to an audience listening to Benjamin Brittan's War Requiem in the Minster during a York Festival is remembered for many things, including setting up a Minster Library Fund and the donation of his priceless collection of Japanese and other pottery to the City Art Gallery. The archivist, Canon J.S.Purvis set up the St Antony's Press in the Borthwick Institute of Historical Research, and, in the midst of cataloguing the archiepiscopal archives discovered and subsequently worked on scripts of the York cycle of Mediaeval Mystery Plays, enabling the cycle to be resuscitated and performed every four years from 1951.

322

Military and Wartime

The presence of military gentlemen in the Yorkshire Club can be explained by York's long history as a garrison city. York's own regiment, the Prince of Wales Own Regiment of Yorkshire was eventually established on the amalgamation of the West Yorkshire and the East Yorkshire regiments in the Imphal Barracks on Fulford Road in 1958. Their Freedom Scroll is in the regimental chapel of the Minster and the regimental museum is on the corner of Tower Street. This was the last of a string of metamorphoses dating from the foundation of the 14th foot, one of several regiments set up in 1685 by James II after Monmouth's Rebellion, and continuing across the centuries, with the absorption into what has been called a 'regimental family' of the local bands of militia and later the Volunteer Battalions. York Volunteer Rifles had been founded by the Lord Mayor in 1859, using a drill ground in Lowther Street and Bootham Stray for shooting practice. Eventually, with the creation of the Territorial Army in 1908, they became the Territorial Battalions of the regiment.

In 1873 Gladstone's War Minister, Edward Cardwell, had attached the West Yorkshires to the North York district, and five years later the regimental depot was transferred from temporary quarters in Bradford, upon the building of the Cavalry Barracks at Fulford. Regiments of Hussars made the Cavalry Barracks their home, and stories are told of how, during the change from a cavalry to an armoured regiment at the time of the Second World War, hussars of the 15th/19th, more accustomed to being on horseback, could be seen frantically practising driving around at the Barracks - the Colonel's driver in an Austin 7, others in trucks or whatever they could lay their hands on. After a short period as a records office, the Cavalry Barracks was handed over to the Police as the Yorkshire Headquarters. The Prince of Wales Own Regiment of Yorkshire maintains its base in the Imphal Barracks next door.

In both 1914 and 1939 all regiments were mobilised; even the Home Guard took its place in the regimental family as the 14th York Battalion in 1940. Although employed on many battlefields in the Second World War, the infantry regiment's most glorious moment occurred in Burma in the battle at Imphal which prevented the Japanese invading India. In recognition of the part played, York City Council gave the new name to the Fulford Barracks, and accorded to the Regiment "the title, privilege and honour of marching through the streets of York on all ceremonial occasions with bayonets fixed, colours flying and bands playing" – an honour also awarded in 1968 to the Royal Air Force at Linton-on-Ouse.

In 1876, the government had purchased Strensall Common for military training, where the Queen Elizabeth Barracks today houses the Army Medical Centre for the area, as well as providing training ranges.

Several handsome memorials in the city bear testimony to the part York citizens played in the wars of the 20th century. The memorial of 1905 by the Minster opposite the Dean Court Hotel is dedicated to those who fought in 'the South African War'; the memorials originally designed by Lutyens beside the arched bridge near the station and in Leeman Road commemorate the fallen of both World War I and II.

During the Second World War, York was scarcely on the front line. Elderly residents remember how the railway station, on the north-south line for the large camps at Catterick and Richmond, was constantly milling with troops on the move; they talk of how offices downstairs in the De Grey Rooms supplied ration books and baby milk and cod liver oil; while the dance hall upstairs supplied, it was rumoured, further necessary comforts to the troops. At the end of the war, York was the North of England depot for demobilisation. Christopher Hassall's moving poem paints a picture of men queuing there to receive their de-mob suits:

> Arriving at a counter heaped with hats,
> "Here comes another head," thought I. "So shrinks
> Their number as more heads approach, and we
> Don our old differences, hat by hat.

A hideous journey brings us to this halt.
How many have dropped out! The rest, once more
Parading, take their choice, then finally
Diverge into the oblivion of freedom."

Unlike Hull or Sheffield which bore the brunt of the blitz, York could be said to have come through relatively unscathed. James Lees Milne, who was travelling round the country inspecting its possessions for the National Trust, tells of how, staying in a York Hotel on Thursday 24 September 1942 he heard a siren in the night. The following morning he decided to climb to the top of the Minster Tower, and on descending, was told by a verger that he ought not to have gone up. ' "There was no notice to that effect," I said. "No," he said, "but a live bomb was dropped close to the tower during the night and has not been defused yet."

In fact, York did suffer bombing in 1916, and in the Second World War 87 inhabitants were killed in bombing raids and about 9,500 houses destroyed. The most significant raid occurred on April 24th 1942 in which the railway station was bombed, the ancient Guildhall (since rebuilt) was gutted leaving only a shell, the school infirmary of the Bar convent in Blossom Street was destroyed, and St Martin le Grand in Coney Street was reduced to half its former size although, under George Pace's restorative skill, it is still worthy of its grand name. This raid is reckoned to have been one of the so-called 'Baedecker' raids which the allies were then imposing on German towns of historic or tourist importance. Yet, in spite of James Lees-Milne's unexploded bomb in the Minster, maps in the Reference Library which plot the path of the bombs, show how they stopped just short of the Minster towers – although these must surely have presented a clear target. One can only presume that some Luftwaffe pilot appreciated the architecture. A brass plaque on the wall of Platform Three at the Station commemorates the raid.

It was in many ways surprising that York was not the target for many more raids. It had of course no industrial importance, but situated on the plain of York it was in the midst of a superb area for airfields and pilot training. When the Royal Air Force Voluntary Reserve was founded in 1937, Linton-on-Ouse became a RAF station, and since 1957 the Number One Flying Training School has been based there to train, in addition, pilots for the Fleet Air Arm. When the Council gave Linton-on-Ouse the freedom of the city in 1968, the Lord Mayor of York was C.W. Oliver who had been an early trainee there and had flown Hurricanes during the war and been awarded the Order of Lenin by our Russian allies.

York's connection with the RAF airfields all round the city is retained in the legend of 'Betty's Mirror', which now figures in a play of the same name, first performed at the Theatre Royal. Other than the De Grey rooms, the great meeting place for Air Force personnel was the oak-lined restaurant in the basement of Betty's in St Helen's Square. It became a habit for aircrews to sign their names in lipstick on a large mirror in the restaurant before setting off on missions, with the poignant sequel of those mates who had returned from the raid, coming back the following day to wipe off the names of those who had 'bought it'.

The Watershed

The two wars, and in particular the second halfway through the century, made a watershed between the old and the new York. Until then, a friendly provincial atmosphere persisted that could have featured in the pages of *Cranford*. People came in from the country to buy their pies in Wright's or have their shoes mended by Cox in the Shambles, to get their light fittings from Cussins and Light, their camera equipment from Saville's; their furniture was moved by Whitby Oliver. For 144 years, until it moved out to Murton on the edge of the city in 1970, as many as 6000 sheep and fat cattle had been herded every week into the 44 stalls of the cattle market, under the walls where the Barbican now stands. When the University arrived in 1962, animals were still to be seen being driven to the market along the streets of York, generously contributing their ordure for the enhancement of the citizens' little gardens. The arrival of the University was a

326

main catalyst for change, but change was coming anyway, due to the problems of getting around York or coming to and from work in the city. This was the problem of traffic.

Communications

Placed in the centre of the country, halfway between London and Edinburgh on the old Great North Road, York was, as far back as Dick Turpin, taken for granted as a centre of communications. Perhaps this is the reason why, at the start of the 21st century, it has still not bothered to build a bus station, and coaches still start from Rougier Street, which lacks proper facilities for long-distance coaches.

The railways were another matter. George Hudson, who had started the railway boom, brought York into its ambit when in 1835 he persuaded George Stephenson to route the line from Newcastle to London through York instead of by-passing the city as it ground its way to Leeds and on to the industrial Midlands, as had been originally planned. By the time the Railway King's shady dealings in promoting the railways had exploded on the public scene in 1849, he had established York as, after London, the basic centre for railways in the country. Hudson had controlled 30 miles of railway in 1839; ten years later he controlled 1,450 miles, a third of the total railway mileage in the country. By the end of the century, the railways in York employed 5,500 in engine, wagon and carriage works, in the station and the railway offices.

As in the rest of the country, the Beeching Report on the railways resulted in the closing and demolition of many little branch lines that had linked the surrounding area to the city; and towards the end of the century, the privatisation of the railways embroiled York and Yorkshire in the effects of an underfunded, under-maintained service, which erupted in the scandals of train crashes such as the Selby crash of 2001.

Transport within the city had a less successful story. In 1900, tramcars were still battling their way through the streets of the city. In 1909 the Corporation bought the trams from the York

327

Tramways Company and in the same year electrified them. Even so, the trams presented constant problems, especially where they had to make their way over old bridges or past defensive walls or through the gates and bars. In 1915 therefore petrol buses were added to the trams and in 1935 the trams were discarded altogether.

It was the age of the motorcar. The first had been seen in the streets of York in the first years of the century. The growth of wheeled traffic was so great that by the end of the Second World War local surveys and advice from central government showed that serious action must be taken to ease congestion, particularly on the main route from the south-west to the north-east, the old Roman route which came from Tadcaster, passed through the centre via the station, Lendal Bridge, Deangate and Goodramgate and went out towards Malton.

All British cities were affected by the traffic problem in the first half of the century, but in York it posed special difficulties. There was the question of bridges over the rivers and canals; the old streets were narrow and twisting; above all they went past   buildings of historic importance which could not be easily removed to push through new routes. Traffic was to cause the creation of ring roads round the city, but also to affect the spread of housing areas and, eventually the building of a ring of supermarkets and large businesses on the outer edges of the city.

In 1903 Deangate was built curving past the Minster and dividing it from the Choir School and other Minster buildings, such as its stone yards and stained glass repair shops. A lobby for the recovery of the cathedral precinct continued throughout the century, but it was not until after the major restoration work on the Minster had shown the ill effects of heavy traffic thundering past its walls, that, under the auspices of the Civic Trust, Deangate was closed to traffic in 1989.

The Advisory plan of 1948 had proposed that a bridge be built across the Ouse at Water End in Clifton. The bridge, ultimately built in the 1960s, acts as a link between suburban areas but not as a by-pass to the city. To provide such a by-pass the authors of the report recommended that a new Outer Ring

Road should be built further away from the built-up area, beyond Skelton Village in the north, beyond Naburn village in the south.

The outer ring road was eventually completed slightly closer in to York in 1987 and has proved essential in relieving the city centre of west-east traffic from the West Riding to the East Riding, and on the south to north route. In several areas, two lanes proved insufficient as soon as it was built, and the road is constantly being worked on with new roundabouts, priority lanes and crossings.

The inner ring road to relieve cross-traffic within the city, following the medieval walls but set about 250 yards from the walls themselves, has only been built in sections. The proposal to buy up properties and the possible, maybe inevitable destruction of some properties in Victorian or Georgian Streets such as Gillygate was opposed by a very strong lobby of conservationists, many from the University, who formed themselves into a pressure group, York 2000.

Within the walled area a pedestrian priority zone was established in 1987 whereby certain streets are closed to all wheeled traffic after 10 o'clock in the morning. A reasonable route from east to west through the centre of the city via Blake Street, Davygate, Parliament Street and Piccadilly already existed. What was now needed was an improved route through the middle of the city from south-west to north-east, avoiding Deangate and the narrow streets round the Minster. To that end a new road was built – Stonebow, linking the end of Micklegate and High Ousegate to Peaseholm Green and ultimately to the Malton Road. Stonebow turned out to be one of the city's few concessions to the concrete jungle architecture of the modern cities. (There have been recent moves among a small group of sixties aficionados to have this eyesore listed as typical of the period; one can only hope this never happens.) Parliament Street, with its famous weekly market in the middle of the road, was to become a roadway again and a new market was to be created in the area between Parliament Street and the Shambles. Originally car-parking was permitted in Parliament Street, but by the end of the century this was limited to taxis and vehicles for the disabled;

a circular fountain was placed in the centre of the area and wrought-iron gates pointed the way to the market. The underground lavatories were removed and two imposing chalets with pillars along the front, badly designed so that the queues from the Ladies' straggles out onto the   road, were built amid much civic amusement and given the cognomen of 'the splash palaces' by the citizens.

The official development plan for the city was published in the form of a survey in 1951 and the plan itself in 1956. It incorporated many of the earlier proposals and provided a framework for the development of the city in the subsequent decades. It also reiterated some basic principles, insisting, for example, that 'If the character of old York is to be retained – and this is the intention of the Planning Authority - traffic difficulties in the city centre cannot be resolved by extensive road widening.' It concluded that links were needed between those streets, such that the building frontages on the streets would not be affected, and that a solution must be found to the central area by diverting non-stopping traffic. The plan also took note of the fact that approximately 15,000 bicycles a day passed the intersection of the A64 and the A19 in the centre of the city.

York, by nature of its flatness, is the perfect bicycle city, and in the days before the closure of the carriage works, a river of bicycles, five or six abreast, streaming out of the gates on Leeman Road at the end of the factory day presented one of the sights of the city. For some decades, bicycles were not so much in evidence, but towards the end of the century, as the problems of moving in and out of the city centre proliferated due to escalation of traffic and the lack of parking, and as the policy of the Labour Government and the environmentalists encouraged other forms of transport to reduce car flow, bicycles are again beginning to play a major part in York. The Planning Authority of the Council working alongside Sustrans, the national sustainable transport body, covered the city with 'traffic calming' measures and bicycle lanes down the side of even quite narrow streets. Fathers and mothers are again to be seen with children in little seats on the back of their bikes.

The Civic Trust and Conservation

These measures are in tune with York's move into the age of conservation. It became - not surprisingly when one considers its rich historic and cultural heritage – a leader in the national move to conservation. In 1968 four enterprising University students led by Pamela Ward got together to host one of the first major conferences on conservation in the country under the aegis of the Institute of Advanced Architectural Studies in the King's Manor in which the Institute was then housed. Lord Harewood chaired the conference; everybody prominent in the world of conservation throughout the country was invited.

Conservation was distinguished from mere 'preservation' as 'the preservation and enhancement of buildings and the environment' - the emphasis on 'enhancement' being of significance. York was particularly fortunate in having a Civic Trust which was a model of guardianship for the city. York Civic Trust was founded in advance of the London Civic Trust on 18 July 1946 by a group of far-sighted and concerned local citizens which included J.B.Morell and Oliver Sheldon of Rowntrees and the Dean of York. They were to have an important influence on the development of the city and later to be instrumental in the foundation of the University. The Civic Trust's terms of reference included 'everything which might profit the history, the beauty, the reputation and the happiness of York whether of its outward scene or its cultural life.' Its objects were 'To preserve for the benefit of the public the amenities of the city and neighbourhood, to protect from dilapidation, disfiguration or destruction, buildings and open spaces of beauty and historic interest; to acquire land or buildings for that purpose, to hold or develop them themselves, or to hand them over to the City or to the nation; to encourage good design and craftsmanship in new erections and to create new beauty within and without the walls.' It was to be the beginning of a new phase in York's story: historic York became one of the important tourist and academic centres for the country.

Lord James of Rusholme

Norwich Union Insurance Offices, Lendal Bridge

Scarcely any new building of quality was erected in York in the post-war burst of building - clearance of 19th century slums and blitz damaged buildings - that characterized most cities in Britain for two decades after the Second World War. In order to speed up the solution of the housing problem, handsome Government subsidies were offered to authorities who would build high. They were flatly turned down by a Labour Alderman, Bill Burke, then Chairman of the Housing Committee. In good blunt Yorkshire fashion when the offer of subsidies was being discussed in a Council meeting he declared: "Over my dead body will we have bloody tower blocks in York." To him is owed the fact that York is almost unique among the country's great cities in having no high-rise buildings. The main concrete atrocity blotting the city remained the Stonebow - that parade of shops on the new connecting road from Peaseholm Green. On the other hand virtually the only building of quality from this period of adventurous concrete is Patrick Gwynne's extension to the Theatre Royal.

As well as cleaning up buildings, erecting plaques on houses to record the life and activities of the people who had inhabited them, the erection of statues and monuments (such as the Roman column standing across the road from the south door of the Minster and the statue of Constantine outside that door, erected for the millennium), as well as the painting and lighting of monuments, gates and railings of interest, the Civic Trust has benefited York in more fundamental ways. It played a decisive part in fostering Lord Esher's report about the conservation of the historic city of 1967.

In his book *Our Selves Unknown* Lionel Brett, Lord Esher, gives a memorable description of accepting the commission for this Report:

'Two years earlier, impressed by the public outcry at the damage done to the heart of Worcester by redevelopment, (Richard) Crossman had decided to commission some studies of major historic city centres as exemplars of how such places might survive the stresses of the twentieth century. After some argument with local authorities, not all of which wished to be

333

Whitehall guinea-pigs, I was offered the choice of Chester, Bath or York. York, I was told, would be the most worthwhile but difficult as the City Council was hostile. So I chose it, on the understanding that this would not be just another exercise on paper, but a live demonstration with Government money (two million was spoken of) of conservation and renewal in action. My arrival in York fulfilled all expectations. I was smuggled into the Guildhall by a back door for fear I might meet the Press, then told by Mr Burke (railwayman and Leader of the Labour Council) in his solid Yorkshire drawl, "We don't like consultants here."

The conservative boss was, if anything, more unfriendly. Mr Bellhouse, the City Engineer and Planning Officer, was correct but inevitably resented my appointment as a criticism of his department's performance. However we set up an office in Micklegate with Harry (Teggin) in charge, David Lloyd on historic buildings and Nat Litchfield on the economics. Citizens high and low, professionals, students in large numbers, were roped in. As the months went by and our proposals were gradually unveiled at public meetings, allies and enthusiasts materialised. The most stalwart was John Shannon, Chairman of the Civic Trust, a passionate lover of the walled city and a splendid speaker... The support of Archbishop Coggan, as President of the Trust, was also much more than *ex officio*. Another essential ally was the local paper, *The Yorkshire Evening Press* and eventually as personalities changed on the Council and among its senior officials I found friends there too. We never got the government money, so implementation had to wait upon the rates and the market...'

Lord Esher's report laid down five objectives. They were:

1. That the commercial heart of York should remain alive and able to compete with its neighbour cities, new and old.
2. That the environment should be so improved by the elimination of decay, congestion and noise, that the centre will become highly attractive as a place to live in for families, students and single persons, and for the

334

retired.

3. That land uses which conflict with these purposes should be progressively removed from the walled city.

4. That the historic character of York should be so enhanced and the best of its buildings so secured that they become economically self-conserving.

5. That within the walled city the erection of buildings of anything but the highest standards should cease.

Supported by Lord Esher's new friends, particularly the Civic Trust and societies like York Archaeological Trust and York Georgian Society, many of these objectives were adhered to; some were not. The conservation study had envisaged an 'inner enclave' in which streets would be restricted to pedestrians, paved from wall to wall and closed to vehicles from 10 a.m. to 5 p.m. The designation of footstreets was begun in 1971. Stonegate, the mainly mediaeval street on the line of the original Via Pretoria of the Roman legionary fortress, was closed to traffic for most of the day. Stonegate was paved over in 1975. Many years later, in 1989, another of Esher's hopes became a reality when Deangate, the road thrust round the Minster wall in 1905, was bollarded off to traffic, thus once again uniting the two sides of the Minster precinct.

Several of the York building firms built delightful little schemes of houses with mini-garden-beds and vivid window boxes, in the Bedern area in the heart of the city. These houses tended to be bought up with a view to retiral by business people from London, one of the problems for the ordinary householder being that the small shops for everyday goods – the grocers and butchers and bakers and chemists – had found themselves forced out of business in the centre, both by the increasing values in the city centre as gentrification moved apace, and by the competition of the supermarkets, then beginning to encircle the city. This had not been envisaged by Esher. One of Esher's proposals that no building should be erected in York with a roofline higher than the aisle of the Minster, had already been broken by the erection of a hotel on the south side of the Ouse, but has remained a useful rule of thumb for additions to the city.

Two years before the publication of the Esher report, conservation was already being put into practice in one area of the city, namely the Minster. Bernard Feilden had been appointed Surveyor of the Fabric of York Minster, in succession to Sir Albert Richardson who had died in the post. Many names were put forward and examined by the appointment committee, including the name of one architect who was already dead! Bernard Feilden had done an excellent preservation job on Heslington Hall and the King's Manor for the University; he already cared for Norwich Cathedral and had restored many churches and had considerable experience of the conservation of religious buildings. He called in Ove Arup and Partners as consulting engineers, the Archaeological Trust to plot the Minster's historic origins, and when work began, Shepherd's as builders. An exhaustive study of the entire Minster was put in hand: core borings to examine the foundations, 'tell-tale' glass strips to measure the widening of cracks, etc. All investigations had to be conducted with the utmost delicacy to avoid further damage to the fabric and ensure the safety of the workmen. The water-table under the building had been lowered due to the use of water in housing and businesses, causing erosion to the foundations; the main piers of the central tower had settled into the ground to a deeper level than the adjoining structure; the transepts were listing; the stonework was in a parlous condition, the great east window was hanging forward at the top. The final solution was to prop up the tower while a crypt was dug away underneath; the entire foundation structure was made into a stable compressed concrete raft on which a mesh of stainless steel rods connected the concrete collars wrapped round the bases of the columns. An appeal had been launched under the chairmanship of the Earl of Scarbrough, and over two million raised for the work carried out between 1967 and 1972.

The Minster was reopened by Her Majesty Queen Elizabeth. It was decided that the foundation work should be exposed to visitors to the crypt, along with elements from the Roman legionary fortress, and the footings of the Norman cathedral of

Thomas of Bayeux, Archbishop of York, which had been discovered.

Credit for this restoration goes to the many skilled craftsmen who contributed to it, and above all to the tenacity and character of Bernard Feilden himself. As a keen sailor, he would sometimes arrive to supervise the work by water, sailing his rubber dinghy, the Zodiac, up round the coast from his Coastguard's house at Morston in Norfolk, then pack it up on the staithe below the Guildhall to be collected by one of his architectural assistants, who would them drive him on to the next job. Since this was the way the Romans had come to York, up the Ouse from the Humber, and the very waterway route that had been used by Vikings and for the traffic of the Middle Ages, he felt this approach to the city brought him into the continuing saga of York and the Minster's history. His enthusiasm led him to work long hours, and it was said that the Dean, Dr. Alan Richardson, hosting a dinner party in the Deanery beside the Minster, would indicate a rare treat to his guests: the sight of the Minster architect crawling along the ridge of the roof.

More money had to be raised in 1984 when York Minster's third great fire occurred, the previous two having been in the 19th century. The south transept, including the rose window was destroyed. The tragedy could have been of much greater proportions, involving the whole Minster, had not a brave decision by the chief fireman to open up the transept roof, prevented the flames reaching the crossing and rushing up into the central tower. A four year restoration programme took place under Dr Charles Brown, Surveyor to the Fabric, involving not only the restoration of the glass but the total replacement of the roof and vaulting - in timber as before, but reinforced with metal mesh and stainless steel bolts. The bosses were recarved and painted, and include six bosses, depicting conservation, the space race and other aspects of the contemporary scene designed by the winners of a competition set up by Blue Peter, the BBC children's TV programme.

The York Archaeological Trust has played an important part not only in the Minster restoration, but in the conservation of

337

the city. Its origins lay in the Yorkshire Philosophical Society, founded in 1822 with the intention of building a geological and archaeological museum to house finds of historical interest which had been unearthed in the area surrounding York. During the building of the Museum on land granted to the Philosophical Society in what is now Museum Gardens, sufficient remains from the adjoining mediaeval Abbey of St Mary (including the King's Manor, originally the Abbot's house, and after the Reformation, the headquarters for the Council in the North) had been mapped, and in 1962 the Royal Commission on Historical Monuments produced Volume 1, of its Inventory for the City: *Eburacum: Roman York*. Many finds displayed in the Museum were bit by bit recognised as belonging to Anglian and Viking York, and writing by authorities in 1924 and 1949 on those periods drew attention to the importance of York as Jorvik, a Viking kingdom. The 4th Viking Congress was held in York in 1965. The street line from Micklegate across Ousebridge to Pavement was shown to be Viking in origin, and Coppergate to be a Viking Street. And so between 1976-1981, the Coppergate project under Peter Addyman unearthed the working Viking city – markets, workshops, wells, latrines; and on these remains were reconstructed the Jorvik Viking Centre, instituting a quite new kind of participatory museum, where visitors 'went back in time' seated in the carriages of a little train, and 'experienced' life in a Viking town, moving through models of markets and harbours, scented with appropriate smells, and besieged by the guttural sounds of Vikings gossiping and squabbling.

A rival attraction to Jorvik with over a million visitors a year is the Castle Museum. It is older than Jorvik, dating back to 1935 when Dr. John Kirk, a general practitioner from Pickering in North Yorkshire (then the North Riding), handed over to York the collection he had made over the years of farm implements, musical instruments, furniture, shop signs and other objects from Yorkshire life in previous centuries. His vast collection, which included a hansom cab, a fire engine and a hearse, over-spilled his outhouses and was so great that it took three years to move everything into York. The city decided to accommodate it in the

Women's Prison, a building by John Carr, opposite the same architect's magnificent Assize Court building, and it speedily took over the next door Debtor's Prison, another 18th century building reputed to be by an associate of Vanbrugh, the architect of Castle Howard. Cobbled streets and shops and houses from past centuries – chemist's with coloured bottles filled with strange liquids, a blacksmith's forge, a saddler, and a sweet shop where sweets are made - have been reassembled within the museum confines. At the end of the 20th century the spotlight has again turned to the so-called 'Eye of York' due to Council plans to develop the area.

New Uses for Old Buildings

If the Castle Museum and the Viking Centre are the most popular, they are not the only tourist attractions that have grown up in York in the second half of the century. Under the auspices of the Archaeological Trust, a redundant church in St Saviourgate has been turned into the ARC – the Archaeological Resource Centre. Specially attractive to schoolchildren – or to their teachers - the finds are laid out in exploratory manner, so that each pupil is given a segment of a round table within which resides a collection of objects – pieces of wood and iron, bones and stones – which they have to identify, and then speculate on their former uses. Since, directly across the road from the ARC. stands the impressive and commodious Methodist Centenary Chapel which is used for a number of social as well as religious purposes – (breakfast for the down- and-outs, lunch for pensioners, premises for meetings and WEA classes) the two buildings have joined forces: primary schoolchildren come by bus into the city, spend their learning time in the ARC and then retire to the Methodist complex to eat their sandwiches and have access to lavatories.

History classes are much more practical these days. On the edge of the city at Murton, attached to the Farming Museum, is an Anglian village, where the children can help to thatch huts, cure skins, care for goats and hens, build fires on which to cook soup which they then consume at long tables in an Anglian hall, washed down by draughts of lemonade from tankards which may be banged on the tables to summon the pot boy.

Social uses have been found for many of York's redundant churches, like St Sampson's near the market, a day centre for elderly people which distributes hundreds of cups of tea each day; but an obvious new use for such churches was to turn them into museums. The ARC was one. Another was St Mary's, Castlegate, which for many years housed The York Story, another Civic Trust venture. Indeed, most historic churches are places of beauty and could be said to be natural museums in their own right. During the York Festival, tours are arranged round these churches, particularly to look at York's treasury of stained glass, often led by Peter Gibson who was for many years chief glazier to the Minster

York architects have therefore made a speciality of restoring historic churches and adapting them to new uses. Because English Heritage and grant-giving authorities insist that the historic fabric must not be tampered with, a method has been evolved for churches like the ARC of preserving the outer shell intact, and then building a framework within the building, from which access can be obtained to upper galleries, offices, shops and small conference rooms.

The churches have, of course to be 'secularized and alienated' as was done to St John's Ousebridge, when it was converted by the Civic Trust to house the Institute of Advanced Architectural Studies that preceded the start of the University. Another redundant church, St Michael's in Spurriergate, flourishes as an excellent café selling healthy homemade and vegetarian food.

At the end of the century another redundant church, St. Margaret's, was given a new use as the National Early Music Centre. The church is situated off Walmgate which had been a run-down area in the early decades of the century, but towards the millennium entered a period of rejuvenation. An important fillip to this process was given when the *Yorkshire Evening Press* moved its works into a new building that backed onto the stretch of the Foss known as Wormald's Cut. The Press had for long

St Sampson's Centre for the Elderly

New flats at Bishop's Wharf

341

occupied dilapidated premises on the Ouse in Coney Street (now the site of the new cinema), with foundations so old that stories are told of how during the war, journalists taking their turn at fire-watching at night, would hear the armour of a mediaeval knight clanking around in the basement. By the second half of the century, the Ouse had ceased to be much used for commercial traffic. One of the last of these enterprises, the coal wharves at King's Staith had ceased to be used and *The Evening Press* was one of the sole survivors, still transporting the massive rolls of paper up the Humber and Ouse by barge to the wharf below the offices. In the early years after moving to Walmgate the tradition was retained - a train of barges being skilfully manipulated up Humber, Ouse, Foss and cut, almost as far as the narrow passage was clear of silt and weeds, to deliver to the great doors on the wharf at the back of the new offices. Later it was considered to be no longer economically viable and the last traditional use of York's river passed away.

The Walmgate area has continued to improve, and the superb restoration and reconstruction of St Margaret's has contributed to this. York has for long had a reputation for good music. Several orchestras, of which the York Symphony Orchestra which celebrated its centenary in 1999 and the Guildhall Orchestra were perhaps best known, had operated for many years; and after 1963, one of the first departments of the new University to be nationally recognised, both for performance and composition under names such as Wilfrid Mellor, was its Music Department. Owing to the vitality and enthusiasm of Delma Tomlin, York has staged an annual Early Music Festival, out of which, with the acquisition of St Margaret's in 1994, grew the Early Music Centre of which Delma Tomlin is the Director. It was opened formally in 1999.

The church had been in a state of total dilapidation, and was leased to York Theatre Royal to store scenery. When Delma took it over the Theatre was able to remove its stores to another building that gave the required height - the disused water tower on Siward's Howe on the hill behind the University. The interior of the church now provides a light and roomy concert hall, with a series of acoustic baffles down the walls which can be opened or closed to suit different reverberation times. There is ample space in the entrance hall to accommodate buffets, bars or milling space for audiences; and off this opens the necessary services and the offices, practice rooms, mini-performance studios, and the room housing the archives of early music. It stands in its intimate graveyard, now fully landscaped. If, other than the extension to the Theatre Royal, York has lacked show-pieces of contemporary architecture, the centre, combining so perfectly the old and the new, makes good that want.

The removal of shop fronts or other accretions constantly exposes the mediaeval heart of York. Restorations include small houses like Barley Hall or the Medical Society Rooms both in Coffee Yard off Stonegate, and the York Guild houses, the Merchant Adventurers' Hall and the Merchant Taylors' Hall.

The National Trust took over the Treasurer's House behind the Minster precinct in 1930. Originally the house of the Minster treasurer, and having passed through many a reincarnation, it was bought about 1900 by Frank Green who set about restoring it – or, perhaps converting it to his own exacting historical standards. Francis Green had made his money in the West Riding by inventing and selling an improved heating boiler called the 'Green's Economiser'. He decided to disburse his fortune in what Peter Addyman has called 'a flurry of conservation' which also included St William's College. York academics are still arguing about whether he was correct to remove the ceiling of the Great Hall in the Treasurer's House and make an upper gallery along it. Mr Green himself suffered from no such doubts. When, during the war, James Lees Milne visited him about an entirely different matter, he would only speak of the National Trust's treatment of the House. 'The old tyrant,' writes Lees-Milne, 'lay in a large fourposter, wearing a striped dressing-gown and a woollen nightcap with a bobble on the end of a string. The bobble bounced up and down his nose as he spoke. His face is that of a rugged, wicked John Bull. It is an eighteenth century, Rowlandish face. Was he to understand that someone had dared to shift the furniture in one of the rooms? Did I not realise that he

343

had put little studs in the floors to mark the precise spot on which every piece of furniture in the house was to stand? He looked me full between the eyes in an accusatory manner. I flinched under the awful gaze. "There!" he cried out, "*You* are guilty. I knew it," and the bobble on the string flew around his cheeks and on to his mouth. "Mark my words," he went on, "I am an old man. I may not have very long to live. But I warn you that, if ever you so much as move one chair leg again, I will haunt you to your dying day."' The Treasurer's House boasts not of Frank Green's ghost but of a Roman centurion riding a horse, only visible from the knees upwards, because the road level has been raised.

Hans Hess, the curator of the Art Gallery in the 60s, used to bemoan that York was so boring, there must be orgies going on somewhere if we could only find where! By the turn of the millennium, it is estimated that four million tourists visit the city each year; that they bring in an income of £250 million. A measure of York's metamorphosis into a tourist city can be seen from the change of uses of York's most staid buildings. A bank in St Helen's Square has been redecorated as a restaurant which has an atmosphere that would not be out of place in Aspen, Colorado; one of the two National Westminster banks in Coney Street, the one with the ceiling moulded in a wreath of fruit and flowers, in the bank's day vividly painted, is now a white and chrome Starbuck's Seattle coffeehouse; Lord Burlington's Assembly Rooms, restored to their former Georgian glory by the City Council with help from the Civic Trust, is now a pizza parlour, as is the Yorkshire Club. The lovely little Lady Anne Middleton's Hospital set back from the riverside in Skeldergate, still in 1939 used for its original purpose and modernised to accommodate ten alms people and a warden, is now a hotel. Coffee houses, mammoth booksellers and Internet cafes are springing up everywhere. In a burst of good weather, one can occasionally see cafes setting out tables and chairs on the pavement.

Arts and Leisure

In the middle of the century, York was in need of cultural revitalization. In moving the city from respectable – and possibly somewhat self-satisfied - stagnation to the position of a leading European City of Culture (as it was to be by the end of the century), a crucial part was played by the Curator of the Art Gallery, Hans Hess, who came to York in 1947. A German refugee, whose father had entertained the Bauhaus artists, he would occasionally show his family visitors' book with its drawings by Kandinsky, Paul Klee and Feininger. This book was so valuable that when, on leaving York to take up a Readership in Art History at Brighton in 1966, the proceeds from its sale were sufficient to buy a very attractive house in Lewes in Sussex. His left-wing politics (he was a Marxist), his inflexibility on standards in art, and his conviction that the grants given to encourage the arts in this country by city councils and the government were shamefully low were, perhaps, too revolutionary for York at that time, and he was frequently attacked in *The Yorkshire Evening Press*, and eventually in a more direct way when a right-wing arsonist set fire to his house. To Hans Hess York owes the biggest cultural impetus in the 20th century until the arrival of the University. He was involved, along with Dudley Holland, the Principal of the Art School, in the launching in 1951 of the York Festival, whose reputation was, at the time, probably second to the Edinburgh Festival in this country.

From 1954 Hans Hess was the Festival Director. The centrepiece was the York cycle of Mystery Plays, not performed in the city for four hundred years. Using Canon Purvis' text, the Festival committee staged the early performances in the Museum Gardens. There was a core of professionals to the huge cast of local amateurs, and many top professional actors made their debut or came to public notice by appearing in the Mystery plays. These included Mary Ure who was to marry John Osborne, a schoolgirl from the Quaker Mount School, Judi Dench who played the Virgin Mary, and Christopher Timothy who played Christ. The ruins of St Mary's Abbey made a superb backdrop to the stage, and the timing ensured that, while the audience watched, the sun would sink, flushing the sky behind the ruins, and the final scenes would be lit by flaming torches and candles.

The Hillsborough disaster at Sheffield when so many spectators were killed in a crowd stampede, put an end to the outdoor performances; the police and the City Council felt they were not prepared to take the risk of evacuating large crowds from the stands in an emergency. For two years the Theatre Royal, itself resuscitated from extinction at a time when theatres all over the country were 'going dark', stepped into the breach; it saved the tradition from being broken, but everybody was aware that the confines of a Victorian stage with a proscenium arch did not afford the correct milieu for a play sequence originally performed on carts at various stations throughout the city. In the Millennium year, Dean Ray Furnell who had taken over from the present writer as Chairman of the Theatre Trust, was able to arrange a much more suitable setting - the Minster itself. Delma Tomlin brought all the resources of the Early Music Centre to support the scheme which was backed by the City Council and the Civic Trust. Banks of raked seats were erected facing the choir, and stepped platforms formed the stage, rising up to the rood screen. Music was written for the performance by Richard Shephard, the Headmaster of the Minster Choir School. The Duke of York, Prince Andrew, attended the first performance. Highlights such as the flood waters indicated by heaving waves of blue silk lapping their way up the chancel steps, and the colours of the rainbow projected onto the choir vault will long remain in people's memory as one of the great experiences of their lives.

Other than the Festival, York at the end of the century is well provided with drama. The Rowntree Theatre houses smaller performances and lively and enthusiastic amateur shows, such as the productions of the York Light Opera Society. After weathering a difficult time in the eighties, York's ancient Theatre Royal is a flourishing concern. Later a disused theatre down by the river, The York Opera House, was opened and run by a private entrepreneur.

Both tourists and citizens have benefited from the extension of sports facilities. York has a long history as a racecourse, with the Ebor Handicap one of the well-known fixtures in the racing calendar. Facilities at the racecourse were several times updated during the century; a new stand was built, and the Gimcrack Rooms multi-purpose facilities make it a welcome addition to the social premises in the city.

After the market moved to Murton, the Barbican Centre was built to house entertainment, particularly large pop concerts for which before that York had no sufficiently large hall, and many sporting activities – from swimming, squash and badminton courts to climbing walls. In the growing complex of supermarkets and businesses at Monks Cross beyond the northern ring road, Water World provides the children with all sorts of exciting additions - waves and flumes - to the usual swimming pool provision.

Cricket goes back to the 18th century in the city but has never aroused the passion evoked by the game in wider Yorkshire, where husbands are reported to have rushed their wives over the border to give birth in the county so that the offspring would be eligible to play for Yorkshire. Rugby was prominent from the mid 19th century and in 1898 split between Rugby Union and Rugby League. York City Football Club which was founded in 1922, has nationally carried the flag for the city's sport, particularly in 1955 when the team beat Arsenal and took part in the semi-finals of the F.A. Cup. It came to prominence again in the 1990s, and in the same decade refurbished the ground with higher stands.

Education

It is in many ways surprising that York had to wait until half way through the twentieth century before founding a university. Not only is it an ancient cathedral city but it boasts a proud lineage of education.

At the beginning of the century, York was well provided with secondary schools, at any rate for a small section of the

347

community. If there are other contenders for St Peter's claim to being the country's oldest school it must certainly be one of the longest running, although its present handsome Gothic building dates only from 1838. A gloss of romance is added to its academic reputation by numbering Guy Fawkes among its past pupils. From this stems the tradition of not celebrating November the 5th – "We don't burn old boys."

The Bar Convent, next in age, yielded to economic and other pressures, by moving by stages from being an exclusive fee-paying school for girls, initially largely for boarders, to becoming All Saints, a Catholic comprehensive for both sexes, and eventually by the end of the century, moving the secondary school out of the Convent buildings altogether to be housed in what had been Mill Mount Girls' School, off the Mount, thus providing a secondary Catholic school for boys up to GCSE Higher standard in the city for the first time.

More recent, but equally honourable, is the Quaker contribution to education through Bootham School for boys, and the Mount School for girls, which grew out of an original teacher training college. Both St Peter's and Bootham have contributed to York's meagre store of good 20th century buildings with St Peter's science block of 1903 by Brierley, and Bootham's assembly hall, built in 1966 by Trevor Dannat whose excellent updated technological facilities make it a popular centre for lectures and meetings. To these schools, one must add the Blue Coat school for boys and the Grey Coat School for girls, both starting as charities and both coming to an end in 1946.

York was pursuing its own educational policy in the latter years of the 19th century, not directly related to Forster's Education Act of 1870. Of Walter Brierley's four Council Primary Schools with their eye-catching brick boiler towers and internal planning that grouped classrooms and washrooms round a large upstairs central hall, two, Haxby Road (partially rebuilt after a fire in the 1990s) and Poppleton Road, both of 1904, are worthy of note. There was not a great increase in the number of primary schools between 1900 and 1939, due to the unexplained fact that, in an increasing population, the number of children of primary school age had decreased. Thus a survey of 1938 shows twelve municipally funded elementary schools and twenty voluntary schools (15 Church of England, 4 Roman Catholic and one Nonconformist) providing some 12,000 pupil places; but all but one of these voluntary schools had been built in the previous century and, according to a report at the time, "lacked conveniences necessary for health and physical development." Sir Joseph Rymer who was Chairman of the Council Finance Committee between 1900 and 1913, waged an uphill battle for more generous grants from the 'imperial government', insisting that the burden of these expenses should be carried by central government, and not by the Corporation or ratepayers of the city.

From the Education Act of 1902 which replaced elementary school boards with education committees of the authority, the movement throughout the century was away from fee paying or voluntary schools to schools financed and controlled by the Local Authority. The abolition of tuition fees in maintained secondary schools demanded by the 1944 Act, propelled the movement further. As the century progressed, the direct responsibilities of the Education Authority extended enormously, so that when a local headmistress Miss M.G. Willoughby contributed a paper on education to a survey produced for the visit of the British Association to the City in 1959, she could list among the bodies under its control, the School Health Service, a School for the Educationally Sub-normal, a Child Guidance Clinic, a School Meals Service, an open-air school for delicate children, and a Youth Employment Service. By 1948 there were thirteen secondary modern schools in York, eight of them built since the war.

The movement for free secondary education for all can be charted by examining two prestigious York schools: Queen Anne's and Archbishop Holgate's. Queen Anne's, which started as a pupil-teacher centre in 1905 was, within the year titled 'the municipal secondary school for girls and fee-paying pupils' and passed its male students over to Archbishop Holgate's. In 1909 it moved into York's first new-build secondary premises in Queen Anne's Road in Clifton. The ancient Archbishop's, started under

Cardinal Pole in 1529, and moved to a city centre site by the Archbishop after whom it is named in 1858, amalgamated with the Yeoman's School, a school founded in 1845 by the Church of England 'to supply a liberal education at moderate cost to the sons of the middle classes of the agricultural and manufacturing districts of Yorkshire' which was used for teaching practice by the next-door training college of St John's. In 1920 the school became a municipal boys' school, and although in 1948 it lost its Direct Grant status and chose to become the city's fourth City Grammar School, it eventually moved out to York's first fully up-to -date school buildings on the Hull Road as a comprehensive. Two schools of distinction, Nunthorpe Grammar School for boys and Mill Mount for girls, after a period under the education authorities fell prey to educational contraction.

St John's College was set up as a teacher training college in 1845 in Lord Mayor's Walk next door to Archbishop Holgate's, and when, in the seventies, the government contracted the number of teacher training establishments in the country as a response to the falling birth rate, it joined up with the training college in Ripon and became Ripon St John on a double site. At the start of the 21st century, preparations are being made to reunite both halves of the College on the much extended York site, and give up the Ripon buildings. The College has by now diversified and offers a wide selection of courses and degrees which are validated, not, as might have been expected, by York University but by that of Leeds.

The University

A significant and seminal event in the movement from the old York to the new was the foundation of the University. The need for a university had been many times proposed from 1840s onwards, but after the Second World War it was revived by men such as John Bowes Morrell (a Director of Rowntrees, the Chairman of the Westminster Press and, in good Dick Whittington fashion, twice Lord Mayor of York), once immediately before the First World War, and again shortly after the Second. The Civic Trust had from its inception formed an academic development committee with the intention of founding a university in the city of York. Indeed many had for a long time felt how strange it was that this beautiful cathedral city should lack a university. Other names credited by the present Vice Chancellor, Ron Cooke, in a paper he gave on the University and the City, as being instrumental in pushing the project from an idea to a reality and supporting the University after its inception include Oliver Sheldon, Jack Birch, Sir Donald Barron, Ken Dixon and Lewis Waddilove from the Rowntree Company and Trusts, the Morrell family, the Rymers, the Gladwyns, the Burtons, the Shepherds, Jack Lyons and Noel Terry.

The government was not encouraging at first, but indicated that if further universities were to be created, they would give preference to those cities which had shown themselves to be involved in academic studies. The Civic Trust made two immediate experiments. The first was the Borthwick Institute of Historical Research, placed in St Antony's Hall, one of the late mediaeval guildhalls within the walls, which sheltered a collection of diocesan and provincial archives deposited there by the Church and extended significantly as a result of endowments. The second was the formation in St John's Church, Micklegate, a mediaeval parish church then derelict and scheduled for demolition, of the Institute of Advanced Architectural Studies. The purpose of this Institute was at first to supply courses on the protection and repair of historic buildings; to those were later added many other courses, particularly on the management and technology of architecture and building for architects, planners and builders. The two academic institutes formed the nucleus of what was to become the University of York.

In April 1960 governmental approval was given for its establishment. A year later Robert Matthew Johnson Marshall and Partners, a firm affectionately to become known as Rumjum, were appointed development architects.

In January 1962 the first Vice-Chancellor, Lord James of Rusholme, and the first members of the academic staff of the new

University arrived in York. The first registrar, John West-Taylor was already in York, having been Secretary to both the Borthwick and the Architectural Institute and to the Academic Trust and the University Promotion Committee.

Eric James was a graduate of Oxford who had taught first at Winchester where he and a colleague wrote the standard textbook of the time: *James and Hall's Elementary Chemistry,* and had then become High Master of Manchester Grammar School. His name was well-known as a member of *The Brains' Trust* on radio; he received first a knighthood and later a life peerage. His registrar was a Cambridge graduate and friend of Henry Morris who had pioneered an open idea of education for a lifetime in his Village Colleges in Cambridgeshire.

The early members of staff were hand-picked, not necessarily from those who had already worked in the higher education sector, but were people of diverse backgrounds who were concerned with the pursuit of learning, and the dissemination of knowledge.

Several aspects of the University emerged from the close collaboration of these founding members. The motto chosen for the University: *In limine sapientiae (On the threshold of wisdom)* reflected this. It was decided that the University was to be a collegiate institute - what Eric James referred to as a 'socio-academic' body, which included all the university staff personnel, the students and even their partners and families. Inevitably, as the university grew, it became impossible to retain quite such an open-house policy, but it provided an opportunity in the early days for the entire university family to be involved in this exciting enterprise.

Both the collegiate ideal, and the broader ideals of an education in which the students would encounter other minds working on different subjects or disciplines were reflected in the physical form of the University. The chief architect Stirrat Johnson-Marshall, had in turn recruited Andrew Derbyshire (now Sir Andrew) as project architect to develop the site of nearly 200 acres (the size required by the government for the establishment of any new university) round Heslington Hall to the immediate south-east of the city boundary. Johnson-Marshall's inspiration of draining the water-logged site by digging out a great bowl of fourteen acres to make a lake, established the basic form of the site. Round it were scattered the colleges, comprising both living and teaching quarters and to one of which each student and staff member belonged. Under Frank Clark, Reader in Landscaping for the Architectural Department of the University of Edinburgh, hundreds of trees were planted to add to the existing landscaping round Heslington Hall which was at first used for teaching quarters and later became the administration centre for the University. Wild life was added to the site in the form of various species of ducks and geese, bought from Sir Peter Scott's Wildlife Centre.

The crucial analysis of the needs of a growing seat of learning was the work of Andrew Derbyshire, and included the linking of the separate buildings by covered pedestrian routes, so as to encourage what somebody called the 'maximum number of happy accidental encounters' between people from different disciplines. These routes would run not *between* but *through* colleges. Because of the condition of the site, it was decided that, with the exception of certain specialised buildings like the central hall for assemblies and examinations and the laboratories for chemistry, physics and biology all the colleges would be built of a prefabricated system originally developed for schools in conditions of mining subsidence. The system was called CLASP, an acronym for Consortium of Local Authority Special Programmes, but jokingly referred to by the architectural fraternity as 'collection of loosely-assembled steel parts', since it consisted of steel frames clothed in concrete panels. It was not the cheapest method of building, (plain brick walls with as few openings as possible would have been cheaper), even though, for reasons of economy, plain grey concrete panels were chosen, but it did mean that the buildings were in budget and on time. "I am not prepared ", said Lord James, "to stand on York station and say to the students as they arrive, 'I'm terribly sorry, but your buildings are not ready.'"

The buildings served their original purpose well, but have not been easy to adapt to new requirements in the following forty years. The flat roofs have leaked; the space beneath the roofs through which the electrical systems were run, have proved difficult to maintain, and a fire-hazard. Because no buildings were more than four storeys high no lifts (expensive items) were put in. It was considered that it would do their young occupants no harm to climb a few stairs. With provision for the disabled in recent years, this has had to be rectified. It was also considered that bathrooms and small kitchens with an electric kettle installed at the end of each short corridor would be quite acceptable to students, but once the University entered into the conference business in the holidays, washbasins had to be introduced into the rooms, and they are now all being built *en suite*. It was of course not anticipated that York University would become such a popular location for conferences – so popular that more of the University income is derived from conferences rather than student tuition fees.

Across the years the University has continued to grow in size and popularity (8,502 students in 2000). In a lecture to the Civic Trust in 2000, Ron Cooke, the 4th Vice-Chancellor, noted that the University is ranked second only to Cambridge in externally assessed teaching quality; is among the top ten in terms of research quality and near the top in terms of research links with industry. The research figures and the relationship with industry are at the end of the century crucial factors in the allotment of government subsidies – a situation which played no part in the founding days of the University. With over 2500 employees, the University is the third largest employer in the city, after Nestlé and the City itself, and new jobs are constantly being created through the Science Park, the Innovation Centre, the Bioscience Initiative (whose existence must have helped to encourage the move of the Central Science Laboratories, under MAFF - (the Ministry of Agriculture, Food and Fisheries) - to come together from all over the country to a new shining complex at Sand Hutton on the northern edge of York), as well as Inward Investment. The attention-catching subjects of research in the

University cover a wide field from osteoporosis, multiple sclerosis, dyslexia and safety critical systems on Rolls Royce engines, to preventing ice cream from crystallizing in a freezer and opera composition. These developments have necessitated new buildings occupying many of the previously vacant parts of the site, and are of many shapes and colours which do not concur with the original uniformity of the early CLASP buildings, and sometimes fail to preserve the vistas carefully planned in the original development plan.

Ron Cooke sees the future of the city and the university as being intimately bound together, and feels that, just as York played a leading part in the railway communication of the 19th century, it must assume a position of leadership in the telecommunications of the 21st century, in the 'electronically networked world' of the future. He considers York and the University excellently placed to become a centre for 'knowledge-based industries' which are 'data rich and data dependent' on such centres of expertise as York, and which can operate globally. All this presages a York whose life is part of the commercial and industrial world of the future, in which tourism and its historic heritage may take second place.

The Millennium

York will always be the York of history, subject in the 20th century, as in all earlier times, to its topography and climate; and, no doubt, these are the things that matter and will live in the memories of many of its population. . The rivers still play a vital part in the life of city - from the occasional freeze-up, when it was possible to walk on the Ouse for a stretch between the Lendal and Ouse Bridges, to the great floods at the end of the century - the worst flooding in the 400 years since records were kept - which devastated the flat Plain of York, southwards into the Selby area and northwards in the Malton area. Any citizen who lived through the floods will retain a vivid memory of the photographs in the local press of Tony Blair, the Prime Minister, and governmental officials wading in thigh boots through the lake

The Millennium Bridge

that islanded Clifford's Tower. *[monochrome plate 16]* York has had to institute building works to control these floods, many of which proved successful in the second round of floods at the end of 2000. These included the flood-water pumping station on the river below the Castle which prevents melt-waters coming down from the Dales into an overloaded Ouse backing up the Foss into the city itself; and the 5 million worth of barrier walls on the river at Clifton which in 2000 protected (by an inch!) residential streets from flooding.

It is now possible to contemplate the Ouse less as a possible threat and more as a potential source of pleasure. When Coney Street was first built, the Ouse was tidal and acted as the town's sewer and refuse system; inevitably the houses turned their backs on this unsightly and odiferous waterway, with job-lot fenestration littered with pipes and patchy boarded-up walls. Now in the 21st century there is hope that the river will become

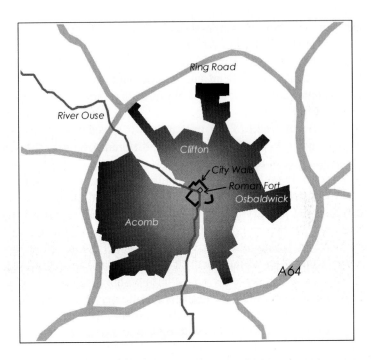

York 2000. From Fortress to Ringroad

one of the amenities of York. In his visionary tract *The City of our Dreams* J.B.Morrell had hoped for a riverside walk. Although far from complete, the riverside walk is beginning to take shape. The opportunity afforded by pulling down the old Westminster Press offices has been taken by the designers of the new cinema and the restaurants which are its neighbours to create a stretch of boardwalk along the river behind Coney Street. An even more impressive piece of river walk has been made between New Walk Terrace and the Blue Bridge in a project associated with York's Millennium Bridge.

This beautiful state-of-the-art contribution to the city spans the Ouse south of the other bridges, linking together the residential area near the Rowntree Park with Fulford, and so providing a cycle and pedestrian route from the other side of the city through to the University. The bridge is in the form of a fine arch made of shining stainless steel structural components, and further excites admiration because it is built on a curve and is tilted to one side. The approaches along the river path to either end of the bridge have been landscaped with seats and look-out points, steps and pieces of sculpture that speak of York's geological foundations.

So at the end of the millennium it is sensible to ask, in what way is York, the city and district, different from what it was at the beginning of this chapter.

York is no longer looking only to a commercial future; it is the most celebrated centre of conservation and environmental prestige in the country and possibly in Europe. As Britain at the turn of the century is confirming its membership of Europe and playing an increasingly effective role in its affairs, so York, the ancient capital city of the north of England, has to offer what it has consciously preserved – a visible three-dimensional complex of monuments and a city centre of supreme quality. There have always been arguments about its development, about its bridges and parks as well as great buildings, and no doubt they will continue.

York is as well cared for, as fascinating and handsome as it has ever been. The poverty found by Rowntree at the beginning of the century is, at its end, confined to small pockets, for which, in many cases, individuals rather than the system is to blame. But in subtle and not very obvious ways York is changing: no longer a proud provincial town, no longer merely an internationally recognised centre for history and conservation, it is possible that in the 21st century, York can take its position as a global centre for business, research and development. Until now, the very things York had to offer to visitors - ancient winding streets, the river and the bridges - had precluded industrial development and the large-scale traffic that goes with it. Now the city and the university together have at their disposal, through the internet highway, a bank of information, invention and research that make possible the development of the commercial and industrial projects of the future - a challenge for continuing discovery.

Bibliography

CHAPTER 1 - Roman York

Addyman, P.V., 1984. 'York in its archaeological setting', in P.V.Addyman and V.E.Black (eds), *Archaeological Papers from York Presented to M.W. Barley* (York) 7-21

Brinklow, D, Hall, R., Magilton, J. and Donaghey, S., 1986. *Coney Street, Aldwark and Clementhorpe, minor sites and Roman roads*, The Archaeology of York 6/1 (London)

Buckland, P.C., 1976. *The Environmental Evidence from the Church Street Roman Sewer System*, The Archaeology of York 14/1

Carver, M., Donaghey, S. and Sumpter, A., 1978. *Riverside Structures and a Well in Skeldergate and Buildings in Bishophill*, The Archaeology of York 4/1 (London)

Hall, A. R., Kenward, H.K. and Williams, D. 1980. *Environmental Evidence from Roman Deposits in Skeldergate*, The Archaeology of York 14/3

Hall, A.R. and Kenward, H.K., 1990. *Environmental Evidence from the* Colonia: *Tanner Row and Rougier Street*, The Archaeology of York 14/6 (London)

Hall, R.A., 1997. *Excavations in the* Praetentura: *9 Blake Street*, The Archaeology of York, 3/4 (York)

Kenward, H.K., Hall, A.R. and Jones, A.K.G., 1986. *Environmental Evidence from a Roman Well and Anglian Pits in the Legionary Fortress*, The Archaeology of York 14/5

Monaghan, J., 1993. *Roman Pottery from the Fortress*, The Archaeology of York 16/7 (London)

Monaghan, J., 1997. *Roman Pottery from York*, The Archaeology of York 16/8, (York)

Ottaway, P. 1993. *Roman York* (London)

Ottaway, P. 1996. *Excavations and Observations on the Defences and Adjacent Sites 1971-90*, The Archaeology of York 3/3 (York)
Ottaway, P. 1996. *Romans on the Yorkshire Coast* (York)
Ottaway, P.1999. 'York: the study of a late Roman colonia' in H.Hurst (ed.), *The Coloniae of Roman Britain: new studies and a review*, Journal of Roman Archaeology, Supplementary Series 36, 136-51
Perrin, J.R., 1981. *Roman pottery from the Colonia: Skeldergate and Bishophill*, The Archaeology of York 16/2
Perrin, J.R., 1990. *Roman pottery from the Colonia 2: General Accident and Rougier Street*, The Archaeology of York 16/4 (London)
Phillips, D. and Heywood, B., 1995. *Excavations at York Minster, volume 1: From Roman Fortress to Norman Cathedral* (HMSO, London)
Royal Commission on Historical Monuments, 1962: An Inventory of the Historical Monuments in the City of York 1: *Eburacum, Roman York* (London, HMSO)

CHAPTER 2 – Anglo-Saxon and Viking-Age York

Introductory surveys and background are provided by
R.A. Hall *Viking Age York*.1994. B.T. Batsford/English Heritage.
J.D. Richards *Viking Age England* 2nd edition 2000 Tempus.
The Archaeology of York series (edited by P.V. Addyman) contains several volumes detailing discoveries and interpretation of buildings; artefacts of all sorts, including well preserved examples of rare materials such as wood, textile and leather; human burials; the environment; animal bones; and coins. Volume 1, *Sources for York History to AD 1100*, by D.W. Rollason, is an important compilation of written references to York.
Details of *The Archaeology of York*, and new discoveries, are posted on the internet at www.yorkarchaeology.co.uk

CHAPTER 3 - York in the Early Middle Ages

Lesley Abrams (1994) 'Eleventh-century Missions and the Early Stages of Ecclesiastical Organisation in Scandinavia', *Anglo-Norman Studies* XVII, pp 21-40.

Robert Bartlett (2000) *England under the Norman and Angevin Kings 1075-1225* (Oxford, OUP)

Majorie Chibnall (1973) *The Ecclesiastical History of Orderic Vitalis* (Oxford, OUP)

P. H. Cullum (1991) *Cremetts and Corrodies: Care of the Poor and Sick at St Leonard's Hospital, in the Middle Ages* (York, Borthwick Paper 79)

Christopher Daniell (1995) 'Family, Land and Politics: Ralph Nuvel and Twelfth Century York', *York Historian* 12, pp 2-20.

Christopher Daniell (2001) 'Battle and Trial: Weapon Injury Burials of St Andrew's Church, Fishergate, York', *Medieval Archaeology* Forthcoming

A. G. Dickens (1953) 'Norman and Angevin York: Some Suggested Revisions', *The Yorkshire Architectural and York Archaeological Society Annual Report 1952-3*, pp 35-45

A. G. Dickens (1955) 'The 'Shire' and Privileges of the Archbishop in Eleventh Century York', *Yorkshire Archaeological Journal*, Vol XXXVIII, pp 131-47

R. B. Dobson (revised 1996) *The Jews of Medieval York and the Massacre of March 1190* (York, Borthwick Paper 45)

William Farrer (1914) *Early Yorkshire Charters, volumes I-IV* (Edinburgh)

Margaret M. Faull and Marie Stinson (eds and trans) (1986) *Domesday Book: Yorkshire* (Chichester, Phillimore)

Ian Friel (1995) *The Good Ship: Ships, Shipbuilding and Technology in England 1200-1520* (London, British Museum Press)

Eric Gee (1979) 'Architectural History until 1290' in G. E. Aylmer and Reginald Cant, (eds) *A History of York Minster* (Oxford, OUP) pp 111-148

A.R. Hall, H. K. Kenward, D. Williams and J.R.A. Greig (1983) 'Environment and Living Conditions at Two Anglo-Scandinavian

Sites', *The Archaeology of York 14/4* (York, Council for British Archaeology)

Rosalind M. T. Hill and Christopher N. L. Brooke (1979) 'From 627 until the early Thirteenth Century' in G. E. Aylmer and Reginald Cant, (eds) *A History of York Minster* (Oxford, OUP) pp 1-43

Charles Johnson (ed and trans) (1990) *Hugh the Chanter, The History of the Church of York 1066-1127* (Oxford, Oxford Medieval Texts)

Charles Kightly and Rachel Semlyen (1980) *Lords of the City* (York, York City Council)

J. M. Lilley, G. Stroud, D. R. Brothwell and M. H. Williamson (1994) 'The Jewish Burial Ground at Jewbury', *The Medieval Cemeteries, The Archaeology of York* 12/3 (York, Council for British Archaeology)

Christopher Norton (1998) 'The York Fire of 1137: Conflagration or Consecration', *Northern History,* Vol XXXIV, pp 194-204

Christopher Norton (1999) 'The Design and Construction of the Romanesque Church of St Mary's Abbey, York', *Yorkshire Archaeological Journal*, Vol 71 pp 73-88

David Palliser (1997) 'The Birth of York's Civic Liberties c. 1200-1354' in Sarah Rees Jones (ed) *The Government of Medieval York* (York, Borthwick Studies in History 3)

Derek Phillips (1985) *The Cathedral of Archbishop Thomas of Bayeux: Excavations at York Minster,* Vol II (London, HMSO)

H. Richardson (1961) *The Medieval Fairs and Markets of York* (York, Borthwick Paper 20)

Henry T. Riley (trans) (1853) *The Annals of Roger de Hoveden* (London, Bohun Antiquarian Library)

Michael Robson (1997) *The Franciscans in the Medieval Custody of York* (York, Borthwick Paper 93)

Alberic Stacpoole (1972) *The Noble City of York* (York, Cerialis Press)

Joseph Stevenson (trans) (reprint 1956) *The History of William of Newbrugh* (Felinfach, Llanerch Publishers)

H. G. Ramm et al (1971) 'The Tombs of Archbishop Walter de Gray (1216-55) and Godfrey de Ludham (1258-65) in York Minster, and their Contents' *Archaeologia* CIII pp 101-47

P. M. Tillot (ed) (1961) *The Victoria History of the Counties of England. A History of Yorkshire: The City of York* (Oxford, OUP)

Christopher Wilson and Janet Burton (1988) *St Mary's Abbey, York* (York, Yorkshire Museum)

CHAPTER 4 - York in the Later Middle Ages

A. Original Sources

R. Davies, *Extracts from the Municipal Records of the City of York during the Reigns of Edward IV, Edward V and Richard III* (London 1843)

The Fabric Rolls of York Minster, ed. J Raine (Surtees Society, 35; 1859)

Records of Early English Drama: York, ed. A. Johnston and M. Rogerson (Manchester, 1979)

Register of the Freemen of the City of York, ed. F. Collins (Surtees Society, 96, 102; 1897-9)

Testamenta Eboracensia: a selection of Wills from the Registry at York, ed. J. Raine (Surtees Society. 4, 30, 45, 54, 45, 54, 79, 106; 1836-1902)

York City Chamberlains' Account Rolls, 1396-1500, ed. R.B. Dobson (Surtees Society, 192, 1980)

York Memorandum Book, ed. M. Sellers and J.W. Percy (Surtees Society, 120, 125, 186; 1911-73).

The York Mercers and Merchant Adventurers, 1356-1917, ed. M. Sellers (Surtees Society, 129; 1918)

B. Secondary Sources

L. Attreed, *The King's Towns: Identity and Survival in Late Medieval English Boroughs* (New York, 2001)

G.E. Aylmer and R. Cant, eds, *A History of York Minster* (Oxford, 1977)

D.J.F. Crouch, *Piety, Fraternity and Power: Religious Guilds in Late Medieval Yorkshire, 1389-1547* (York Medieval Press, 2000)

R.B. Dobson, 'Mendicant Ideal and Practice in Medieval York,' in *Archaeological Papers from York presented to M.W. Barley,* ed. P.V. Addyman and V. Black (York Archaeological Trust, York, 1984)

R.B. Dobson, 'Richard III and the Church of York', in *Kings and Nobles in the Later Middle Ages,* ed R.A. Griffiths and J. Sherborne (Gloucester, 1986)

R.B. Dobson, *Church and Society in the Medieval North of England* (London, 1996)

F.Drake, *Eboracum* (London and York, 1736)

B.F. Duckham, *The Yorkshire Ouse* (Newton Abbot, 1967)

T.French, *York Minster: The Great East Window (Corpus Vitrearum Medii Aevi)* (Oxford 1995)

P.J.P. Goldberg, *Women, Work and Life Cycle in a Medieval Economy: Women in York and Yorkshire, c 1300-1520* (Oxford, 1992)

J Harvey, *York* (London, 1975)

R. Horrox, ed., *Richard III and the North* (Hull: University of Hull Centre for Regional and Local History, 1986)

J. Kermode, *Medieval Merchants: York, Beverley and Hull in the Later Middle Ages* Cambridge, 1998)

E. Miller, 'Medieval York', in *Victoria History of the County of York: The City of York,* ed. P.M. Tillott (Oxford, 1961), pp. 25-116

A. Raine, *Medieval York: a topographical study based on original sources* (London, 1955)

S. Rees Jones, ed., *The Government of Medieval York: Essays in commemoration of the 1396 Royal Charter* (Borthwick Studies in History, 3, 1997)

Royal Commission on Historical Monuments (England), *An Inventory of the Historical Monuments in the City of York,* 5 vols. (London, 1962-81)

CHAPTER 5 - Tudor York

A. G. Dickens in his chapter on 'Tudor York' in P. M. Tillot ed., *The Victoria History of the Counties of England. A History of Yorkshire: The City of York* (1961), pp. 117-159 provides a succinct account of the city in the sixteenth century and this volume as a whole includes invaluable information on the fate of the city's institutions and buildings during the period.

D.M. Palliser, *Tudor York* (Oxford, 1979), primarily a very detailed economic and social history of the city, in addition lucidly places York in its geographical, administrative and cultural setting in sixteenth-century England, while in *The Reformation in York 1534-1553* (Borthwick Paper 40, York, 1971) the same author more briefly relates the progress of the early Reformation in the city. In three further articles he has significantly augmented his monograph: 'Epidemics in Tudor York' *Northern History*, VII (1973), pp. 45-63, 'A Crisis in English Towns? The Case of York, 1460-1640', *Northern History* XIV (1978) pp.108-125 and 'Civic Mentality and the Environment in Tudor York' *Northern History*, XVIII (1982), pp. 78-115.

Chapter V of G. E. Aylmer and R. Cant, *A History of York Minster* (Oxford, 1977) describes changes in the Minster at this period.

In *Catholic Recusancy in the City of York 1558-1579* (Catholic Record Society Monograph 2, 1970) J. C. H. Aveling considers the development of Protestantism as well as the revival of Catholicism in the city.

Information on York monks, friars and nuns dispossessed at the Reformation is contained in C. Cross and N. Vickers, eds., *Monks, Friars and Nuns in Sixteenth Century Yorkshire* (Yorkshire Archaeological Society, Record Series CL (1995).

C. Cross, 'The Genesis of a Godly Community. Two York Parishes 1590-1640', *Studies in Church History*, 23 (1986), pp. 209-222 turns the spotlight on the parishes of All Saints, North Street and St John's, Ousebridge.

R. R. Reid, *The King's Council in the North* (1921), remains the best account of the Council in the North, though there are now more recent biographies of two of its most influential presidents:

A. G. Dickens, *Robert Holgate Archbishop of York and President of the King's Council in the North* (Borthwick Paper 8, 1955) and C. Cross, *The Puritan Earl. The Life of Henry Hastings, Third Earl of Huntingdon 1536-1595* (1966).

Detailed excerpts from the corporation's records from 1474 to 1591 have been printed in A. Raine ed., *York Civic Records 1-8* (Yorkshire Archaeological Society, Records Series, XCVIII, CIII, CVI, CVIII, CX, CXII, CXV, CXIX, 1939-1953) and D. Sutton ed., *York Civic Records 9* (Yorkshire Archaeological Society, Records Series, CXXXVIII, 1978).

Half of *Catholic Recusancy in the City of York* is given over to detailed summaries from the High Commission Act Books, the House Books, the Assize records and other sources for recusant history.

In *The Lives of our Catholic Forefathers related by themselves*, Third Series (1877) J. Morris has edited the contemporary life of Margaret Clitherow by John Mush.

CHAPTER 6 - Stuart York

York has been fortunate in its historians and there is no need to repeat the names which have already been mentioned in earlier chapters, except to say that the history of the city produced in this period, *Analecta Eboracensia* by Sir Thomas Widdrington, though written in 1662, was not published until 1829. The chapter on 17th-century York by G. C. Forster in *The City of York* volume edited by P. M. Tillott for the Victoria County History (1962) remains the starting point for the present day researcher, along with the four volumes on the city, vols 2-5, so far published by the Royal Commission on Historical Monuments which record and illustrate the surviving architectural features from the period. The social and demographic history of the city is covered by C. Galley, *The Demography of early modern towns: York in the 16th and 17th centuries* (1998), and detailed treatment of the plague in 1604/5 can be found in D. M. Palliser, 'Epidemics in Tudor York' *Northern History* 8, pp. 45-63. He has also written on the period before the Civil War, 'A crisis in English Towns: the case of

York 1560-1640' *Northern History*, 18, pp. 108-25, and, with Mary Palliser, compiled an excellent collection of contemporary visitors' impressions of the city, *York as they Saw It, from Alcuin to Lord Esher* (1979). The building works of Sir Arthur Ingram are discussed by C. Gillett, 'Ingram's Almshouses, York' and R. M. Butler, 'York Palace; a lost Jacobean Mansion' in volumes 1 and 13 of *The York Historian* respectively. The conflicts between Minster and City in the early part of the century are dealt with in a chapter by M. C. Cross, 'From Reformation to Restoration' in G. E. Aylmer and R. Cant eds, *A History of York Minster* (1979), and politics are also discussed in A. Warmington, 'The Corporation of York in Peace and War, 1638-45', *York Historian* 9, pp.16-26. The central event of the Civil Wars in the city is examined in detail in L. P. Wenham, *The Great and Close Siege of York, 1644* (1970), and the ensuing battle is analysed in P. Newman, *Marston Moor, 2 July 1644: the Sources and the Site* (1978). The political and religious backgrounds to the wars are discussed in D. Scott, 'Politics and Government in York, 1640-1662' in R. C. Richardson, ed., *The English Revolution in Town and Countryside* (1992) and by M. C Cross, 'Achieving the Millennium: the church in York during the Commonwealth' in *Studies in Church History,* 4 (1967), and her 'A man of conscience in 17th-century urban politics; Alderman Hoyle of York' in J. Morrill, P. Slack and D. Woolf eds, *Public Duty and private Conscience in 17th-century England* (1993). The Restoration years are discussed in P. Withington, 'Views from the Bridge: Revolution and Restoration in 17th-century York' *Past and Present,* 170 (2001), pp.121-51 and D. Scott, *Quakerism in York 1650-1720* (1991). Catholicism is comprehensively treated by J. Aveling, *Catholic Recusancy in the City of York 1558-1792* (1970), and the social and intellectual milieu of the late 17th-century is discussed in T. Brighton, *Henry Gyles, Virtuoso and Glasspainter of York* (1984) and J. Malden, 'Elusive Virtuosi, Thomas and Joshua Mann', *York Historian,* 6. For an insight to local and national politics at the end of the century, the edition of *The Memoirs of Sir John Reresby,* published by the Royal Historical Society in 1991, provides a contemporary source.

CHAPTER 7 - 18th Century York

Defoe Daniel, *A Tour through the Whole Island of Great Britain*, The Promotional Reprint Co. Ltd; 1992

Drake Francis, *Eboracum; or the History and Antiquities of the City of York, 1736*

Hutchinson J & Palliser D M, *York*, Bartholomew City Guides, 1980

Morris C, ed. *The Journeys of Celia Fiennes*, London, 1949

Murray H, *Scarborough, York and Leeds: The Town Plans of John Cossins 1697-1743*, Sessions Ltd, The Ebor Press, York; 1997

Victoria County History, P M Tillott (ed), *A History of Yorkshire: the City of York*, London, 1961

Wittkower, R "Burlington and his Work in York", in W A Singleton ed. *Studies in Architectural History*, 1954

White E ed. *Feeding a City*, Prospect Books, 2000

Wragg, B ed. by Giles Worsley, *The Life and Works of John Carr of York*, Oblong 2000

York City Art Gallery, *York through the Eyes of the Artist*, City of York Council; 1990

York Georgian Society Occasional Paper no.1; 1945

York Historian:-

N J Arch, "To stop this dangerous mischief': York and the Jacobite Rebellion of 1745", vol.3, 1980;

Jeremy Black, "The City itself is but poor': York in 1721", vol.7, 1986;

Jeremy Black, "Whig Popular Propaganda in the early C18: a Yorkshire Example", vol.7, 1986;

R M Butler, "York Palace, a vanished Jacobean mansion", vol.8, 1988;

A Davison, "A Genuine and Superior Article: the last two centuries of Brewing in York", vol.10, 1992;

David Griffiths, "Music in the C18 York Theatre", vol.15, 1998;

Brett Harrison, "William Gossip's House in Ogleforth, York, 1733-1808", vol.15, 1998;

B R Hartley, "Thomas Griffith of York, 'once Governor of the Castle and now a Debtor from the same'", vol.11, 1994;

David Haxby and John Malden, "Thomas Haxby of York (1729-1796) - an extraordinary musician and musical instrument maker", vol.2, 1978;

David Haxby and John Malden, "Thomas Haxby - a note", vol.3, 1980;

Jennifer Kaner, "York and the Battle of Jersey", vol.6, 1985; p.72

John Malden, "A Secret Diary", vol.17, 2000;

R J Malden, "Combmakers of York", vol.8, 1989;

H Murray, "Sedan Chairs In York", vol.17, 2000;

Corita Myerscough, "The Fishers of York: a Family of Sculptors", vol.7, 1986;

Jonathan Oates, "York and the Rebel Prisoners, 1745-52", vol.17, 2000;

W B Taylor, "The Rise and Decline of the Wholesale Butter Trade of York in the C18", vol.9, 1990;

W B Taylor, "The Workshops and Manufactories of York in the Second Half of the C18", vol.10;

W B Taylor, "A History of the Tadcaster-York Turnpike", vol.12, 1995;

W B Taylor, "Banking in York in the 18th Century", vol.14, 1997;

Barbara Whitehead, "York and the Jacobite Rebels: some events and people in the York of 1745 to 1747", vol.6, 1985;

Young Arthur, *A Six Months Tour through the North of England*, London, 1771

CHAPTER 8 - 19th Century York

Armstrong, Alan, *Stability and Change in an English County Town. A Social Study of York, 1801-1851*, Cambridge University Press, Cambridge, 1974

Aylmer G. E. and Cant, Reginald, eds, *A History of York Minster*, Clarendon Press, Oxford, 1977

Bailey, Brian, *George Hudson. The Rise and Fall of the Railway King*, Alan Sutton, Stroud, 1995

Baines, Edward, *History, Directory & Gazetteer of the County of York*, vol. 2, E. Baines, Leeds, 1823

Benson, George, *An Account of the City and County of the City of*

York: from the Reformation to the Year 1925, Cooper & Swann, York, 1925

Brett, Peter, *The Rise and Fall of the York Whig Club, 1818-1830*, Borthwick Papers no. 76, University of York, York, 1989

Camidge, William, *Ye Old Streete of Pavemente (York)*, "Yorkshire Gazette", York, [1893]

Digby, Anne, *Madness, Morality and Medicine. A Study of the York Retreat, 1796-1914*, Cambridge University Press, Cambridge, 1985

Digby, Anne, *From York Lunatic Asylum to Bootham Park Hospital*, Borthwick Papers no. 69, University of York, York, 1986

Durey, Michael, *The First Spasmodic Cholera Epidemic in York, 1832*, Borthwick Papers no. 46, St Anthony's Press, York, 1974

Feinstein, Charles, ed., *York 1831-1981. 150 Years of Scientific Endeavour and Social Change*, William Sessions, York, 1981

Finnegan, Frances, *Poverty and Prostitution. A Study of Victorian Prostitutes in York*, Cambridge University Press, Cambridge, 1979

Finnegan, Frances, *Poverty and Prejudice. A Study of Irish Immigrants in York, 1840-1875*, Cork University Press, Cork, 1982

Fitzsimmons, Linda, 'The Theatre Royal, York', *York History* 4, pp. 169-92, York Educational Settlement, York, n.d.

Gillman, F. J., *The Story of York Adult Schools from the Commencement to 1907*, [York 1907]

Hargrove, William, *A History and Description of the Ancient City of York*, 2 vols, William Alexander, York, 1818

Hills, R. I., *The Inevitable March of Labour? Electoral Politics in York, 1900-1914*, Borthwick Papers no. 89, University of York, York, 1996

Howard, John, *Historical Sketch of the Origin and Work of the York Incorporated (Church of England) Sunday School Committee*, The Committee, York, 1887

Jones, Ian, *Brass Bands in York, 1833-1914*, Borthwick Papers no. 85, University of York, York, 1995

Knight, Charles Brunton, *A History of the City of York*, Herald

Printing Works, York, 1944

Leak, Adrian, *The Liberty of St Peter of York, 1800-1838*, Borthwick Papers no. 77, University of York, York, 1990

Lyth, John, *Glimpses of Early Methodism in York*, William Sessions, York, 1885

McGregor, G. P., *A Church College for the 21st Century? 150 Years of Ripon & York St John*, William Sessions, York, 1991

Manchester Statistical Society, *Report of a Committee of the Manchester Statistical Society on the State of Education in the City of York in 1836-1837*, James Ridgway and Son, London, 1837

Pevsner, Nikolaus and Neave, David, *Yorkshire: York and the East Riding*, The Buildings of England, Penguin Books, London, 1995

Ratcliffe, Barrie M. and Chaloner, W. H., eds, *A French Sociologist Looks at Britain. Gustave d'Eichthal and British Society in 1828*, Manchester University Press, Manchester, 1977

Report from His Majesty's Commissioners for inquiring into the Administration and Practical Operation of the Poor Laws, *Parliamentary Papers* 1834 (44), Appendix A, part 1, pp. 870a-874a (Report on York by J. D. Tweedy)

Reports from Commissioners. Corporations, England and Wales, *Parliamentary Papers* 1835 (116), Appendix to the First Report, part III, on the City of York, pp. 1735-1766 (Report on the City of York)

Reports from Commissioners. State of Large Towns and Populous Districts, First Report, *Parliamentary Papers* 1844 (572), pp. 93-129 (Report on the State of York by Thomas Laycock)

Reports from Commissioners. State of Large Towns and Populous Districts, Second Report, *Parliamentary Papers* 1845 (610), Appendix, part II, pp. 307-8 (Report on the Condition of the City of York by James Smith)

Rowntree, B. Seebohm, *Poverty. A Study of Town Life*, London, Macmillan, 4th ed. 1902

Royle, Edward, *The Victorian Church in York*, Borthwick Papers no. 64, University of York, York, 1983

Royle, Edward, *Nonconformity in Nineteenth-century York*, Borthwick Papers no. 68, University of York, York, 1985

Schools Inquiry Commission, *Parliamentary Papers* 1867-8 (3966), IX pp. 103-423 (General Report on the West Riding of the County of York, by J. G. Fitch); XVIII pp. 413-28 (St Peter's), 676-79 (Elmfield), 680–4 (Bootham), 692-5 (The Mount) (Reports, Digests of Information, &c., City of York, by J. G. Fitch)

Sessions, William K. and Sessions, E. Margaret, *The Tuke Family of York - Mainly an Account of Three Generations*, William Sessions, York, 1971

Stackpoole, Alberic, and others, eds, *The Noble City of York*, Cerialis Press, York, [1972]

Swift, Roger, *Police Reform in Early Victorian York, 1835-1856*, Borthwick Papers no. 73, University of York, York, 1988

Taylor, W. B., *Blue Coat: Grey Coat. The Blue & Grey Coat Schools and St Stephen's Home of York, 1705-1983*, Sessions Book Trust, York, 1997

Tillott, P. M., ed., *A History of Yorkshire. The City of York*, The Victoria History of the Counties of England, Oxford University Press, Oxford, 1961, reprinted Dawson, Folkestone. 1982

Vernon, Anne, *A Quaker Business Man. The Life of Joseph Rowntree, 1836-1925*, George Allen & Unwin, London, 1958

Webb, Katherine A., *"One of the most useful charities in the City": York Dispensary, 1788-1988*, Borthwick Papers no. 74, University of York, York, 1988

Whellan, T., *History and Topography of the City of York and the North Riding of Yorkshire*, Whellan & Co, Beverley, 1857 and re-issue by J. J. Sheahan (John Green, Beverley, 1871).

White, William, *History, Gazetteer and Directory of Yorkshire*, 3 vols, W. White, Sheffield, 1840

Wright, Sheila, *Friends in York. The Dynamics of Quaker Revival, 1780-1860*, Keele University Press, Keele, 1995

CHAPTER 9 - 20th Century York

Adshead, S.D., Minter, C.J, Needham, C.W.C., *York, A Plan for Progress and Preservation,* York, 1948

Allison, K. J., Sigsworth, E.M., and Tillott, P.M., *The City of York* (Victoria County History Series), O.U.P., 1961

Benson, G., *An Account of the City and County of York from the Reformation to the Year 1925,* York, 1925. Reprint 1968

Briggs, Asa, *A Study of the work of Seebohm Rowntree, 1871-1954,* London, 1961

British Association, *York, a Survey,* York 1959

Brockbank, J.L. and Holmes, W. M., *York in English History,* London, 1909

Brunskill, Elizabeth, *The York Mystery Plays,* York, 1963

Esher, Viscount, *York, A Study in Conservation* (Report to the Minister of Housing and Local Government and York City Council), HMSO, 1968

Esher, Viscount, *A Broken Wave – The Rebuilding of England 1940-1980,* London, 1981

Fife, Michael and Walls, Peter, *The River Foss – its History and Natural History,* York, 1973

Hutchinson, J. and Palliser, D.M., *York,* 1980

Hutton, Barbara, *Clifton and its People,* York 1969

Knight, C.B., *A History of the City of York,* 1944

Knowles, John A., *The York School of Glass Painting,* London, 1936

Morrell, J.B., *The City of Our Dreams,* London, 1940

Morrell, J.B. and Watson, A.P., *How York Governs Itself,* London, 11928

Morris, J.E., *York,* London, 1924

Nuttgens, Patrick, *York* (City Buildings Series), London 1970

Nuttgens, Patrick, *York...The Continuing City,* York, 1976,1989, 2001

Radley, J. and Simms, C., *Yorkshire Flooding – Some effects on Man and Nature,* York, 1970

Rowntree, B.Seebohm, *Poverty, A Study of Town Life,* London, 1901

Rowntree, B. Seebohm, *Portrait of a City's Housing* (Rebuilding Britain Series), London 1945

Rowntree, B. Seebohm, *Poverty and Progress,* London 1941

Royal Commission on Historical Monuments, *An Inventory of the Historical Monuments in the City of York,* Vol. III, IV,V, HMSO 1972-1981

Stacpoole, Alberic (ed.) *The Noble City of York,* York, 1972

Timmins, Nicholas, *The Five Giants – A Biography of the Welfare State,* London, 1995

Vernon, Anne, *A Quaker Business Man – The Life of Joseph Rowntree,* London 1958

Wenham, L.P., *York,* London, 1971

York Archaeological Trust, *Interim Bulletins,* 1973 to date

York City Council, *Development Plan Survey,* 1951; *A Guide for Developers,* 1966; *Inner Ring Road Study,*1967; *Report on Proposed Conservation Areas,* 1968; *Report on Parking,* 1969; *Central Area Traffic Schemes,* 1970; Other papers to date

York Civic Trust, *Annual Reports,* 1946 to date.

York Georgian Society, *Occasional papers, 1-8; Annual Reports,* 1944 to date.

York Group for the Promotion of Planning, *The Strays and Ways of York,* York, 1968

York Institute for Architectural Study, *Studies in Architectural History,* (ed. A. Singleton), York, 1954,1956

York Redundant Churches Commission, *New Uses for Old Churches*, York, 1967

York and East Yorkshire Society, *Year Books,* especially 1956-7

York Archaeological Society, *The Yorkshire Archaeological Society Record Series,* 1885 to date

Yorkshire Philosophical Society, *Annual Reports,* 1825 to date

Index

Illustrations are indicated in **bold** type

Acomb 250, 253

Acomb Church 207

Addyman, Peter 338, 343

Adult Schools 300

Adwick le Street 159

Aelia Severa **26,** 27

Aelle (King) 50-1

Aese 58

Aethelberht (Archbishop) 44-45

Aethelred 'the Unready' 40, 66

Agricola (Roman governor) 12

Ainsty 144, 149, 249-50, 266

Albany, Leeman Road (Primitive Methodist Chapel) 280

Albion Street (Wesleyan Chapel) 272, 274

Alcuin 45-6, 48

Aldam, Thomas 201

aldermen, office of 183, 192, 203, 204, 265

Aldwark 36, 58, 123, 272, 282

alehouses 182

Alexander III, king of Scotland 106

Alexander, William 218, 261, 265

Alfred (King) 40

All Saints Church, Fishergate 62

All Saints Church, North Street 101, 129, 136, 184 - 5, 187-188, 245

All Saints Church, Pavement 61, 179, **184, 185,** 195, 245

All Saints Comprehensive School 348

All Saints, North Street 289

Allanson, William, almshouses 183, 194

Allen, Edward 233

Allen, William 164, 166

Ammianus Marcellinus 36

Andrews, George Townshend, architect **252, 260,** 285

Aneley's Building Firm 315

Anglian Tower 34 - 5, 46, 60, **Monochrome Plate 2.**

Anne Middleton's Hospital 201, 293

apothecaries 208

Archaeological Resource Centre 339

Archbishop Holgate's school 156, 160, 168, 283, 284, 349, 350

archbishop's palace and prison 191

Arciacus (Roman god) 18

Argles, George, clergyman 277

army 275, 296

Ashe, Simeon 197

Aske, John 148

Aske, Robert 147, 148

Askwith, Robert 172

Assemblies 226, 231, 240, 295

Assembly Rooms **214,** 226, 227, 233, 242, 243, 295, 297-8, 315, 344

Assize Courts 219, 227

Aston, John 191

Athelstan (King) 52, **53**

Atkinson, Francis 180

Atkinson, James, surgeon 297

attendance at church 274, 278

Atys (Roman god) 19

Augustinian Friary 148, 150, 152, 153, 155, 158

Ayscough, Henry 185

Baines, Ald. Henry 229, 232

bakers 181

Bakewell 52

Baltic 57, 175

Bamburgh 44, 65

Banks 255

Bannockburn, battle 107-8

Baptists 204, 272, 275, 279

Bar Convent 205, 217, 238, 276, 321, 325, 348

Bar Convent School 217, 238, 282, 285

barbers 208

Barbican Centre 347

Barker, Robert 193

Barnes, Mrs 164

Barnes, Richard 163

Barron, Sir Donald 351

Barwicke, Richard 152

basilica 41, 46

Bath Houses (Roman) 8 - 9, 14, 16, 24

Battle of Fulford Gate 78

Battle of Stamford Bridge 67, 78

Battle of the Standard 76

Baynes, Thomas 152

Bean, John 169

Beckwith, Ralph 155

Beckwith, Sir Leonard 155, 160

Bedern 187, 253, 265, 279, 280

Bedern (National) School 283

Beedham's Court **273**, 291

Bellasis, John 195

Bellerby, George 152

Bellerby's Paint Works 315

Bellhouse, City Engineer and Planning Officer 334

Beningborough Grange 150

Bernicia 44, 65

Best, Charles, physician to York Asylum 294

Betty's Restaurant 326

Beverley 62, 147, 194

Bilborough 144

Birch's Building Firm 315

Birchill, John 185-6

Bishop Fields 192

Bishophill 19, 44, 63, 249, 261, 275

Bishophill (British) School 282

Bishop's Wharf **341**

Bishopthorpe, palace 108, 109, 131

Black Swan Inn, Coney Street 240, 242

Blackburn, Nicholas, Jr, mayor 129-30, 138

Blackburn, Nicholas, Sr, mayor 129-30, 136, 138

Blair, Tony **Monochrome Plate 16.**

Blake Street 47, 59

Blossom Street 10, 206, 246, 249, 276

Blue Coat (Charity) School 236, 282

Blues, the 220

Board of Health 267, 291 – 2

Bolton castle [Castle Bolton] 165

Bond of Association of 1584 173

Book of Sports 186

bookbinders 182

Booksellers 208, 261

Booth, Robert, dean 132

Bootham 134, 188, 189, 197, 249, 293

Bootham (Quaker) School 285 - 6, **306,** 348

Bootham Bar 8, 47, 66, 108, 112, 245

Bootham Ward 265

Borthwick Institute of Historical Research 322, 351, 352

Bosa (Bishop) 44

Bosworth, battle 114, 116, 140-1

Botterill's Horse Repository 318

Bourchier, Sir John 228

Bowes, William 223, 231

Bowet, Henry, archbishop 133, 139

Bowles, Edward 200

Bowman, William 169

Bradford, Tong Hall 208

Braithwaite family 178-9

Brearey family 183, 186

Breda 200

Brenz, Johann 158

Brett, Lionel, Viscount Esher 333

brewers 182, 183

bridges 265

Bridlington Priory 149

Brierley, Walter 283, **284**, 312, 315, 322, 348

Brigantes 5

Bristol 102, 116, 142

British and Foreign Schools Society 282

British Association for the Advancement of Science 297, 298

British Sugar Corporation 316

Brooke, Robert 155, 172

Brooks, Thomas 233

Brown, Dr Charles Surveyor to the Fabric 337

Brown's Drapers 315

Bruce, Robert 107 – 8

Brunanburh 52

Bulkeley, Stephen 193

Bullinger, Heinrich 158

Bunney, Edmund 184

Burgesses of York 90

Burke Bill, Chairman of the Housing Committee 333, 334

Burlington, Lord 224, 226, 228 **Colour Plate 12.**

Burton Family 351, 352

Burton, Dr John 230, 234

butchers 181

Butter trade 232, 242

Byzantium 57

Caesar, Julius 4

Calton 208

Calvin, Jean 158

Cambridge university 168

Canon J.S Purvis, Minster Archivist 322, 345

Canterbury 163

Caracalla (Emperor) 14, 29

Carlisle, Earl of 224, 228

Carmelite Friary 150, 152, 155

Carpenter, Samuel 207

Carr, John 219, 223, 227, 231, 238, 312, 339

Carr, John, mayor 137

Cartimandua (Queen) 5

carvers 206

Cassius Dio 14, 29

Castle *see* York Castle

Castle Mills 262

Castle Mills Bridge 268

Castle Musuem 338, 339

Castle Yard 218-220, 228

Castlegate 61, 204, 248, 263, 272

Castlegate House 238, **241**

Castlegate Postern 246

Castlegate Ward 265

Catholics *see* Roman Catholics

Cavendish, Lord John 223, 230

Cawood, palace 131, 139

Celerinius Vitalis 6

Cemeteries (Anglian) 38

Cemeteries (Roman) 24 - 9, 33

Centenary (Wesleyan Chapel) 272, 277, 279, 339

Central Laboratories of MAFF, Sand Hutton 354

Chamberleyn, Joan 135

Chambre, John, glazier 126

Chantries 129, 133, 136 - 8

Chapter House Street 8

Charlemagne 45

Charles I 185, 186, 192, 193, 194

Charles V 161

Chaytor, George 180

chemists and druggists 254, 261

378

Christchurch 45, 63

Christianity 32 – 3

Christmas Interludes 166

church courts 181, 186

Church of England 271, 274, 276-9, 280-1, 283, 285

Church Street 8

churches and chapels 246, 274, 277

Cistercians 86

City walls 245-7, 265

Civic Trust 321, 328, 331- 340, 344, 351, 354

Civil Wars 192-200

Clark, Frank 355

Clarke Ald. Samuel 224, 225

Claudius (Emperor) 4

Claudius Hieronymianus 19

Clay, George 182

Clayborough, William 160

Clayton, Robert 158

Clementhorpe 35, 62, 261, 263, 277

Clementhorpe Priory (nunnery) 134, 146, 147, 150, 152, 155, 164; fields 113

Clifford Street 248, 266, 287, **Colour Plate 13.**

Clifford, Henry, second earl of Cumberland 165

Clifford's Tower 69, **70,** 71, 77, 148, 210, 247

Clifton 250, 253, 294

Clifton (Wesleyan Chapel) 277

Clifton Ings 192, 198, 208

Clifton Proprietry School 284

Clitherow, John 170

Clitherow, Margaret (née Middleton) 169, 170

clockmakers 182, 261

Close The 161, 164

Cnut (King) 40, 66

coffee houses 209

Coggan, Archbishop of York 334

Colan, John, goldsmith 122

Colet, John 156

Colliergate 61, 261

Collins, Lancelot 147, 148

colonia 47

Columba (Saint) 44

Comber, Thomas 208

Commission for Regulating Corporations 203

Coney Street 10, 24, 61, 144, 145, 158, 206

confectionary and cocoa 263 - 4, 300

Congregationalists *see* Independents

Constantine (Emperor) 1, 31 – 2

Constantius I (Emperor) 7, 32

Cooke, Ambrose 169

Cooke, Ron 351, 354-5

Cooke, Thomas, clock manufacturer 261

Cookridge 207

Coppergate 53-5, 60-1, **Monchrome Plate 3, 4.**

cordwainers 181, 183

Cornwell, Ald.William 223, 229

Corporation (after 1835) 256, 257, 262, 265 - 8, 270, 283, 287, 298, 299

Corporation (before 1835) 254, 256, 264 - 6, 268, 270, 291, 295

Corpus Christi 145, 166

Corpus Christi plays 101, 112, 126-7

Cossins, John 225, 226, **Monochrome Plate 12.**

Cottesford, Thomas 160

Council in the North 149, 158, 162-163, 166, 168, 173, 176, 181, 189 - 91, 199, 206

County and Borough Police Act (1856) 266

Coupland, William 164

Coventry 175

Cowper, Edmund 195, 199

Cox, Shoemakers 326

crafts and guilds 120 – 6

Cragges, Robert 160

Craven 43, 174

Craven, Thomas and Mary Ann, confectionary manufacturers 263, 305

Creed Play 164

Cripling, Robert 168, 169, 171

Cromwell, Oliver 201

Cromwell, Richard 201

Cromwell, Thomas 146

Crossman, Richard 333

Culloden, Battle of 213, 221

Cumberford, Henry 167

Cumberland 149, 165

Cumberland House 229

Cumberland Street 61

Cumberland, Duke of 221, 229, 230

Cumberland, earl of *see* Clifford, Henry

Cumbria 180

Cussins and Light 326

Cuthbert, Saint 51

Dalbie, William 195

Danby, Lord 220

dancing masters 208

Danelaw 66

Danes 64

Dannat, Trevor 348

Danzig 128

Darcy, Thomas, Lord 147

Davies, Lord Llewelyn 311

Davy Hall 187

Dawson, Brian 204

De Grey Rooms 296, 324, 326

Dealtry, Dr John 231, **Monochrome Plate 13.**

Dean Court Hotel 324

Dean's Park 44, 191, 251

deanery 192, 284

Deangate 248, 328, 329, 335

Debtors' Prison 218, 219, 228

Defoe, Daniel 225, 226, 230, 232, 239

Deira 43

Demetrius 14

Dench, Dame Judi 345

Derbyshire, Sir Andrew 352, 353

Dickinson family 183

Dineley, John 168-169

diseases 289 – 92

dissent *see* nonconformity

Divelinestaynes 63

Dixon, Kenneth 351

Dobson, William 225

Dodsworth Schools 293

Domesday Book 58, 73-5, 80, 89

Dominican Friary 148, 150, 152, 155, 158

Doncaster 159, 258, 294, 295

Douai 167-168

Doughty, James 233

Douglas, James the Black 108

Downes, Geoffrey 162

Drake, Francis 225, 226, 227, 230, 232, 243

drapers 183, 209

dressmakers 208

Dringhouses 14, 144, 250

Dublin 52-3, 63

Dudley, John, duke of Northumberland 158

Duke of York 88

Duke of York Street Mission, Layerthorpe **273,** 280

Duncombe Place 248, **252,** 276, 293, **Monochrome Plate 15**

Duncombe, The Hon. Augustus William, Dean of York 248, 276, 279, 321, 322

Durham 51, 163, 165, 195

Durham, bishop 110; cathedral 133

Eadred (King) 53, 57

Eadwig (King) 57

Earl of York, Wm Aumale 88

Earlsburgh 66

East Anglia 52

Eastern Association, army of 197, 200

Eastland Company 181

Ebenezer, Little Stonegate (Primitive Methodist Chapel) 274

Eborius (Bishop) 1, 33

Ebrauke 144

economy 254 - 64, 295

Edgar (King) 57, 63-4

Edinburgh castle 207

Edmund (King) 52, 66

education 280 - 8, 300, 301

Education Act (1902) 288

Education Act (1870) 283

Edward the Confessor (King) 40, 66

Edward the Elder (King) 52

Edward I 103 - 7, 114, 130

Edward II 106 – 8

Edward III 106, 108 – 9

Edward IV 113

Edward VI 156, 158, 159, 160

Edwin (King) 53, 57

Egberht (Archbishop) 45

Eidsborg 57

Eleanor, queen of Edward I 130

elections 264, 265, 269 - 71, 283

electricity supply 267 – 8

Elizabeth I 139, 155, 158, 160, 162, 164, 165, 166, 171, 173, 174, 175, 176, 177

Ellerker family 164

Elmet 43

Elmfield College (Primitive Methodist) School 288

English Martyrs School, (Blossom St) (Dalton Terrace) 276, 321

engravers 206

Eoforwic 48, 50

Erasmus, Desiderius 158

Eric Bloodaxe (King) 53, 57, 65

Eric of Hlathir (Earl) 66

Escrick Park 183

Etteridge's Hotel 241, 242

Etty, William 231

Evelyn, John 200-01

Ewbank, George 229

Exclusion Crisis 205

Exeter 142

Fair 93 – 4

Fairfax House 197, 321

Fairfax, family 204; Charles 201 - 2; Sir Thomas 193, 196 – 201

Fairfax, Lord 108

Fairfax, Sir Nicholas 148

Fairfax, Viscount 228

Falkirk, battle 107

Farming Museum, Murton 339

Farnley Church 207

Fauconberg, Lord 208

Fawkes, Guy 184

Feilden, Sir Bernard, Surveyor to the Fabric 336, 337

Female Prison 219

Festival Concert Room 298

Fetter Lane 14

Fiennes, Celia 210-11, 224, 227, 239

Fine Arts and Industrial Exhibition (1866) 298

Fine Arts and Industrial Exhibition (1879) 298, **299**
Fire 95

fire brigade 248, 252, 267

Fisher, John 231

Fishergate 50, 53, 55, 58, 62, 150, 254

Fishergate (Board) School 283

Fishergate Bar 245, 291

Fishergate Postern 245, 247, 249

Fishpool 71 – 2

Flemyng, Nicholas, mayor 108

Fletcher, John 168

flour milling 262

food supply 22-3

Ford, John, Quaker head master 285, 297

Fortress Baths 8 - 9, **Monochrome Plate 1**; Defences 9, 13, 34; Headquarters 6 - 8 **Colour Plate 1**

Foss Bridge 61, 197, 247, 255, 266, 282

Foss Islands 257, 292

Foss Islands Road 267

Foss Navigation 257, 262 - 3, 268

Foss, River 2, 24, 49, 53, 60, 61, 135, 247, 249, 253, 257, 262-3, 267-8, 289-90

Fossgate 61, 128, 136, 150, 181

Fountains Abbey 133

Fox, George 201, 223

France 50

Franciscan Friary 150, 152, 153, 155, 158

Freez, Fridericus, printer 122

Friargate 61, 205

Friars 86

Friendly Societies' Dispensary 248

Frisians 48

Frost, William, mayor 112

Fulford 62, 67, 198, 250, 251, 268, 277

Fulford Cross 149

Fuller, Thomas 211

Furnell, Raymond, Dean of York 346

Gale, George 160

Galmanho 66

Galmanlith 66

Games 96

Garden Place, Hungate **262**, 281, 282

gas supply 265, 267, 270, 274, 296

Gaunt, John of 110

Geldart family 183

Gent, Thomas 233

George Hudson Street 16, 246

George Inn, Coney Street 241, 242

George Street 62

Germany 63, 175

Gild Merchant 89

Gilliot, Sir John, mayor 137

Gilliot, William, mayor 137

Gillygate 329

Gimcrack Rooms,York Racecourse 347

Gisburne, John, mayor 112

Gladwyn, Arthur Family 351

glass works 254, 256, 261

Glenton, Peter 157

Gloucester, duke of *see* Richard III

Godfrey's Booksellers 315

Godwin 66

Goldie, George 321

Goldsmiths 182

Goldthorpe, Richard 155

Goodramgate 47, **111,** 245, 248, 256, 275

Goose Lane 228

Gordian (Emperor) 30

Gordon Riots 213, 223

Graa (Gray) family, merchants 129, 138

Graham, John, clergyman 297

Grape Lane (various Nonconformist Chapels) 272, 274

Gray Dodsworth and Cobb 318

Gray, Jonathan 297

Grayson, Thomas 158

Grayson, William 158

Green, Francis 343

Green, Laurence 155

Gregory (Pope) 43, 45

Gresham, Sir Richard 155

Grey Coat (Charity) School 236, 237, 282

Grey, Lady Jane 159

Griffiths, Thomas 235

Grim 58

Grindal, Edmund 166, 168, 170, **Monochrome Plate 8.**

grocers 209

Groves 253

Groves (Wesleyan Chapel) 277, 299

Gryme, William 152

Guildhall 47, 101, **125,** 127, 135, 144, 150, 195, 199, 202, 207, 266

Guildhall Ward 265

Guilds 93

Gunpowder Plot 184

Guthfrith/Guthred (King) 51-52

Gyles, Edmund 207; Henry 207 – 8

Haberdashers' Guild Hall 189

Hadrian (Emperor) 12

Hainault, Philippa of, queen 109

Hale, John 182

Halfdan (King) 51

Halifax 142

Hanseatic League 119, 121, 128

Hansom, Joseph, architect 275

Harald 'Fairhair' (King) 52

Harald Hardraada (King) 66-7

Hargham, Norfolk 151

Hargrove, William, printer and journalist 276

Harley, Lord 228

Harold (King) 67

Harper family 155

Harrington, John, common clerk 121

Harrington, William 147

Harrison family 183

Harrying of the North 71

Harsnett, Samuel 185

Hartrigg Oaks 309, 310

Harwood, Richard 171, 172, 184

Hassal, Christopher 324

Hastings, Henry, third earl of Huntingdon 166, 167, 168, 170, 171, 173,

Monochrome Plate 9.

Hastings, Sir Francis 173

Haxby Road (Board) School 283

Haxby, Thomas 233

Head Pot **Colour Plate 2**

Heath, Nicholas 160, 162, 163

Hemsworth 156

Henrietta Maria, Queen 195

Henry IV 112 – 13

Henry V 113

Henry VI 113, 128

Henry VII 119, 141, 142, 144, 145, 174

Henry VIII 133, 145, 146, 147, 148, 149, 155, 156

Herbert family 183

Hercules (Roman god) 24

Herring, Archbishop Thomas 216, 217, 219, 220 221, 230

Hess, Hans 344, 345

Hewley, Dame Sarah 204, 236

Hewley, Sir John 204

Heworth 43, 246, 250, 253, 277, 283, 288

Heworth (Wesleyan Chapel) 277

Heworth moor 193

Heywood, Oliver 204

High Commission Court 163, 166, 168, 169

High Ousegate 24, 61

Hildyard, Christopher 209

Hildyard, Francis 225

Hills, Rodney, Leader of the Council 319

Hinxman, John 233

Hodgeson, John 152

Holgate 250-253, 259, 280, 301

Holgate, Robert 149, 156, 158, 159

Holme, Robert, merchant 129, 138

Holme, Thomas, merchant 129, 138

Holy Trinity Church, Goodramgate 101, 129, **143,** 178, 180, 196, 278

Holy Trinity Church, Heworth 277

Holy Trinity Church, King's Square (King's Court) [Christchurch] 61, 170, 247

Holy Trinity Church, Micklegate 45, 63, 152, 246, 275; Parish 289

Holy Trinity Priory 134, 146-147, 150, 152, 153, 155

Holy Wisdom Church 44

Hope Street (British) School 282, 300

Horsefair 160

hospitals and asylums 291, 294, 296

Hothams Brewery 234

housing 246, 247, 249, 251, 259, 289 - 90, 292, 294, 295 **Colour Plate 15.**

Howard, Ebenezer 308

Howard, John, first duke of Norfolk 141

Howard, Katherine 149

Howard, Thomas, third duke of Norfolk 148

Howard, Thomas, fourth duke of Norfolk 165

Hoyle family 186; Thomas 194, 200

Hudson, George 246, 257-8, 270, 285, 319, 327

Huguenots 172

Hull Road 62

Hull *see* Kingston upon Hull

Humber 163

Hundred Years' War 109 – 10

Hungate 135, 249, 262 - 3, 267, 280, 290

Hungate Mission **262,** 280

Huntingdon, earl of *see* Hastings, Henry

Hutton, Matthew 163, 164, 170 184, 185, 188

Hutton, Mrs 164

Imphal Barracks 323, 324

Improvement Commission 265 - 7, 290

Independents 204, 206, 220, 270, 272, 281

Ingram, Sir Arthur 189, 191, 192, 193, 237, **Monochrome Plate 11A.**; Sir William, 183

Ingram's Hospital 189

innkeepers 181, 182

Institute of Advanced Architectural Studies 331, 340, 351

instrument makers 182, 261

insurance 255 – 6

Iona 44

Ipswich 48, 50

Irish, Ireland 52, 57, 63, 249, 253, 255, 269, 270, 274, 275, 291

iron works 254, 261-2; *see also* railways

Irwin, Lord 225, 226, 228, 237

Istanbul 57

Jackson, John 233

Jacobite rebellion (1715) 219, 220

Jacobite rebellion (1745) 219

Jacob's Well 164, **Colour Plate 8.**

James II 182, 204, 205

James the Deacon 44-5

James VI and I 177

James, Eric, Lord James of Rusholme 351, **332**

Jersey, Battle of 221

Jervaulx Abbey 149

Jewish Massacre 78 – 9

Jews of York 107, 121

Johnson, Francis 321

Johnson, Godmondr', Icelander 121

Johnson, Peter 231

Johnson, Robert, mayor 137

Johnson-Marshall, Stirrat 352

joiners 181

Jonson, Ben, Printers 315

Jorvik 56

Jorvik Viking Centre 338

Jubbergate 272

Judges' Lodgings 228, 231

Julia Domna 14, 29

Julia Fortunata 18

Julia Velva **27**, 28

Kearne, Andrew 207

Keirincx, Alexander 192, **Colour Plate 9.**

Kelke, Christopher 161

Kelsaye, Guy 151

Kemble, John Philip 227

Kempe, Margery 138

Kendrick, John, Unitarian tutor 286

Kent 64

Keregan 227

King Street 61

King, General 196

King's Manor 133, 163, 170, 171, 174, 177, 186, 208, 217, 226, 237, 238, 319, 331, 336, 338, **Colour Plate 10.**

King's Square 47, 54, 61, 247, 255

King's Staithe 61

Kingston upon Hull 107, 120, 124, 128 - 9, 163, 171, 174, 178, 244, 254, 256, 262, 263, 298

Kirk, Dr. John 338

Kirkdale 66

Kirke, George 207

Knavesmire 122, 169, 227

labourers 182

Lady Hewley's Hospital 204, 293

Lady Peckett's Yard 275, 281, 300

Lady Peckett's Yard (Wesleyan Methodist Association Chapel) 275

Lambert, John 208

Lamel Hill 197

Lancaster, Nicholas 141

Lancaster, Walter 160

Lancastrian dynasty 144

Lawson, Sir George 148, 155

Laycock, Thomas, surgeon 289 - 292, 295, 297

Layerthorpe 61, 197 280, 282, 289

Layerthorpe Bridge 246, 289, 292

Layerthorpe Mission (Wesleyan) 280

Layerthorpe postern 246

Lee, Edward 146, 156

Lee, Roger 167

Leeds 142, 171, 244, 246, 255, 256-8, 276, 297-8, 300

Leeman Road 259, 280, 300

Leeman, George, solicitor and politician 270, 271

Lees Milne, James 325

Leetham's Flour Mill **262**, 268, 315

Lefwin son of Thorulf 75, 94

Leicester 175

leisure 295 – 301

Leland, John 153

Lendal Bridge 246, 247, 275, 298

Lendal Chapel (Congregational) 272, 281

Leprosy 98

Leven, Lord 196

Liberty of St Peter 265

libraries 281, 287, 298, 300

Lichfield 167

Lincoln 64, 148

Lincolnshire 147

Lindisfarne 44

Lister Kaye, Sir John 225

Lister, Martin 207

Little Blake Street (Lop Lane) 248, 272, 287

Llandaff 149

Lodge, William 208

Lollardy 161

London 48, 50, 64, 101 - 4, 110, 112, 115, 119, 128, 130, 136, 142, 148, 155, 174, 177, 178, 246, 247, 256-8, 263, 296

Lord Mayors Walk 228

Low Countries 50

Low Ousegate 61

Low Petergate 245

Lucius Duccius Rufinus 6

Lucius Viducius Placidus 24

Lumley, George 148

Lumley's Boarding School 236, 237

Lutterworth, Leics 139

Lyons, Jack 351

Malmesbury, William of, chronicler 103

Malton, Old 156

Manchester Academy (College) 218, 285, 286

Manchester, earl of 197-198, 200

Manklin, Richard 225

Manor (National) School 282

Mansion House 224, 231, 238, 243, **Colour Plate 11.**

Marcus Aurelius Lunaris 17, 24, 29, 30

Market Street 301

Markets 94, 97, **260**

Marlborough, Duchess of 226

Marse, Thomas 151

Marshall, Roger 162

Marshall, Thomas 183

Marston Moor, battle of 198

Mary I 159, 161-162

Mary, Queen of Scots 165

Marygate 66, 134, 179, 197, 250, 268, 299

Masham, prebend 131

Mason, Canon William 227, 230, 231

masons 183

Matthew, Tobie 184

mayor, office of 90, 183, 192, 203, 205

Mechanics Institute, see York Institute

Medical Society Rooms, Coffee Yard 343

Mediterranean 57

Meek, James, business man 256, 261, 270, 276

Melbourne Terrace (Wesleyan Chapel) 277

Mellor, Professor Wilfrid 342

Mercers and merchants 101, 127 - 30, 139

Merchant Adventurers' Hall 128, 147, 181, 293, 343. **Monochrome Plate 6.**

388

293, 343, **Monochrome Plate 6.**

Merchant Adventurers' Company 174 – 5, 254

Merchant Taylors' guild 101, 123, 180, 181; Hall, **105**, 123, **202**, 207, 282, 343

Merchants 181, 183

metalworkers 181

Metcalfe, Anthony 172

Metcalfe, Margaret 172

Methodist Centenary Chapel 339

Methodists 256, 270, 272, 274 - 5, 276, 277, 278, 279 – 80, 281, 282, 288, 299
Micklegate **17**, 19, 46-7, 54, 61 - 2, 144, 147, 150, 152-153, 171, 207, 246, 261, 275, 289

Micklegate Bar 10, 47, 113, 118, 198, 245, 246, 276, 282

Micklegate House 228

Micklegate Ward 249, 253, 265, 272, 276, 291

Middleham 141

Middleham, castle 114

Middleton, Margaret *see* Clitherow

Midlands 52

Militia Act 213, 221

Mill Mount Girls' School 348, 350

Millennium Bridge **356**, 357 – 8

Miller, Prof. Steuart 3

Milner, Sir William 226

Milner-White, Eric, Dean of York 322

Minster 3, 7, 30, 34, 41, 43, 47, 51, 59, 67, 72, 79, 80 - 2 - 3, **81**, 91, **92**, 100 - 1, 112 -

100-1, 112-14, 118, 130-3, 138-9, 145, 146, 147, 152, 153, 156, 157, 158 - 163, 166, 167, 172, 173, 184, 186, 187, 196, 198, 199, 201, 203 - 4, 216, 228 244, 245, 248, **252**, 271, 279, 297, 321 - 325, 328, 329, 333 - 337, 340, 343, 344, 346, altars 123; canons 131 - 3; chantries 114, 133, 137; chapter house 109, 130; dean and chapter of 187, 203; library of 158, 188; vicars choral 132 - 3. **Colour Plates 5, 6. Monochrome Plate 15**

Minster Gates 286

Minster School 153, 160

Minster Yard 187, 193, 209, 247 - 8, 265

mint 209

missions 277, 279 – 80

Mithras **18** – 19

Monck, General 202

Monk Bar 245, 248, 253, 275, 277, 282

Monk Bar Chapel (United Methodist Free Churches) 275

Monk Ward 196, 265

Monkgate 189, 197, 249, 267, 285, 286

Moore, John 173

Moray, earl of 108

Morell, John Bowes 331

Morton, William 178

Mosaics (Roman) 35 - 6

Mount (Quaker) School 286

Mount, The 19, 25 - 6, 38, 43, 246, 268, 292
MP for York 178, 183, 199, 203, 266, 270-1, 297
Multangular Tower 1, 3, **4**, 13, 34, 60

Municipal Corporations Act (1835) 264 – 6

Musculus, Wolfgang 158

Museum Gardens 3

Museum Street 298

music teachers 208

musicians 182

Myers, John 195

Mystery Plays 96

Myton-on-Swale, battle 108

Naburn 2, 162

Naburn Asylum 294

Naburn Banqueting House 242, 268

National Covenant (1644) 199

National Early Music Centre 340, 342, 346

National School 237, 238, 282

Near East 57

Neile, Richard 185

Nelson, Thomas, mayor 137

Nessgate 24

Nestlé 305

Neville family 141

Neville, Anne, Lady 113

Neville, Charles, sixth earl of Westmorland 165

Neville, George, archbishop 131

New Earswick 308 - 9, **317**

New Street 255, 272, 293

New Street Chapel (Wesleyan) 256, 272, 277

New Walk 228

Newburgh Priory 158

Newby Park 183

Newcastle, marquis of 194-198

Newcastle-upon Tyne 110, 120, 128, 142, 163, 170-1, 256-7

Newgate 61

Newton, John, Minster canon 132

Ninth Legion 1, 2, 6, 8, 12

nonconformity 204 *and see under* Baptists, Independents, Presbyterians and Quakers

Norfolk 151

Norfolk, dukes of *see* Howard

Norman, Anthony 159

North and East Riding Asylum 294

North Street 63

North Street Mission (Wesleyan) 280

North Street postern 246

Northampton 175

Northrop, James 233

Northumberland 165

Northumberland, duke of *see* Dudley, John

Northumberland, earls of *see* Percy

Norway 52, 67

Norwich 142, 175

Norwich Union Insurance Office **332**

Nottingham 162, 194

Nun Appleton Hall 207

Nunnery Lane 206, 245, 259

Nunthorpe Grammar School 350

Nutt, S and J 233

Olaf Guthfrithsson (King) 52

Olaf Sihtricsson (King) 52

Old Baile 246

Oldcorne, Thomas 168

Oldfield, Joshua 229, 232

Oldfield, Wilson, Smith, Hartley & Tweedy 229

Oliver Sheldon House 207

Oliver, C.W., Lord Mayor of York 326

Orkney 76

Osberht (King) 50-1

Oswald (King) 44, 64

Oswin (King) 44

Oswulf I (Earl) 65

Otterburn, battle 110

Our Lady's, Acomb 321

Ouse Bridge 47, 105, 144 **154,** 174, 246, 266, 268

Ouse Navigation 265, 268

Ouse Navigation Act (1727) 265

Ouse, River 1, 2, 10, 14, 16, 20, 49, 53, 60-3, 196, 198, 248, 257, 269, 289, 290

Ousegate 210

Ove Arup and Partners 336

overseas trade 181, 206

Oxford, University College 207

Pace, George 314-15, 325

Pacocke, Robert 171

painter/stainers 182, 207

Palace, Archbishops' 44

Palladio, Andrea 226, 238

Palmes family 204

Palmes, George 162

parishes 265-7, 268-9

Parisi 5

Park Grove (Board) School 283

Parker, Barry 308

Parkyn, Robert 159

Parliament 104, 110, 127, 129

Parliament Street 60, 247, 255, **260,** 272

Parliamentary Reform Act (1832) 271

Parmentier, Jacques 208

Paulinus 43-4

Pavement 61, 247, 255, 263, 275

Peasants' Revolt (1381) 112, 116

Peasholme Green 12, 254, 255

Peasholme Green, Aldwark (Wesleyan Chapel) 272

Peckitt Street (Methodist New Connexion Chapel) 274,

Peckitt, William 228

Peirson, Major Francis 221

Penty's Animal Feeds 315

Percy family 110; Sir Henry (Hotspur) 110

Percy, Henry, fourth earl of Northumberland 142, 145, 148

Percy, Sir Thomas 148

Percy, Thomas, seventh earl of Northumberland 165, 170

Perepointe, William 160

Peter (Saint) 43, 45, 51

Petergate 8, 34, 46, 206

Petilius Cerialis 1

Phawghney, Ferdinando 172

physicians 208

Piccadilly 247

Pickering, John 148

Pickerings, Booksellers 315

Picts 57

Pilgrimage of Grace 146-147, 149, 156, 165

Place, Francis 208

Place, Thomas 231

plague 177-9, 206; of 1604 - 5, 177-9

plasterers 206

Plays 161, 166

Plutarch 16

Pole, George 169

Pole, Reginald 161

police 248, 265 - 6, 267

Poll Taxes 103, 116

Pontefract 147-8

Poor Law Amendment Act (1834) 268, 293

poor relief 188, 265, 269, 292, 298

Popish Plot 205

Poppleton Road (Board) School 283

population 248 - 53, 264, 269, 275, 277, 290, 292

Portyngton, Thomas, Minster canon 132

Postgate, Oliver 205

Poteman, William, Minster canon 132

poverty 244, 288 - 95, 301

*Poverty (*Rowntree*)* **Monochrome Plate 15.**

Presbyterians 204, 206; *see also* Unitarians

Presbyterians (Scottish) 275

Prince John 219

Prince of Wales Own Regiment of Yorkshire 323

Prince Rupert 197, 198

printers 193, 208

Priory St (Baptist Chapel) 275, 279

Priory St (Presbyterian Chapel) 275

Priory Street 246, 274, 275, 282

Priory Street (Wesleyan) School 282

prisons 249, 265 - 7 *see also* York Castle

Pritchett, James Pigott, architect 255, 272, 274, 284, 291, 295

Privy Council 159, 174

public health 267, 268, 288 – 95

Public Health Act (1848) 267, 291

Public Health Act (1872) 267

public houses 299 – 300

Public Libraries Act (1851) 287

392

Purey-Cust, A.P., Dean of York 322

Purey Cust Nursing Home 322

Pursglove, Robert 156, 162

Quakers *see* Society of Friends

Queen Anne's School 349

Queen Elizabeth Barracks 324

Queen Street 246, 259

Queen's Staith **Monochrome Plate 14.**

Radcliffe, Thomas, third earl of Sussex 166

Ragnall (King) 52

railway stations 14, 25 - 6, 246 - 7, 248, 249, 258, **260**, 268, 293

Railway Street (George Hudson Street) 301

railway workshops 259, 280, 299, 301

railways 246, 256 - 9, 264, 268, 275, 296

Ralph Nuvel 87, 89, 94

Red House, The 224, 230, 238

Red Sea 57

religion 271 – 80

Reresby, Sir John 205, 220

Retreat, The 238, 285, 293 – 4

Revolt of the Earls (1569) 165, 166, 167, 171

Rhine 50, 56

Riccall 62, 67

Richard II 102, 110 - 13, 115 - 16, 128

Richard III 107, 113 - 14, 116, 132, 141, 144, 149

Richardson, Alan, Dean of York 337

Richardson, Thomas 158

Richmond, archdeacon of 132

Richmondshire 174

Ripon 165

Ripon Minster 207

river transport 256-7, 262, 268, **Monochrome Plate 14**

road transport 246, 256, 258

Roads (Roman) 9 - 10, 20, 38

Robert Matthew Johnson Marshall 351, 353

Robin Hood 109, 134

Robinson family 183

Robinson, Laurence 172

Robinson, Sir William 223, 224, 238

Rockingham, Marquis of 219, 226, 230

Roger de Mowbray 78

Roger of Pont l'Évêque 82

Roger of Wendover 64

Roman Catholicism 184, 187, 204, 205, 265, 272, 274, 275-6, 278, 282, 285

Rome 41, 165, 168

Romeyn, John le, archbishop 130

Rougier Street 16, 20

Rowntree & Co. 232, 263 - 4, 299, 301

Rowntree Mackintosh 305

Rowntree, B. Seebohm 278, 294 –5, 300, 301, 304, 305 - 9, **306**

Rowntree, Henry Isaac 263

Rowntree, John Stephenson 300

Rowntree, Joseph (junior) 263 - 4, 295, 300, 308

Royal Air Force Base. Linton-on-Ouse 324, 326

Royal Regiment of Hunters 221

Rump Parliament 201

Ruskin, John 131

Rutland, Duke of 225, 228

Rymer, Sir Joseph 349

Salem Chapel (Congregational Church) 272, 280, 281

Salisbury 142

Salvation Army 279

Samarkand 57

Samuel 189, 195

Sandys, Edwin 170

Savile, Sir George 227

Saville family 155

Saviourgate 61

Sawley Abbey 149

Scandinavia 57

Scarborough Castle 161

Scarbrough, Earl of 336

Scarcroft 251

Scarcroft (Board) School 283, **284**

School Board 248, 283, 287, 301

School of Design 287

Scone, coronation stone 106

Scotland 44

Scots 52, 65, 121, 275

Scots army 195, 196, 197, 199

Scott, Thomas 145

Scottish Border 163

Scottish Wars 76 - 7, 104, 106 – 10

Scrooby, Notts 131

Scrope, Lord, of Upsall 135

Scrope, Richard, archbishop **111,** 112 – 13

Seamer 157

Selby 62, 195, 256-8

Selby, William, mayor 138

Septimius Severus 7, 14, 28

Serapis (Roman God) 19

Sessions, William, printer 261, 315

Shambles 61, 170, 245, 247, **Monochrome Plate 7.**

Shannon, John 321, 334, 339

Shaw, John 231

Shawe, John 195

Sheffield, Edmund, Lord 191

Sheldon, Oliver 331, 351

Shepherd's Building Firm 315, 316

Sheriff 88

Sheriff Hutton 141, 183, 189

Sheriff Hutton, castle 114

sheriff of York, office of 183; of Yorkshire 183

Shetland 57

Ship Money 185

Shipton Street (Board) School 283

shopkeepers 206, 254, 263, 286

Siddons, Mrs 227

siege of York (1644) 196-199

Sihtric Caoch ('Squinty') (King) 52

Silvanus 6

silversmiths 207

Simnel, Lambert 144

Sir William Fitzherbert 84 –5

Siward (Earl) 66

Sixth Legion 12, 19, 22, 23

Skeldergate 54, 201, 291, 293

Skeldergate Bridge 248

Skeldergate Mission (Wesleyan Chapel)
273

Skeldergate postern 246, 261

Smith, Melchior 171

Smith, Sir Thomas 161

Society of Friends (the Quakers) 200, 201,
204, 205, 238, 248, 261, 263-4, 265, 272,
282, 285 - 6, 297, 300

Solway Firth 107

South Bank 253, 277

South Sea Bubble 212

Southampton 48, 50

Southlands (Wesleyan Chapel) 277

Sowerby, Robert 237

Spain 168, 173

Speght, Robert 153

Spinning School 282

sports 299-300

Spurriergate 61

St Aelred, Tang Hall 321

St Andrew's Priory (Gilbertine) 134, 146,
150, 151, 152, 155

St Andrew, Fishergate 58, 62

St Andrew, St Andrewgate **154**, 283

St Andrewgate 293

St Anthony's Hall 188

St Clement 62

St Clement (1874) 277; schools 280, 283

St Crux 61, 136, 189, 247, 272, 277

St Cuthbert 61, 186; parish 289-90; schools
282

St Denys / Dennis 61-2, 152, 289, 291;
schools 283

St George 204; parish 249, 253, 291

St George (Catholic Church) 275, 276,
282, 307, 321; schools 282

St George (Wesleyan Chapel) 272; schools
282

St George Parish 249, 253, 272, 291

St George's House 188

St Gregory, Micklegate 45

St Helen, Fishergate 62

St Helen's, Stonegate 158

St Helen's Square 8, 246, 255, 263, 286

St Helen-on-the-Walls 58

St James the Mount 144

St John, Ousebridge 172, 189, 320, 340

St John's (Diocesan Training College) 284, 285, 350

St Joseph, Water Lane 321

St Lawrence 158, 197, 277; schools 280, 283

St Leonard's Place 245, 287, 296, 298

St Leonard's Hospital 67, 97, 98, 134 - 5, 146, 150, 151, 152, 153, 155, 161

St Margaret, Walmgate, now the National Early Music Centre 289, 340, 342; parish 282

St Martin cum Gregory, Micklegate 63, 169, 185, 207

St Martin le Grand, Coney St 158, 170, 179, 325

St Mary, Bishophill Junior 45, 152, 275, 277; vicarage house 203

St Mary, Bishophill Senior 45, 63, 253, 277, 280, 282, 320; parish 277, 282

St Mary's Castlegate 36, 58, **59**, 152 158, 245, 276, 340

St Mary's Abbey 66 - 67, 73, 82, 86, 91, 98, 132 - 4, 146, 148, 150, 151, 153, 155, 163, 296, 338, 345 **Colour Plate 7**; tower of **190**, 197

St Maurice 277, 278; parish 253

St Michael le Belfrey 44, 136, 248, 178, 179, 321, 322

St Michael, Spurriergate 61, 193, 203, 204, 340, **Monochrome Plate 5**

St Nicholas 197

St Olaf / Olave 66, 136, 178

St Paul Holgate 277; school 156

St Peter the Little 158

St Peter's School 184, 237, 283 - 4, 286, 287, 300, 348

St Quintin, Matthew 225, 228

St Sampson 164, 168, 197, 255, 274, **341**

St Sampson's Square (Thursday Market) 60, 247, 255

St Saviour, 61, 152, 185, 272, 274, 320

St Saviourgate 272, 275, 287, 293

St Saviourgate Chapel (Presbyterian/Unitarian) **190,** 206, 271-2, 281, 286

St Sepulchre 160

St Sepulchre's College 157

St Thomas in the Groves 277

St Thomas Play 147

St Thomas's Hospital 161, 171, 188

St Wilfrid's (Catholic Church) 152, **252, 260,** 275-6, 321, **Monochrome Plate 15**

St William of York 130, 138

St William's College **125,** 133, 157, 193, 237

St. John's Ousebridge 320, 340

Stainforth, Ald. John 224

Stamford Bridge 62, 67

Standeven, Thomas 164

Sterne, Dr Jaques 221, 230

Sterne, Rev. Laurence 230, 233, 234

Stirling, castle 107

Stonebow 329-3

Stonegate 46, 144, 206, 209, **317**

Stonegate 8, 32

Strafford, earl of *see* Wentworth, Thomas

streets 289, 294, 299

Stuart dynasty 176

Stuart, Charles Edward, the Young Pretender 220, 230, 234

Stubbs, Ironmongers 315

suburbs and villages 248 - 250, 253, 265, 276, 277, 278, 280, 283, 290 295, 301

Suchard 305

Sunday schools 277, 280-1

Sussex, earl of *see* Radcliffe, Thomas

Svein Forkbeard, King of Denmark 66

Swann family 232

Sycamore Terrace 33

Tacitus 5, 12

Tadcaster 144, 196

tailors 181

Tancred family 183

Tanner Row 20, **21**, 22, 47, 124, 246, 293

Tees, River 65

Teggin, Harry 315, 334

Telemark 57

Tempest, Pierce 208

Temple Newsam 189

Temples (Roman) 17

Terry's of York 232, 235, 263, 305

Tessimond, William 169

Test and Corporation Acts 265

textileworkers 181

Thanet 64

The Barbican 326, 347

The Black Swan, Peasholme Green 210, **Monochrome Plate 11B.**

The George, Coney Street 209

The Star, Stonegate 209

The Tower 159

Theatre Royal 295-6, 297, 298, 310, 326, 333, 342, 343, 346

Thirsk 145

Thomas Agar's Hospital 189

Thomas Becket 84

Thomas de Ultra Usam 89

Thomas of Bayeux 72, 76, 80, 83, 337

Thomas Watter's Hospital 189

Thompson, Edward 183, 205, 226; Henry 210

Thor 51

Thored (Earl) 66

Thoresby, Ralph 207

Thornton, John, glazier 126

Timothy, Christopher 345

Tobacco cutter 182

Todd's Warehouse 233, 237

Todde, William 145

Toft Green 19, 35, 135, 150, 249

Tolbooth 170

Tomlin, Delma 342, 346

Topham family 186

Tostig (Earl) 66-7

Towton, battle 119

Trade 10 -11, 23 - 4, 31, 254-5, 257, 262, 263, 264

Trajan (Emperor) 8

trams 268 *see also* York Tramways

Treasurer's House 191, 237

Trentholme Drive 25

Trinity Lane 164

Tuke 232, 234

Tuke, Samuel 293-4, 297

Tunnock, Richard, mayor 126

Turner, Charles, of Kirkleatham 223

Turpin, Dick 218, 227

Tyburn 169, 170, 205

Tyler, Wat 112

Tyne, River 50

Ugthorpe 162

Unitarians 206, 271 -2, 281, 286, 297

University of York 199, 312, 318, 319, 326, 329, 331, 336, 340, 342, 345, 350 - 55, 357, 358

University Science Park 312, 354

Unwin, Raymond 308

Ure, Mary 345

Uzbekistan 57

Vale of York 1

Vaux, John 193, 194, 195

Vavasour family 204

Vavasour, Dr Thomas 167

Vavasour, Mrs 170

Vavasour, William 153

Venice 208

Venutius 5

Verecundius Diogenes 17

Vernon, William 297

Vespasian (Emperor) 5

Victoria Bar 245, 275

Victoria Bar (Primitive Methodist Chapel) 275

Villas (Roman) 23, 26

Waddilove, Lewis 351

Wakefield 142

Wakefield, battle 113

Wakefield, William 218, 231

Walker, John, iron founder 261 -2

Walker, Peter 160

Wallace, William 106

Walmgate 61 - 2, 77, 152, 179, 188, 196, 206, 249, 272, 275, 280, 282, 290

Walmgate Bar **105,** 197, 245, 255, 277, 285, 291, 292

Walmgate stray 197

Walmgate Ward 249, 253, 255, 265, 270, 291, 292

Walpole, Sir Horace 230

Walpole, Sir Robert 212

Wandesford, Mary 236

Ward, Caesar 230, 233

Ward, Isabel 164

Ward, Mary 206

Wartre, Sir Richard, mayor 137

Water Lanes **222**, 248, 253, 272, 274, 280, 292

water supply 8 - 9, 20, 265, 267, 289, 290, 295

Watson, Anthony 173

Watson, Rev. David 322

Watson, Robert 160

Webster, John 234

Weddall, William 189

Wellbeloved, Charles, Unitarian minister 218, 286, 297

Wellington Row 10, **11, 21**, 20, 35

Wensley 172

Wensleydale 165, 180, 183

Wentworth, Barbara 159

Wentworth, Sir William 228, 229

Wentworth, Thomas, earl of Strafford 179, 191

Wesley Place (Wesleyan) School, Garden Place 282

Wesley, Charles 218

Wesley, John 218

Wesley, Priory Street (Wesleyan Chapel) 274, 275, 277, 280, 282, 299

Wessex 52

West Riding 194

West Riding Militia 223

Westminster 106 - 7, 109, 114, 131, 159, 164, 176

Westminster, Synod of 160

Westmorland 165

Westmorland, earl of see Neville, Charles

West-Taylor, John 352

Wetherby 196

Weymouth, Dorset 117

Whickham, Tobias 187

Whitby 44

Whitby Oliver 326

White Swan Inn, Pavement 241, 242

White, John, Grace 233

Widdrington, Sir Thomas 100, 203, 209

wigmakers 208

Wilberforce, William 219, 287

Wilby, Norfolk 151

Wilcock, Edward 173

Wilfrid 44-5

Wilkinson, John, theatre manager 295

Wilkinson, Tate, theatre manager 227

Wilkinson, Thomas 219

William III and Mary II 205

William of Malmesbury 52

William the Conqueror (King) 67-69, 71

Williams, Henry 160

Willoughby, Francis 229

Willoughby, Miss M.G. 349

Willoughby, Raper, Clough & Swann 229

Wilson, Dorothy 236, 237, 238

Wilson, Miles 160

Wilson, Thomas 160, 229, 233, 238

Wilson's Green Coat (Charity) School 236, 237, 238, 282

Wilton Rise, Holgate (Wesleyan Chapel) 280

Winterscale's Hospital 236

Wintour, Samuel 193

Wintringham 157

Wintringham, Dr Clifton 230, 231

Wistow 162

Wolstenholme, John 233, 237

Wolsthrope, Sir Oswald 148

Woodhouse, Ald James 223

Worcester 175

workhouses 268 - 9, 294

Wormald, Samuel 242

Wortley Montagu, Lady Mary 220

Wotton, Nicholas 163

Wright, James 189

Wright, John 169

Wright's, Butchers 326

Wyatt, Sir Thomas 161

Wycliffe, John 139

Wyman, Henry, mayor 121

Wynne, Sir Rowland 227

Yeoman School 284

York Archaeological Trust 333, 336-7, 339

York Asylum (Bootham Park) 238, 293-4, 298

York castle **81,** 90, 109, **140,** 150, 169, 201, **214,** 245, 251

York Castle gaol 246, 247

York Choral Society 297

York Chronicle Newspaper 256

York Church High School 288

York City Football Club 300, 347

York City Friaries 107, 127, 135, 140

York City officials: aldermen 104, 112-15; chamberlains 115; common clerk 115, 121; mayor 104, 112, 127; recorder 100; sheriffs 112

York College for Girls 288

York Co-operative Society 301

York County Hospital 230, 238, 289, 293, 297, 298

York Courant Newspaper 233, 256

York Dispensary 289, 293

York District Hospital 31, 312

York Flint Glass Company 261, 315

York Georgian Society 335

York Herald and Advertiser Newspaper 233, 247, 256

York High School for Girls 288

York Institute of Art, Science and Literature 248, 286, 287, **Colour Plate 13**

York Journal Newspaper 233

York Medical Society 297

York Mercury Newspaper 233

York Opera House 346

York parish churches 117, 126, 135 – 8

York Police Act (1825) 265

York Public Cemetery Company 291

York races 208, 280, 295

York residents: aliens 120-2; craftsmen 123-6; freemen 114 - 5, 117, 123 –6, 254, 265, 266, 270-1; women 122 – 3

York Saving Bank 255

York Subscription Library 286 – 7

York Tavern, St Helen's Square 240, 246

York Tramways Company 328

York Volunteer Rifles 323

York, plague and population 103, 116 - 20, 122

York, Richard duke of 113

York, Sir Richard, mayor 137

Yorkist dynasty 144, 176

Yorkshire 149

Yorkshire Antiquarian Club 297

Yorkshire Architectural Society 297

Yorkshire Association for Parliamentary Reform 219, 220

Yorkshire Central Agricultural Association 297

Yorkshire Club 298, 318 - 19, 323, 344

Yorkshire East Riding 147, 157, 250, 297

Yorkshire Evening Press 334, 340, 342, 345

Yorkshire Gazette Newspaper 256, 270, 276

Yorkshire Insurance Company **252,** 255 - 6, 267

Yorkshire Mission 217

Yorkshire Museum 296, 298, **Colour Plate 14.**

Yorkshire Music Festival 297 – 8

Yorkshire Naturalists Club 297

Yorkshire North Riding 145, 162, 250, 297

Yorkshire Philosophical Society 286, 296, 338

Yorkshire Rising (1659) 201

Yorkshire School for the Blind 287-8

Yorkshire West Riding 142, 156, 174, 194, 250, 254, 257, 294, 297

Yorkshireman Newspaper 256

Young King's Revolt 78

Young, Arthur 243

Young, Sir George 191

Young, Thomas 163, 164, 166, 171

Zouche, William de la, archbishop 117

401

University of York
Central Hall   Patrick Nuttgens 1987